MOVING FROM WINDOWS TO LINUX

MOVING FROM WINDOWS TO LINUX

CHUCK EASTTOM

CHARLES RIVER MEDIA, INC.
Hingham, Massachusetts

Acquisitions Editor: James Walsh
Production: Paw Print Media
Cover Design: The Printed Image

CHARLES RIVER MEDIA, INC.
10 Downer Avenue
Hingham, Massachusetts 02043
781-740-0400
781-740-8816 (FAX)
info@charlesriver.com
www.charlesriver.com

This book is printed on acid-free paper.

Chuck Easttom. *Moving from Windows to Linux.*
ISBN: 1-58450-280-0

Library of Congress Cataloging-in-Publication Data

Easttom, Chuck.
  Moving from Windows to Linux / Chuck Easttom.
     p. cm.
  ISBN 1-58450-280-0 (acid-free paper)
 1. Linux. 2. Microsoft Windows (Computer file) 3. Operating systems
(Computers) I. Title.
QA76.76.O63E233 2003
005.26'8—dc22

                    2003022787

Printed in the United States of America
03 7 6 5 4 3 2 First Edition

CHARLES RIVER MEDIA titles are available for site license or bulk purchase by institutions, user groups, corporations, etc. For additional information, please contact the Special Sales Department at 781-740-0400.

Contents

Introduction

This book is targeted towards a Windows® user who wants to migrate to Linux. That means that this book is written with the Linux novice in mind. However, although you may be a novice to Linux, it is assumed that you are certainly not a novice to Windows. This book assumes you are an experienced Windows users, what many would call a Windows power user. You have probably spent some time experimenting with Windows, changed options in the Control Panel, changed screen resolution, and perhaps even added some new hardware.

Many, if not most, Linux books are written for very technical people. In blunt terms, they are written for computer nerds like the author! Don't worry, most technical people don't consider the appellation *nerd* to be derogatory. The reason why so many books for Linux are so technical is that for many years Linux has been the exclusive purview of the tech heads. Linux has been used as the operating system of choice for Web servers and for computer science enthusiasts. As the Linux operating system moves more into the mainstream of computing, more people who are not extremely technical want to learn about it. This necessitates books like this one that bring Linux to the masses.

The purpose of this book is to take what you already know as a moderately experienced Windows user and apply that knowledge to Linux, thus making you a knowledgeable Linux user. Frequently, concepts in Linux will be related to their counterparts in Windows, thus helping Windows users learn Linux.

This book makes only few assumptions about you, the reader. It assumes that you are an experienced Windows user who has used a computer for some time on a somewhat regular basis, perhaps in your office or at home. It assumes that this computer was most likely running some version of Microsoft Windows. It assumes that you have used Web browsers, e-mail, and probably some business applications such as a word processor or spreadsheet tool. In essence, it assumes that you are a fairly competent PC/Windows user. You probably use a PC and some applications at work or school and are a fairly savvy computer user. It does not assume that you have any extensive knowledge of hardware or operating systems, but you do know what a hard drive is and may have even added some hardware to your PC at some point. It does not assume that you are a system administrator or any type of computer professional, although some professionals may also find this book useful. Basically, if you are an experienced Windows user who has been curious about Linux but have been reluctant to take the plunge, this book is for you. The reason why you must be experienced with Windows to follow this book is that most topics are compared and contrasted with their Windows counterparts. If you are well acquainted with Windows, this book will be easy for you to follow, and you will quickly become a competent Linux user.

To put it more simply, and directly, if you can easily get onto and navigate the Internet, know what RAM is, know what a folder is, understand the fundamentals of using a personal computer, and are pretty comfortable with your computer, you probably will be able to follow along with this book. The enthusiastic and experienced Windows power user is perfectly suited for this book.

If you are completely unfamiliar with basic PC hardware, you may find Appendix D to be useful. It is designed to give a basic overview of PC hardware to novice PC users. If you feel that your understanding of hardware is too scant to effectively understand the Linux operating system, perhaps you should consider starting with that appendix.

The more computer experience you have, the quicker you will absorb the material in this book. It must be clear that this book is aimed primarily at a computer user who has a fair amount of experience. Novice computer users will struggle with some material in this book, but they should be able to follow along with most of it. They will need to re-read some sections and perhaps spend more time practicing techniques shown. Computer professionals, network administrators, and programmers might find some of this material a bit remedial. Such people will probably be able to skim over some sections of the book and will absorb material quite quickly.

Although this book is not a textbook, per se, it does have some features much like a textbook. Every chapter ends with a brief summary and a set of review questions. These are provided for two reasons. The first is as a study aid to ensure that you are getting the salient points of the chapter. Second, while not specifically intended as a textbook, this book could be used as an introductory Linux text.

It is very important to note that, while this book uses Red Hat Linux 9.0 as an example, the only real difference between Linux distributions is the installation process and the extra software that comes with the distribution. All software mentioned in this book comes with Red Hat 9.0. If you are using some other version of Linux that does not include one or more of these applications, you can download that application from the Internet. The Web site for each of these applications is included in the appendixes at the back of the book. If you are using a Linux distribution other than Red Hat, your installation process might be slightly different, but it should be very similar. The rest of the topics we discuss will be common to all Linux distributions.

The following note is so critical, that it is partially repeated near the end of Chapter 2. Each Linux distribution (SuSE, Red Hat, Mandrake, etc.) has the same core operating system and functionality. However, each distribution may bundle different applications with Linux. As you go through this book, you will be introduced to several applications that are used in Linux. If you do not include the appropriate packages during the installation, or if you are using a different Linux distribution or a different version of Red Hat, you will not have all of the applications installed. However, most of these applications can be downloaded from the Internet for free. When each application is introduced, the appropriate Web address is provided if one is available. Many applications for KDE can even be found at www.kde.org/.

One final note. Some computer terms are used interchangeably throughout the computer industry. Therefore, they are used interchangeably here. Every effort is made to mention this directly in the text, so as to avoid confusion. However, a few terms are shown here:

Program—Also called an application or software. Very small programs, particularly those that perform some system task, are sometimes called utilities.

Desktop Environment—This is the graphical user interface that you see and interact with. It is sometimes called simply the desktop, a graphical environment, or a GUI (graphical user interface).

Web Address—A Web address is in the format *www.chuckeasttom.com* and is also called a URL (uniform resource locator).

Memory—Your computer's memory is also called its RAM (random access memory)

User—The person using a computer, program, or Web site is often called the user.

Linux Fundamentals

This section is designed to give you your first exposure to Linux. All of the basic concepts are explained in detail. No prior knowledge of operating systems or installations is assumed. The only assumption made is that you are a competent computer user with experience with Windows, the Internet, and some office applications. As you read through the chapters in this section, you will be shown the fundamentals of the Linux operating system.

Chapter 1 introduces you to the concepts underlying the Linux operating system. You are given a brief history of the operating system, as well as a basic introduction to the world of Linux. Perhaps most importantly, this chapter gives you a comparison between Microsoft Windows and Linux.

Chapter 2 takes you step by step through the entire process of installing Red Hat 9.0, the most popular Linux distribution. Each step is carefully explained, with pictures showing you what you will see during your install. Underlying concepts such as disk partitions and boot loaders are explained.

Chapter 3 introduces you to some basics of the Linux operating system. You will learn about shells and graphical user interfaces. You will also learn to do a few simple shell commands and learn how to find things on the KDE desktop.

1

Making the Move from Windows to Linux

In This Chapter

- What Is Linux?
- Where Did Linux Come From?
- How Does Linux Compare to Windows?
- Linux Distributions
- Where Is Linux Going?

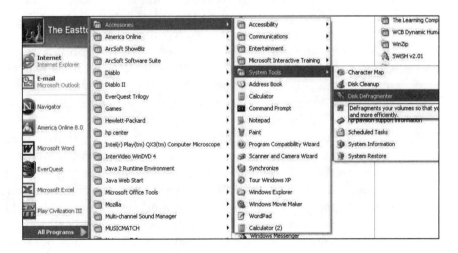

INTRODUCTION

If you are reading this book, then probably you are a Microsoft® Windows® user who is considering switching to Linux®. You may be considering this change for any number of factors. Perhaps your employer is starting to use Linux. Or it might be that you are intrigued by all the media attention Linux has received recently. Whatever your reasons for considering changing from Windows to Linux, it is likely that you are contemplating this change with a fair amount of trepidation. You have probably grown quite comfortable with Microsoft Windows, and regardless of any advantages Linux may have or how curious you may be, you probably have a lot of questions. Will the transition be difficult? Will you be able to do all the things you want to do with your computer? Will you need to be a complete computer geek in order to understand Linux?

The answers to those questions, in order, are no, yes, and no. It won't be difficult. You will be able to do all the things you want to do. The best part about transitioning to Linux is that you don't have to be a computer wizard or a computer professional to be able to do so. You do need to be comfortable with computers. An experienced Windows user who routinely uses a computer for work or recreation will probably suffice. In fact, this book simply assumes that you are a relatively experienced computer user with some exposure to Microsoft Windows, the Internet, and some office applications such as word processors or spreadsheets. The reader for whom this book was designed is a competent and experienced computer user, one who is comfortable with some basic configuration tasks such as changing screen resolution, finding items in the Control Panel, and perhaps even adding on some hardware. Perhaps the best description for the target audience of this book would be a Windows power user. However, you don't need to be a computer professional to use this book.

One common misconception about Linux is that it is hard to understand and difficult to use. This simply is not true. Contrary to what you may have heard, Linux is no more difficult to use than Windows or Macintosh®. It just takes a little guidance, which this book will endeavor to provide, and some patience on your part. The purpose of this book is to answer your questions about Linux and ease you through that transition. This chapter is the beginning of your journey.

This chapter is designed to introduce you to the world of Linux. That means that this chapter is a sort of smorgasbord of Linux concepts and terminology. The concepts you see will be introduced here briefly and expounded upon in more depth later in the book. The purpose of this chapter is to give you an initial overview of Linux. That means a few advanced topics will be touched upon in this chapter. If you feel that some topic in this chapter is still not completely clear to you, don't worry—it will be explained in much more detail in a later chapter.

The following pages will take you through the fundamental concepts of Linux. You will find out what Linux is and what it is not. You also will be introduced to a brief history of Linux and a few thoughts on its future. Some of the information in this chapter may already be familiar to you, but it is hoped that you will learn a few new things about Linux. This material will set the stage for subsequent chapters. Therefore, it is imperative that you thoroughly master the concepts of this chapter before proceeding with subsequent chapters.

WHAT IS LINUX?

Linux is one of the hottest buzzwords in the world of computers, but beyond that, what is it? Simply put, Linux is an operating system. Which of course begs the question, "what is an operating system?" In simple terms, an operating system is software that runs your PC. Microsoft Windows is another operating system, as is the Apple OS X®. Of course, you are familiar with the various applications you run on your PC, such as word processors, graphics utilities, spreadsheets, and even games. An operating system is like these other applications, except that rather than create a document or play a game, it actually runs your PC. When you move a file, delete a file, create a directory, load software, etc., it is your operating system that performs all of these tasks. Without an operating system, your PC is really just a pile of useless circuits, worth less to you than a toaster. The operating system is what is running your machine. In addition to communicating with your printer, displaying output to your monitor, and running your CD-ROM, it has other functions. Your operating system provides a context within which your applications run. For example, your favorite word processor must run within the context of your computer's operating system. When you print, your word processor talks to the operating system, which in turn handles the printing. The operating system is, essentially, the soul of your computer.

There are other operating systems available for you to use. You are probably familiar with Microsoft Windows (Windows 98, 2000, or XP). Windows is a very popular operating system for home users and small businesses. In fact, in its various versions, Windows is the predominant desktop operating system. It is hard to find a modern office without computers running Windows. Most home users have a Windows PC. This is obvious when you go to any store that sells computer software. Most commercial software stores carry predominantly Windows software, with only a small selection of titles for other operating systems. Another popular operating system is Apple Macintosh OS (short for *operating system*). As of this writing, the Macintosh OS is up to version 10, popularly referred to as *OS X*. Macintosh is easy to use and has been particularly popular with the graphics and computer animation industries. Many very high-end computer graphics companies use Apple computers. Many of the special effects you see in movies were probably created, or at least augmented, with Apple computers. Another operating system that generally is used for high-end servers, not for desktops, is Unix, which is known for its stability and security, but also for its expense.

This brings us to Linux. Linux is a variant of Unix. In fact, many people now use the term *nix* to refer to Unix and its variants. Linux is an operating system that has some rather unique features. First, it is very stable and robust, being based on the time-honored Unix operating system (more on that in the next part of this chapter). Second, it is distributed under an open source license. Open source licensing is rather simple, yet elegant. *Open source* means that once you obtain a piece of software, it is yours to do with as you please. Would you like to make a copy or change the source code? Under open source, the source code of the software is open to the public, and when you purchase a product, it is yours to do with as you will. In case you did not realize it, this is radically different from Microsoft, Oracle®, Sun®, and most commercial software. For example, when you buy Microsoft Windows, the manufacturer's licensing agreement that comes with the product places rather significant restrictions on what you can do with that product. Violating that license agreement can result in losing the license to that software and, in some extreme cases, in lawsuits. Each vendor's licensing agreement stipulates what is acceptable use of its software and what is not. Most commercial vendors do not allow you to alter their software, nor do they allow you to have access to the source code for the software. Most vendors also do not allow you to make or distribute copies of their software after you purchase it. One example of software licensing restrictions is that if you purchase a computer that comes with Windows, you cannot later sell that copy of Windows, even if you have disposed of the machine. Several eBay® sellers have been shut down by Microsoft for just that sort of activity. Also, you most certainly do not have access to its source code. With open source software, you can do anything you want with the software once you get it, and you have complete access to the source code.

For those readers who may not know what source code is, it is the programming commands that were written to create a piece of software. With commercial software, source code is usually carefully guarded. With open source software, it is freely distributed.

Access to source code may not be particularly intriguing to many readers. You have to be a rather highly skilled programmer to make much use of it. However, if you have skilled programmers on staff, they can take the Linux source code and make modifications to customize the operating system for your particular needs.

One note of caution is in order. What you can do with open source software is not completely unlimited. For example, you cannot put your own label on open source software and resell it. The open source license does not give you this right. If you put Red Hat® Linux and your name on a CD-ROM and then started selling copies, you might find yourself the target of litigation and possible criminal charges. The author does not claim to be an attorney and recommends that with any software, you read the licensing agreement carefully. Open source software has the least restrictive licensing of any software you can find, far less restrictive than commercial software. However, there are still some limitations. It is recommended that you look at *www.opensource.org/* to see a wealth of information and links on open source software.

One advantage of an open source operating system is that a lot of the software written for the operating system also is open source. This means that, although the software selection for Linux in an average retail store might be slim, the selection of freely downloadable software on the Internet is vast.

You will also find that the Linux community is rather supportive of itself. You will find several links in the appendices of this book, and it is even possible that you might find a Linux users group in your area, especially if you live in a major metropolitan area. These people can be quite helpful to the Linux novice.

WHERE DID LINUX COME FROM?

Linux is essentially a clone of the Unix operating system. This means that its commands, file structure, and behavior are a lot like Unix. In fact, in many cases they are exactly like Unix. This also means that our story must begin with the history of Unix. This history could be quite lengthy. However, for our purposes, we just need to cover the highlights.

Unix was the creation of the legendary Bell Laboratories. For those readers who are not familiar with Bell Laboratories, it is famous for a plethora of technological and scientific breakthroughs, including the discovery of the first evidence of the Big Bang and the creation of the C programming language. At the time that Unix was developed (late 1960s), operating systems were written for a specific machine's hardware. This meant that even if you were an expert on a given operating system, the odds were that your expertise would not transfer to other machines. Unix was an attempt to create an operating system that could run on various hardware, and it turned out to be an unequivocal success. Unix was first released in 1971, and more than 30 years later it is still a top-notch operating system. In the world of computing, five years is often considered woefully out of date, and any technology a decade or more old is likely to be considered a quaint antique. For an operating system to survive and flourish for over 30 years speaks volumes about that operating system's stability and functionality. Unix is used around the world, particularly on high-end systems that must service a large number of users. It is renowned for its efficiency and stability. Most experts agree that even today there is no operating system more stable than Unix. Unfortunately, Unix is also known for its high cost. A Sun Solaris® Unix machine or an SCO® Unix machine is quite expensive.

SCO and Solaris are simply brand names for individual companies' versions of Unix. SCO is an acronym for Santa Cruz Operation, and Solaris is made by Sun Microsystems, which also created the Java programming language.

Sun Solaris machines cost from $3,000 to more than one million dollars. That is a lot more expensive than your standard Windows PC or even a high-end Windows server. Of course, Sun Microsystems would probably like to point out that their higher-end Unix servers are in a completely different class than a Windows server running on a standard PC. They are able to handle much more work than any Windows/PC server. These Unix servers are designed for very intensive projects, thus their expense.

This cost, combined with the perceived complexity of Unix, prevented it from becoming a player in the desktop operating system market. Unix was primarily an operating system for high-end servers. The advent of the open source movement would eventually change this. Open source, briefly described earlier, was first brought to the public forefront by Richard Stallman, who in 1985 published his famous "GNU Manifesto," a document outlining the parameters for open source licensing. Stallman had begun working on his own operating system in 1983. He called this system GNU (GNU is Not Unix). His goal was to create an open source version of Unix. Stallman's Free Software Foundation later created the GNU General Public License that today allows Linux and other software to remain completely free. This open source movement was the start of a really big idea. An idea others ran with.

In 1987, Andrew S. Tanenbaum created Minix, an operating system quite similar to Unix. Minix was a fairly stable and functional system and a reasonably good Unix clone. Although Minix failed to gain the popularity of some other Unix variants, it was an inspiration for the creator of Linux.

The story of the Linux operating system starts with a young computer science graduate student named Linus Torvalds. Torvalds was introduced to Minix and, while still in graduate school, decided to create his own open source Unix clone. Torvalds found many things he liked about the Minix operating system, but he believed that he could make a better Unix variant. He chose the name Linux, as a combination of his first name and the end of the word Unix. He began by posting the operating system code on an Internet discussion board, allowing anyone to use it, play with it, or modify it. Finally, he released Linux 0.01 on the Internet under a GNU public license. Torvalds not only released the operating system for free, he released the source code and even invited other programmers to lend a hand in making the system more workable.

Over the years, Linux's popularity has grown. It has moved from a hobby operating system for computer enthusiasts to a full-fledged business operating system. Vendors like Red Hat, SuSE, and Debian have released popular distributions of Linux that bundle the operating system with useful programs and a graphical interface. You can find out more about the history of Linux at any of these Web sites:

- *http://ragib.hypermart.net/linux/*
- *www.li.org/linuxhistory.php*
- *http://linuxrefresher.com/additional/history.htm*

You may be wondering how these vendors make money. If the operating system can be downloaded for free from the Internet, it would seem that any Linux company would have a very narrow profit margin. The first way they make money is by selling their operating systems in neatly packaged boxes with manuals and easy-to-install CDs. If you download a free version of Linux from the Internet, you do not get any manuals or CDs, installation can be quite tricky, and the download time will severely tax even a high-speed cable connection. These vendors also make money by selling support for Linux. If you purchase Red Hat Linux, you also can call their support line for help on a fee-per-call basis.

HOW DOES LINUX COMPARE TO WINDOWS?

Since you have used Windows and are now at least thinking about moving to Linux, it might be prudent to compare the two operating systems. What does one offer that the other does not? What do they have in common? Why would you move from Windows to Linux? Let us first set aside some of the operating system wars that you find in Internet discussions. Those of you who are not familiar with the raging Internet debates between proponents of different operating systems are probably fortunate. Many an Internet discussion group or chat room has become bogged down with proponents of Linux/Unix and proponents of Microsoft hurling accusations and insults at each other. At times these arguments get quite nasty. The purpose of this book is not to bash one operating system or to exalt another. Both Windows and Linux have their place. The author has both a Windows XP machine and a Red Hat Linux machine at home and a dual boot on his laptop (*dual boot* means you have both operating systems installed, and at startup you are prompted to pick the one you want to use). Some people seem to have an almost religious fervor regarding their operating system of choice. That is not the tone of this book. Still, there are significant differences in the two operating systems. Differences that should be examined thoroughly.

Advantages of Linux Over Windows

First, let's take a look at the advantages of using Linux as opposed to Microsoft Windows. The most obvious advantage is cost. If you purchase a commercial version of Linux, you can expect to spend about $50 for Red Hat 9.0 Personal Edition®, as opposed to about $200 for Windows XP Personal Edition. You also can download several versions of Linux for free from the Internet. Simply by purchasing Linux rather than Microsoft Windows, you immediately save money. You also don't have to worry about licensing fees. If you are using a Windows 2000 or XP server in your small business, you are required to purchase a license for each machine that will connect to it. With Linux, the number of machines you connect is irrelevant—you don't need any licenses. This is an something that gets many small businesses in trouble. If you set up a Windows server and connect 10 employees to it, you are supposed to purchase 10 licenses. If you don't, you are in violation of copyright laws and subject to criminal and civil penalties. With a Linux server, you can connect as many machines as you want.

You also can install your copy of Linux on multiple machines. This is not the case with Windows. When you buy any version of Windows, it is illegal to install it on more than one machine at a time. Linux has no such restriction; you can install it on every machine in your office if you want.

To continue our scenario of an office with 10 machines and one server, this could all be done for about $50 with Linux. With Windows, you need 10 copies of Windows XP at $200 each, one copy of Windows XP Server (over $500), and 10 licenses for the 10 machines to connect to the server. You need well over $3,000 worth of software and licenses! That is a lot of money, probably as much as you spent for the computers themselves or very close to it. Clearly, using Linux saves you money.

You also save money on applications. After you have purchased Microsoft Windows, you then will need to pay for a variety of applications to run on it. You will need to purchase Microsoft Office (about $500) in order to do word processing, spreadsheets, presentations, small database work, and so on. If you need large-scale databases, you have to first purchase Microsoft Windows XP Server instead of the Home or Professional edition, and then purchase Microsoft SQL Server® for about $3,000. With Red Hat Linux 9.0, you get Open Office® for free. Open Office has a complete office suite, including word processor, spreadsheet, and presentation tools. You also get MySQL®, which is a complete large-scale database server. You can purchase Star Office® for under $60 or Corel Office Suite® for Linux for $150. It would seem that even after buying the operating system, you save even more money on applications with Linux. Linux is the most cost-effective solution for the home user or small business operator.

Saving money is obviously a good thing, but it is certainly not the only criterion you should consider when choosing an operating system. Another consideration is the operating system's stability, which includes a number of factors. The most obvious factor is uptime. How much of the time is the operating system actually running and performing useful work, versus downtime due to crashing? The Linux operating system is stable. Will it work when you need it to? The answer is a resounding yes. In fact, by every standard, both Unix and Linux are far more stable than Windows. You can have a Linux machine running for months and never need to reboot it or defragment it.

Some readers may wonder what is meant by defragmenting a hard drive. You may have heard this process called optimizing a drive, and it is periodically necessary because of the way files are stored. Your hard drive has multiple spinning platters, and when you save a file, segments are saved to the hard drive. These fragments may not be contiguous. This leads to file fragmentation, which means that a single document might be found in pieces scattered all over your hard drive. This fragmentation can make your computer run much slower because it must search throughout your hard drive to find all the pieces of the document, rather than finding them all in one place. When you defragment your hard drive, you will often find that it will run faster.

The way in which an operating system handles the files on the computer depends entirely on the filesystem used by the operating system. A filesystem is exactly what its name implies, a system for storing and accessing files. Put another way, a filesystem organizes the files on your computer. You have lots of files of different types on your PC. You have documents you save, spreadsheets, programs, and so on. All of these are files. The problem for the computer is organizing them in such a way that you can easily find them. This is where the filesystem comes in. It is simply the method the computer uses to organize the files stored on your computer. The filesystem used by Linux, Extended File System (ext), is more robust than the systems used by Windows (FAT, FAT32, and NTFS) and does not need defragmenting.

In Windows you would go to the Start menu, choose Programs, select Accessories, then go to System Tools, where you would find the defragmentation tool, as shown in Figure 1.1.

FIGURE 1.1   Finding the Windows defragmentation tool.

All of the mentioned filesystems for Microsoft operating systems work on a table that relates specific file segments with addresses on the hard drive. The first of these is File Allocation Table (FAT). Windows 2000 and XP use a significantly enhanced filesystem called New Technology File System (NTFS).

Disadvantages of Linux Compared to Windows

It appears that there are some significant advantages to using Linux. It is a very stable operating system that is also very cheap. There also are a few disadvantages to using the Linux operating system, the first being the availability of software. You can get office products such as Star Office and Open Office (which will be explored later in this book). You can find robust graphics programs such as GIMP® (Graphics Image Manipulation Program, also explored in this book). You can even purchase a few games for Linux. However, you cannot get Microsoft Office®, Adobe Photoshop®, or many other popular applications for Linux. At least you cannot get them at this time. You will be able to do all the tasks you are used to, but you may need to do them with new software. You will probably have to seek out alternative applications for some of the products you are used to working with. Fortunately, many of these alternative applications are also open source. In fact, Red Hat 9.0 includes several of these on the installation disks. Even if you are not using Red Hat

9.0, you will find many of these alternative applications are available as free downloads from the Internet.

In addition to learning some new software applications, you will find that some applications simply cannot be found for Linux, and no suitable Linux analog exists. For example, many games have not been ported to Linux. This is changing, but you will still find a great many games that do not have Linux versions. You also will find that some hardware does not have a Linux driver. Most standard CD-ROMs, printers, NIC cards, and such will work under Linux, but more obscure brands might not. If you are using fairly common hardware, this will not be a problem.

One very significant disadvantage for small businesses using Linux is finding appropriate technical staff. Most computer companies that do outsourcing of PC support and repair are trained in Windows, not in Linux. It also is likely that most of your employees have significant Windows experience but little or no Linux experience. This may necessitate retraining your staff in the use of Linux (of course, you could start by simply buying them all copies of this book!). In plain terms, competent technical personnel trained in Windows are very easy to find, whereas competent Linux technical support can be much more difficult to find. This often leads to Linux professionals commanding a somewhat higher salary.

LINUX DISTRIBUTIONS

This book deals with Red Hat Linux. However, there are a number of other brand names associated with Linux. It is important that you know the similarities and differences between these brands. To begin with, they are usually referred to as *distributions*. These distributions have much more in common than they have differences. The various desktops (such as KDE and GNOME), shells, commands, and administrative tasks that you will learn in this book apply to all Linux distributions.

You may be wondering what is different about them. Each distribution, while still distributing Linux, creates its own installation routine and decides what additional programs will be bundled with it. In other words, the real difference between distributions amounts to the installation process and the different applications that will be installed with the operating system. Red Hat Linux, for example, ships with the popular graphics program GIMP, a complete office suite, and a plethora of other applications.

The most important thing to keep in mind is that the actual operating system is the same for all distributions. That means that what you learn in this book will carry over into other Linux distributions such as SuSE, Debian, and Mandrake.

WHERE IS LINUX GOING?

Now that you know where Linux came from and what you can do with it, the next question is, where is it going? Linux is gaining a large share of the Web server market. The fact that it is very inexpensive and comes with both Web server and FTP server software makes it very attractive to people running Web servers. More businesses are turning to Linux for Web servers, file servers, and other servers. America Online and Amazon.com book sellers both use Linux servers. Windows is still king of the home and business desktops, but this is changing. Business owners are tired of paying exorbitant licensing fees for proprietary products. More and more small businesses are looking to Linux and open source software as a low-cost alternative. Clearly, a growing market share of the home and small business community is in Linux's future.

Linux is also becoming popular with makers of high-tech appliances, such as the television viewing product named TiVo®. The low cost and lack of licensing restrictions make it ideal for such operations. It is clear that Linux is growing in popularity and will be taking a growing portion of the market over the next few years.

Recently, Linux has made some fascinating inroads into very high-end computing. Many scientific research endeavors require computing power well beyond the capabilities of any standard server—Windows, Unix, or Linux. This leads some research facilities to purchase supercomputers that often cost millions of dollars. A supercomputer is a very powerful computer. A normal computer running Unix or Windows may have only two or four processors. A supercomputer is essentially a multiprocessor machine, running hundreds or even thousands of processors. All of those processors need very specialized cooling that is quite expensive. In the past few years, some researchers have linked dozens and even hundreds of old PCs with Linux on them, making them work in concert and essentially mimicking the power of a supercomputer. This setup is referred to as a *hive*. This type of setup usually depends on old, often discarded PCs running a free version of Linux. Thus, the only cost is that of connecting the PCs and powering them. This is yet one more way that Linux is making its mark on the world of computing.

SUMMARY

Linux is a powerful and inexpensive operating system that provides a very user-friendly graphical user interface and provides access to a number of software applications. Linux is an open source Unix clone, which means that much, if not most, of what you do in Linux is identical to what you do in Unix. Its price and stability are attracting a growing number of users, but there are still a number of applications that have no corresponding Linux version. It is also important to note that more obscure hardware may not have a Linux driver.

REVIEW QUESTIONS

1. What operating system are both Minix and Linux based on?
2. What does GNU stand for?
3. Who invented Linux?
4. List two advantages of Linux over Windows.
5. List two advantages of Windows over Linux.
6. What filesystem does Linux use by default?
7. What filesystem does Windows XP use by default?

2 Installing Linux

In This Chapter

- Getting Started
- The Install Process
- Disk Partitioning
- Continuing with the Installation
- Choosing Packages
- Completing the Installation

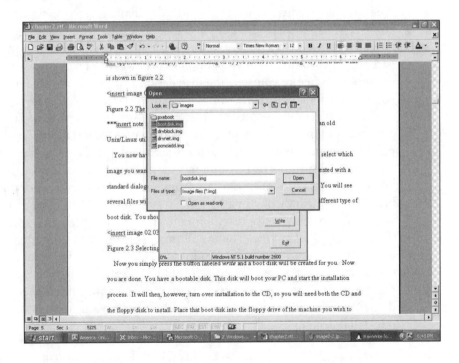

INTRODUCTION

We now have taken a broad overview of the world of Linux, including a brief history and an examination of the advantages and disadvantages of Linux versus Windows. However, we won't be able to do much of anything with Linux unless we install it. Although this is not a particularly difficult process, you should realize that installing any operating system is a very important step.

The most obvious reason is that you cannot use the operating system until you install it. However, there are other reasons why the installation is very important. The manner in which you install the operating system and the options you select during installation will determine what features your operating system has and, to some extent, how it behaves on your machine. For this reason, you must pay very close attention to this process. This process is critical, but it's not particularly difficult if you proceed carefully; still, there are pitfalls you will need to avoid. It is recommended that you read this entire chapter before attempting the install. You should not simply start at the beginning of the chapter and follow along as you read. Read through the entire chapter one time, making certain that you understand all the issues involved, and then go through the chapter a second time while you actually perform an installation. Pay particular attention to any Notes in the text. These Notes are designed to highlight potential problems or specific issues that will require particularly close attention on your part. That way, you will be aware of any potential problems before you start the installation process. If after reading this chapter you still are not comfortable with the install process, it might be a good idea to also read the installation instructions that came with your version of Linux. After you carefully read this chapter and are certain you understand the material, then simply pay attention to the installation process itself and you should do just fine.

It may seem odd to recommend that you pay attention to the installation process, but this admonition comes from long experience. It is not uncommon for beginners to rush through parts of the install and end up doing some things very wrong. If you simply pay careful attention to each screen and read any instructions, you should be fine. The install process is not that difficult; in fact, it is no more difficult than installing Windows and, in same ways, even less difficult. Of course in the worst-case scenario, should you totally botch the installation, you can simply reinstall the operating system. You cannot damage the hardware by doing a bad installation. However, you can render your machine unusable until a reinstall is accomplished.

If you really botch the installation, you will have to repartition your hard drive and reinstall the operating system. This chapter discusses the process of partitioning a hard drive. It is a very good idea either to perform your first Linux installation on

an old machine that does not have any important data or to make sure you have made backups of all your data before beginning the installation process. In fact, if you are not using an old machine that has no data, it is absolutely critical that you back up all data before starting. Failing to do so can lead to a loss of all of your data.

This introduction might have left you frightened. Remember that if you first carefully read the instructions in this chapter and perhaps any documentation that came with your Linux distribution, you should be fine. Most readers who read and follow the instructions carefully will have no problems installing. However, for those readers who just don't want to try it, there are a number of major computer stores that offer PCs that come with Linux already installed. Usually they are much cheaper than a Windows PC. You can always purchase one of those and skip the installation process. The key, if you choose to install yourself, is to read this chapter and your distribution's documentation before installing.

This book uses Red Hat Linux for all examples; however, the installation of other distributions such as SuSE or Mandrake will have a great many similarities. In fact, the installation process of any Linux distribution is likely to have more similarities than differences. If you are using one of the other major Linux distributions, don't worry. The material in this chapter, combined with the documentation that came with your particular Linux distribution, should still be enough for you to install Linux. Also keep in mind that when you are through the installation, the other tasks in this book are common to all major Linux distributions.

Before you embark on the installation of Red Hat 9.0, or any software for that matter, you should make sure that your system will support it. The minimum hardware specifications to run a particular software package are also referred to as its *system requirements*. These minimum requirements are usually determined by the operating system vendor. System requirements are yet another reason to consider moving to Linux. The Linux operating system does not require an expensive high-end PC in order to run. In fact, Linux has been successfully installed and run on machines that literally were thrown away by small businesses. Red Hat puts the specifications for its Professional Edition at a Pentium II 400MHz or faster processor, 28 megabytes of RAM, 1.3 gigabytes of hard drive space, a mouse, and a CD-ROM. The Personal Edition, which this book focuses on, can be installed on a Pentium II 200MHz processor with only 64 megabytes of RAM. To give you a perspective on how low these system requirements are, remember that these are Pentium II machines. Pentium IV is the current model of Intel processor as of this writing. You also would have a difficult time finding a new computer that had less than 128 megabytes of RAM. In fact, even low-end PCs tend to have 256 megabytes of RAM and at least 10 gigabytes of hard drive space. If you purchased a new machine anytime in the last 18 months, Linux probably will install and run just fine on it. In fact, Linux will work on machines so old and outdated that they are not even sold in stores any longer and have not been for several years. This means that you don't need an expensive PC to run Linux or even a new machine.

It is critical that you realize that the manufacturer's minimum recommended hardware is just that, a bare minimum. If you choose to use a PC that only has that bare minimum, you will find that it performs quite sluggishly, although it will work. You will usually want more than the minimum requirements for any software you use. Fortunately, any system purchased new in the last two years is likely to be more than enough for Linux. However, the author's personal recommended minimums, which exceed the manufacturer's minimum standards, are a Pentium III 500, 128 megabytes of RAM, and a 5-gigabyte hard drive. Fortunately, the machine just described would have been considered new in about 1999. That means that you still won't need to purchase an expensive new computer to run Linux. The rule of thumb on any PC, however, is that there is no such thing as too much power. Today you can purchase a brand new Pentium IV with 512 megabytes of RAM and a 20-gigabyte hard drive for less than $500 from virtually any major computer store.

You can obtain Linux from a variety of sources. Most local computer stores such as Best Buy™ and Microcenter™ carry the major distributions of Linux. You also can order or download Linux from the several Web sites, some of which are listed here. Some of these sites offer a Linux distribution for free, and others for a small fee.

These are various distribution Web sites:

- *www.redhat.com/*
- *www.redhat.com/download/howto_download.html*
- *www.mandrakelinux.com/*
- *www.debian.org*
- *www.slackware.com*
- *www.suse.com*

These are generic Linux Web sites:

- *http://linux.tucows.com/*
- *www.linux.com*
- *http://download.com.com/3150-2035-0.html?tag=dir*

These sites offer very inexpensive or free Linux CDs:

- *www.cheapbytes.com/*
- *http://freelinuxcd.org/*

Unless you are a particularly savvy reader, it is recommended that you purchase a commercial version of Linux, such as Red Hat 9.0. The installation is much easier, and there is extensive documentation included. If you download, you will have a more complicated time with the installation. You might need to transfer the installation files to one or more CDs before beginning the installation.

The installation described in this chapter was done with a commercial version of Red Hat 9.0, purchased for about $50 at one of the major computer stores. There was nothing special purchased or added. The author simply bought Red Hat 9.0 Personal Edition off the shelf exactly as you would find it. However, it should be stressed that this installation can be done with Linux versions obtained from other sources, and anywhere you obtain Red Hat Linux, the installation should be much the same. Even other Linux distributions such as Mandrake, Debian, and SuSE should be very similar.

GETTING STARTED

Most computers today can *boot* (start up) from the CD-ROM. This means that if you put disk one of the Red Hat installation disks into your CD drive and *reboot* (restart) your machine, it should start up the Linux installation. However, if it does not, the reason is probably that your PC is not booting through the CD drive. Don't worry, all PCs have their floppy drive somewhere in the boot sequence, so we can do an install from a floppy. Let's begin by examining how this is done.

Making a Bootable Floppy Disk

If your PC boots through the CD drive, you can skip this part. It is for those readers whose machines will not boot through the CD drive. This process is not particularly complicated. Your first step is to find a working PC that you can use to create the bootable disk. If you find a machine with Windows on it like the one you are about to install Linux on, that would be perfect. Simply place the first CD-ROM of your installation set into the CD drive and place a blank floppy into your floppy drive. Using either My Computer or Windows Explorer, find the folder located on your CD that is named \dosutils\rawritewin. If you are using My Computer, you should see something much like what is shown in Figure 2.1a. If you prefer to use Windows Explorer™, then your screen will appear much like what is shown in Figure 2.1b.

You should notice a file named rawritewin.exe. This program is going to make the blank disk you put into your floppy drive into a boot disk for the Linux install. When you launch this application (by double-clicking on it) you should see something very much like what is shown in Figure 2.2.

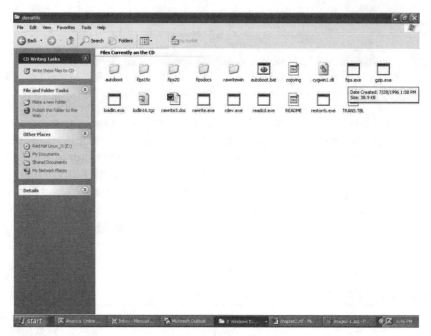

FIGURE 2.1A   The DOS utilities via My Computer.

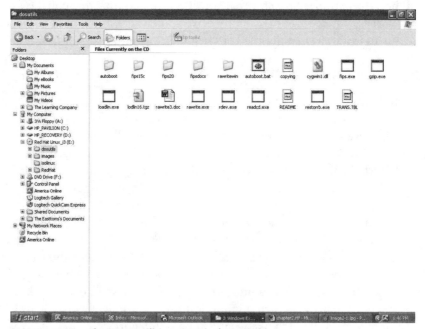

FIGURE 2.1B   The DOS utilities via Windows Explorer.

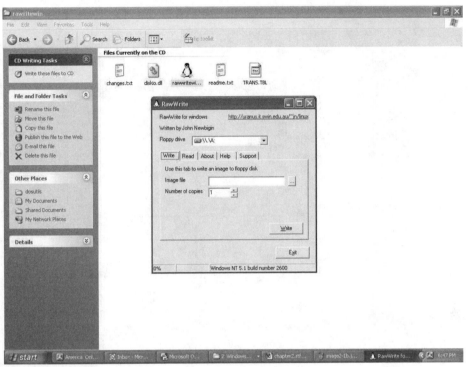

FIGURE 2.2   The rawwritewin application.

rawwritewin *is actually a Windows wrapper for an old Unix/Linux utility called* rawwrite. *That utility is used to write material to disks.*

You now have to use the small button next to the text box titled "Image file" to select the image you want to place on the disk. When you press that button, you will be presented with a standard dialog box that enables you to select a particular file from a specific folder. You will see several files with the extension .img. These are *images*, and each is used to create a different type of boot disk. You should select the bootdisk.img file, as shown in Figure 2.3. On some Linux distribution disks, the file is called boot.img, so if you do not see bootdisk.img, then select boot.img.

Now you simply press the button labeled Write, and a boot disk will be created for you. Now you are done. You have a bootable disk. This disk will boot your PC and start the installation process. It will then turn over installation to the CD, so you will need both the CD and the floppy disk to install. Place the boot disk into the floppy drive of the machine you want to install Red Hat Linux on, and put the first of your installation CDs into the CD drive. Then, reboot your PC and the install process will start.

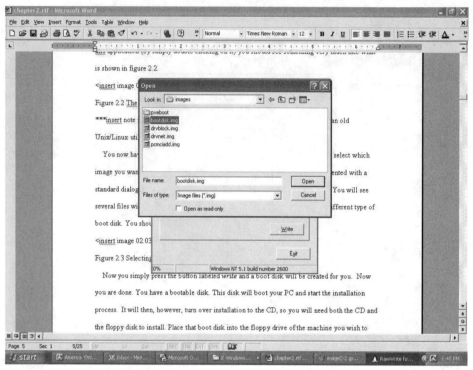

FIGURE 2.3 Selecting the `boot.img` file.

The installation described in this chapter makes some specific choices. These choices will install specific applications. These applications will be covered later in this book. If you do not follow this installation process exactly as it is detailed in this book, you might not be installing all the applications we will be covering later.

Now we are ready to install Linux. Simply place disk one in the CD drive and restart your PC (unless you were using a floppy disk install, in which case your floppy disk and your CD should already be in their respective drives). After it boots up, you will see the opening screen. There is very little information on this screen; it simply notifies you that you are ready to start the installation.

If you have ever watched a Microsoft Windows machine boot up, you will notice that the Linux bootup shows a lot more information. What you are seeing is virtually every detail of the boot process.

You are asked how you wish to proceed with the installation. You almost always will want to choose the first option, Install in Graphical Mode. You can select this option by simply pressing the Enter key. In fact, the only good reason not to use graphical mode would be if your PC were so outdated that it would not support a graphical installation. Of course, if your machine does not support a graphical installation, then it probably will not support most of the really cool graphical Linux products such as KDE*, GNOME, GIMP, and Open Office. If you will recall our earlier discussion about system requirements, then consider that the author has personally installed Red Hat 9.0 with all options in graphical mode on a Pentium II 233MHz with only 64 megabytes of memory. (However, it should be noted that the machine does not perform as well as one might like.) To put this in perspective, a machine like the one just described has not been sold new in stores since about 1998. This means that you probably have a machine that is more than capable of using graphical mode and running everything that Linux has to offer.

This is another strong point in favor of Linux. Unlike Microsoft Windows, it is not resource intensive. Red Hat 9.0 will run on machines that do not support later versions of Windows, such as Windows XP.

With some installation disks you will be asked next if you want to test your CD. Several editions of Red Hat 8.0 and earlier include this screen, particularly installations from third parties. The Personal Edition of Red Hat 9.0 does not include it. If you purchased a packaged version of Linux such as Red Hat, then this is probably unnecessary, and you can select No. If you downloaded Linux onto your own CDs, you probably want to select Yes. The reason for this is simple. If you copied downloaded install files to a CD using your own CD burner, a variety of things may have gone wrong, and it is possible that the CD is not in proper working order. If you are using a packaged installation purchased commercially, it is very unlikely that the CD has any damage.

On the next screen, you will find an introduction to Red Hat Linux. It will explain what is going to happen and tell you a little about Red Hat. If this is your first time installing Linux, it is recommended that you carefully read this screen before pressing the Next button at the bottom of the screen. It will give you an overview of what the installation process will be doing.

The next two screens are very simple. They ask what language you want to use and what keyboard setup you want. Select your language from the options provided. These steps are shown in Figures 2.4 and 2.5. It is interesting to notice the plethora of languages you have to select from. Linux is now available to users in a variety of nations, using a wide range of languages.

The next screen, shown in Figure 2.6a, asks what type of mouse you have. If you don't see your model, select either the two-button PS2 generic mouse or the two-button serial generic mouse. There is also a check box labeled "Emulate a Three Button Mouse" that is checked by default. You can choose to leave it checked or not.

---

*KDE is a trademark of KDEe.V.

FIGURE 2.4 Choosing a language.

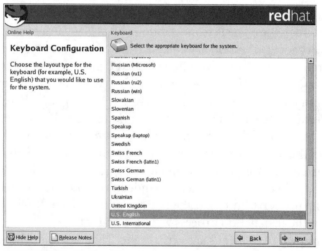

FIGURE 2.5 Keyboard setup.

If your mouse connector (the end that connects to the PC) is a small round plug, then it is a PS2 connector. If it is a horizontal plug with several pins (usually there are nine pins), it is a serial connector. If you are unfamiliar with mice and connectors, you should probably read Appendix D, "PC Hardware," before continuing with this book. It will give you a brief crash course in PC hardware. For readers who do not know how to tell what type of mouse they have, a picture of the connector for each of the three major types is shown in Figures 2.6b, 2.6c, and 2.6d.

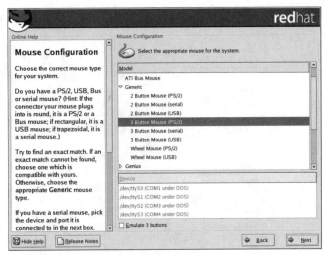

FIGURE 2.6A Select your mouse type.

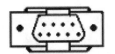

FIGURE 2.6B A serial
mouse connector.

FIGURE 2.6C A PS2
mouse connector.

FIGURE 2.6D A USB
mouse connector.

If the machine you are installing on already has a previous version of Linux on it, then you will be asked whether you want to wipe out the old installation completely and start from scratch or simply upgrade. This is shown in Figure 2.7.

The next step is to select packages. A *package* is a logical grouping of a number of separate applications. The various applications that you can install with Linux are grouped so that you can easily pick the set of applications you are most likely to need, depending on how you intend to use the machine. Your choice of packages will determine what software gets installed on your PC. The options are:

- Personal Desktop
- Workstation
- Server
- Custom

Each of these is designed for a specific type of user. These various package configurations are summarized in Table 2.1.

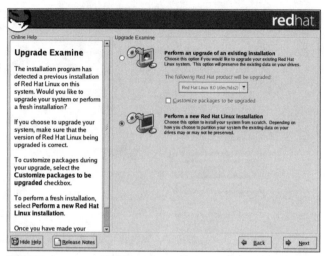

FIGURE 2.7 Installation or upgrade?

TABLE 2.1 Installation Packages

Package	Contents/Purpose
Personal Desktop	This includes things the average home user would want, including Internet software such as Web browsers and e-mail clients. It also includes graphics programs and games.
Workstation	This is intended for the business user and includes productivity tools such as Open Office.
Server	This option is for servers. It will install a Web server, an FTP server, an e-mail server, and other server software.
Custom	This option allows you to pick any packages you want to install.

Each of these packages is provided to make installation for a certain type of machine simple. However, this simplicity comes at a cost. If you choose Personal Desktop or Workstation, you will not be installing the Web server, FTP server, or other server packages. Conversely, if you select Server, you will not be installing many personal use items such as games. Since each of the preset options has some limitations, for our purposes we will choose Custom because we want several elements drawn from more than one package. When you select Custom, you will be prompted during the installation to select individual packages and applications to install. Later in this chapter we will cover the options you should select. For now, select Custom. This screen is shown in Figure 2.8.

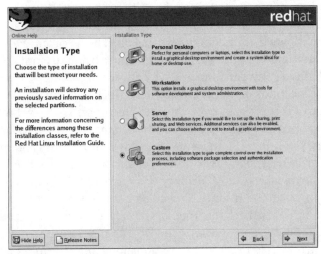

FIGURE 2.8   Selecting packages.

The next screen will take you into the process of disk partitioning. This is probably the most important and complex part of the installation. As such, it warrants a separate part of this chapter, which will explain exactly what disk partitions are and how to partition.

DISK PARTITIONING

The first question you might be asking yourself at this point is: what, exactly, is a disk partition? Partitioning is literally the process of dividing your hard drive into one or more useable segments. Simply put, you can divide your hard drive into several *logical drives*. A logical drive is simply a part of your hard drive that is treated as if it were a separate drive. In other words, you can treat your hard drive as if it were several different hard drives. This is particularly useful for very large hard drives, and in cases where people wish to organize their computer more efficiently. You might have one partition that is designated for business, and another for home use or entertainment. A partition that is created to look like a separate hard drive is called a *logical drive*. Your computer might have only one actual hard drive, but several logical drives. Partitions and logical drives are not applicable only to Linux. All operating systems have partitions and can be divided into logical drives. Even if you are not going to partition your hard drive into multiple logical drives, you will still need to partition it. The only difference is that you will partition it into a single logical drive.

This brings us to the topic of partitioning a hard drive that will run Linux. Your hard drive must have at least one main partition. This primary partition is the starting point when your computer turns on. This is called the *root partition*. It must also have one swap partition. This of course brings us immediately to the question of what is a swap partition and why do you need one? A swap partition is a pretty incredible innovation. Essentially, it is a small segment of your hard drive that is set aside as a sort of backup for your PC's memory. The way it works is rather simple. As you open up programs, they are loaded into memory. So, as you open more programs, you utilize use more and more of your memory and there is less free memory for other programs to use. When a program has been idle for a while, the program is taken out of memory and moved to this swap file. If you later activate that program, for instance by clicking on it, it is moved from the swap file portion of the hard drive back into memory. By placing it into a special segment of the hard drive, it can be more quickly reloaded into memory than if you simply loaded it off the normal hard drive partition. Thus the name "swap," since it swaps programs from memory to a special segment of the hard drive.

All operating systems support swap partitions. The swap partition's size should be at least equal to the amount of RAM your machine has, but no more than two and one half times the RAM. That means if you have 128 megabytes of RAM, your swap partition should be at least 128 megabytes in size but no more than 320 megabytes.

Now that you understand disk partitions, at least in a rudimentary fashion, you are ready to partition your hard drive. You will notice that the Red Hat Linux installation gives you three options. The first is to partition your hard drive automatically. You can choose this option if you have no intention of dual booting your machine.

CAUTION

If you choose to automatic partition, all existing partitions will be erased and one root partition, one boot partition, and one swap partition will be created.

The second option is to use Disk Druid. Disk Druid is a graphical disk partitioning program specifically designed for Linux.

The final option is FDisk. FDisk is a program that will be familiar to some Windows users because it is used to partition Windows machines. However, it is rather complicated to use and does not provide a nice graphical interface. For our purposes, we will use Disk Druid.

While it is certainly possible to dual boot a system with both Windows and Linux, it is much simpler just to have a Linux machine. Less-experienced readers would probably have an easier time using their entire machine for a single Linux partition, using the Automatic Partition option. Those readers who want to dual boot are advised to read the following paragraphs and any documentation that came with their Linux distribution carefully.

When you select Disk Druid, you will be taken to a screen displaying your current partitions. There are two courses of action you might take. First, if you are not going to dual boot your system (have more than one operating system on it), then it is probably best to highlight each partition, one by one, and delete it. Then you can start fresh. Then you will choose the New button, which will take you to a screen where you can set the parameters for this new drive. This is shown in Figure 2.9a.

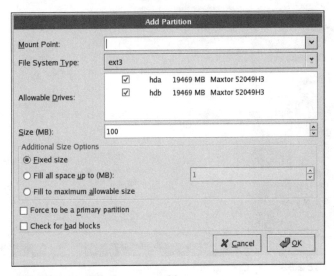

FIGURE 2.9A Setting up partitions.

You also are taken to this screen if you choose to edit an existing partition.

If you are planning to dual boot with an operating system that is already installed—for example, should you wish to install Linux on your Windows machine and keep both operating systems—then you will *not* delete all the existing partitions. You will delete all partitions except for the one that contains Windows. This means that when we are done you will have one Windows partition and one Linux partition.

The important point to remember is that you should leave the partition that has Windows completely untouched. The real question is, how do you know which partition has Windows? Linux and Disk Druid identify partitions differently than Windows does, but both Disk Druid and Windows list the size of the partition. The trick is to boot up your system before you begin the install and use My Computer to note the size of the partition you want to install Linux on. For example, consider Figure 2.9b.

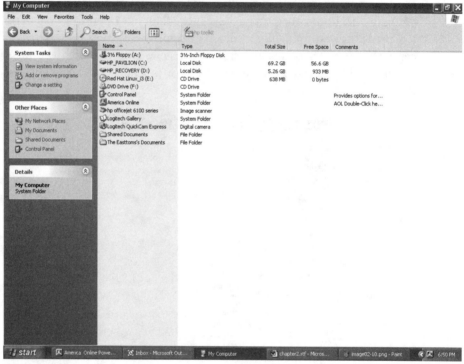

FIGURE 2.9B My Computer.

This is one more reason why you were advised to read this entire chapter before attempting to perform the installation.

Here we see there is a single large partition of 13.6 gigabytes, and it is called the C drive. When you start the Linux install and get to Disk Druid, you will not see a drive labeled C, but you will see a drive that is about 56.6 gigabytes in size.

The best way to do a dual boot with Windows is to have a separate partition created to hold Linux. This partition should be created before you begin the Linux installation. If you are uncomfortable with partitioning your hard drive, you might consider using a commercial product such as Partition Magic™, available from www.powerquest.com. *If that were present on the machine depicted in Figure 2.9b, you would also see a D or an E drive. Also note that it is much simpler to have one operating system per machine. In other words, it's easier and simpler to have a separate Linux and Windows PC than to try to install both on one machine.*

One significant problem with Disk Druid, however, is that you cannot resize the partitions. If your machine already has two partitions of about the right size to handle Windows and Linux, then this is fine. If it does not, you could be in for a problem. As we already discussed, one of the easiest and relatively least expensive routes is to obtain some utility such as Partition Magic, install it in Windows, and resize your partitions as you see fit. Then when you reboot and install Linux, the partitions will already be set up for you. If you want to repartition your machine manually so that you can dual boot, the best option for you is to follow Microsoft's recommendations. The Microsoft Web site *www.microsoft.com/exchange/tech-info/tips/StorageTip2.asp* may be of some help to you.

Another option is to use the FDisk utility, previously mentioned, to repartition your drive. FDisk does not actually allow you to resize your partitions as you need to. However, it does let you delete one partition and create one or more partitions from that freed space. One of the best Web pages on the Internet on the FDisk utility can be found at *www.computerhope.com/fdiskhlp.htm*. You can also access the Linux FDisk manual at *www.die.net/doc/linux/man/man8/fdisk.8.html*. FDisk is more versatile, but also more complex. For this reason, this book will focus on Disk Druid. Readers who want to learn more about FDisk are encouraged to use the Web sites previously mentioned and perhaps do a search in their favorite search engine for FDisk for even more resources.

Assuming that you are not dual booting, you will probably want to use Disk Druid to create only two partitions: a swap partition, described earlier, and a single large partition for your operating system. This is the simplest setup and is highly recommended for beginners. Once you have made those selections, you click to tell Disk Druid you are done. You also can select a check box indicating that you want the installation process to check the actual physical disks before creating the partitions. This is a very good idea. It is time consuming, but it ensures that you won't be installing Linux on a bad hard drive.

CONTINUING WITH THE INSTALLATION

Once you have finished with Disk Druid, there are still some steps to take before installation is complete. The next screen will list the operating systems on your PC. If you are not dual booting, you should see just one, Linux. If you are dual booting, you can select which operating system you want to be the default. This is shown in Figure 2.10.

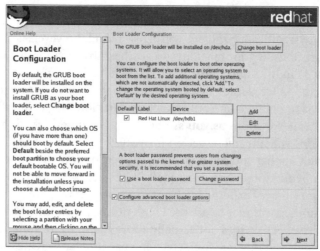

FIGURE 2.10   Selecting an operating system.

When your machine first starts, you will be given a display listing these operating systems, and you will be given a few moments to select one. If you do not make a selection, the default will be selected for you. You should note that what this screen is doing is configuring your *boot loader*. A boot loader is just a small program that loads the operating system into memory. During your boot phase, it loads the operating system, thus the name boot loader. Many Linux distributions use the *LILO* (Linux load) boot loader software. Red Hat 9.0 uses a newer boot loader, *GRUB* (Grand Unified Boot Loader). Among other things, GRUB makes dual booting much easier.

The next stage of the installation is to configure your network adapter. The network adapter, also called an NIC (network interface card), is simply the card that you plug a network cable into. If this is a stand-alone home machine, leave the default settings shown in Figure 2.11.

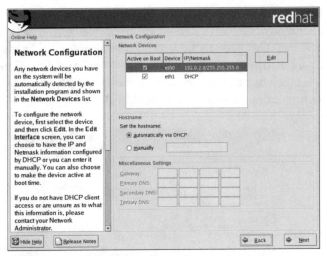

FIGURE 2.11 Network configuration.

If this is not a stand-alone machine but instead is a machine that will be used on a network, you will need to set the IP address assigned to you by your network administrator.

If you are not on a network but are going to log on to the Internet, the chances are that your Internet service provider (ISP) assigns you an IP each time you log on (this is referred to as a dynamic IP). This is the default setting for Linux, so you should be fine. If your ISP assigns you a static IP, a rather unusual step for an ISP to take, it will have to tell you what that IP address is.

An IP address consists of four numbers, each between 0 and 255 and separated by periods. An example of an IP address is 10.32.0.43.

Don't panic if you either don't know the proper network settings right now or put them in wrong. You can change them at any time, once you have Linux up and running. Chapter 4, "System Configuration in KDE," shows you in detail exactly how to do it.

After you have configured your network card, the next phase is to set up the firewall. You might be wondering what a firewall is. A *firewall* is a barrier between your computer and the outside world. It is your first line of defense with hackers. A firewall can be a separate device (such as a router or another PC) or software that filters incoming packets. In this case it is software that filters incoming packets. If you do not have extensive knowledge of firewalls, your best bet is to leave the default settings. This firewall, however, is one more of the many strengths of the Red Hat Linux distribution. It is bundled with and installs a firewall, and that makes your PC much more secure from the various dangers posed by the Internet. The default configuration is shown in Figure 2.12.

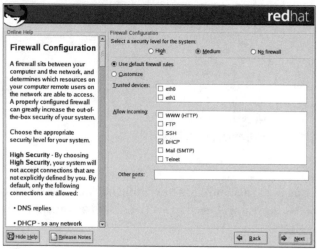

FIGURE 2.12   Firewall configuration.

 The network interface cards (NICs) in your PC are listed in order as eth0, eth1, *and so on.* eth *is short for Ethernet. Most home PCs have only one card.*

Once you have set up your firewall, the next screen will ask if there are additional languages you want to install. You can have support for multiple languages on your Linux PC. If you are using only one language, you won't need to do anything at this stage.

The next few screens are very simple. In fact, they are pretty self explanatory, but we will discuss them briefly. The very next screen has you select your time zone. If you get this wrong, don't worry; as with the network configuration, you can reconfigure this after your PC is up and running. You can see the time zone screen in Figure 2.13.

The next screen is simple but important. Here you do two things, set the root password and add user accounts. The main action taken at this point and depicted in Figure 2.14 is to set the root password.

This is critical. In Linux and Unix, root is like the system administrator in Windows. Anyone who logs on to your PC as root can do anything to the machine. This

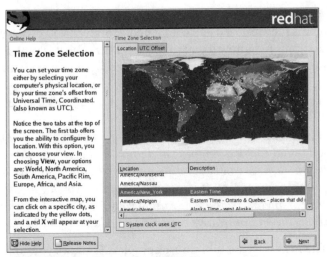

FIGURE 2.13   Selecting the time zone.

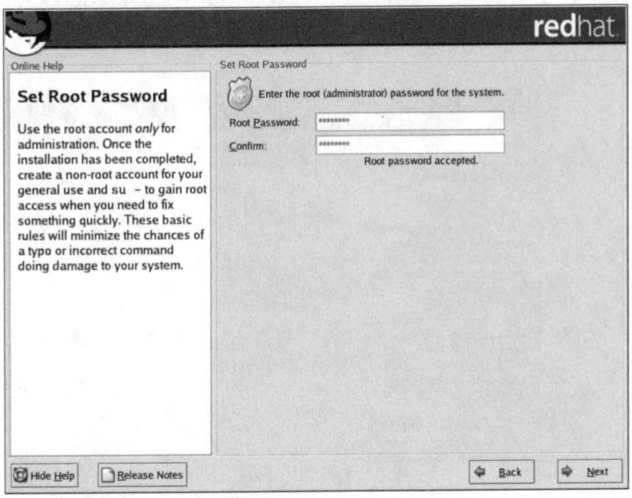

FIGURE 2.14   Setting the root password.

means you must select a good password. It should be at least eight characters in length and contain a combination of letters and numbers. Make certain you write it down somewhere. If you forget it, you are in really deep trouble. Your only option will be to reinstall completely and wipe out the previous Linux installation.

On this screen, you also can add user accounts. These are important because you can define users with specific permissions, allowing them to do only the tasks you want them to do. You must set a root password before leaving this screen, but adding users can be done later if you prefer. In fact, many Linux administrators add users after the machine is fully installed and configured. However, you do have the option of adding user accounts right now if you so desire. Either way, it is probably a good idea to take a minute and add a user account for yourself. That way, you can log on without needing to do so as root. A common system for usernames is to use the first initial of the first name with the last name. For example, the author's username might be `ceasttom`.

It is usually unwise to simply log on as root every time you use your PC. The reason is that root has complete and unfettered access to the entire system. However, in this book we will be covering some basic administrative duties that will require you to log on as root. It is recommended that you log on as the username you just created anytime you are just using your Linux machine, but log on as root when trying the administrative exercises found later in this book.

The next screen is a bit more complex. It allows you to set various encryption schemes for your PC. Unless you have some significant understanding of these various encryption methodologies, you should leave the default settings and move past this screen, which is shown in Figure 2.15.

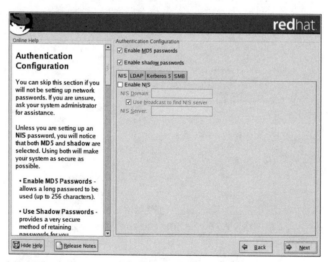

FIGURE 2.15 Setting encryption schemes.

After setting up the encryption schemes, you will be on to choosing packages. This is a rather lengthy topic in itself and will be covered in the next section. You are now, however, done with the essential configuration of your PC and have reached a significant milestone in the installation process.

CHOOSING PACKAGES

What packages you choose to install is a very important topic. Next to the Disk Druid, this is probably the most important part of the installation. There are a number of packages you could select, each with a different purpose. They are divided into categories such as desktops, servers, and development. Each of those categories will be explored in this part, and specific package groups will be explained. At the end of this section is a list of the packages it is recommended you select. The Package Group Selection screen is shown in Figure 2.16.

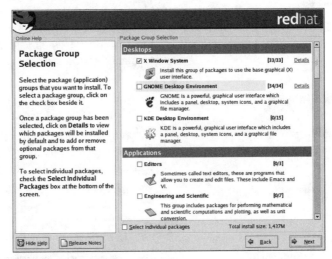

FIGURE 2.16 Package selection.

Desktops

You can use Linux in a simple command-line mode (also called shell mode). This means that you type in everything on a plain black screen, but why would you want to? As a Windows user, you are used to a rich graphical interface, and you probably want to continue using such an interface. Linux not only provides you with a very easy-to-use graphical interface, it provides you with more than one to choose from. There are three packages listed in this section: X Window System, GNOME (GNU Object Model Environment), and KDE (K Desktop Environment). Each of these is a complete graphical window interface that operates in a fashion similar to Microsoft Windows. Which one you choose is a matter of preference. In this book we will use the KDE user interface. Whether you choose KDE or GNOME, it should be chosen in conjunction with X Window System. In order to follow along with this book, you should select GNOME, KDE, and X Window System.

Applications

This part is going to be very important to you. It lists the various types of applications Linux can install. Most of it is self explanatory. For example, the Office Productivity package includes word processors, spreadsheets, and so on. The Games and Entertainment package includes games for Linux. A complete list, with explanation, is provided in Table 2.2.

TABLE 2.2 Application Packages

Package	Purpose
Editors	This package provides a variety of text editors, many of which have functionality far beyond text editors such as Notepad, which you may have used.
Engineering and Scientific	This package contains a number of programs for scientist and engineers.
Graphical Internet	Including this package will provide you with access to a variety of Internet tools, including a Web browser, chat software, and e-mail clients.
Text-Based Internet	You will need this package only if you will be running without a desktop graphical user environment. It will allow you to check e-mail and do some Internet activities.
Office Productivity	This package includes a wide array of word processors, spread sheets, presentation tools, and more.
Sound and Video	Installing this package gives you access to several programs used to record sound and video, play video, and more.
Authoring and Publishing	These programs are specifically for desktop publishing and Web page development.
Graphics	In this package you will find applications for image manipulation. Some of these applications are on a par with commercial products such as Adobe Photoshop.
Games and Entertainment.	Red Hat Linux 9.0 comes with several games you can use to amuse yourself

Servers

There are a number of different server-related packages available. These include Web servers, database servers, and news servers. Some of these packages will apply only to network servers, but some may be applicable to small business and personal use. The individual packages are described in Table 2.3.

TABLE 2.3   Server Packages

Package	Purpose
Server and Configuration Tools	This is a vital package that contains many tools for configuring a server. If you are installing any of the other server packages, it is a good idea to install this one as well.
Web Server	This package contains the software you will need to turn your PC into your own personal Web server.
Windows File Server	This contains software that will enable you to share files with machines that are running Windows. If your Linux PC will interact in a heterogeneous network environment (a network with more than one operating system), you will probably need this package.
DNS Name Server	If your Linux server is going to be a DNS (Domain Name System) server for a network, you will need this package.
FTP Server	This package enables you to upload and download files to and from your PC over a network or the Internet.
SQL Database Server	This is a very robust, fully functional database server. If you are running a small-to-medium size business, you may need this package.
News Server	This package enables you to host discussion groups/newsgroups on your PC. This is not recommended for most users.
Network Servers	This package includes a variety of applications used in running a network server.

Development

If you are a programmer, then you will absolutely love Red Hat 9.0. It offers a wide range of development tools that you can install for free. You will have everything you need to develop Linux software of your own. The individual packages are described in Table 2.4.

TABLE 2.4   Development Packages

Package	Purpose
Development Tools	This package contains a number of generic development tools for creating programs in C, C++, Lisp, Java, and other programming languages. Compilers, editors, and all required tools are in this package.
Kernel Development	This package contains the tools and the code to the Linux kernel. If you are a skilled programmer and want to alter the Linux operating system, you can do it.
X Software Development	This package is specifically for developing software to run with X Window System.
GNOME Software Development	This package includes everything you need to develop software to run with GNOME.
KDE Software Development	This package has everything you need to develop software that runs with KDE.

System

The various system packages are useful for administering your Linux PC. It is recommended that you install each of the three packages. They are administrative tools, system tools, and printing support.

Miscellaneous

This is not really a set of packages so much as it is two additional choices. If your PC is short of hard drive space, you can select Minimal. With this option, you won't get many of the interesting and useful applications that come with Red Hat, but you will have the bare essentials. The other option, Everything, is exactly what you think it is, all packages. This option requires over four gigabytes of hard drive space.

Different Linux users will find different combinations of packages to their liking. However, this book concentrates on certain applications that you must install. For that reason, please ensure that you select everything in Table 2.5.

TABLE 2.5   Recommended Packages

Part	Packages
Desktops	X Window System
	KDE
	GNOME
Applications	Editors
	Graphical Internet
	Office Productivity
	Graphics
	Games and Entertainment
Servers	Server and Configuration Tools
	Web Server
	FTP Server
	SQL Database Server
Development	None
System	All packages
Miscellaneous	None

This set of packages is a good mix of server, workstation, and personal options. You have the office productivity of a business workstation, the entertainment and graphics of a personal workstation, and the Web and FTP server software of a server. Together, these packages, many of which will be covered in this book, will give you a wide range of applications you can choose from. However, if your hard drive is significantly larger than five gigabytes, as many current ones are, you would be well advised to select the Everything option and install all packages. Of course, this will make your installation take longer.

It is also very important to note that packages can be added and removed after Linux is in operation. The procedure to add or remove packages will be described later in this book. Chapter 14, "Miscellaneous Linux Applications," includes a section on adding and removing packages.

As you go through this book, you will be introduced to various applications that are used in Linux. If you do not include the appropriate packages, you will not have those applications on your machine. However, you can either add a package or download the application from a Web site. In most cases, you are given the Web site when you are first introduced to the product. It is also possible that readers using a different Linux distribution or a different version of Red Hat will not have all of the applications installed.

COMPLETING THE INSTALLATION

At this point, the installation will run unattended for several minutes. Depending on the speed of your PC's processor and the number of packages you selected, this could take anywhere from a few minutes up to 30 minutes or more. At some point the CD-ROM door will open and you will be prompted to insert disk two. When that disk is done, there are just a few basic configuration items you need to take care of. As your disk is installing, you will see a screen displaying the progress of the installation. That screen is shown in Figure 2.17.

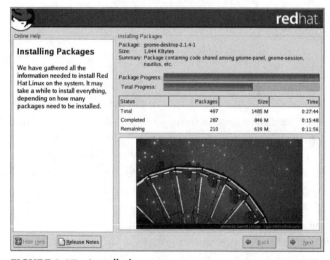

FIGURE 2.17 Installation progress.

The more packages you select, the longer the installation will take. An installation that includes all available packages can take over two hours.

You will be asked to set the current time zone. This is relatively easy; there is a list of major cities around the world, and you should pick the one closest to you. You also can select your time zone from a map of the world. You will be asked if you want to create a boot disk. This is highly recommended. This is an emergency disk that can get your machine up and running in the event of a catastrophic failure. You also will be asked whether you want Linux to boot to graphical mode automatically or to a shell. You should choose graphical mode. Finally, you will be prompted to remove any disks from your system, and the PC will restart. You have successfully installed Linux and are ready to start using it.

In normal operations it is not recommended that you log on as the root user. Remember that the root is the same thing as an administrator in Windows. However, for the purposes of this book, you should log on as root. That way, you will have access to all the features of Linux, including administrative tools. This will be critical when we cover administrative tools later in this book.

SUMMARY

This chapter walked you through the installation of Red Hat 9.0 Linux. You were shown the steps needed to install Linux successfully. This chapter also explained the concept of partitioning and gave suggestions as to how you should partition your drive. Finally, each of the major packages was explained, and you were given a list of what packages you should consider installing. It is recommended that you read this chapter carefully before attempting to install Linux on your PC.

The installation process requires some practice. The chances are that once your PC is up and running with Linux, you will not have occasion to install Linux again for quite some time. In fact, you may not install Linux again unless someone asks you to help him install it. For this reason, it is a good idea for you to repeat the entire installation process once or twice. Once your PC is in use, you will have data on it that would be wiped out by a reinstallation. If you want to practice the installation a few more times, do it now, before you personalize your PC or begin to save any data. If you choose not to practice the installation, you should at least read this chapter once thoroughly before you install and review it again after the installation. This will help to ensure that you have a firm understanding of the installation process.

REVIEW QUESTIONS

1. What are the four options for selecting packages?
2. If your PC has two NICs, what would the second one be named when you look at firewall or network configuration?
3. What is Disk Druid?
4. What is the minimum size for your swap partition?
5. What is the maximum size for your swap partition?
6. What is GRUB?
7. What is LILO?
8. What is a NIC?
9. What is RAM?

3

Basics of the Linux Operating System

In This Chapter

- Desktops and Shells
- Shell Basics
- Moving Around in KDE

INTRODUCTION

Now that you have made it through the installation of Linux, you are probably anxious to begin using it. This chapter is sort of a tour of Linux basics. Many useful features and some fundamental concepts and terms will be introduced in this chapter. The primary goal of this chapter, however, is simply to get you comfortable with Linux. With that in mind, it is recommended that you not simply read this chapter but also do some exploring. When you see something, play with it a little. The goal is that at the end of this chapter and this section you will be comfortable with Linux.

You will see a wide range of topics in this chapter. Each will be introduced and explained briefly. You may feel that some topics are given too brief an explanation, and that you are not getting enough detail. Don't let this trouble you. Each of these topics will be expanded upon in subsequent chapters.

This chapter also marks the end of Section I, "Linux Fundamentals." By the time you have completed this chapter and this section, you should be basically familiar with simple Linux concepts, know how to maneuver in the Linux graphical user environment, and have a basic understanding of Linux terminology. You won't be a guru, and you probably should refrain from applying for a job as a Linux system administrator, but you should be comfortable and ready to move deeper into the world of Linux.

DESKTOPS AND SHELLS

If you followed the instructions in Chapter 2, "Installing Linux," chances are that you are working from within the KDE desktop. If you are not in KDE, or are not sure, when you first boot up and go to the login screen, there are several words at the bottom, such as *system*. If you click on these you will see that they have menus. You can go to the system menu and select the desktop environment you want to use. If you followed the instructions in Chapter 2, you will have other desktop options, such as GNOME. You should select the KDE environment. Throughout most of this book, we will be working with the KDE environment.

Before we begin exploring desktops and shells, it would be prudent to get a firm grasp of exactly what a shell is and what a desktop environment is. A desktop environment is simply a graphical environment such as Windows. This means that your interaction with the computer is done via a graphical interface. You push buttons, click drop-down menus, and do most of your maneuvering with a mouse or a similar pointing device. It may not have ever occurred to you that there are other ways to interact with your computer. For most PC users, the graphical Windows interface is the only thing they have known since the early 1990s.

Even after the discovery of alternative means of interacting with a computer, most people prefer the graphical environment because it is more intuitive and user friendly. Early versions of Linux suffered from a lack of a graphical interface. Fortunately, that is no longer the case. In Linux you now have several desktop environments to choose from. We will delve into desktops later in this chapter, and much of this book will concern itself with using desktop environments and some of the applications you can run in the Linux desktop environment.

A shell is simply a command-line interface. A command-line interface is one in which you type commands, and the operating system types out responses. The interface is text only, usually a simple white font on a black or blue background. There are no user-friendly graphics, no buttons or drop-down menus. If you have ever used the DOS prompt in Windows 95 or 98 or the command prompt in Windows NT, 2000, or XP, then you have used a command-line interface. During the early years of computing, the command-line interface was the only way to work with any computer. In fact, Microsoft originally used a command-line interface–based operating system called Microsoft DOS® (disk operating system). Unix originally worked only via command-line interfaces as well. Apple was the first company to bring graphical desktop environments to the public, and Microsoft soon followed with Windows. Many people have become so accustomed to using a rich graphical environment that they are not even aware of command-line interfaces. You might think that such an interface is now outdated and of no use. While it is true that most users and even most administrators prefer the easy-to-use graphical interface, it is not true that the command-line interface has no use.

Now that you know what a shell is, you might wonder why anyone would ever choose to use one when there is a rich graphical desktop environment available. There are several reasons to use a command-line interface instead of a graphical user interface. One reason is that the command-line interface uses less of your computer's resources. Since the command-line interface is not creating a graphical user interface, it does not require as much memory or processor power. Displaying all those colorful and easy-to-use graphical elements (such as buttons, toolbars, and drop-down menus) takes memory and processor speed. If you are working on an older machine that has limited resources, you may choose not to use a graphical user interface. With Linux, you can dispense with the graphical user interface altogether and use only the command line, if that's what you want.

Another reason you might consider working with the command-line interface is that it is more streamlined. You can do anything with a command typed in directly. You do not need to go through a series of graphical steps such as selecting a drop-down menu, then a submenu, then choosing an option. You simply enter the appropriate command. A person who knows the proper commands can often accomplish a task faster in the command-line interface than via a graphical interface. It is also true that command-line interfaces, while less user friendly, are far more stable. In essence, they almost never crash or freeze up.

Linux has a command-line interface called a shell. It looks very similar to the DOS prompt or command prompt from Windows. However, Linux takes the command-line interface to a whole new level. With Windows you have a single command-line interface that has a limited repertoire of commands. With Linux you have several different shells you can use and a host of commands to work with. Each shell looks pretty much the same, and the vast majority of shell commands work in any shell. We will examine many of those commands in this book, and you should become increasingly familiar with them as you progress through this book.

However, there are interesting and useful features in each of the various shells that are unique to that shell. One useful feature that is common to all shells is that you can write scripts in them. A *script* is a short program that executes one or more tasks. In Windows you can write batch files for the DOS or command prompt, but there is a limited number of functions you can write into a batch file. The term *batch file* stems from the fact that it is a batch of commands being executed in sequence. Linux and Unix administrators write scripts to automate repetitive tasks. With a Linux script, you can write either a simple script, quite similar to a DOS batch file, or a fairly complex script that is essentially a program. These scripts have all the options that most programming languages do. We will be writing some scripts in a later chapter, in the final section of this book.

There are multiple shells you can use, each with specific advantages. One of the oldest is the Bourne shell. This was followed by an updated version called the Bourne-again shell (often simply called *bash*). The bash shell is the default used in Linux. There are other shells, each with its own advantages and disadvantages. The most commonly used shells are summarized in Table 3.1.

TABLE 3.1   Linux Shells

Shell	Features
Bourne	One of the oldest shells for Unix or Linux. It was created in the late 1970s by Steve Bourne and was included in the seventh edition of Bell Labs Unix.
Bourne-again (bash)	This is an updated version of the Bourne shell. It is the default shell used in most Linux distributions.
Korn	This shell was developed by David Korn at the AT&T Bell Labs. This shell is very popular with Linux administrators.
C	This shell is of particular interest to programmers. With it you can write and run programs written in the C language. You can write the code right in the shell and run it.

The list of shells in Table 3.1 is not exhaustive. These are the most commonly used shells, and any Linux enthusiast should at least be aware of their existence. In this book we will use the bash shell because it is the most commonly used Linux shell. Remember, however, that most of the basic commands and simple scripts work the same in all shells. It is only the more advanced techniques that are specific to certain shells. That means that what you learn about bash in this book can be applied to the other shells.

With Linux you have the option of having your machine start up in graphical mode or in shell mode. Even if you choose graphical mode, you can launch a shell, just as you can launch a command prompt in Windows 2000 and Windows XP. Once you have a shell open, you can then type commands as you want. If you followed the installation instructions in Chapter 2, your machine starts up in graphical mode. Let's start by examining how you open a shell if your machine starts in graphical mode.

This chapter will mention the Windows command prompt several times and compare various Linux shell commands to the equivalent Windows command prompt commands. Many, but not all, Windows users have used command prompt commands. If you have never used a command prompt, it is found in Windows by clicking on the Start menu, choosing Programs, finding Accessories, and then clicking on the Command Prompt.

Assuming your machine starts up with a graphical interface, you will have to start your shell manually. Before you can start working with shell commands, you must first start up a shell. At the bottom-left corner of your screen you should see a Red Hat icon.

This assumes you are currently using the KDE interface. If you are not, then you should log out, and at the login screen change to the KDE desktop. It also is true that many distributions will put some other symbol here. In earlier versions of Red Hat you saw a K in this location.

Clicking on the Red Hat icon is much like clicking on the Start button at the bottom-left corner of Windows. When you click on the Red Hat icon, you are given access to a number of options. You can see the Windows Start menu and the KDE start menu in Figures 3.1 and 3.2.

You can see that the menus are very similar. This should give you some level of comfort. The KDE interface is not that different from Windows, and you should be able to get comfortable with the KDE interface in a short time. We will go into more depth on how to maneuver in KDE later in this chapter. For now we just want to find the shell. Click once on the Red Hat icon and then move up the options until you see System Tools. If you let your mouse hover over this for a second or two, you will see suboptions that are part of the System Tools group. One of these options is

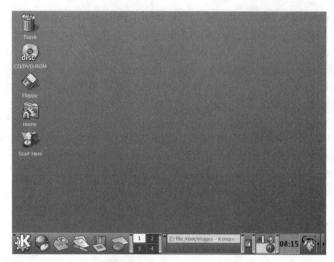

FIGURE 3.1   The KDE start screen.

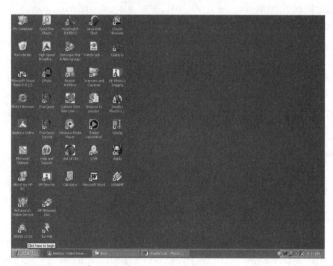

FIGURE 3.2   The Windows Start screen.

labeled Terminal. By clicking on Terminal, you will launch a shell. It should look much like what you see in Figure 3.3.

As you can see, this looks a lot like a command prompt in Windows 2000 or Windows XP, or like a DOS prompt from Windows 95/98. This is to be expected, since a shell is basically a command-line interface. The next section will take you on a tour of some shell basics.

SHELL BASICS

The first thing you must do is get comfortable with a shell. You may have used DOS commands in a Windows command prompt, and this is not going to be much different. If you never used any DOS commands, don't worry, this section will walk you though the basics. First you should note the default command prompt shown in Figure 3.3. The default command prompt tells you who is logged in currently. The user's name and the domain he is logged in to are shown in the command prompt. In our example, it is root@localhost root. This means that the root user is logged on to this local machine. Don't forget that the root user is the same as a Windows administrator and has full privileges to change anything in the system.

As was previously mentioned, bash is the default Linux shell. Fortunately, all shells share a lot of common commands. Now would be a good time to walk you through a few of these and compare them to DOS commands you might use in Windows. Keep in mind that these commands are case sensitive. That means that if you capitalize something you shouldn't, it will not be recognized. For example, the command to show who is currently connected to your Linux machine is done by entering who. If you enter Who, WHO, or wHo, it will not work. When in doubt, go with all lowercase.

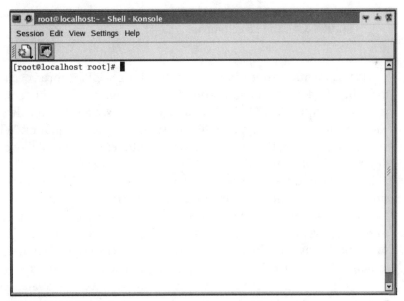

FIGURE 3.3 The shell.

One of the simplest commands is the command to list all the contents of your current directory: the ls command. This is very much like the dir command in Windows. Both commands list the contents of the current directory. You simply type ls, in all lowercase letters, and press the Enter key. You will see the contents of that directory, as shown in Figure 3.4.

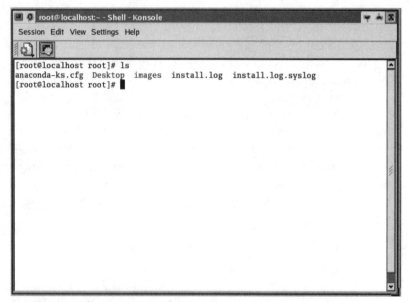

FIGURE 3.4   The ls command.

It was mentioned previously that the Linux shell is more versatile and robust than the Windows command prompt. You can see this in the ls command. When you use the equivalent DOS command, dir, you see a list of the directory content with no clue as to what types of files or subdirectories it contains. When you enter ls you might notice that some items are in different colors. All files are in black, all directories in blue, and all executable files or scripts are in green. This color-coding of items makes it easy to identify and use certain items. This is just one example, a simple one that illustrates some of the added features in Linux.

Now that you have seen how to list the contents of a directory, let's look at some other shell commands. This should help you get started with the basics of shell operations. This brings us to creating directories, changing directories, and moving files. Directories are designed to give you an organized way to store your files and programs. From time to time, you may need to create new directories, navigate through directories, or move files around. This is not much different than it was in the Windows command prompt, where you create a file by typing md di-rectoryname. For example, if you wanted to create a directory named stuff, you would enter md stuff. In Linux you do this with the mkdir command (short for Make Directory) like this: mkdir stuff. Simply type mkdir stuff in the shell, and then run the ls command to see the content of the directory you are in. You should see a new subdirectory named stuff. You can see this demonstrated in Figure 3.5.

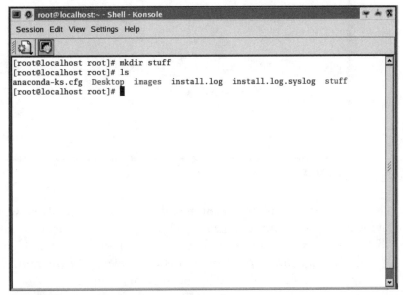

FIGURE 3.5 Using the mkdir command.

Changing directories is not much tougher than that. Before we change to our new directory, perhaps we should put something in it. You may have noticed that when we ran the ls command, there was a file named install.log. This is a log of what happened during the installation of Linux on this machine. We are going to copy that file to our stuff directory. This is a simple process using the cp command. Simply type cp filename target directory (the name of the file you want to copy and the directory you want to copy it to). Enter cp install.log stuff, as you see in Figure 3.6.

This command is very similar to copying files in a Windows command prompt, where you enter the word copy followed by the file and target directory. If we were performing this copy in Windows, we could enter copy install.log stuff.

If you want to see if the file was actually copied to the directory in question, you will need to change to that directory and run the ls command. You can

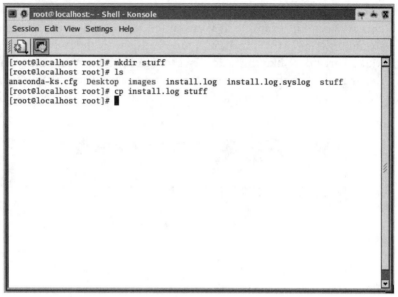

FIGURE 3.6 Copying files.

change directories with the cd command by simply typing cd followed by the name of the directory. In our case that would be cd stuff. Then enter ls and you will see that the file has been copied to that directory. This is shown in Figure 3.7.

The change directory command is the same as it is in Windows command prompts. You type cd followed by the directory name.

You will note that in several instances we examine commands that are very similar or identical to Windows command prompt commands. It is important to remember that Unix existed decades before DOS or Windows, and it was Windows that copied the commands from Unix, not vice versa. This is important because Linux beginners often wonder why Linux did not simply use the same commands Windows uses.

You may have noticed that the previous commands are not displayed in the figures in this chapter, just the command that is being discussed. When you type this into your shell, you probably see everything you have entered so far. This may lead you to ask how to get rid of the old stuff you no longer want to view. Just type the word clear, and the shell screen will clear. The same thing can be done in the Windows command prompt by typing in cls (short for clear screen).

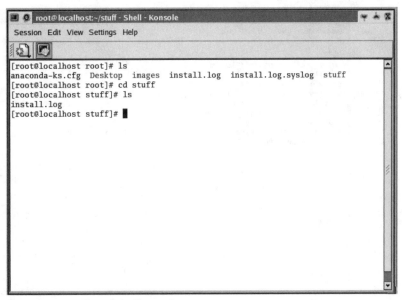

FIGURE 3.7   Changing directories.

What happens when you want to get rid of a file or a directory? You must delete all files in a directory before you can get rid of that directory, so let's discuss removing files first. In Windows you probably used the `del` command, simply typing in `del filename`. The process is very similar in Linux, only the command is `rm` (for remove). You enter `rm filename`. In our case, we want to enter `rm install.log`. You will then need to be out of the directory you are in, back in the root directory, to delete the directory `stuff`. In a Windows command prompt you enter `cd\`; in Linux, simply typing in `cd` will take you to the root directory. So now you type in `cd`, and you are back at the root and ready to remove that directory. In the Windows command prompt, you can use the `rd` (remove directory) command. In Linux you use the `rmdir` command (remove directory). The format is `rmdir directoryname`. In our case, that would be `rmdir stuff`. The entire process, from removing the file to removing the directory, is shown in Figure 3.8.

Table 3.2 lists some basic Linux shell commands with an example of using each command, an explanation of the command, and the equivalent Windows command prompt command.

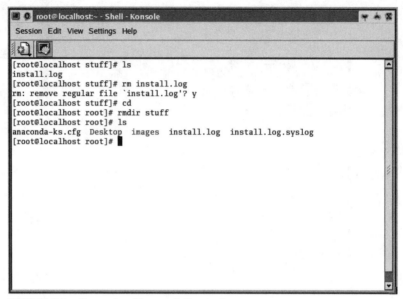

FIGURE 3.8   Removing files and directories.

TABLE 3.2   Linux shell command and Windows command prompt commands

Linux Command	Explanation and Example	Windows Command Prompt Equivalent
ls	List the content of the current directory. Example: ls	dir Example: dir
cp	Copy a file to another directory. Example: cp filename.txt directoryname	copy Example: copy filename.txt directoryname
mkdir	Create a new directory. Example: mkdir directoryname	md Example:md directoryname
cd	Change directories. Example: cd directoryname	Identical.
rm	Delete or remove a file. Example: rm filename	del Example: del filename
rmdir	Remove or delete a directory. Example: rmdir directoryname	rd Example:rd directoryname
clear	Clear the screen. Example: clear	cls Example: cls

This list is by no means comprehensive, but it does contain the basic shell commands you must be familiar with. It is recommended that you take some time to experiment with these commands and get comfortable with them. Section V, "Advanced Linux," deals extensively with using the shell. Chapter 18, "Linux Shell Commands," discusses a host of shell commands at some length. Chapter 19, "Linux Administration from the Shell," shows you how to perform administrative tasks using the shell. Chapter 20, "Basic Shell Scripting" teaches you the basics of writing your own shell scripts. For now all you need is a basic understanding of what a shell is, and how to accomplish some basic tasks in the shell.

There is one last simple but very useful feature of the shell that needs to be covered before we continue. The shell has access to Linux manuals built into it. These are frequently called *man pages* (short for manual). Man pages enable you to look up the specifics for any Linux command. For example, if you forget how the `mkdir` command works, you can simply enter `man mkdir` at the shell, and you will be shown an entire section of the Linux manual on this command. Man pages are very useful, and no Linux aficionado would dream of not using them.

MOVING AROUND IN KDE

Shell commands are very useful, but frankly not that user friendly. You have to type them in exactly, and if you make any mistake, even in capitalization, they fail to work. In addition, most Windows users want a cool graphical interface. Fortunately, Linux provides several to choose from. The two most popular are GNOME and KDE. For this book we will use KDE because it is more commonly used and is the preferred graphical interface of the author. However, in Chapter 7, "The GNOME Interface," we will take some time to explore GNOME and some of the applications and utilities that ship with it.

NOTE
You will see several terms used interchangeably throughout this book, and throughout all Linux documentation. The terms desktop, desktop environment, *and* graphical interface *are all referring to the graphical user interface you are using. This could be KDE, GNOME, or some other interface.*

You have already seen the KDE interface. It was used in the preceding section to locate and launch the shell. You may have noted that it is not too different from the Windows interface you are used to. To begin with, on the desktop you should notice a taskbar at the bottom of the screen with a K in the left corner. This is shown in Figure 3.9.

The bottom taskbar looks quite similar to the one in Windows. The icons on the left side are shortcuts to Open Office, an office productivity suite that we will

FIGURE 3.9 The KDE desktop.

examine in detail later in this book. On the right side of the taskbar you should see a clock displaying the current time. The shortcut icons in the taskbar are simply some common applications you might need. Let's examine how to add a shortcut or delete an existing one. Deleting is quite simple. You simply right-click on an icon with your mouse and choose Remove from the menu that appears. This is shown in Figure 3.10.

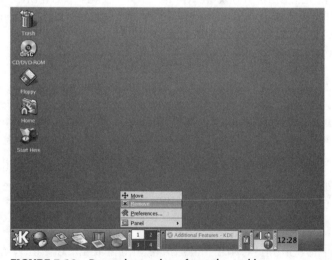

FIGURE 3.10 Removing an icon from the taskbar.

Adding a shortcut is not particularly difficult, either. Right-click on the taskbar and choose Add. Then select what you want to add. We will explore all of these options later in this book, but for now the Button option is the only one we are interested in. You will see a menu exactly like you see when you select the Start menu by clicking the Red Hat icon. For our example, select System Tools and Terminal. This is shown in Figure 3.11a.

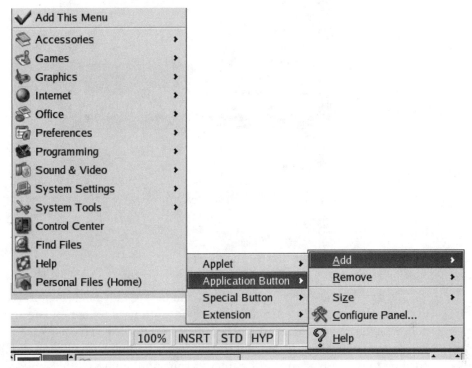

FIGURE 3.11A Adding a button to the taskbar.

Of course, you can create shortcuts only for applications you have already installed, and you'll want only the ones you use most frequently. How do you find other applications? What you need is a brief tour of KDE so that you can find various programs easily when you need to later. Later in this book we will explore many of these features and applications in some depth. Right now, let's just get comfortable.

When you click on the Red Hat icon, you see a menu of items, much like what you are probably used to in Windows. Applications are grouped in sections based on their functions. The section on System Settings is shown in Figure 3.11b, and we will explore that section in detail in Chapter 4, "System Configuration in KDE."

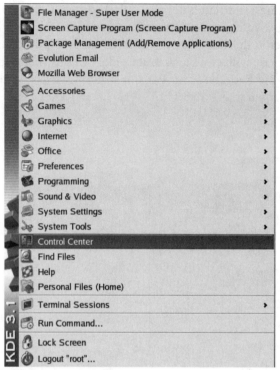

FIGURE 3.11B The menu.

Each of these groups of applications contains logically related applications. For example, the Graphics group contains applications used to manipulate and generate various graphical images. What specific applications you have in each grouping will depend on what packages you chose when installing Linux. If you installed according to the instructions in Chapter 2, you should have all the applications we will discuss in this and later chapters. Let's take a brief tour of each of these logical groupings and see what we have available.

At the very top you will see the applications you most recently used. In Figure 3.11, that includes the Paint program, the Screen Capture program, and the File Manager. On your machine, that would include any applications you have used recently. You will then see a horizontal line, and beneath that are the various program groups.

The first group is Accessories. Windows also has an Accessories group, and it contains items similar to what you might find in the Linux Accessories group. You will find a Print Monitor that monitors items being sent to the printer. You will also find a scientific calculator, a tool for formatting floppy disks, and an alarm clock. The items in Accessories are basically interesting applications but nonessential. For example, the scientific calculator would be of interest only to those working with math, physics, or some related topic. However, it is interesting to note the rich set of applications that Linux gives you. An item such as KDict, which is an online dictionary, might be of use to almost any user.

KDict is an online program, and you must be connected to the Internet for it to work.

In many older versions of KDE, after Accessories, the next category you see will be Extras. If you are using the very latest version of KDE, you will not see this category. It was folded into the other categories. Instead of seeing a separate Extras category, each category has a subcategory called Additional. In some distributions this is called More, rather than Additional. For example, there is an Additional Graphics item under the Graphics category. If you are using Red Hat Linux 9.0, you should have the more recent version of KDE. If you are using an earlier version, you may not. If you want to get the latest KDE, you can download it from *www.kde.org*. If you have an older version of KDE and want to stay with it, you should become familiar with the Extras section. This is a very interesting category. It contains applications that properly belong in one of the other categories but were added as extras.

Some readers might ask why we spend time investigating Extras if that category no longer exists in the newest versions of the KDE interface. One reason is that many readers might be using older versions of Linux. Unlike Windows users, it is not uncommon to find Linux users sticking with an older version. New versions of Linux are not radical departures from previous versions. The changes are usually subtle, and therefore there is often no pressing drive to constantly upgrade to the newest version. Another reason to discuss the Extras category is that every application in that category still exists with Red Hat 9.0 but has simply been moved. They have been moved back to the appropriate categories; for example, Extras games are now found under Games.

If you are looking for something you think belongs in a given category but cannot find it, you probably should check in Extras. There are some very interesting applications in this category. Under the Extras Games subcategory, you can find an interesting chess game, as well as a racing game called *Tux Racer*.

Tux is the name of the penguin logo/mascot for Linux. In Tux Racer, *the penguin races down snow-covered mountains.*

Of more practical interest are some of the applications you will find in the Extras System Tools subcategory. You will find, among other things, a File Manager. This File Manager is very much like the one that began in Windows 3.1 and was carried through subsequent versions of Windows. This tool will be of great importance in later chapters, so it bears exploration. When you launch the File Manager, it looks very much like a Web browser, and it begins by pointing to the home directory of the user who is currently logged in. If you are logged in as root, then you will be pointing to the root directory, as shown in Figure 3.12.

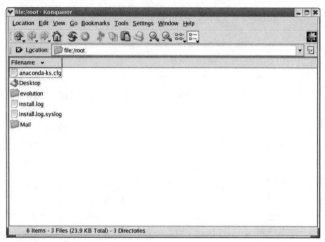

FIGURE 3.12   The File Manager.

Standard practice is to NOT work logged on as root unless you absolutely require administrative rights to perform the task you are performing. Except for the chapters that deal directly with administrative tasks, it is recommended that while working through this book you log in as the user account you created in Chapter 2. It is recommended that you not proceed logged on as root.

This brings up the question of what a home directory is. For that matter, some readers might be wondering what a directory is. Your computer has lots of files. If you save a document, that is a file. If you create a spreadsheet, that is a file. If you save a picture to your computer, that is a file. If you install a program, it probably has several files. These files are organized into groups called directories. A directory is exactly the same thing as a folder in Windows. If you have ever used Windows Explorer to peruse the folders and files on your computer, keep in mind that looking through directories on a Linux machine using the File Manager is very much the same.

You can use the arrow keys on the left side of the toolbar to move up a level or down a level. The three keys farthest to the right change the way you view items in the File Manager. The view shown in Figure 3.12 is the icon view and is selected by the third button from the right. Selecting the second button from the right will choose tree view, which is shown in Figure 3.13.

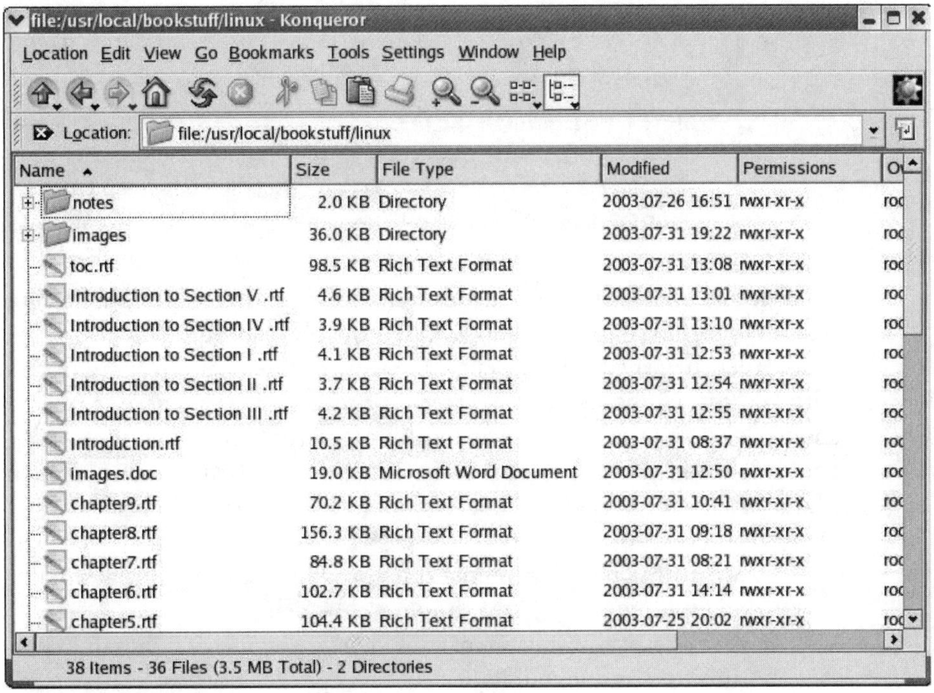

file:/usr/local/bookstuff/linux - Konqueror

Location Edit View Go Bookmarks Tools Settings Window Help

Location: file:/usr/local/bookstuff/linux

Name ▲	Size	File Type	Modified	Permissions	O
notes	2.0 KB	Directory	2003-07-26 16:51	rwxr-xr-x	roo
images	36.0 KB	Directory	2003-07-31 19:22	rwxr-xr-x	roo
toc.rtf	98.5 KB	Rich Text Format	2003-07-31 13:08	rwxr-xr-x	roo
Introduction to Section V .rtf	4.6 KB	Rich Text Format	2003-07-31 13:01	rwxr-xr-x	roo
Introduction to Section IV .rtf	3.9 KB	Rich Text Format	2003-07-31 13:10	rwxr-xr-x	roo
Introduction to Section I .rtf	4.1 KB	Rich Text Format	2003-07-31 12:53	rwxr-xr-x	roo
Introduction to Section II .rtf	3.7 KB	Rich Text Format	2003-07-31 12:54	rwxr-xr-x	roo
Introduction to Section III .rtf	4.2 KB	Rich Text Format	2003-07-31 12:55	rwxr-xr-x	roo
Introduction.rtf	10.5 KB	Rich Text Format	2003-07-31 08:37	rwxr-xr-x	roo
images.doc	19.0 KB	Microsoft Word Document	2003-07-31 12:50	rwxr-xr-x	roo
chapter9.rtf	70.2 KB	Rich Text Format	2003-07-31 10:41	rwxr-xr-x	roo
chapter8.rtf	156.3 KB	Rich Text Format	2003-07-31 09:18	rwxr-xr-x	roo
chapter7.rtf	84.8 KB	Rich Text Format	2003-07-31 08:21	rwxr-xr-x	roo
chapter6.rtf	102.7 KB	Rich Text Format	2003-07-31 14:14	rwxr-xr-x	roo
chapter5.rtf	104.4 KB	Rich Text Format	2003-07-25 20:02	rwxr-xr-x	roo

38 Items - 36 Files (3.5 MB Total) - 2 Directories

FIGURE 3.13   The tree view of the File Manager.

The KDE File Manager has some features not found in the Windows File Manager. One of the most useful features is the capability to bookmark a location. In any standard Web browser you can bookmark (or add to Favorites) any Web site you want, and then you have quick access to it later. Because the KDE File Manager operates like a browser, you can bookmark directories. You simply open that directory, select Bookmark from the drop-down menu, and click Add Bookmark. Figure 3.14 shows how to bookmark a folder, and Figure 3.15 shows that item in the File Manager bookmarks.

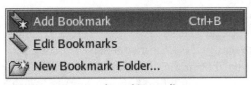

Add Bookmark	Ctrl+B
Edit Bookmarks	
New Bookmark Folder...	

FIGURE 3.14   Bookmarking a directory.

FIGURE 3.15 A new item in Bookmarks.

The File Manager is not the only item in Extras that you might find interesting, but it is one of the most useful. It would probably be prudent for you to spend some time experimenting with the File Manager to make certain you are comfortable with it. You will be using it in later chapters. However, there is one caveat you should keep in mind. If you are logged on as root, which you probably are, you could delete important system files. When you are experimenting with the File Manager, it is recommended that you adhere to the following rules:

1. Most of your experimentation should consist of simply moving around and finding things. You should not be deleting any files.
2. If you want to experiment with deleting or moving files, first create a new directory and a couple of new files for that purpose. Then, you won't be hurting any system files.
3. If you are in doubt about what something is, or what it does, leave it alone.

If you follow these three simple rules, you should be able to take a rather extensive tour of the File Manager without harming your system.

After Extras we come to Games. There are a number of games included with Linux. It is beyond the scope of this book to explore and explain these games, but you should be aware that there is a plethora of amusing pastimes included with the standard installation of Red Hat Linux.

This is one area where the various Linux distributions might differ. The number of games included varies from distribution to distribution.

The category following Games is Graphics. In this category you will find some very useful applications, such as GIMP. GIMP is an acronym for *graphics image manipulation program*. It is a full-fledged graphics program comparable to Adobe Photoshop. An entire chapter is devoted to GIMP later in this book. Also in the Graphics section you will find a screen capture tool. This was used to capture most of the images for this book. If you are using a different Linux distribution and

GIMP was not included, don't worry. When we get to that chapter, you will be told where to download it for free.

After Graphics we come to Internet. Most readers will probably find this very useful. In this section you will find an e-mail client, a Web browser, and an instant messenger client. All of these will be explored in detail in a later chapter. At this point, it is simply necessary that you realize that they are there and where you may find them.

After the Internet category we have Sound & Video. This category has a number of useful applications in it. It has an audio player, volume control, and sound recorder, all of which you might expect because you find the same items in Windows. What you may not expect is the sound mixer program. It works just like a sound mixer on an equalizer for your home stereo, but it adjusts sounds you record or work with on your Linux computer.

One of the most commonly used categories is Office, This comes right after the sound and video category and contains a rich suite of office programs. If you followed the installation instructions in Chapter 2, you installed Open Office (don't worry if you did not; you will be shown where to obtain Open Office for free). Open Office contains all you might need, including presentation programs, word processors, spreadsheets, and project management software—truly a complete suite of office products. Several chapters of this book are devoted to walking you through the intricacies of this software.

The next category is Preferences. You are given a plethora of choices on how to organize and view things in KDE. This section is replete with applications that enable you to personalize virtually every aspect of your computing experience with Linux. You will be walked through the basics of many of these applications later in this book.

The following category, Programming, is of interest only to those readers who are programmers or who want to be. It is beyond the scope of this book to delve into programming. However, you can find a number of Web sites and books that will help you get comfortable with Linux programming. Simply keep in mind that if you are a programmer or develop an interest in programming, there are many very powerful programming tools available for Linux. Most are completely free, and many come with the Red Hat 9.0 installation.

The next three areas—Server Settings, System Tools, and System Settings—are used to perform various administrative tasks in Linux. These will be examined in detail in the chapters on Linux administration. Suffice it to say that there are a number of useful applications that make system administration much easier.

After these comes the Control Center, which is a convenient grouping of the most commonly used items from the previous four categories. This makes it easier for you to find those programs used most frequently to set your preferences or to administer your system.

The last category we want to view is the Help category. If you select this, you are provided a rich array of helpful information and tips on how to use Linux and KDE. As you can see in Figure 3.16, there is an extensive array of documentation, including manuals for the operating system, KDE, and various applications commonly used. It also provides information on where to get technical support and how to find useful Web sites.

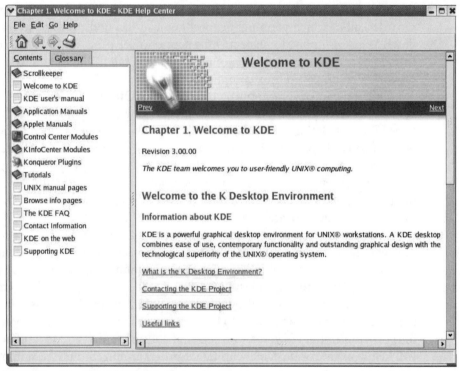

FIGURE 3.16 The KDE Help screen.

In addition to the wide assortment of applications you find in the Start menu, you probably noticed a few icons on the left side of your screen. These are commonly used, essential shortcuts. The first is the Trash Bin. This works very much like the Recycle Bin you have used in Windows. It's a last chance to change your mind about deleting a file. You empty it by right-clicking on it with your mouse and choosing Empty Trash Bin.

The CD/DVD ROM and Floppy icons are shortcuts to your CD-ROM drive and your floppy disk. They provide quick and easy access to these devices. The Home icon will open the File Manager, beginning in your home directory. Finally, we have the Start Here icon. This provides a convenient starting point for exploring the basics of KDE.

SUMMARY

As we have seen, there are two ways to approach using Linux. You can use the shell commands or you can use a graphical interface such as KDE. Most Windows users find that KDE has a familiar feel and is easier for them to adjust to. However, a basic working knowledge of shell commands is essential for many basic administrative tasks, which we will delve into later in this book.

It is important that you be familiar with the material in this chapter before proceeding to subsequent chapters. Being comfortable with finding what you need in KDE, and at least a cursory familiarity with the shell, will be essential later in this book. It is recommended that you take some time now to go back and experiment a little with both the KDE and the shell, just to ensure that you are comfortable with both.

REVIEW QUESTIONS

1. What does the man command do?
2. What is the shell command to delete a directory?
3. What is the default shell used by Linux?
4. What is the Linux command to delete a file?
5. What is found in KDE under Extras?
6. What is the Linux equivalent of the Windows Recycle Bin?
7. The File Manager in Linux operates much like what other type of application?
8. What is the Linux command to view all the files in a given directory?

II The Linux Graphical User Interface

If you are used to Microsoft Windows, you are used to the ease of a graphical user interface. There are several such interfaces available for Linux. The two most popular are KDE and GNOME. This book will emphasize the KDE interface but also introduce you to GNOME. In this section you will find out how to navigate through the KDE interface, how to administer your system via the KDE interface, and how to do many of the common tasks you used to do in Windows. Finally, you will get a brief introduction to the GNOME interface.

After finishing this section, you should be comfortable with KDE. This means you should be able to perform basic administrative tasks with KDE, know where to find applications you need, and be familiar with a few of the programs that are included with KDE. You should also have at least a passing familiarity with GNOME.

4 System Configuration in KDE

In This Chapter

- Desktop Preferences
- Setting Preferences
- Hardware Information
- Configuring Network Settings
- Configuring Internet Settings

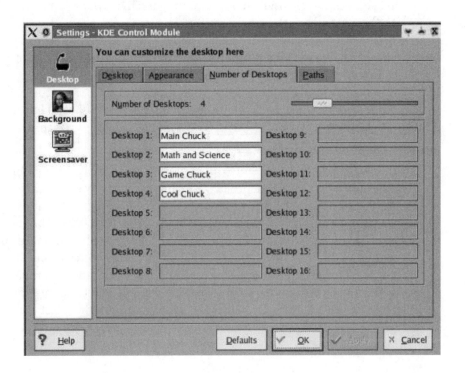

INTRODUCTION

Any computer system that you might purchase will require some configuration. Whether it is a Windows system, Apple Macintosh, or Linux, you will still need to configure it so that it recognizes and uses your hardware. During the installation, most operating systems, including Linux, will detect and configure many types of hardware. However, you might still need to reconfigure certain settings at a later date. Reconfiguration can be required because you add new hardware, change your Internet connection, or simply want a different look to your interface. For this reason, knowing how to configure your system properly is critical.

This chapter will walk you through the essential configuration tasks you might need to perform in Linux. In this chapter you will learn to reconfigure your desktop settings, set up hardware, configure your network, connect to the Internet, and more.

This chapter will focus on using the graphical interface, KDE. If you followed the installation instructions in Chapter 2, "Installing Linux," then your machine should boot up to KDE automatically. If you choose at some later date to use GNOME as your graphical interface, you will find most of the same features, only they may be in different locations. Also recall that we discussed what to do if your machine has KDE installed but is booting to GNOME or some other interface. Go to the Start menu (the large K or Red Hat symbol in the bottom-left corner of the screen) and log out. Once you are logged out, you will be at the login screen. Find the word *System* at the bottom of the screen and click on it. You can then choose which of the installed desktops you want to use.

Throughout this book, the graphical interface we will be concerned with is KDE. However, Chapter 7, "The GNOME Interface," will give you a brief overview of the GNOME graphical interface.

Before we get too far into our exploration of KDE, perhaps a brief history lesson is in order. The KDE project, which is the primary graphical interface used in this book, was founded by Matthias Ettrich in 1996. KDE stands for K Desktop Environment. The first version was released in July 1998. The most recent version, 3.1.2, was released in May 2003. KDE is simply a modern, user-friendly, graphical desktop environment for Unix or Linux workstations. KDE seeks to fill the need for an easy-to-use desktop for Unix workstations, similar to the graphical interface PC users can find with Microsoft Windows or Apple Macintosh. You can find out more about KDE history and get the latest version of KDE at *www.kde.org*.

DESKTOP PREFERENCES

Configuring your desktop to be appealing and convenient is a task most computer users eventually have to undertake. The more you use your computer, the more important it will be to have it configured in a manner that you find convenient and aesthetically pleasing. With earlier versions of Linux, those prior to KDE or GNOME, your graphical user interface options were limited. However, with recent versions you have a very rich graphical user interface, one that you can easily reconfigure and adjust to meet your personal preferences. Inside KDE are a number of options for altering desktop appearance and behavior. We will start with the simplest and most commonly used.

Just as in Windows, KDE enables you to right-click on the desktop and select Configure Desktop. This is one more thing that you will find works in Linux just as it did in Windows. You can then set a wide array of settings. This is shown in Figures 4.1 and 4.2.

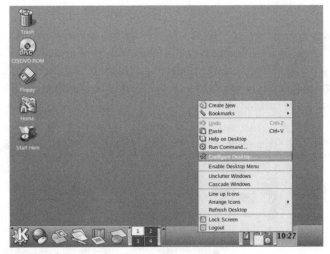

FIGURE 4.1   Right-clicking to configure the desktop.

As you can see, the first tab, Desktop, enables you to set what occurs when a particular mouse button is selected, what files to display, and how to display them. Most people will leave these with the default settings, but you can reconfigure them to behave in any manner you think is appropriate or convenient for you. You have probably noticed that the Desktop section has several tabs. The second tab enables you to set up the appearance of your desktop, including font and text color, as

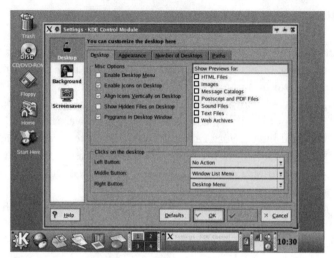

FIGURE 4.2 Desktop configuration.

shown in Figure 4.3. This tab is very useful if you want to customize the look of your desktop. While many users, this author included, stick with the default settings, being able to change them is important. Not only can a different font make your desktop more appealing, it can also make it more readable if the default configuration is difficult for you to read.

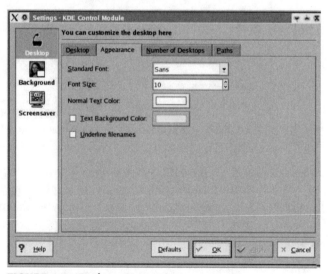

FIGURE 4.3 Desktop Appearance.

Setting fonts and icons is something you probably are familiar with from Windows. You can set all of that using KDE as well. However, KDE offers some features that Windows does not. One such feature is the use of multiple desktops. This is a feature that many Linux users find to be very useful. You can have more than one desktop and simply switch back and forth between them. The third tab on the Desktop screen enables you to configure the number of desktops and name them. You probably noticed that in the taskbar is a series of squares numbered 1 through 4; these enable you to set the various desktops. You can see the number of desktop settings as well as the Desktop options in the taskbar in Figure 4.4.

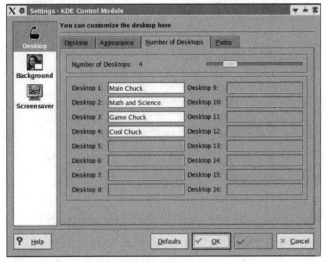

FIGURE 4.4 Number of Desktops.

We will explore setting different desktops in just a moment. First, we must finish examining the desktop configuration. You should also notice a fourth tab, labeled Paths. The paths simply tell you where on your hard drive the Trash Bin, Desktop, and other items are stored. For the most part you need not alter these settings at all. However, if you should need to change the path to trash, the desktop, or documents, this is where you would do it. A word of caution here. If you don't have a compelling reason to alter these paths, it is better that you don't. An error could make your Trash Bin or some other item unreachable.

On the far left side of the screen you probably noticed that you can set the background for the desktop. You can even set different backgrounds for each desktop. You simply highlight the name of the desktop and set the background. We will set the backgrounds for Desktop 1 and Desktop 4 so that you can see how it is done.

Simply uncheck the Common Background check box and click once on the desktop you want to alter. It is critical that you uncheck that box because if you leave it checked, it tells KDE to use the same background for all desktops. Next, select a mode and color. For our example we will choose Pyramid Gradient with gold and blue for the colors, as shown in Figure 4.5.

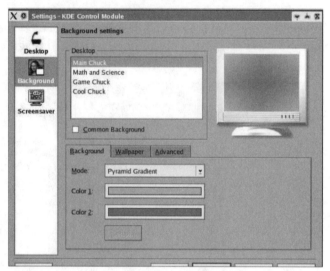

FIGURE 4.5   Setting the background for Desktop 1.

Now we will set the background for a second desktop and examine how that looks. Simply click once on the fourth desktop, and then choose the Wallpaper tab. Then, click the Single Wallpaper button and use the Browse button to find any appropriate image on your machine you like. When you finish, it should look much like what is shown in Figure 4.6.

Now click the Apply button. You should see the background change behind your Desktop configuration screen. That should be the background for Desktop 1.

That brings us the last option on the desktop configuration, that of screensavers. This is probably somewhat familiar to you because it is quite similar to selecting and configuring screensavers in Windows. You simply select the screensaver you want and the number of minutes KDE should wait before launching the screensaver. For our example, we will pick six minutes. You then decide whether or not to require a password. At this point, your screen should look very much like the one shown in Figure 4.7. KDE has a number of different screensavers already in it, and you can find other screensavers written for Linux on the World Wide Web.

At this point, simply click the Setup button to configure the individual screensaver you chose. Each screensaver has different options, depending on the type of

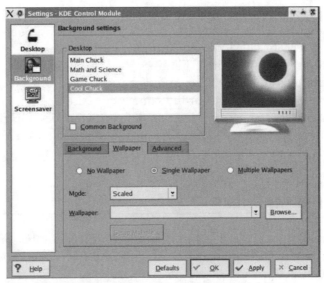

FIGURE 4.6   Setting the background for Desktop 2.

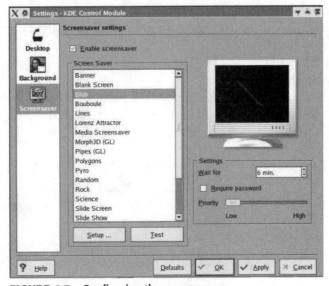

FIGURE 4.7   Configuring the screensaver.

screensaver you selected. For example, the Star Field screensaver enables you to select how many stars are displayed and how fast they move.

As you can see, you have all the options for configuring your desktop that
you are used to accessing in Windows. You also have a few additional options

you probably are not used to, since those options do not exist in Windows. One such option is the capability to use multiple desktops. You can now switch desktops merely by clicking on the number in the taskbar. By default, you have four desktops to choose from. This gives you the option of setting up different desktop configurations for four different users. Of course, you might simply have multiple configurations for the same user to use in different situations.

Now you have seen how to configure your desktop preferences, establish screensavers, and even switch between multiple desktops. This information should enable you to configure your KDE desktop in the manner most appealing to you.

SETTING PREFERENCES

In addition to desktop settings, there is a variety of other preferences you might want to set. These preferences can be found under the Preferences group in the Start menu. Under the Preferences category you will find numerous subcategories. The first of these is File Browsing. In this subcategory you can select what files are associated with what applications. For example, you might want all files ending in a .pdf extension to be opened with Adobe Acrobat Reader®.

The second subcategory is Information. This category provides a lot of useful information regarding various hardware devices in your computer. This will be dealt with in some detail in the next section. For now, we will move on to the third subcategory, Look & Feel.

You will notice that under Look & Feel you can set some of the same settings you accessed by right-clicking your mouse on the desktop. You can set the desktop settings, backgrounds, and even screensavers. However, you also can set a few other

FIGURE 4.8   Taskbar settings.

items here. For example, if you select Taskbar, you have several options you can set regarding the look and behavior of your taskbar. These options can be seen in Figure 4.8. They include whether to group similar tasks, whether windows should be shown on all desktops, and how the mouse behaves when a certain mouse button is clicked.

HARDWARE INFORMATION

You can find all the detailed information you might need by looking in the Preferences category, under the Information subcategory. You can see the various hardware options shown in Figure 4.9.

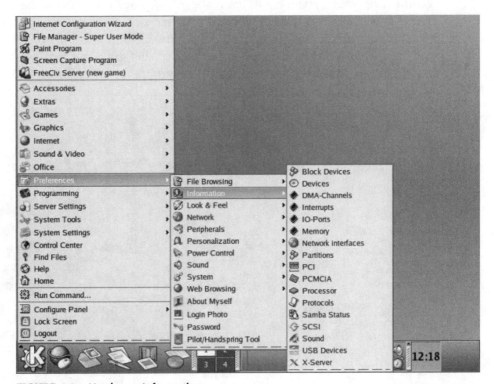

FIGURE 4.9   Hardware Information.

We will not delve deeply into these various settings because they depend on a thorough knowledge of PC hardware, and that is beyond the scope of this book. A good rule of thumb to remember on any computers settings is if you don't know much about it, leave it alone. You are more likely to cause problems than you are to improve your system.

You may wonder why this is even mentioned, since it is given such cursory treatment. The answer is twofold. To begin with, should you ever be speaking to a technical support person over the phone, he will probably ask about your hardware settings. You should at least know how to find them. Second, some readers will choose to expand their PC knowledge and learn more about PC hardware. The PC hardware is the same whether you run Windows or Linux. However, most PC hardware books have a strong bias toward Windows and will probably tell you where to find these settings in Windows but not in Linux.

Configuring Network Settings

Configuring your network settings is something you will probably have to do. Whether your PC is connected to a local area network (LAN) or simply connected to a cable modem or DSL (digital subscriber line) modem, you will need to configure your network settings. There are two ways to configure your network card settings. Both are found under the System Tools group, shown in Figure 4.10.

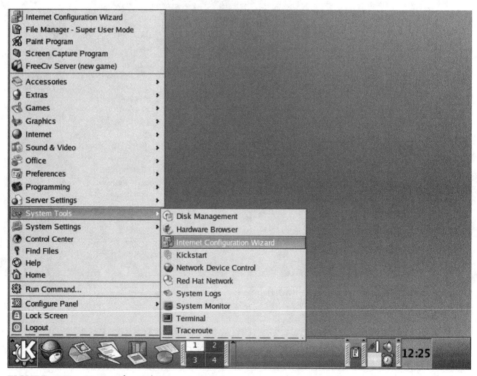

FIGURE 4.10 Network settings.

The first method is to go to Network Device Control and manually set all the parameters there. The second is to use the Internet Configuration Wizard. In this section, we will examine both methods.

Let us begin with the Internet Connection Wizard. We begin with this option because it is the easiest to follow, and because you certainly will want to get on the Internet as soon as possible. As with any wizard you have used in Windows, this wizard is simply a series of screens that walk you through the required steps to accomplish a goal. It is assumed that you have minimal knowledge of the task at hand, so the wizard helps you. The first screen of this wizard is shown in Figure 4.11. The entire purpose of any wizard is to walk you through some process in an easy-to-follow, step-by-step manner.

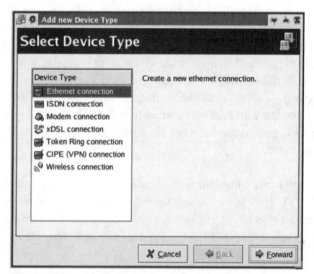

FIGURE 4.11 The Internet Configuration Wizard, screen one.

The first step in this wizard is to select what type of Internet connection you have. The list contains several items, and some are more likely to be found on the typical machine than others. We will walk through the most commonly used Internet connections step by step so that you will be able to set up your Internet connection regardless of the network connection type. There are three types we will not look at. The first two are the Token Ring connection and the VPN (virtual private network) connection. It is highly unlikely that you have either of these in your home, and if it is a work environment, you will need your network administrator to assist in setting up either of them. Token Ring, in particular, is an older technology that was popular with certain companies, notably IBM, but is not widely used in business any longer. It is also virtually unheard of to have a Token Ring network in a home. We also will not discuss the ISDN because it is not very uncommon in the U.S., and if it is used in Europe you will need to contact your Internet service provider to find out what settings to use.

Let us begin with the Ethernet connection. Ethernet is the most common type of network connection. Most office networks and virtually all home networks use Ethernet. Ethernet connections are the basic network cards you probably have seen many times. The connection to an Ethernet card is an RJ-45 connection. RJ-45 connectors essentially look like rather large phone connectors. In fact, they are very much like the telephone connector, except that RJ-45 connectors have eight wires in them, whereas the standard telephone connector has four wires. Just for your information, the standard telephone connector is called an RJ-11. The RJ stands for *Registered Jack*. If you use a cable Internet connection, it probably comes into your home and connects with normal coaxial cable (the same cable used for television, round wire about 1/4-inch thick with a connector that has a single needle-like protrusion in the middle) to a box, and then a network cable (also called CAT 5—category 5—cable) comes to your computer's network interface card (NIC). This means you have an Ethernet connection. You also are using an Ethernet connection if your PC gets to the Internet via a local area network (LAN) such as in an office environment.

If you are not familiar with these hardware terms, remember to look in Appendix D, "PC Hardware," which provides a basic crash course in PC hardware. It won't make you a trained PC service technician, but at least it will make you a computer user who understands basic PC hardware and terminology.

The next screen takes you to a list of the network cards that Linux has detected on your PC. You should see your card somewhere on the list. If you do not, your card may not be supported in Linux. That means that you will need to contact your card's manufacturer to find out if it supports Linux and, if so, where to obtain the appropriate driver for the network interface card. This screen is shown in Figure 4.12.

You will see the terms network card, NIC, NIC card, *and* Ethernet card *used interchangeably in most computer books. They all refer to the same thing.*

The next screen is used to configure your IP address. All computers on the Internet must have a unique IP address. Your Internet service provider (ISP) either assigns you an IP dynamically each time you log on or assigns you a static IP address that is always the same. If the former is true, simply select the option Automatically Obtain IP Address Settings with: DHCP. DHCP stands for Dynamic Host

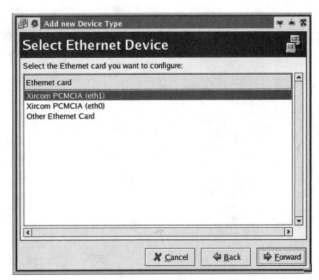

FIGURE 4.12   Selecting your Ethernet card.

Configuration Protocol. It means that when you dial up to your ISP or log on to your network, an IP address is assigned to your PC automatically from a pool of available addresses. If your IP address is permanently assigned, referred to as a static IP, then select Statically Set IP Address. You will then need to set the three fields with information that your ISP or network administrator gives you. The final screen, shown in Figure 4.13, simply verifies your settings and lets you apply, cancel, or back up and change something.

That's it; your network card is set up and ready to go. Congratulations! That wasn't that hard, was it?

The next most commonly found connection type in homes and small offices is a modem connection. If your phone line plugs into the back of your PC, you are using a modem. When you select the Modem option on the first screen of the wizard and then move forward, you will be presented with a list of modems detected on your PC. Like the Ethernet configuration, it is possible that your modem will not show. If that is the case, you will have to contact the manufacturer of the modem to verify that your modem is supported by Linux.

The next screen asks you to set modem properties. This screen is shown in Figure 4.14.

The first setting is the Modem Device. Linux refers to all modems as tty followed by a number. For example, your modem might be tty1. If you have two modems, you will have tty1 and tty2. If you have more than one modem, you can select the one you want to use here. The other two settings, Baud Rate and Flow

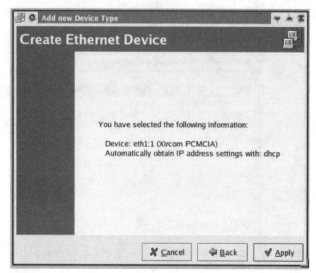

FIGURE 4.13   Confirming your settings.

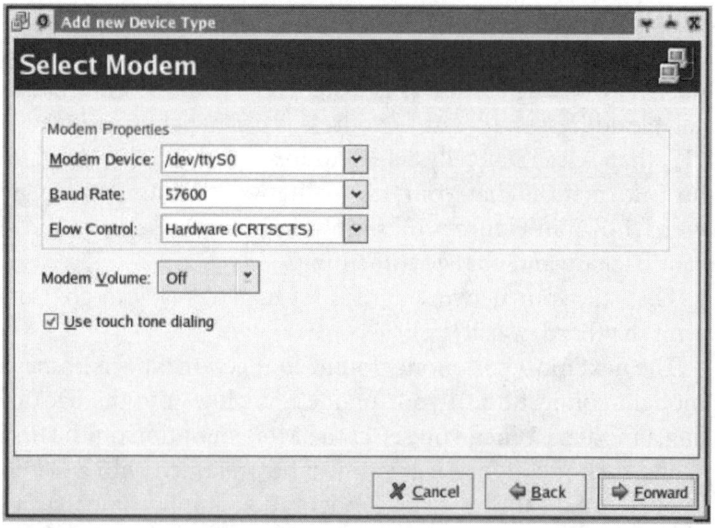

FIGURE 4.14   Selecting modem settings.

Control, are specific to your modem. The box it came in or the owner's manual would have that information. Next you set Modem Volume to whatever setting you prefer (it will work the same either way). Finally, you may notice that the Use Touch Tone Dialing setting is selected by default. Very few people have rotary phones these days, but if you do, deselect this option.

Now press the Forward button, and you are taken to information regarding your provider. This is shown in Figure 4.15.

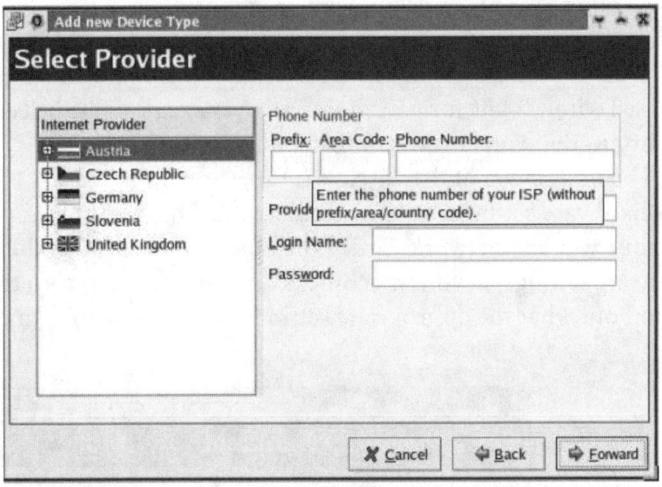

FIGURE 4.15 Your provider settings.

You can select a particular nationality here, if that is appropriate for your situation. Then you enter the phone number your ISP gave you to dial for Internet services. You will then put in your provider's name, and the login name and password that your ISP provided. This is shown in Figure 4.16.

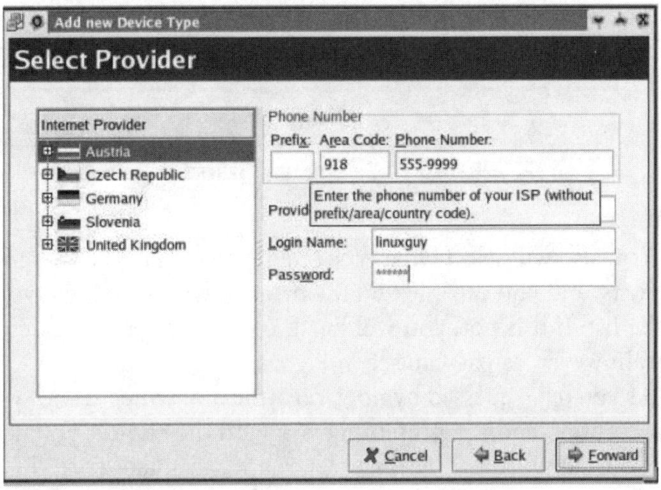

FIGURE 4.16 Entering the appropriate provider settings.

You are then taken to a screen that is identical to the final screen of the Ethernet setup. You will see the setting you selected and have a choice to apply the settings, cancel the settings, or back up and change your settings.

Another type of connection you might have is wireless. In the coming years, the odds of you using a wireless connection will increase. More and more businesses and even homes are going to wireless networks. Most consumer electronics stores now sell wireless kits for your home at a very reasonable price. For this reason, it is important that you know how to set this up in Linux.

The first screen of the wireless setup, shown in Figure 4.17, asks you to set various hardware settings for your connection. These settings include the IRQ and IO for your wireless network card. Previously we discussed where you could find all hardware settings on your machine. You may need to return to that section in KDE to find out what the appropriate settings are for your machine.

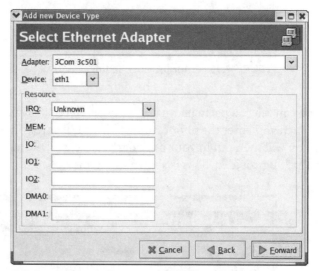

FIGURE 4.17   Setting up a wireless connection.

You also will select what type of adapter you have. There are several that Linux supports, and you can click on the drop-down list to see if your wireless adapter is on the list. If it is not, you will need to contact the manufacturer. The list is fairly large, however, as you can see in Figure 4.18.

As you have guessed by now, regardless of which device you are setting up, the wizard always ends by presenting you with the choices you made and giving you a chance to apply those settings, back up and make changes, or cancel the entire process. Setting up your Internet connect, as you have seen, is not particularly dif-

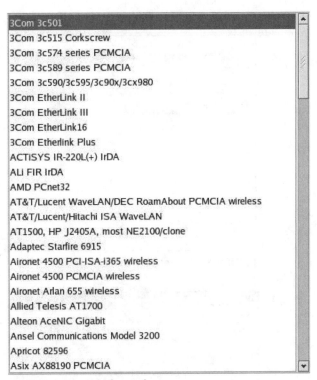

FIGURE 4.18   Wireless adapters.

ficult. However, there are times when it is not sufficient. For example, if you purchase a new network card and install it, you will need to configure it before you can connect to the Internet.

Fortunately, the Internet Configuration Wizard is not the only way to configure Internet or network settings. There is also Network Device Control. This is found under System Tools just like the Internet Configuration Wizard. The initial screen of the Network Device Control shows any network cards you have, their names, and their current status. This is seen in Figure 4.19.

You will notice the buttons on the right side. With these you can activate or deactivate the network device or configure it with a single click. Obviously, it must be properly configured before you can successfully activate it. Let's click on the Configure button and take a look at how to configure a network card in Linux. When you click on the Configure button, you are taken to a screen such as the one in Figure 4.20. The plethora of choices, buttons, and tabs may seem daunting at first, but don't worry, we will walk through all of them.

FIGURE 4.19 Network Device Control.

FIGURE 4.20 The Devices tab of Network Device Control.

The first tab, Devices, lists the various network cards on your machine and their current status and types. In case you were not aware, it is entirely possible to have more than one network card in a PC, although most home PCs probably only have one NIC card. The second tab, Hardware, is where one goes to add, change, or delete a particular network card. This screen is seen in Figure 4.21.

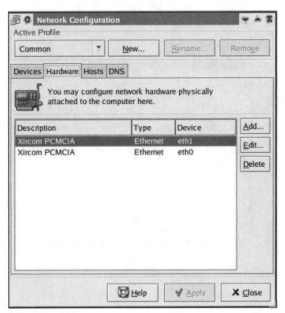

FIGURE 4.21   The Hardware tab of the Network Device Control.

The last two tabs, Hosts and DNS, are where your configuration takes place. The Hosts tab is where you will set the IP address for your network card.

All PCs have what is called a loop back address, which is 127.0.0.1. Linux treats this address as an actual physical network card. That way, even if you have only one NIC in your machine, you will see two Ethernet devices listed.

To set the IP address for your NIC manually, select Add or Edit, depending on whether you are adding a new IP address or editing an existing one. You will see something much like what is shown in Figure 4.22.

If you clicked Add, the three fields will be blank. If you highlight an existing Ethernet device and press Edit, the three fields shown will have that device's current settings. You can then enter whatever IP address and hostname you have been assigned by your ISP or network administrator. Aliases can be any name or names you select. This is simply a name that should be easy for you to recall.

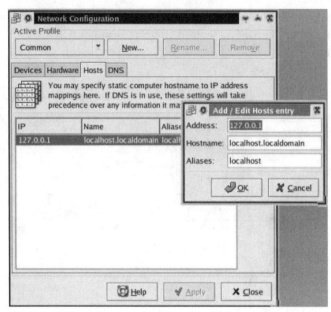

FIGURE 4.22 Adding and editing IP addresses.

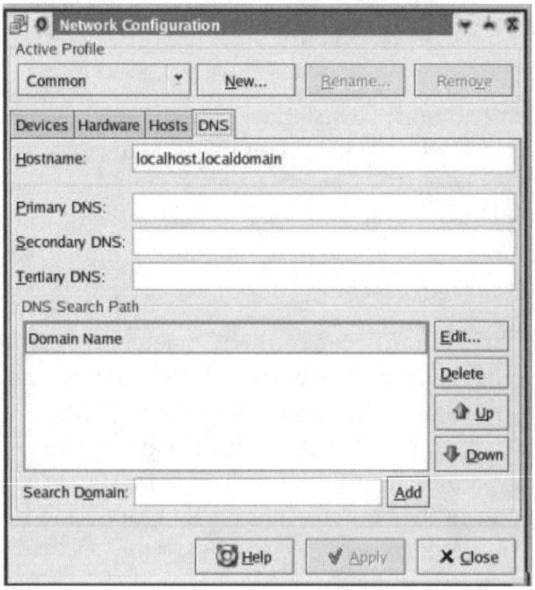

FIGURE 4.23 Setting the DNS settings.

Virtually all local area networks must use DNS service in order to use the World Wide Web. DNS is a networking protocol that translates the URL you enter (such as *www.chuckeasttom.com*) into an IP address. If you are on a network that uses DNS, you can enter the settings for it on the DNS tab. These settings will be provided by your network administrator. The screen is shown in Figure 4.23.

Your network card should now be configured. You can communicate on your local network, if you are on one. As you can see, this is not particularly difficult.

INTERNET SETTINGS

You might be thinking that we already covered this when we went through the Internet Connection Wizard. What that wizard did was set up your connection to the Internet. However, the various Internet software that you might want to use, such as a browser or an e-mail client, will also need to be set. There are a number of Internet-related software packages that either ship with Red Hat or can be downloaded for free. Many of these will be covered later in this book, but most readers will want to be able to surf Web pages and check their e-mail right away. With that in mind, we will examine how to configure the default browser (Mozilla) and the default e-mail client (Evolution) that come with Red Hat Linux 9.0. That way, you can start using the Web and e-mail right away. However, keep in mind that what we cover here is just the basics for these Web applications, enough to get you started. There also are a number of really useful Web sites in Appendix A that you can use to expand your Linux knowledge, but of course, your browser will be essential to accessing those sites.

If you are a Microsoft user, you probably use Microsoft Internet Explorer to visit Web sites. There is good news and bad news for the reader who is used to Internet Explorer. The bad news is that there is no version of Internet Explorer for Linux. The good news is that there is a plethora of other browsers you can use (Netscape, Mozilla, Opera), all of which are free. In this section we will examine the basic configuration of Mozilla. If you do not have Mozilla, you can go to a machine that is connected to the Internet and download it from *www.mozilla.org*.

If you use Red Hat Linux 9.0 (or even an earlier version) and followed the instructions in Chapter 2, "Installing Linux," then Mozilla is already on your machine. You simply need to go to K, then Internet, and then Web Browser. When you first launch Mozilla, it will look much like what you see in Figure 4.24. First it displays a Red Hat Linux help page. It is probably a good idea to bookmark this page for later use. Bookmarks in Mozilla work just like Favorites in Internet Explorer. You simply go to the drop-down menu at the top of the browser and select Add Bookmark. You can also use the shortcut key Ctrl-D.

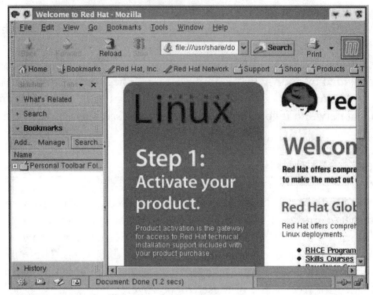

FIGURE 4.24 Mozilla's opening screen.

The most important thing to learn is how to set up the browser's home page and make certain it connects to the Internet properly. With Internet Explorer, you accomplished this by going to Tools and then selecting Internet Options. The same thing is accomplished in Mozilla by going to Edit on the drop-down menu and selecting Preferences. You will then see something like what is depicted in Figure 4.25.

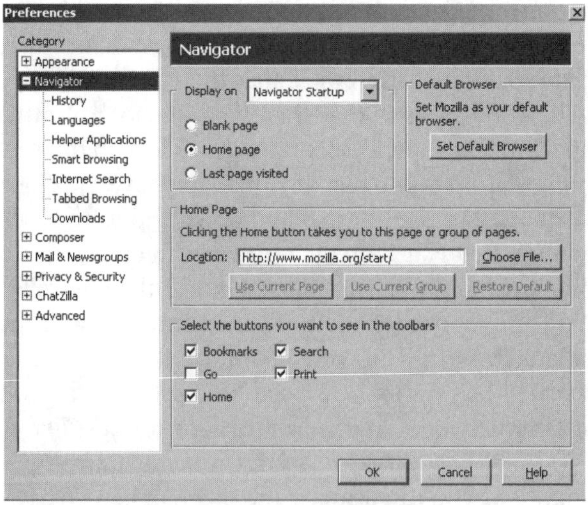

FIGURE 4.25 Preferences in Mozilla.

You can see that you have a host of settings you can configure at this screen. We will not attempt to explore all of them, just the ones you will most likely need. On the main Preferences screen you can set how Mozilla starts up, what home page is displayed, and what buttons are displayed. You select a home page simply by typing it in the Look In box in the middle of the screen. You can also use the page you are currently on by clicking on the Use Current Page button. This will cause the URL of the current page to be displayed in the location box.

If your PC is on a local area network, it is very likely that your network has a firewall and a proxy server. A proxy server is a device that hides all the internal IP addresses from the outside world. You must go through it in order to connect to any Internet resource. In essence, the proxy server is your gateway to the Internet and its gateway to you. If you first select Edit from the drop-down menu, then Preferences, and choose Advanced and then select Proxies, you will be at a screen that looks like Figure 4.26, and you can enter the settings for your proxy server. Normally, you will need to enter the IP address of your proxy server only into the HTTP Proxy and FTP Proxy boxes. You will also need to enter a port number. You can get the IP and port numbers from your network administrator. Usually, FTP is on port 21, and HTTP on port 80.

If you are not using a proxy server, you will select the Direct Connection to the Internet button at the top of the screen. Of course, all of this talk of proxy servers may

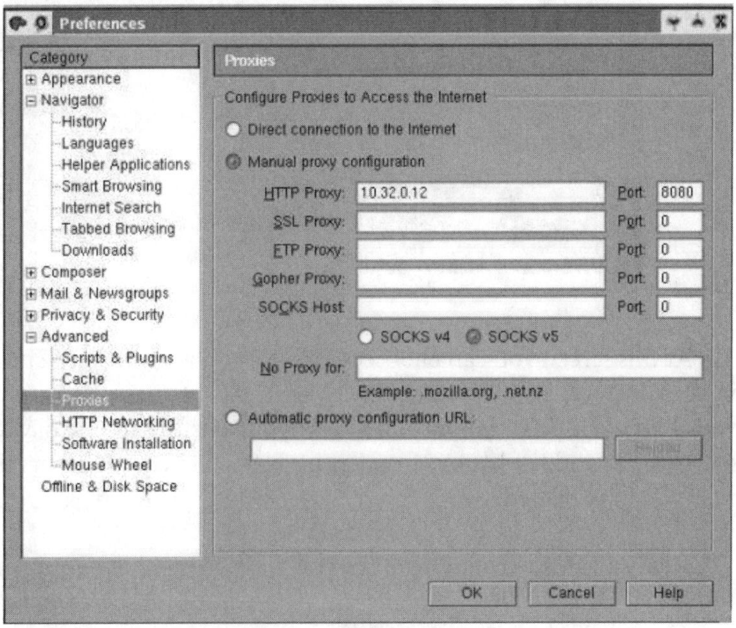

FIGURE 4.26 Proxy settings.

be leaving some readers scratching their heads and wondering what in the world a proxy server is. A proxy server is a device that provides a barrier between a network and the Internet. You will find a proxy server in many, if not most, business networks. The outside world can see only the proxy server and cannot see the network behind it. The computers on that network get all of their external access through the proxy server and receive only the packets that the proxy server lets through.

Another important setting you will want to look at is the History setting. That screen is found by selecting Navigator and then History, and you will see something similar to Figure 4.27.

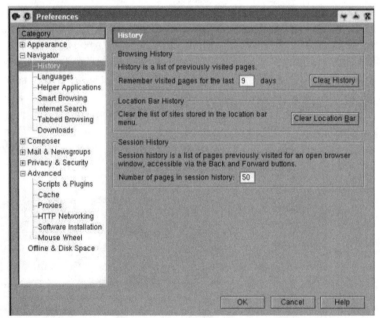

FIGURE 4.27   History settings.

At this screen you can choose how long you want to keep sites you have visited in your history. You can clear the location bar of sites you have entered and clear your history. If privacy is a concern, set your History to one day and then clear the location bar and the history frequently. This will prevent others from determining sites you have visited.

If your company is using a proxy server, most proxy servers are capable of logging every site you visit. You will not be able to prevent that. This should make you reconsider visiting any illicit sites from your office computer; Big Brother may be watching.

This should enable you to use your browser to navigate Web pages. It probably is a good idea with this browser, or any software you are unfamiliar with, to explore and experiment a little bit.

Configuring the e-mail client is even easier. When you go to the Start menu and select Internet and select E-mail, the Evolution Setup Assistant will start. You should see something much like what is in Figure 4.28. At this point, simply click the Next button and get ready to enter your e-mail settings.

FIGURE 4.28   Starting the Evolution Configuration Wizard for e-mail.

Of course, your e-mail settings will be different from any other user's. However, to assist you in following along, this text used the author's e-mail settings as an example. This also will help should you want to e-mail the author. The first screen asks you to enter your full name and your e-mail address. You also can connect to a signature file. A signature file can be either a text document or an HTML document that contains a signature block you would like to appear at the bottom of all of your outgoing e-mails. This screen is shown in Figure 4.29.

The next screen asks you to enter information about your incoming e-mail servers. The e-mail server is a machine at your ISP or in your company that handles incoming and outgoing e-mail. The overwhelming majority of e-mail servers use Post Office Protocol (POP) for incoming e-mail, and it usually works on port 110. POP is simply the protocol that computers use to receive e-mail. Some computers use a protocol called IMAP. Conversely, all computers use Simple Mail Transfer Protocol (SMTP) to send e-mail, and that protocol works on port 25. You will find

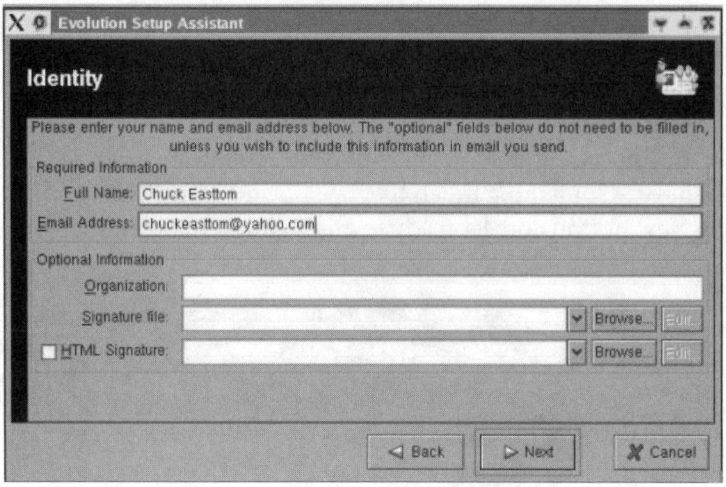

FIGURE 4.29 Entering your e-mail address.

that there is a protocol for every type of communication between one computer and another. The e-mail server screen is seen in Figure 4.30. The screens for setting up your SMTP server and POP server are identical.

The next screen, shown in Figure 4.31, asks your preferences regarding checking e-mail. You are asked to indicate how often you want to check for new e-mail and whether to leave a copy on the server. This means that even after you read your e-mail, it is still on the server. This is usually preferred by people who might check

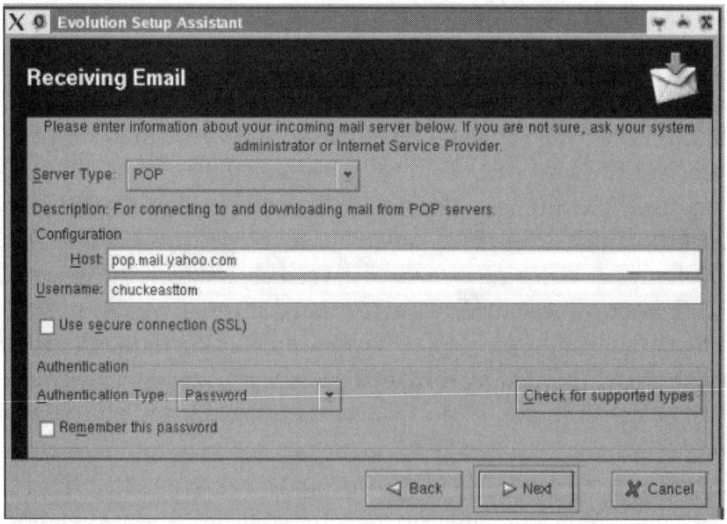

FIGURE 4.30 Your incoming e-mail server.

their e-mail from more than one machine. If you leave the e-mail on the server, you can access it from any e-mail client on any machine. Of course, if you get a large volume of e-mail, this volume might exceed limits that your ISP or network administrator has set on your e-mail inbox.

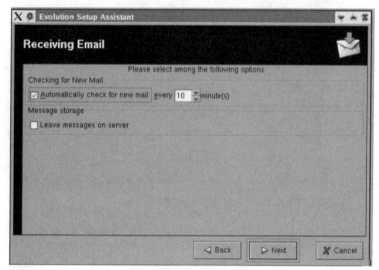

FIGURE 4.31   Preferences for receiving e-mail.

The following screen, shown in Figure 4.32, is to set up your outgoing e-mail. Recall that we previously mentioned that e-mail is sent using SMTP, which usually works on port 25.

The next two screens have you enter your e-mail address and select your time zone. You are now ready to start using the Evolution e-mail client. In fact, you will be taken to the main e-mail client screen, shown in Figure 4.33. In the future, when you launch the e-mail client, you will go directly to this screen.

You can see that using Evolution for your e-mail client will be no more difficult that using Microsoft Outlook® or Outlook Express®. In fact, the initial setup is considered easier by many people. This is just one of many alternative applications that were mentioned in previous chapters.

There is an option you may have noticed, called Leave messages on server. This is just a little check box that you either check or uncheck. It simply directs the e-mail software to leave the e-mail on the server, even after you have read it. If you intend to check your e-mail from more than one PC or e-mail client, then you may wish to leave the e-mail on the server. If you don't, then when you log on with another

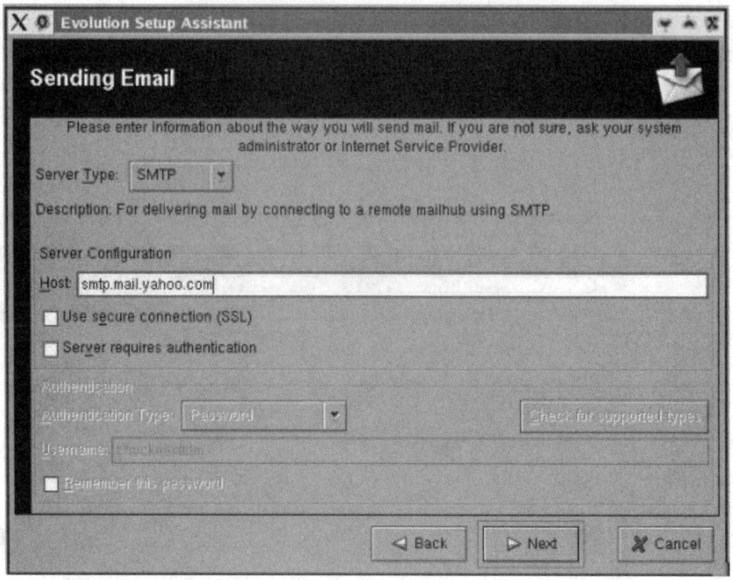

FIGURE 4.32 Outgoing e-mail settings.

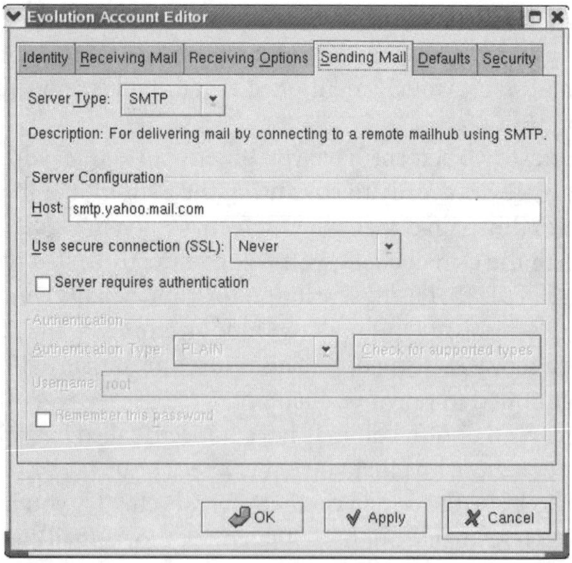

FIGURE 4.33 Your e-mail client.

e-mail program, you won't see any of your e-mails. You might think they are gone! However, they were simply downloaded by the e-mail client Evolution.

The option of whether or not to leave e-mail on the server is hardly unique to Evolution. You are likely to find that option somewhere in almost any e-mail client program you may choose to use.

SUMMARY

This chapter took you through the fundamentals of administering and configuring your Linux PC. You have seen how to get connected to the Internet, how to configure your browser, and how to configure your e-mail. These are critical tasks because most people are particularly interested in Internet access.

In addition to establishing Internet access, you have also seen how to configure your desktop preferences, the look and feel for your desktop, and how to set up and use the multiple desktop feature of KDE. You have also been shown where to find hardware settings.

REVIEW QUESTIONS

1. What are the three most common means of Internet connection?
2. How many different desktops does KDE provide by default?
3. Under Desktop Settings, what does the Common Background setting do?
4. What is the rule of thumb for changing hardware settings?
5. What is the default browser for KDE?
6. In Mozilla, what drop-down menu do you select to set up your Internet connection settings?
7. What is the default e-mail client for KDE?
8. Favorites in Internet Explorer are called what in Mozilla?

5

Using KDE for Everything You Used to Do in Windows

In This Chapter

- Text Editors
- Calculators
- Paint Programs and Screen Capture
- The File Manager
- Accessibility
- Other Office Applications

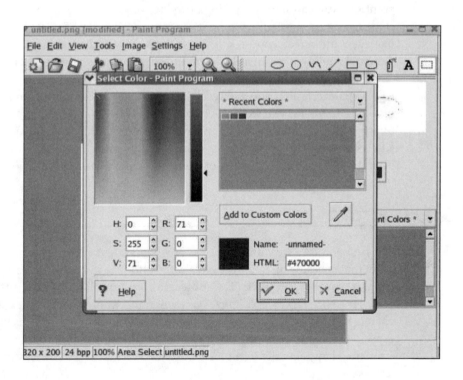

INTRODUCTION

The first four chapters of this book took you through the fundamentals of Linux. At this point, you should have a solid grasp of essential Linux terminology, know how to install Linux, and know how to do some basic configuration of your system. These are the essential functions you will need in order to progress with Linux. The Linux terminology is critical to being able to understand Linux articles and books, use online tutorials, or simply communicate with other Linux users. The capability to install and configure a system is absolutely essential to being able to use that system. However, these are not the things that most users do on a day-to-day basis. You generally install Linux on a PC only one time. You will usually only change the system's configuration when some pressing need arises, such as if you change your hardware or a person with different requirements will use the machine. This brings us to this chapter. In this chapter, we will explore some basic, common tasks that most people will use on a frequent basis.

This chapter will show you how the most commonly used functions in Windows can be accomplished in Linux. The point is to take those common functions you formerly accomplished in Windows and translate them into Linux. We will walk through many of the basic tasks that typical users will do. This should take you to the point that you can start using Linux productively. The tasks we will examine will include using basic text editors to write documents, finding calculators, using a contact manager, and screen captures. In most cases, we will discuss briefly how the task is done in Windows and then show you how to accomplish the same task in Linux.

The applications and utilities we will deal with in this chapter come with the KDE user interface. If you will recall from Chapter 2, "Installing Linux," during the installation process you were asked to select the KDE interface as your default mode of using Linux. KDE has a similar feel to Windows, so it should be no surprise that KDE offers a number of applications that are quite similar to Windows applications. This chapter will review the use of some of the more common of these utilities.

TEXT EDITORS

The first question we should address is, what is a text editor? A text editor is a program that enables you to enter text, alter it, and save it. In short, it is a program that enables you to edit text. To quote from a popular online Unix help page, *www.gw.com/UNIXhelp/editors/*, "you will often want to create a text file and then change its content in some way. A text editor is a program that has been designed especially for this purpose." Text editors enable you to enter text and change the content. They generally don't have advanced formatting or processing capabilities that you find in word processors. A simplified definition might be that a text editor is a very simple word processor. Linux is not limited to text editors. In fact, there are several complete word processors and office suites available for Linux. You can choose from Star Office, Open Office, Corel Word Perfect, and others. All of these are comparable with Microsoft Word. We will look at Open Office extensively later in this book. In fact, several chapters are devoted to Open Office. However, you may be used to having access to simpler text editors that you use for smaller, less demanding tasks. In Windows, you can go to Start, choose Programs (in Windows 2000 or 98 it was Programs, in Windows XP , it is All Programs), then select Accessories, and you immediately have access to both Microsoft Notepad and Word-Pad. Notepad is a very limited text editor. With Notepad you can essentially type in plain text with no formatting options. You can then either save the file or print it. WordPad, while not as feature rich as most commercially available word processors, does include basic word processing features. It is more than adequate for most simple word processing tasks. Simplified word processing applications such as Notepad and WordPad often are called text editors. The difference between a text editor and a word processor is the additional tools available in a word processor. However, there is no accepted demarcation line that indicates when some application is considered a word processor, versus when it is considered a text editor. Some purists would comment that a text editor is entirely separate from a word processor, and at one time that would have been accurate. However, more and more text editors are adding enhanced formatting to their capabilities, and more and more simplified word processors are being released. This has caused the line between text editor and word processor to be blurred considerably.

Now that we have discussed what a text editor is and mentioned some text editors found in Windows, you might be wondering if Linux also has some text editor applications for you to use. The answer is a resounding yes. In fact, when using the KDE graphical interface, you have a few different text editors to choose from.

We also have mentioned that Linux ships with full-fledged word processors. This might lead you to ask why would you use a text editor? There actually are several reasons. The first is that if you want a very simple tool to just type in text, a word processor might have more complexity than the situation warrants, especially if you are not overly familiar with that word processor. Text editors also are useful when you want to enter text that has no formatting at all. If you enter your own HTML code for Web pages, code for compilers, or just shell scripts (which we will do in Chapter 21, "Advanced Shell Functions"), then you need plain text with no formatting at all. Many word processors add formatting that may cause problems when you attempt to use the resulting text as a script or in a compiler. Finally, these text editors are so common in the Linux world that it would be a glaring omission not to introduce you to them.

Now you know what a text editor is, and you know some of the reasons why you might use one. We will now take a look at a few of the more common text editors you have access to in Linux.

Kate

The KDE interface comes with a text editor called *Kate*. Other graphical interfaces (such as GNOME) may have a very similar application called simply *Text Editor*. Whatever your distribution of Linux calls it, it is found in the same place and functions pretty much the same. Kate is a very simple text editor that enables you to enter text and to save that file to some location. It does not enable you to alter fonts or do any type of formatting. With Kate, you cannot align text, insert images, or draw tables and graphs. Kate is limited to entering plain text and saving or printing that text. It is quite a bit like Microsoft Notepad in that regard. To launch Kate, you would to go the K (recall that we mentioned earlier that depending on your distribution, you might have a capital K in the lower left-hand corner of your taskbar, or a red hat), find Accessories and select Kate (or select Text Editor). You should then see something very much like what is seen in Figure 5.1. Enter your text, then select File from the drop-down menu and Save As. You will then be able to save your file with any valid name you want, in any location you choose.

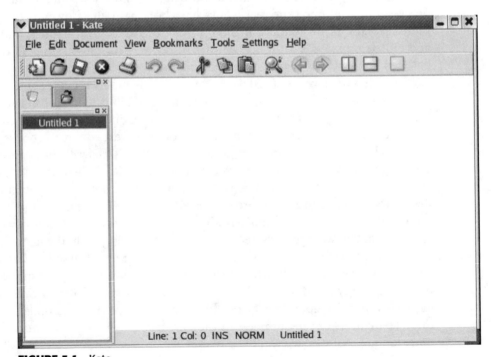

FIGURE 5.1   Kate.

You probably noticed that the toolbar for Kate, as well as many other applications in KDE, looks very much like the toolbar for a Web browser. This is intentional. Many, if not most, KDE applications give you a standardized toolbar that works much like a browser. Once you get used to one interface, it will be the same for most applications. This is quite convenient, especially for the new Linux user who is trying to become comfortable with Linux. You also may have noticed another trend with KDE applications: many of the application names start with the letter *K*. You will quickly find that the Linux community is not without a sense of humor. Beginning KDE applications with the letter K is one example of this; the penguin symbol, named Tux, is another.

Using Kate is remarkably simple. You simply type the text you want on the screen, then select File and Save As. When you select Save As, you will be presented with a standard dialog box that looks very much the same as any other dialog box you may have used before, including the dialog box in Notepad or Word. This should look quite familiar to you, as Windows also uses a dialog box to open or save files. This dialog box enables you to choose a name for your file, as well as a location to save it.

Using Kate, or Notepad for that matter, you cannot do many of the basic word processing functions you may be familiar with. You cannot alter fonts, use bold or italic, insert tables or pictures, or many other standard word processing activities. This might make you wonder why anyone would want to use one of these simple text editors. The answer is that there are many tasks that do not need any of those word processing functions. In fact, for some tasks, those functions are a problem, rather than an asset. Such tasks include writing shell scripts, which we will cover in some depth later in this chapter, as well as writing Web pages in HTML. Either of these tasks requires simple text editing with no special formatting.

Simply because Kate and some other simple text editors lack complex formatting options does not mean that they do not provide you with useful tools. Microsoft's Notepad application provides you with a search utility. If you have a lengthy document and you want to search for a word or phrase, you can simply select Edit and Find, and you will see a search screen, much like the one in Figure 5.2. You can then enter the text you want to search for and run your search.

You have the same functionality in Kate. You even get to the search function in the same way. You select Edit, then Find, and you will be presented with the search screen shown in Figure 5.3. You also can use the shortcut keys Ctrl-F, just like in Notepad. Just as in Notepad, you can search forward or backward.

Kate also has all the additional search options that Notepad offers. The Case Sensitive option is the most commonly used. If you select this option, the search will take you only to text that matches your search criteria in spelling and in case.

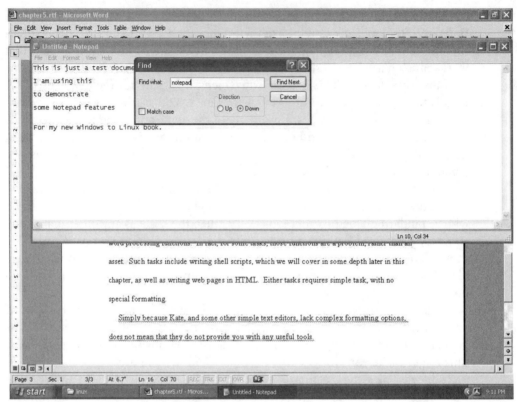

FIGURE 5.2   The Notepad search utility.

FIGURE 5.3   The Kate search utility.

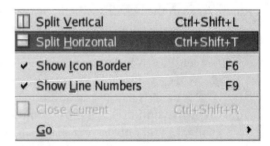

FIGURE 5.4   The Kate view options.

In other words, with this option turned on, Bob is not the same as bob. Of course, you can leave the option turned off, and your search will ignore case.

Kate also offers some interesting options not found in Notepad. If you look under the View option on the drop-down menu, you should notice several options not found in Notepad. You can see the View menu in Figure 5.4.

The first two options enable you to select how Kate will be displayed. You have two panes, one listing the recently opened or used files and the currently open file, and the other displaying the file itself. The next two options determine whether or not you will see the icon border and the line numbers. Figure 5.5 shows both of these options turned on.

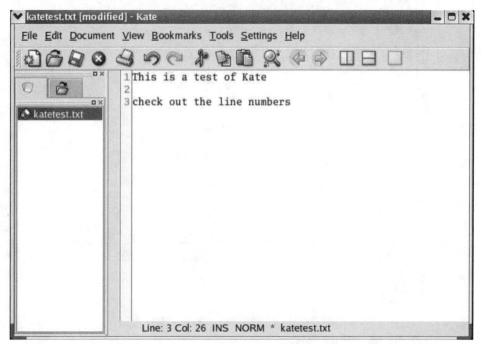

FIGURE 5.5   Icon Border and Line Numbers options turned on.

As you can see, Kate is a fully functional text editor that gives you all the functionality you may have grown used to with Microsoft Notepad and some new functionality not found in Notepad. This is just one more example of what was stated earlier in this book. You may need to use some new applications to accomplish certain tasks, but you will find that you can do everything in Linux that you are used to doing in Windows. You may even find that you can do some tasks in Linux that you were not able to do with Windows.

KWrite

For some Windows users, Notepad simply does not provide the functionality they need. If they don't want to purchase Microsoft Office, they might choose to use WordPad. WordPad is a fully functional word processor that is essentially a scaled-down model of Microsoft Word. It will handle most basic word processing tasks. If you are unfamiliar with WordPad, you can find it on any Windows PC by going to Start, select Programs, choose Accessories. There you will see it, listed with several other useful programs. You can see how WordPad looks in Figure 5.6.

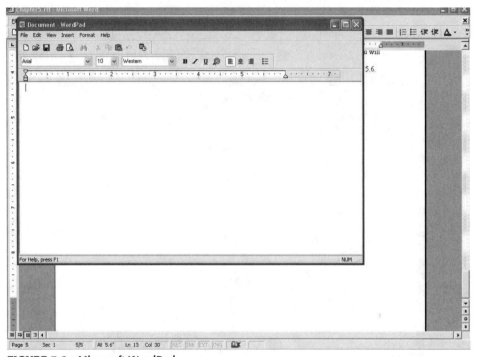

FIGURE 5.6   Microsoft WordPad.

WordPad has a number of formatting options, including the capability to select various fonts, bold, italic, align text, and more. For many basic word processing needs it is more than adequate. Unfortunately, none of the basic text editors that are part of KDE offer this functionality. However, Open Office, which installs with Red Hat Linux 8.0 and 9.0, supports all that functionality and more. We will examine Open Office later in this book. Also, there is a full word processor that is part of the latest version of the KDE interface, called KWord, and we will examine it later in this chapter. In the meantime, there are text editors besides Kate that come with the KDE interface and offer more functionality than Kate. KWrite is probably one of the most commonly used. If your installation does not include KWrite, you can get it from *http://docs.kde.org/en/3.1/kdebase/kwrite/installation.html.* That site also has complete installation instructions. Readers who are using the latest version of the KDE interface can go to Accessories, choose More Accessories, and click on KWrite. If you have an older version of the KDE interface, you get to KWrite by selecting Extras, Accessories, and KWrite. You can see the KWrite screen in Figure 5.7.

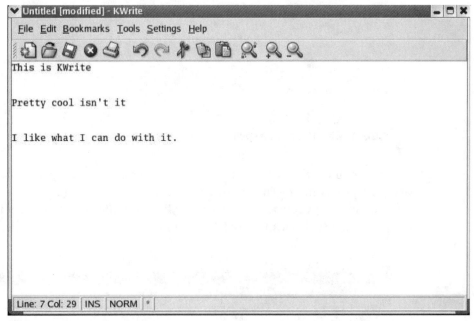

FIGURE 5.7 KWrite.

You probably noticed that the KWrite screen looks very much like the Kate screen. Under the Settings drop-down menu you will see Show Icon Border and Show Line Numbers, just as you did with Kate. The difference between the two is that KWrite offers a few more tools than Kate. To begin with, under the Tools drop-down menu option you will find a spell checker, shown in Figure 5.8. A spell checker, for many people, is an indispensable tool. In fact, without a spell checker, the book you are holding in your hands would not have been possible!

There is another tool available in KWrite that is not available in Kate, Notepad, or WordPad. This tool probably will be of use only to the more technically savvy readers, but it is worth mentioning in any case. If you look under Settings, you will find an option to set Highlight Mode. This mode enables you to direct KWrite to highlight

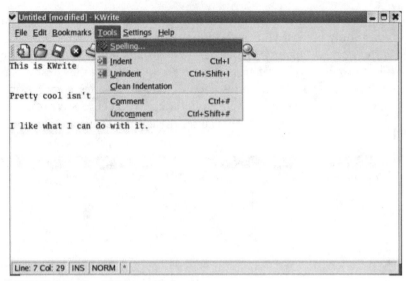

FIGURE 5.8   The KWrite spell checker.

text in accordance with the structure of certain scripting languages, markup languages, and programming languages. This option is shown in Figure 5.9a.

For example, if you want to use a text editor to write your own HTML documents, you can use this feature to detect errors in the document you write.

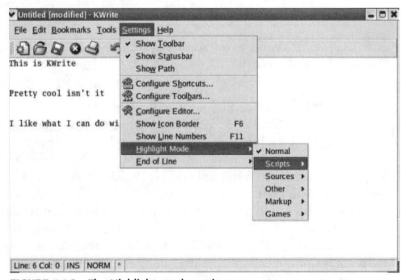

FIGURE 5.9A   The Highlight mode setting.

HTML, or Hypertext Markup Language, is the language that Web pages are written in. If you use one of the popular Web page development tools such as Microsoft FrontPage, Macromedia Dreamweaver, or Adobe PageMill, they are actually generating HTML code for you. If you know HTML or learn it, you can develop your own Web sites using a basic text editor, with no need to invest in an expensive Web development tool.

We have now examined two of KDE's built-in text editors and compared them to Microsoft's WordPad and Notepad. You should now be able to do simple text editing in Linux as easily as you did it in Windows. More technically inclined readers can now use KWrite for editing source code for HTML documents and many programming languages. Please keep in mind that Linux has several fully functioning word processors that are on a par with Microsoft Word. We will be exploring one of these later in this book.

KWord

As mentioned earlier, the latest version of the KDE interface comes with its own word processor, called KWord. You can get to KWord by going to Office, selecting More Office Applications, and clicking on KWord. Remember that, if you are using an earlier version of Linux, you might find this under the older Extras category. When you launch KWord, you will be prompted to choose what type of document to start with. This is shown in Figure 5.9b.

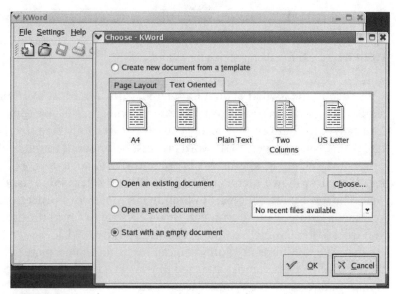

FIGURE 5.9B The opening screen for KWord.

As you can see, you have several options for how to start. For our purposes we will start with an empty plain text document. This takes you to the main working screen of KWord, shown in Figure 5.9c. We will examine some of the options you have available to you to manipulate and format text. First, you will need to enter a few sentences so that we have some text to work with.

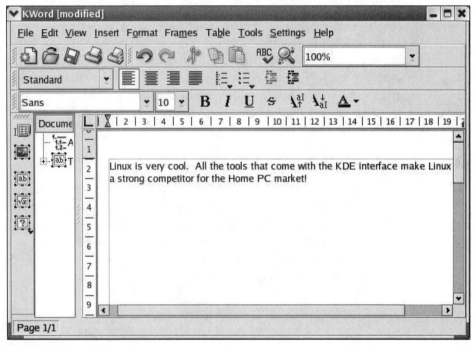

FIGURE 5.9C   The working screen for KWord.

Much of the toolbar should look familiar to you. Most word processors have similar functionality, so all word processors' toolbars also have some commonality. You can see the buttons that enable you to select the font, font size, bold, italic, and underline. These are very basic word processing functions found in almost all word processors, including Microsoft's Word and WordPad, as well as Corel WordPerfect . The drop-down menu at the top of KWord offers some standard options as well. The most interesting part to examine in most word processors is the objects you can insert into your document. If you click on Insert in the drop-down menu, you will see something like what is shown in Figure 5.9d.

Just like in Microsoft Word, you can insert footnotes, pictures, formulas, and tables. If you have a scanner attached to your PC, you can use the Scan Image option to go directly to the scanner, acquire an image, and insert that image into your

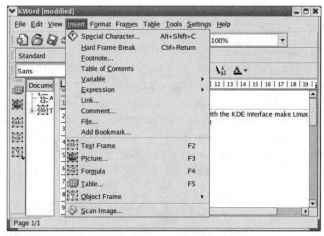

FIGURE 5.9D   The Insert options for KWord.

document. Pictures are frequently added to documents to improve their appearance. If you choose Insert and select Picture, you will be presented with a dialog box that will enable you to select any image from your hard drive and insert it into your document. However, this is one area where Microsoft Word is superior to KWord. Microsoft Word comes with a host of images you can select for various purposes. KWord does not.

Aside from basic formatting and inserting images or formulas, the Tools section is the most important. If you select Tools from the drop-down image, you should see something very much like the image in Figure 5.9e.

There are two options here that are indispensable to most people using a word processor. The first is Spellcheck. Most people, including the author, are very dependent upon their spell checker. The second item that should attract your attention is Autocorrection. This option enables you to turn Autocorrection on or off. With Autocorrection on, your spelling will be corrected as you type.

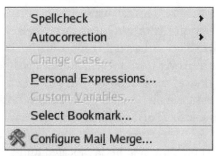

FIGURE 5.9E   Tools.

CALCULATORS

Word processing is perhaps one of the most common activities on any computer. Another very common activity is mathematical calculations of one sort or another. The need for number crunching is a fact of life. We all have occasion to need the accurate processing of numbers. Even if you are not an accountant, you will still need to balance checkbooks, compute interest rates on your credit card, and perform dozens of other functions with a calculator. You have probably used the Windows Calculator program before. This program is found by selecting Start, choosing Programs, going to Accessories, and selecting the Calculator, shown in Figure 5.10.

FIGURE 5.10 The Windows Calculator.

The Windows Calculator is well suited for basic arithmetic operations. The mathematics involved in bookkeeping, computing a loan interest rate, or working with your budget, for example, can readily be accomplished with this calculator. However, if everyday math is not suited to your task, you can select View from the drop-down menu and switch to a scientific calculator, shown in Figure 5.11.

The scientific calculator enables you to work with various exponents, roots, scientific notation, and more. This calculator is appropriate for the mathematics associated with general chemistry courses (either in secondary school or for freshmen college courses) as well as algebra-based physics courses. You have probably already guessed that Linux has an answer to your calculator needs. If you look under Accessories, you will find a scientific calculator, shown in Figure 5.12. An important side note should be made at this juncture. You have probably already noticed that Linux has applications that are comparable to all of the applications you have found in Windows. You should also notice that very often they are even found in the same place! Notice how the calculators in both operating systems are located under Accessories.

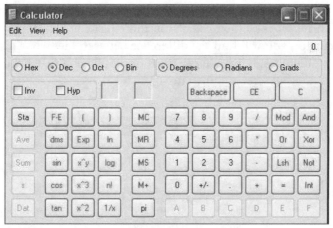

FIGURE 5.11   The Windows scientific calculator.

By examining the Windows scientific calculator and the Linux Scientific Calculator, or simply by looking closely at Figures 5.11 and 5.12, you should note a number of similarities. Both have the option to select hexadecimal, decimal, octal, or binary number systems. Both also give you the option of having angles represented in one of three different ways. This option is of particular interest if you intend to use your calculator for trigonometry. Both give you buttons for basic trigonometry functions (sine, cosine, tangent), raising a number to a certain power, computing the logarithm or the natural logarithm of a number, and more. In fact, you may be tempted to claim that the two have identical functionality and only slightly differing layouts. If you made such a claim, you would be almost correct,

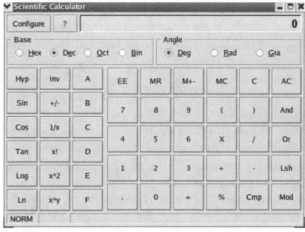

FIGURE 5.12   The Linux Scientific Calculator.

but only almost. If you notice the Configure button that is prominent in the upper-left corner of the Linux calculator and conspicuously absent from the Windows Calculator, you will find the difference between the two. This button may seem a small difference, but it offers a great deal of flexibility. Clicking it takes you to the Configuration screen, shown in Figure 5.13.

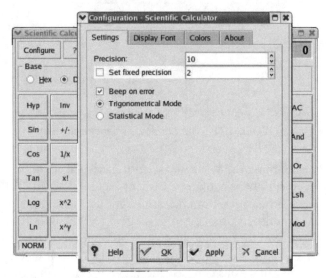

FIGURE 5.13 The Calculator Configuration screen.

There are four tabs on this screen, each enabling you to alter a different aspect of the Linux Scientific Calculator. The middle two options merely alter the appearance of your calculator. You may select any font or color combination that you find appealing. The first tab, Settings, is the one that enables you to change how the calculator will behave. Here you can alter the precision with which mathematical calculations are done. This is of critical importance to students in science classes, where the precision of a calculation is of paramount importance to successfully solve a given. You also can customize the calculator for either trigonometric or statistical use. Finally, you can elect to have the calculator beep if an error occurs.

As you can see, Linux offers all the calculator functionality you have grown accustomed to in Windows. In fact, using the Scientific Calculator that comes with KDE, you have some functionality not present in the Windows scientific calculator. We have found again that in Linux, not only can you perform all the tasks you are used to doing in Windows, but you may even be able to perform some tasks you could not do in Windows. Of course, some readers may be wondering what some of the mathematical functions listed do. You might not be familiar with natural logarithms or measuring an angle in radians. If this is the case, rest comfortably knowing that Linux not only is ready to meet your current mathematical needs, but is capable of doing even more!

PAINT PROGRAMS AND SCREEN CAPTURE

Simple graphics manipulation is another common task. In this age of Web cameras, digital cameras, and even cameras on cell phones, many people find they need to alter digital images. You probably used Windows' built-in graphics program, Microsoft Paint. Simply choosing Start, selecting Programs, going to Accessories, and clicking on Paint takes you to the Paint program, shown in Figure 5.14.

The toolbars on the left and at the bottom enable you to select colors, paint styles, and more. You can then paint simple graphics. You also can open up and alter most basic graphics files, including JPEG, GIF, bitmap, and others. Once open,

FIGURE 5.14   Microsoft Paint.

you can alter them as you see fit. If you routinely use a Web camera or digital camera, you have probably at least used Paint to crop an image before sending it to someone else. Not only do you have access to similar graphics programs in Linux with the KDE graphical interface, you have more than one graphics application to choose from. We will examine a few of the more popular graphics applications available to you with the KDE graphical user interface for Linux.

Simply going to the Start menu and choosing Graphics you can find a plethora of graphics applications. There is a subheading under Graphics labeled More Graphics Applications. In this group you will find many additional interesting graphics programs.

With previous versions of KDE, not all graphics applications were found here. While you will find some graphics-related utilities here, you will not find tools similar to Microsoft Paint. What you will find are very specialized tools. There is a digital camera tool for interfacing with a digital camera that is connected to your PC. There is also a scanning tool for use with scanners, and a screen capture tool, which we will examine later. For the basic graphics manipulation tools included with KDE, those that are similar in function to Microsoft Paint, you will need to look under Extras and Graphics. Here you will see several graphics programs. Let's take a moment to review the features and functionality of a few of these applications.

Paint Program

This is KDE's basic all-purpose graphics program. It is also the KDE application that is most similar to Microsoft Paint. When you launch the Paint program, you will see an image much like what is displayed in Figure 5.15. This looks remarkably similar in many ways to Microsoft Paint.

With KDE Paint, you still have the same basic functionality you had in Microsoft Paint. From the toolbar at the top right you can select to draw ellipses, rectangles, straight lines, curved lines, text, or to simply highlight a portion of the image to crop. For demonstration purposes we will draw a simple picture using the tools on the upper-right side of the toolbar, along with the color selections at the right side. The color on the left is the foreground color. Using the Ellipse tool, we can drag and draw a basic red ellipse. If you then click on the red box, you are shown a dialog screen much like the one shown in Figure 5.16, where you can select whatever color you prefer. We are going to select black.

Use the buttons on the right side of the toolbar or the drop-down menu items found under Tool to select the Pen tool or the Spray Paint tool and begin painting. For our purposes, we will select the Spray Paint tool and being painting in the ellipse. This is shown in Figure 5.17.

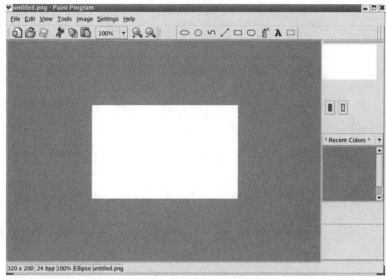

FIGURE 5.15   The KDE Paint program.

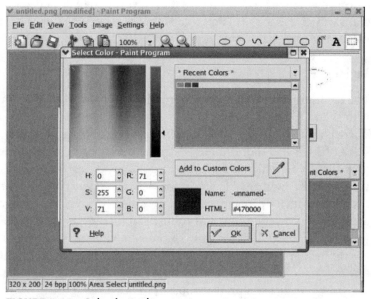

FIGURE 5.16   Selecting colors.

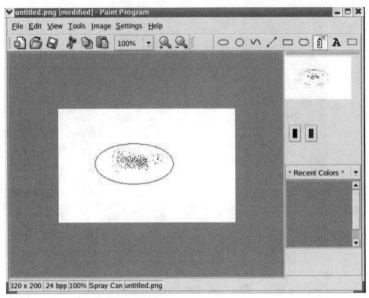

FIGURE 5.17 Using the spray paint tool.

Clearly, this is not a high-end graphics package, like Corel Draw or Adobe Photoshop, but it is comparable to Microsoft's Paint program. It is also adequate for most basic image manipulation activities. You can do some simple image manipulation and drawings with this program. If you select File and Save As, the Paint program will save as a PNG (Portable Network Graphics) image by default. However, you can change that to save it as a TIFF, JPEG, bitmap, or other image type.

Image Magick

The Paint program is not the only graphics manipulation program available to you with the KDE interface. In fact, it is not even the one with the most functionality. There is a more robust graphics application called *Image Magick*. In some earlier versions of KDE it is found under Extras and Graphics. In newer versions it may be found under Graphics and the subcategory Additional Graphics Programs. In other versions of KDE, Image Magick is not included. If your distribution or your installation did not include Image Magick, you can get it from *www.imagemagick.org/*. This application is a very useful and robust graphics program. If it does not come with your version of KDE, it is highly recommended that you obtain a copy. When you launch this application you will see the Image Magick screen. If you then click on the screen, the toolbar will appear on the left side. This is shown in Figure 5.18.

Image Magick is a pretty robust graphics program with a lot of basic functionality for creating or altering images. While it may not be up to the demands of a

FIGURE 5.18   Image Magick. Image Magick logo © Pineapple USA, Inc.

professional graphic artist, it is more than adequate for typical PC users. Let's try a little test run with Image Magick and see what it can do. For the purposes of this book, we will open one of the figures you saw earlier in the book, and you can follow along by opening any image you like on your PC. Simply choose File and Open, and you can use the dialog box to locate and open any image on your PC.

The toolbar with Image Magick is a floating toolbar. This means you can move it around independently of the image you are working with.

Just to see what a few of these tasks do, you should select the button in the toolbar labeled F/X (this option is for special effects) and then select Oil Paint. You will be asked to give a number; for this example, give 15. Your image is altered to look like an oil painting, and this process can take quite a few seconds. We will be converting the image used for Figure 5.5 to an oil painting. You can see the results in Figure 5.19.

This effect is even more startling when used with a digital photograph of a person. It essentially converts the photo so that it looks like an oil painting. This is a really interesting way to add some spice to old family photos! You probably also noticed several other special effect options, such as Charcoal. Each of these different special effects alters the image's appearance in some significant manner. Using these special effect tools, you can do some very exciting things with digital photos. More importantly, none of these options are available with Microsoft's Paint program.

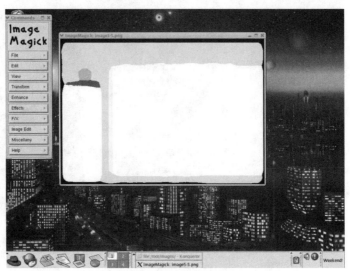

FIGURE 5.19 The Oil Paint effect.

In addition to these special effects, you have several other options available to alter your image's appearance. Before we look at them, let's direct your attention to the Edit button, which is second from the top in the toolbar. You should notice that it has options to undo and redo. This will be particularly useful if you try some special effect and decide you do not like it. You can then use the undo option to correct your mistake.

Next you should look at the View button. By selecting this button you have the option of viewing the image at half size, original size, double size, or some specific size you may prefer.

After the View button is the Transform button. This button is very useful. It enables you to crop an image to just a portion of the original image. You also can rotate the image or flip it. The author used that tool to edit most of the images you see in this book.

The Effects button brings you to a series of effects that can be used to alter your image in some way. None of these effects are quite as dramatic as the options you find under the F/X button, but they can be very useful nonetheless. For demonstration purposes we will take the image from Figure 5.5 again, only this time we will use the Effects button and choose the Emboss effect. This renders an image like what you see in Figure 5.20.

As you can see, you have a number of very exciting effects you can choose from. These tools enable you to alter basic digital photographs in diverse and artistic fashions. You can then use the options under Image Edit to add borders, frames, draw on the picture, annotate the picture, and more.

FIGURE 5.20   The Emboss effect.

This is not an exhaustive treatment of Image Magick. It is likely that an entire book, or at least several chapters of a book, could be devoted to that topic alone. However, you should now be comfortable with the basics of Image Magick. Perhaps you could take some digital image and just experiment with it for a while. Try each of the effects and become comfortable with them. Learn what the various transformations do. An hour or so of experimentation should be enough to make you a competent user of Image Magick.

As you can see again, you can do everything you previously did in Microsoft Windows, and you can even do exciting new things that you where unable to do with Windows. To do in Windows the kind of special effects you have seen with Image Magick, you would need to purchase expensive graphics software. Image Magick is free with many Linux distributions, including Red Hat. To be perfectly frank, Image Magick is in a completely different class than Microsoft Paint, in that it offers a much richer set of functionality. It is more comparable to professional graphics programs than it is to Microsoft Paint.

Screen Capture

Frequently, you may need to capture the contents of the current screen as an image. If you are doing a report or tutorial, this may be especially useful. The images in this book were done by capturing the appropriate Linux screen. In Windows, you press the Print Scrn key, and the contents of the current screen are saved to the system's Clipboard. You then open Paint or some other graphics program and choose Edit and Paste from the drop-down menu. The image will be placed in Paint, where you can alter it or simply save it as is. Using the KDE interface for Linux, you can still do screen captures, but the process is a little more complicated.

If you are using the GNOME interface rather than KDE, you should be able to press the Print Screen button on your key board and a small window will appear asking if you want to save the screen shot. We will discuss GNOME in Chapter 7, "The GNOME Interface."

If you select Graphics and choose Screen Capture, you will launch the KSnapshot program. This is a basic screen capture utility and is shown in Figure 5.21.

FIGURE 5.21 KSnapshot.

There are only a few settings to notice with this program. The first is the check box labeled Only Grab the Window Containing the Pointer. If this is checked, then only the window that has focus will be grabbed. If this option is not checked, the entire screen displayed on the desktop will be grabbed. The other option you should take notice of is the Delay option. This specifies how many seconds after you press Grab to capture the current screen. In some versions of KDE, the button is labeled New Snapshot, rather than Grab. Whatever the label on the button, the functionality is the same.

THE FILE MANAGER

You might be thinking that we already discussed this in a previous chapter. You are correct, we did. However, the File Manager is a very important tool that we will be using later in this book, so it seems prudent to go over it again, perhaps in a little more detail. The File Manager is a program that is literally used to manage files and directories, thus the name. It is commonly used to browse your machine's hard drive, view the contents, open files, create new directories, and more. You have probably used Windows Explorer many times to accomplish similar tasks. The File Manager in KDE has much of the same functionality as Windows Explorer. You can see Windows Explorer depicted in Figure 5.22.

FIGURE 5.22   The Windows Explorer.

In all versions of KDE, you can invoke the File Manager by simply double-clicking on the small icon on your desktop labeled Home. If you have the most recent version of KDE, you can find the File Manager by going to System Tools, then selecting More System Tools, then clicking on File Manager. In some older versions of KDE, the File Manager for KDE is found by going to Extras, selecting System Tools, and choosing File Manager. You can see what the KDE File Manager looks like in Figure 5.23.

As you probably already guessed, with the KDE user interface, you can use the File Manager to do all the tasks you previously did with Windows Explorer. To create a new directory (also called a folder) with Windows Explorer, you simply went to the drop-down menu File, selected New, and then chose Folder. Creating a new directory

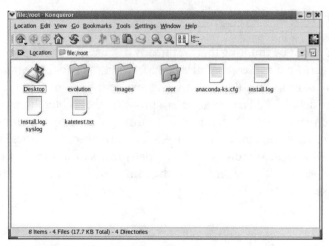

FIGURE 5.23 The KDE File Manager.

with the KDE File Manager is not much different. You go to Edit on the drop-down menu, select New, and choose Directory. With both Windows Explorer and the File Manager, you can use an alternative method to create new folders or directors. That method is to simply right-click on any blank area within the File Manager (or within Windows Explorer), select New, and create a new folder or directory.

You may have noticed the words "directory" and "folder" being used interchangeably. This is because both refer to the same thing. Prior to Windows 95, Microsoft used the term "directory" as well.

You probably noticed that navigation via the toolbar looks a lot like navigating via a Web browser's toolbar. As mentioned earlier, many KDE applications have this common Web browser–like interface. This means that once you become comfortable with one KDE application, learning others will be less complicated than if they had different toolbars and different means of navigation. A fascinating side effect of this Web browser–like interface is that you can bookmark a file or directory just as you might bookmark a favorite Web site. This can be enormously convenient.

ACCESSIBILITY

The term *accessibility*, in the world of information technology, generally refers to making a system more accessible to individuals with some disability. This can be anything from incorporating sound queues, text to speech, or large icons for the visually impaired to using text rather than sound for the hearing impaired. Microsoft Windows XP has made accessibility a prominent feature of its operating system. If you look under Start, Programs, Accessories, you will see a group called Accessibility. It has several options as shown in Figure 5.24.

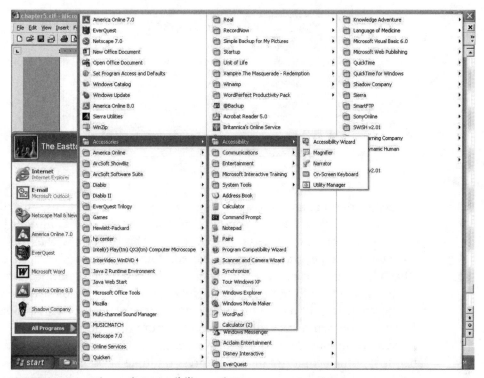

FIGURE 5.24   Microsoft Accessibility options.

Microsoft provides several features to make your PC more accessible to people with various disabilities. One such feature is the Magnifier. When you use this, you can put your mouse over any area of the screen and that portion of the screen will be magnified. This is very useful to visually impaired users. If a user is even more seriously visually impaired, you can turn on the Narrator, which will read all written commands or captions that the user passes his mouse over, provided the application running is designed to work with Windows Accessibility features.

As you can probably guess, Linux also offers some accessibility features to users using the KDE interface. You get to the Accessibility control panel by going to Preferences and selecting Personalization, and then choosing Accessibility. You will then see something like the screen shown in Figure 5.25.

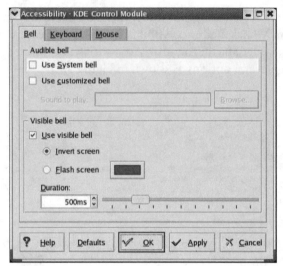

FIGURE 5.25 KDE Accessibility control panel.

The first option that really stands out is that you can select to use an audible or a visual bell for system alerts. You have probably heard your computer beep or make a similar sound when certain events occur. This can be a very useful cue to a person unless that person is hearing impaired. With KDE you can set up visual bells so that a hearing-impaired person can still receive system alert notifications.

The second tab of the KDE Accessibility control panel enables you to change how the keyboard will react. One such feature is sticky keys. You are probably familiar with commands executed by entering more than one key simultaneously. For example, in most programs the shortcut key to copy is Ctrl-C pressed simultaneously. Some people are unable to press multiple keys simultaneously. Sticky keys causes the machine to remember any key press for a few seconds and put it with the subsequent key press if the combination creates a command the software recognizes.

Another accessibility feature that KDE offers is Bounce Keys. Have you ever meant to press a key once but accidentally pressed it two or more times? This is referred to as bouncing. With Bounce Keys turned on, the software will ignore the second press of the same key if it occurs within a specified number of seconds. You set this specified number of seconds by setting the delay. KDE enables you to set it in milliseconds (thousandths of a second).

The third tab enables you to control the mouse using the numeric pad. Some people may lack the motor skills required to operate a mouse, and you can set up their Linux machines so that they can still use the mouse, via the number pad. On this screen you set the speed of response and any other factors that affect mouse performance. These settings will take some experimentation to find the right settings for a particular person.

OTHER OFFICE APPLICATIONS

Perhaps the most commonly used Windows application is Microsoft Office. This suite of applications contains word processors, spreadsheets, presentation tools, database management systems, and more. We have already examined some alternative word processors available with the KDE interface. We have also mentioned that several chapters later in this book are devoted to Open Office, an office suite that is distributed as open source and free of charge. However, there are some other interesting office applications that ship with KDE that are not part of Open Office and are not word processors. Let's examine a few of them. Recall that if you encounter any application in the text that is not included on your system, you can go to Add and Remove Programs and add it.

GNU Cash

Like many Windows users, you might currently use a product such as Microsoft Money or Quicken to handle your various financial accounts. The KDE interface includes a money management application called GNU Cash. GNU Cash is a very interesting open source program that is used to manage personal finances. It has a number of exciting features that we will examine. You can manage all of your personal accounts via GNU Cash. This includes savings accounts, checking accounts, 401(k) accounts, mutual fund accounts, and more. When you first launch GNU Cash, you will see something much like what is shown in Figure 5.26.

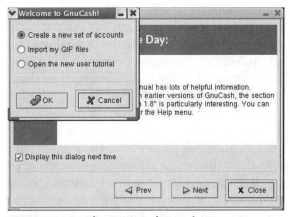

FIGURE 5.26   The GNU Cash opening screen.

If you choose New Accounts, GNU Cash will take you through a very user-friendly wizard that will help you set up your accounts. The first screen of that wizard is shown in Figure 5.27. Notice that some Linux software refers to certain wizards or utilities as "druids." This is one more example of the quirky sense of humor common to the Linux community.

FIGURE 5.27 The GNU Cash Wizard screen one.

The next screen of the wizard, shown in Figure 5.28, prompts you to enter the currency type. For our example we will use United States dollars (USD). However, it is important that you realize that Linux and most applications written for Linux are truly international. If you peruse the currency options available, you will see that virtually every currency type currently in use is represented.

The following screen of the wizard asks what type of account, or accounts, you want to set up. For demonstration purposes, we will set up a simple checking account. This is shown in Figure 5.29. However, you should probably take a look at the wide array of options you have available to you. Virtually any type of financial account can be handled by GNU Cash.

On the next screen you can set a starting balance. This is shown in Figure 5.30. Then you simply press Next, then Finish, and your accounts are created and ready for you to work with. Setting up the accounts, as you can see, is very simple and easy to do.

When you are finished, you should see something much like what is shown in Figure 5.31. You can now begin working on this account using the various options on the drop-down menu. Two important options you might want to look at are the export

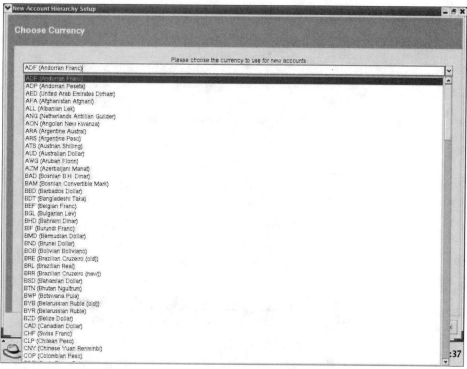

FIGURE 5.28   Currency options.

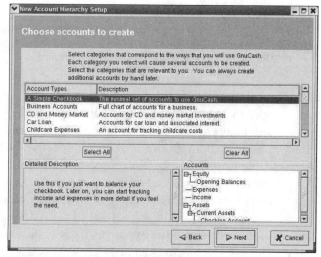

FIGURE 5.29   Selecting account types.

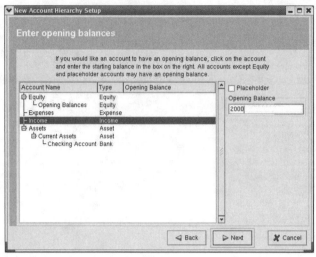

FIGURE 5.30 Opening balance.

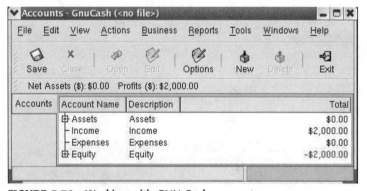

FIGURE 5.31 Working with GNU Cash accounts.

and tax options. Under File, on the drop-down menu, you can select Export and export your account to a number of different formats, including a spreadsheet. Under Edit, you can select Tax Options and alter how taxes are computed on this account.

Perhaps most important, from a financial perspective, is the plethora of reports you have available to you. If you select Reports from the drop-down menu, you should see something like what is shown in Figure 5.32. As you can see, there are a number of reports you can choose from, grouped into logical categories.

Thorough coverage of GNU Cash is beyond the scope of this book. However, you should at least be aware of its existence, its basic functionality, and where to find it. If you are a longtime Quicken or Microsoft Money user, you will probably find GNU Cash a very viable alternative that you can use with Linux.

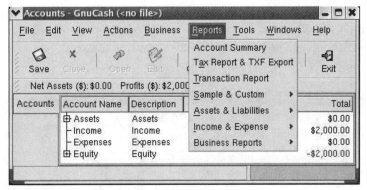

FIGURE 5.32 GNU Cash reports.

KSpread

In addition to word processing, which we explored a bit earlier in this chapter, working with spreadsheets is a very common task among computer users. As a Windows user, you probably are familiar with Microsoft Excel. Like most other products you are used to in Windows, there is a viable Linux alternative to Excel. That alternative is KSpread. You can find KSpread by selecting Office from the Start menu, then choosing More Office Applications. When you first start KSpread, you should see something much like what is shown in Figure 5.33.

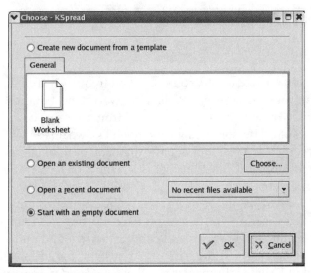

FIGURE 5.33 KSpread.

If you then choose to start a blank spreadsheet document, you will see something very similar to what is shown in Figure 5.34. For Excel users, this should look very familiar. The basic layout is very much like Excel.

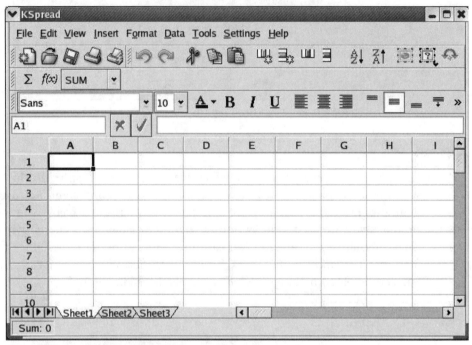

FIGURE 5.34 A blank spreadsheet.

If you are like most Excel users, you frequently need to include various functions in your spreadsheets. Well, don't worry, most of those familiar functions are in KSpread as well. If you choose Insert from the drop-down menu and select Functions, you will see something very much like what is shown in Figure 5.35. As you can see, there is a plethora of basic mathematical functions. You have all the standard trigonometric functions, statistical functions, sum, and so on, just as with Microsoft Excel.

To sort rows, insert new rows, or insert new columns, look under the Data drop-down menu. With Microsoft Excel, sorting was found under the Data drop-down menu, but new rows and columns were found under the Insert drop-down menu. Essentially, all the basic functions you found in Microsoft Excel are supported in KSpread. In many cases they are found in the same place in both appli-

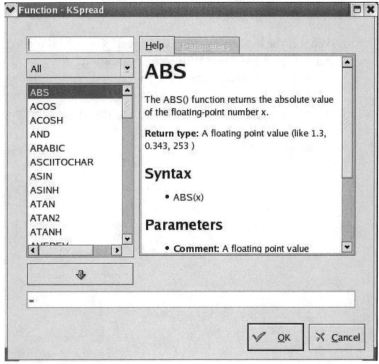

FIGURE 5.35   KSpread functions.

cations. The major difference between Excel and KSpread is that in some cases the functions are found in different locations on the two applications, and you may find that some advanced features of Excel are not present in KSpread. However, KSpread is more than adequate for basic spreadsheets and number crunching.

SUMMARY

In this chapter, we reviewed some common tasks accomplished in Windows and showed you how to do them using the KDE interface in Linux. We have looked at various text editors, graphics programs, calculators, and even accessibility options. By the end of this chapter you should be ready to start using your Linux machine to accomplish useful work. In short, you should be able to do many of the tasks you did in Windows.

REVIEW QUESTIONS

1. What is the biggest difference between Kate and KWrite?
2. Kate is most like what Windows application?
3. Which offers more graphics functionality: Windows Paint or Image Magick?
4. Do you use the Print Screen button to do screen captures in KDE?
5. What are sticky keys?
6. What are bounce keys?

6

Linux Administration from KDE

In This Chapter

- Managing Users and Groups
- Important System Tools
- Using the KDE Control Center
- Scheduling Tasks
- Kickstart Configurator

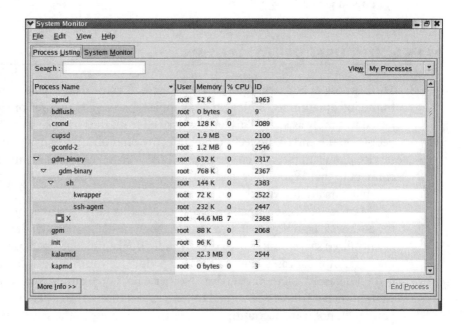

INTRODUCTION

By this point in this book you should be getting quite comfortable with Linux and with the KDE graphical interface. You have installed Linux, configured Linux, and found out how to get on the Internet, and you have been introduced to several basic but highly useful applications. You should now be able to accomplish word processing, spreadsheet applications, use a calculator, and even do simple graphics with Linux. At this point you should be a basically competent Linux user. However, Linux is not always used for a single-user home environment. Many readers will want to use Linux in their small businesses. For this reason it will be necessary for us to cover some basic Linux administration skills.

This chapter is aimed at showing you how to use Linux as a server, perhaps for a small office, and how to administer that server via the KDE graphical interface. We will explore how to add users and groups, how to schedule tasks, and how to monitor the system. All of this will be done with easy-to-use point-and-click applications (in a later chapter, you will see how to perform many of these tasks with shell commands). Even if you are certain that you have no desire to use Linux as a server, it would still be a good idea to at least skim this chapter. It will give you some insight into how Linux works and perhaps a deeper understanding of computer systems in general.

MANAGING USERS AND GROUPS

The purpose of a server is to provide services, files, or data to one or more people. In the information technology field, people who use a computer or system are referred to simply as *users*. This term is derived from the term *end users*, meaning the people on the end of the technology line, the ones ultimately using the product or service. For example, a Web server provides Web pages (data) to any user who can connect to that Web server via the Internet or a local network. The people accessing that data are the Web server's users.

Many offices, even small ones, use a server to store information. That way, all the authorized employees have access to the same data, since that data is located on a centralized server rather than on any individual employee's personal machine. In many if not most cases, you want some people on your network to have access to certain data and not to have access to other data. For example, you would probably want human resources personnel to have access to a person's personal records, but you might not want accounting or sales to have access to the same data. It is therefore necessary to restrict a person's access to only those items that are pertinent to the performance of his job. It is also probable that you would not want general users to have access to system administration tools. They might accidentally or even intentionally change important system settings. This could be annoying, or it could shut down your system.

With the Linux operating system, each time a user logs on, the settings in his user account determine what files and directories he has access to and what ones he does not. The place to start managing users and groups is with user accounts. Using the KDE interface, you would go to System Settings and select Users and Groups. You should then see a screen that looks very much like the one in Figure 6.1.

The options on the toolbar should be fairly self explanatory. If you prefer to use drop-down menus rather than toolbars, you can access these same items by choosing File from the drop-down menu. Under that you will see Add User, Add Group, and the other options shown on the toolbar.

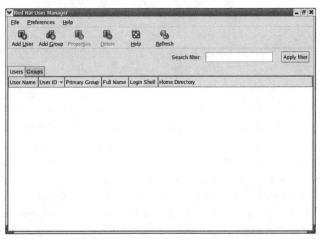

FIGURE 6.1   Red Hat User Manager.

Let's add a user just to get the feel of how it's done. You begin by clicking the Add User button on the toolbar, or selecting File and then choosing Add User from the drop-down menu. Regardless of which method you use, you should then see something very much like what is shown in Figure 6.2.

The first two fields are obvious. In the first field, you simply enter a username. What you select for a username is a matter of personal preference, but many organizations use the person's first initial and last name. For example, the username for the author would be ceasttom. You then enter that person's full name in the second field. Next you need to enter a password. You will be required to type this password twice to ensure that the password was correctly entered.

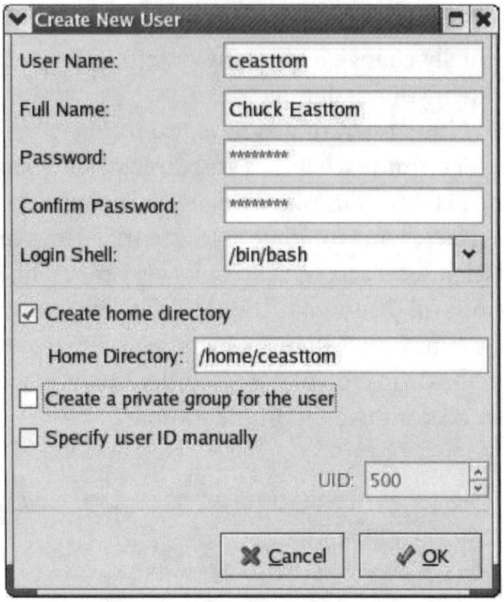

FIGURE 6.2 Create New User.

If you want your system to be secure, there are a few guidelines regarding passwords you must follow. To begin with, there are programs freely available on the Internet that are used to guess passwords. For this reason your password should never be any common word or any word associated with you. It is foolish to use the names of your children, spouse, your anniversary, or other such items as passwords. Another good rule to follow is to mix letters and numbers. For example, if your password were banana, you should consider using something like banana189 instead. Finally, the longer your password is, the harder it will be to crack. Many system administrators make all users pick passwords between 5 and 20 characters long.

The next step is to check whether or not you want a home directory for this user. In most cases, the answer will be yes. This is the default directory that user will have access to when he logs on. It is where he will store files and data. All home directories are subdirectories of the directory home. It is a common practice to name the user's home directory the same as the username. In fact, this user utility will by default create a home directory name that is the same as the username. So, for example, the default home directory for the author would be /home/ceasttom. If you do not want to use the default name, then you will have to manually change it. You do that by typing in the alternative directory you want to use. You then have two check boxes that need to be unchecked. One is labeled "Create a private group for the user," and the other is labeled "Specify user ID manually." The first setting would create a private group for your user and place him in it (more about groups in just a bit). The other would require you, the administrator, to create a unique user ID number for that user. That number is how the Linux system recognizes the person. Usernames are for people to read and understand. If you choose to do this manually, you will need to keep track of all user IDs and ensure that you never try to use the same one twice. It is far simpler to let Linux handle that.

There is one more item on the Create New User screen that we purposely left to last. That is the Login Shell setting. Most users will want to use the bash shell, which you may recall is the most commonly used Linux shell and is selected by default. However, you can select from a list of shells, and any one of them can be the default shell for a particular user. When you are finished adding a user, the screen should look something like what you see in Figure 6.3a. All you need to do now is press the OK button, and you will have created a new user account.

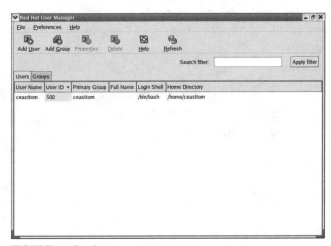

FIGURE 6.3A A new user account.

If you restart the machine and log on with this username and password, you will notice a few changes. The first is that your starting directory would be that user's home directory rather than the root directory. The only reason why root is your current starting directory is because you have logged on as root. The second change would be that you would find that when you attempted to use many administration functions, you would be asked to supply a superuser password. *Superuser* is a term in Linux that denotes someone logged on to a regular user account who is using administrative privileges. To do this, you must have the root password. In short, superuser mode is being logged in as a normal user but using the root password to have temporary access to root privileges.

You have now established a user account, but what does this user have access to? The answer is, not much. At this point he will have access to his home directory and not much else. In Linux, users are put into groups, and those groups are assigned access to certain resources. The access rights a user has depends entirely on what groups that user belongs to. When you double-click on a user account (or if you single-click on it and select Properties from either the toolbar or the drop-down menu), you are presented with a User Properties screen. This screen has four tabs. The first is the account information you provided. This includes username, password, home directory, and login shell. The other three tabs are where we will determine important parameters about this account, including what groups that user belongs to.

The second tab, Account Info, is shown in Figure 6.3b. This tab allows you to set an expiration date for the account or even to lock out the account. If you have a temporary employee, you definitely want to set an expiration date for that employee's account. Should you terminate an employee, you must immediately lock out his account.

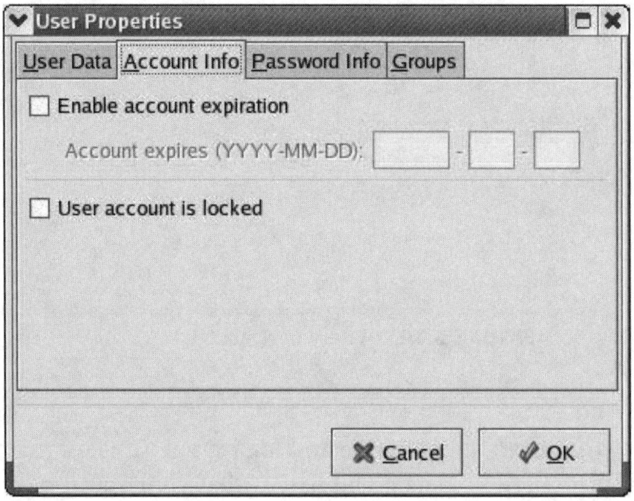

FIGURE 6.3B   The second tab of the User Properties page.

The third tab contains information about a user's password. One important security precaution you can take is to require that users change their passwords periodically. In Figure 6.3c you can see the screen where you would set the expiration date of the account if you wanted to. The user in question will get a warning that his

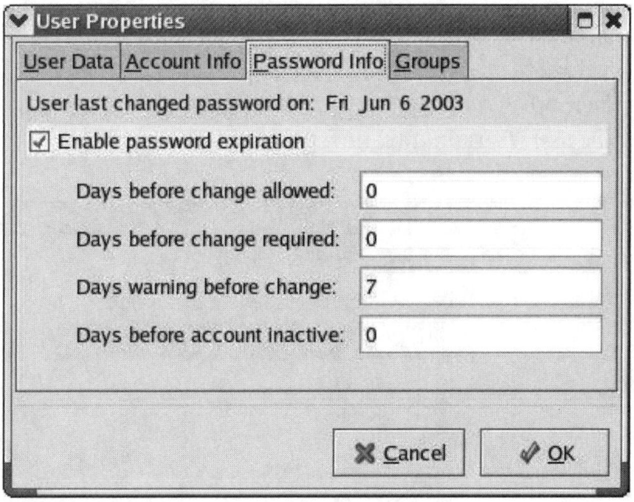

FIGURE 6.3C Password settings.

password is about to expire every time he logs in for five days preceding the expiration date. These are very useful features you probably will want to turn on. Having the password expire after a given period of time forces users to change their passwords from time to time. This definitely heightens security in your system. If you are going to force the user to change his password, you should remind the user that his password's expiration date is drawing near. This gives him time to think of a new password. Many organizations have policies regarding acceptable passwords. These policies often include a minimum password length. A good basic password policy, if you don't already have one, is to require passwords to be at least five characters long and include both numbers and letters.

The fourth tab of the User Properties screen is where we establish the groups a user belongs to. Select this tab and you will see the Group Properties screen, which is shown in Figure 6.3d. You can see a long list of groups; some may make sense to you, and others will make more sense as you move forward in this book. There are several groups listed, and some may seem quite obscure to you. One that will probably make sense to you is the adm group. This group is for administrators. If you add a user to this group, that user will have some administration privileges. Contrary to what you might think, though, this group does not have the unlimited administration privileges of the root user. To practice, you may want to add the user you just created to the adm group. You can see that one of the easiest ways to grant a user access to certain items is to add him to the appropriate group. For example, if you want him to have access to the Web server, you add him to the apache group.

Apache is the name of the Web server that ships with Red Hat Linux. Using Apache is covered in a later chapter. You may be interested in knowing that Apache runs as a daemon. A daemon is a program that runs in the background and is not visible to the user. In Windows, such programs are referred to as services.

FIGURE 6.3D   Adding a user to groups.

In some cases you will want to create your own new groups. This is just as easy as creating new user accounts. To add a new group, click on the Add Group button on the toolbar or select File from the drop-down menu and select Add Group. You will then be prompted to assign the group a name, as shown in Figure 6.4. It usually is a good idea to use logical names for your groups, names that indicate the type of group it is.

You will need to click on the Groups tab to see the new group you have added, as well as any groups that were previously added. Once you do that, you can click once on your group to highlight it and then press the Properties button in the toolbar. You can also select File from the drop-down menu and choose Properties. Whatever method you use to get there, you will finally arrive at a screen much like the one in Figure 6.5. You should then click on the Group Users tab so that you can see what users are assigned to the group.

You will notice that, in addition to the user you added, there are a number of users already on the list. Some of these users are actually applications. Many

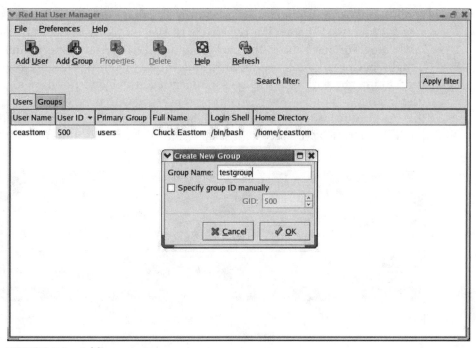

FIGURE 6.4   Adding a group.

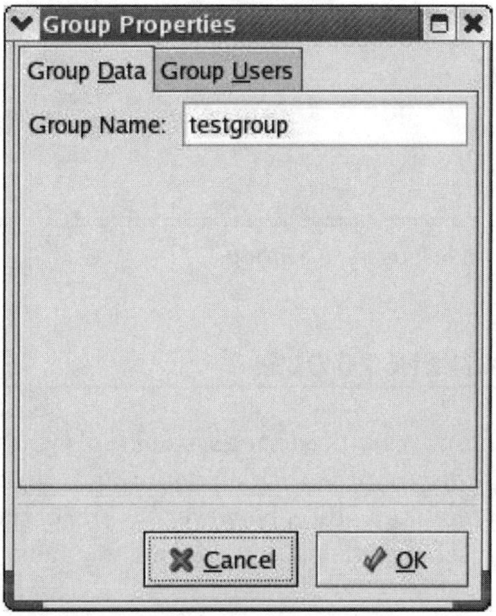

FIGURE 6.5   Group Properties.

applications run as daemons. We previously said that a daemon is much like a service in Windows. Whether it is referred to as a daemon or a service, it is essentially just a program that runs in the background and has certain tasks it must fulfill. Usually, daemons handle system functions, things that the average PC user has no need to interact with. For this reason, daemons usually do not have a graphical user interface. For now, you need not be concerned with these other user accounts that are already loaded into the system. Simply find the username you added and put a check by it, as you see in Figure 6.6, and click the OK button.

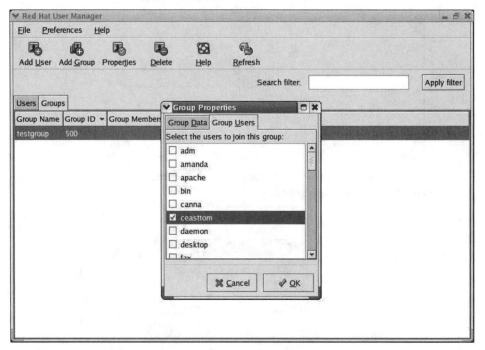

FIGURE 6.6   Adding users to a group.

IMPORTANT SYSTEM TOOLS

There are a number of important system tools you will want to become familiar with. These tools are of particular importance if you are using your Linux machine as a server for an office. However, several of these tools can be useful for the home Linux user as well. We will examine the most important system utilities in this section.

The System Monitor

By going to System Tools and selecting System Monitor, you will find the System Monitor utility, shown in Figure 6.7a. This is a very important system utility. It allows you to see how your system is performing.

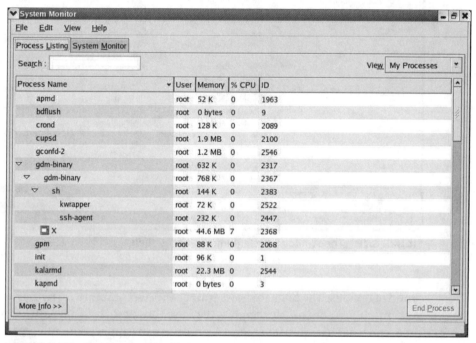

FIGURE 6.7A   The System Monitor.

If you did not follow the install instructions in Chapter 2, "Installing Linux," you may not have the System Monitor installed on your system.

You may have previously used the System Information option in Windows to get similar information about your Windows system. If you have not used that feature of Windows, you can go to the Start menu, select Programs, choose Accessories, then select System Tools and click on the System Information option. The System Information screen, shown in Figure 6.7b, will then be displayed.

Although both the Windows System Information screen and the KDE system monitor provide access to similar information, their layouts are quite different. The KDE System Monitor is displayed via tabs, with each tab representing a different

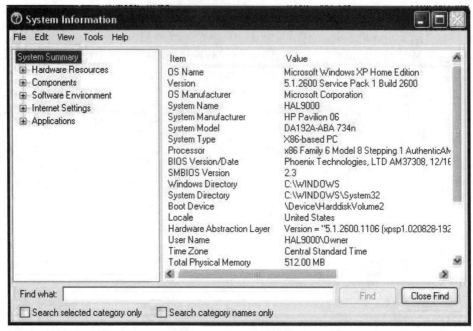

FIGURE 6.7B The Windows System Information screen.

group of options. The first tab shows you the processes that are currently running on your machine, how much memory they use, how much of the CPU's processor time, and what user initiated them. A process is any application, utility, or daemon running on your machine. If your machine is performing sluggishly, you might want to see if there are any processes that don't need to be running and can be shut down. System administrators often examine running processes of a system to look for telltale signs of a hacker attempting to infiltrate the system. Strange processes running may indicate some virus on your system or some malicious program that a hacker has loaded onto your system.

The second tab will be more useful. This tab is shown in Figure 6.8 and is labeled System Monitor. On this tab you see a neat little graph displaying the current CPU and memory usage. This is a very useful diagnostic tool. You can see if your system needs more memory. As a rule of thumb, if you are consistently using more than 80 percent of your memory, you probably want to consider adding more memory.

At the bottom of this screen you can see how much of your hard drive space is being used. In Figure 6.8 we are using 4.8 gigabytes of a 9.0-gigabyte hard drive. Since we are using only a little more than half of our hard drive space, we don't

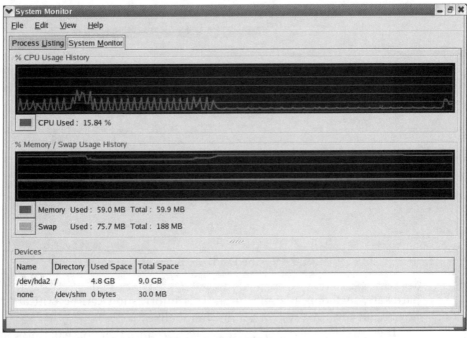

FIGURE 6.8   The second tab of the System Monitor.

need to consider a new hard drive. However, notice that we are using 56.1 megabytes of our memory and we only have 59.9 megabytes total. It would probably be prudent to consider purchasing additional memory.

Whether you are a system administrator for your organization or a casual home user, the System Monitor is an invaluable tool. It can be quite useful for diagnosing shortcomings in your system. Don't go out and invest money in more memory or a new hard drive if it's not needed. Use System Monitor to see if your current memory, CPU, or hard drive is inadequate for your system's needs.

The Hardware Browser

The Hardware Browser is located by going to System Tools and selecting Hardware Browser. When you do this, you should see something like what is shown in Figure 6.9. This is a very important yet easy to understand and use utility. With the Hardware Browser you can see what devices are on your machine. This includes disk drives, network cards, sound cards, and pretty much any piece of hardware you can put on a PC. In many cases, this utility will even display the specifications of the

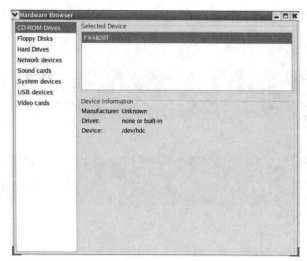

FIGURE 6.9   The Hardware Browser.

hardware, including manufacturer. This information can be critical to the PC novice and advanced system administrator alike.

If you are a novice user, there is a good chance that you will find some occasion to contact a technical support representative. This might be technical support from your Internet service provider, your PC manufacturer, or from Red Hat Linux itself. Whatever the reason you contact them, technical support personnel often ask you questions about your system's hardware. These are questions that many novices cannot answer. The Hardware Browser will give you access to all of this information.

If, on the other hand, you are a technically savvy system administrator, you will find a veritable gold mine of valuable data under the Hardware Browser. You can get specifications on every piece of hardware on a machine. You can then use that information in myriad ways. For example, you might take the manufacturer information from a video card, do a Web search to find that manufacturer's Web site, and look for the latest drivers for Linux that the vendor offers.

Under the device information for all hardware devices, the last item is Device. You may note that all devices appear to be paths, just like the path to a file in a directory. They also all start with /dev/. Linux views all devices as if they were files or directories within the /dev/ directory. Hard drives always start with hd, floppy drives with fd, and network cards with eth.

Security Level

This utility is so important that it would be a grave injustice not to introduce you to it. However, it is found under System Settings rather than System Tools. When you were installing Linux, you had the opportunity to establish a number of configuration settings. Recall that you were admonished to leave the firewall settings at default. However, if in the interim since that installation you have picked up a little knowledge on the subject, you can now customize security for your system. Even if you have not learned much more about network security, you should be aware of a few basics. The Security Level Configuration screen is shown in Figure 6.10.

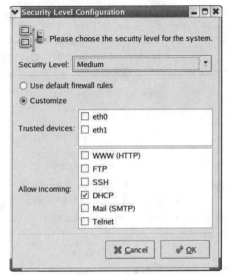

FIGURE 6.10 The Security Level Configuration screen.

Before we can discuss the security settings, it would be prudent to have a brief introduction to how networks and the Internet communicate. In short, data is broken down into packets that are sent using various protocols. A protocol is simply a standardized way of communicating. There are a number of protocols used in networks and on the Internet, each with its own purpose. It is not necessary for a casual home user to memorize these, but since some readers might be their office system administrators, the most commonly used protocols are described in Table 6.1.

TABLE 6.1 Protocols

Protocol	Description
HTTP	This is Hypertext Transfer Protocol. It is the protocol used by Web browsers such as Netscape Navigator and Mozilla to communicate with Web servers and display Web pages.
FTP	File Transfer Protocol. This protocol is used to upload and download files. If you have ever downloaded a demo game, music, or any file from the Internet, it was probably done with FTP.
SMTP	This is Simple Mail Transfer Protocol and is used to send e-mails.
POP3	This is Post Office Protocol, which is used to retrieve incoming e-mails from an e-mail server.
DHCP	Dynamic Host Configuration Protocol is used to get an IP address from a server.

Notice that the Trusted Devices category includes your machine's own network cards. If you select a device as a trusted device, that means that packets from that device will not be screened. You should think very hard before selecting any device as trusted. As you learn a little more about how networks work, you might consider customizing your security settings.

Adding and Removing Applications

From time to time you may find that you don't use an application that you have installed, and you may want to remove it to free up more space on your hard drive. You may discover that you forgot to install some application. The Add and Remove Applications screen, found under System Tools, is what you need for either task. You may recall that in Chapter 2 you were told that if you forgot any applications, they could be installed later. This utility is how you go about doing that.

When you first launch this utility, it will take several moments to load. This is because it is checking your system to see what applications are already installed. While it is loading, you will see a screen giving you the status of the process. This screen is shown in Figure 6.11.

Once the utility is loaded, you will have a list of all possible packages that you might install. Applications that are already installed on your system will have a checkmark beside them. Items that are not installed will not have the checkmark.

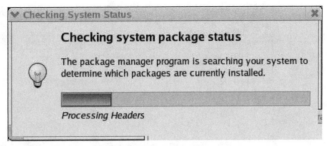

FIGURE 6.11   Checking System Package Status.

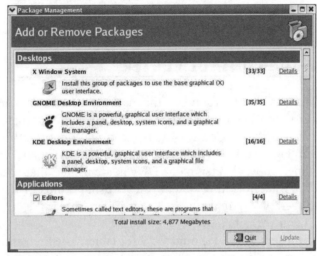

FIGURE 6.12A   Adding and removing applications.

You may check the packages you would like to install and uncheck packages you want to uninstall or remove. Then simply click the Update button. Depending on the choices you made, it might take several minutes to add and remove various applications. Also, if you chose to add applications, you will be prompted to insert the appropriate installation disks. You can see the utility's main screen in Figure 6.12a.

KDiskFree

KDiskFree, shown in Figure 6.12b, is a rather simple utility. It shows you various drives, including floppy and CD-ROM, as well as hard drives. In the display it will show how much space is still free, what percentage is in use, and the Linux device name and initial size of the storage device.

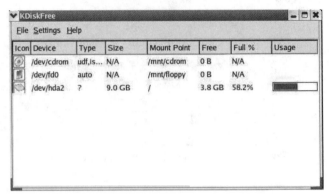

FIGURE 6.12B   KDiskFree.

USING THE KDE CONTROL CENTER

The Control Center is found on the main Start menu. It is, as the name implies, a centralized location from which to control many important features of KDE. When you first launch the Control Center, you will see something much like what is shown in Figure 6.13. In the main screen on the right side, you should notice that it is telling you what version of KDE you are using, what user account is currently logged in, what operating system you are using (Linux or Unix), and what version of that operating system you are using. The release is the version of the Linux kernel that you are using.

On the left side you should see three tables. The first, entitled Index, is a listing of all the various items you can control through the Control Center. The second tab is a Search tab allowing you to search for a particular item. The third is a Help tab where you can look up help on various KDE topics.

Many of the items you can control from the Control Center are items we previously covered. Things such as appearance and themes, Internet and network, and desktop are all items that we explored previously. The Control Center provides a convenient single location from which to work with many of the various configuration utilities available with KDE. We will not cover the items we have previously examined. They work exactly the same way from the Control Center as they did previously. However, we will look at a few interesting items in the Control Center that we did not examine previously.

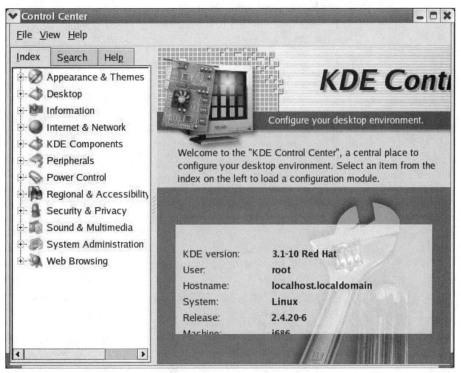

FIGURE 6.13 The Control Center.

Power Control

If you look under Power Control and select Display Power Control, you will see something much like what is displayed in Figure 6.14. The settings shown here allow you to conserve energy. You can tell your PC to suspend operation after a certain amount of time or to completely power off after a given amount of time. That way, if you walk away from your PC and leave it running, it will eventually shut itself off.

There is also a Laptop Battery section that is specifically for laptop users. This section enables you to determine how to warn the user if his laptop battery is getting low. If you are installing Linux on a laptop, you would be very wise to set up your laptop battery settings. This screen is shown in Figure 6.15.

The first tab establishes whether or not to display a battery status icon and how often to check the status of the battery. The second tab is very much like the Power Control settings we previously examined. It allows you to shut down the system power after a given amount of time. You can have a different amount of

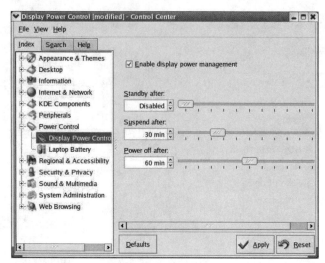

FIGURE 6.14   Power Control settings.

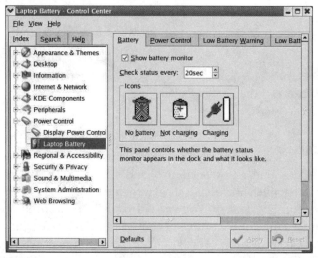

FIGURE 6.15   Laptop Battery settings.

time selected, depending on whether your laptop is plugged into an outlet or running off battery power. This is a very useful setting and can prevent you from leaving your laptop running and running down your battery. The final two tabs determine how and when the user will be warned about a low battery. If you are using Linux on a laptop, it would be a mistake for you not to become familiar with these settings and to ensure that they are set up in such a manner as to maximize your use of the Linux operating system and your laptop.

SYSTEM ADMINISTRATION

You may have noticed a section entitled System Administration. This section is for some of the more common system administration tasks. We will take a look at the ones that are most likely to be of use to you on a routine basis.

Login Manager

The Login Manager allows you to establish how the login screen is presented to the user when he logs in. This screen has six tabs that enable you to specify every aspect of the login process and appearance. You can see the screen in Figure 6.16.

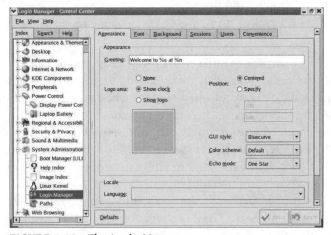

FIGURE 6.16   The Login Manager.

The first tab allows you to set the greeting, whether or not to show the logo (Tux the penguin), to show a clock, and what color scheme to use for the login screen. You can also change what character appears when someone is typing in a password. Most people are used to seeing one asterisk appear for each character they type, so it's probably a good idea to stick with this format, but you can change it if you want. The next two tabs allow you to further customize the login screen by setting the font and the background. These tabs handle purely cosmetic properties of the login screen and should be set to whatever you find pleasing.

The fourth tab, labeled Sessions and shown in Figure 6.17, is not cosmetic at all. This tab deals with the options the user will be presented with when he gets to the logon screen and what he can do from this screen.

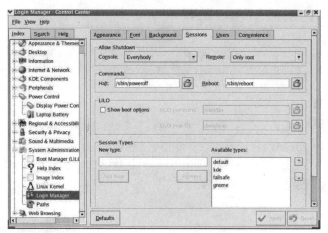

FIGURE 6.17 The fourth tab of the Login Manager.

As you can see, the first two settings allow you to determine what users can use the console/shell and what users can log on remotely. The second set of options, Commands, determines what happens when you halt or reboot. You should leave these with the default settings unless you have some very compelling reason to alter them. The third section simply determines whether or not to show the boot options on the login screen. This will make very little difference unless your machine is set to dual boot with two or more alternative operating systems (such as Linux and Windows).

The fourth section is the most interesting. Here is where you decide what startup options the user has. You will note that under Available Types there are four different settings for the user interface. As was mentioned earlier, while KDE and GNOME are the most popular graphical user interfaces, they are not the only ones available for Linux.

The Users tab allows you to select an image to display and to choose whether or not to show a list of users for the person to pick from. This would mean that instead of simply typing in their usernames and passwords, they could pick from a list of users and then enter the appropriate password.

This sixth and final tab, labeled Convenience, allows you to set some items that you may find convenient. However, you should remember that convenience almost always comes at a price. On this screen you can choose to allow people to log on without a password. Unless the machine is a home machine, such an option would be very foolish. Even if it is a home machine, you should think very hard before choosing this option. Do you really want your 10-year-old to be able to log on as root and have complete system administration privileges?

REGIONAL AND ACCESSIBILITY

This section allows you to set some accessibility options, which we have examined previously. However, it also allows you to reconfigure your machine for a given region. After you have chosen Regional & Accessibility, click on Country/Region & Language, and you should see a screen much like that in Figure 6.18.

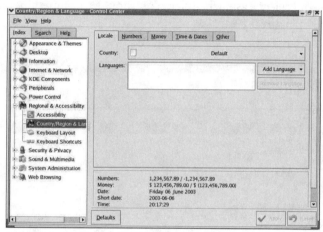

FIGURE 6.18   Country/Region & Language.

The first tab, Locale, allows you to set what nation and language settings to use. You can see at the bottom of this tab that your current settings are shown. The second tab determines how you will display numbers. The third tab is probably the most important for setting up your machine for a different country. This tab allows you to change how money is displayed. Obviously, currency is quite different from one nation to the next, so this tab can be quite important. The fourth tab establishes how you will display times and dates. This tab is more a matter of preference than regions. The final tab will allow you to choose paper format and measurement systems. If you are traveling abroad, you should remember that most countries use the metric system.

SCHEDULING TASKS

One very useful feature of Linux is the capability to schedule certain tasks to take place at some future date and time. If you will recall, earlier we discussed programs that run in the background and accomplish tasks. In Linux and Unix these are referred to as daemons, and in Windows they are called services. Most daemons in Linux end in a letter d. The daemon that is responsible for handling scheduled tasks is called *crond*, for chronological daemon. You can completely manage crond via shell commands, and we will visit that topic in Chapter 8, "Moving from Microsoft Word to Open Office," but right now we will see how to do this through the KDE interface. Like most tasks, scheduling tasks via the KDE interface is a lot easier and more user friendly than doing it via shell commands. To get to the Task Scheduler, you can go to System Tools and select Task Scheduler. You should see something much like what is displayed in Figure 6.19.

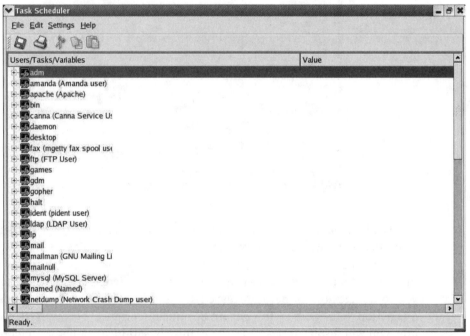

FIGURE 6.19   The Task Scheduler.

To schedule a new task, you simply expand the category appropriate to your task and right-click on New Tasks, as shown in Figure 6.20.

When you do this you will see a screen like the one shown in Figure 6.21. On this screen you can decide when you want this task to run. You can pick months, days, time of day, even down to the exact minute when you want the task to run. Then use the Browse button to select the program you want to run.

That is all that is required to schedule any task. You can have any program you want run automatically at a certain time and date. This is very useful for system

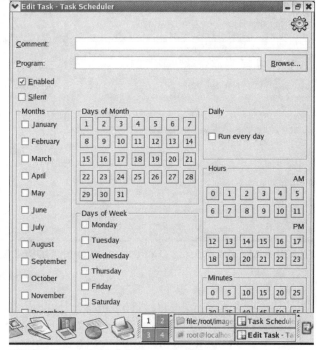

FIGURE 6.20   New Tasks.   **FIGURE 6.21**   Scheduling a new task.

administrators who want particular programs or scripts to run when they are away. This allows you to have certain cumbersome administrative tasks take place when you are away from the computer.

KICKSTART CONFIGURATOR

Linux, being a descendent of Unix, was designed with a powerful high-end server in mind. For that reason, Linux, like many Unix variants, comes with a wide assortment of configuration utilities. Some of these, such as the System Monitor, have Windows analogs you can relate to. However, some utilities, such as Kickstart Configurator, do not have any close analog in the Windows world. The Kickstart Configurator is a very useful KDE program. It is found under System Tools, and the main screen is shown in Figure 6.22. The Red Hat official documentation describes Kickstart in this manner: "Kickstart Configurator allows you to create a kickstart file using a graphical user interface, so that you do not have to remember the cor-

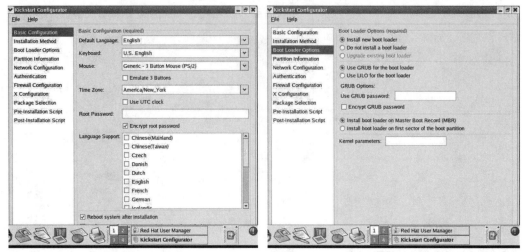

FIGURE 6.22 The Kickstart Configurator screen. **FIGURE 6.23** The Boot Loader Options screen.

rect syntax of the file." This means it allows you to generate a configuration script via a very easy to use graphical interface. It allows you to reconfigure all the things you set up in Chapter 2. It is often used by system administrators to create a single install script to be used for installs across an organization. From the basic configuration screen, you can change the language, mouse, keyboard, time zone, and other important settings.

The next screen that is of particular interest to us is the Boot Loader Options screen, shown in Figure 6.23. As you can see, this screen allows you to choose which boot loader to use. Even though GRUB is the newest boot loader, you don't have to use it. You can use LILO if you so desire. You can also choose to have a password on GRUB if you like.

After that, you come next to the Partition Information screen, shown in Figure 6.24. This screen should be used with great caution. You can readily see that one option is to remove all existing partitions. If you select this, you would wipe out your entire hard drive. This screen is of use only in certain restricted cases. For the most part, you will want to avoid altering anything on this screen.

The next two screens, Network Configuration and Authentication, provide yet another way to configure options we have already explored. We have seen three different ways to configure your network card after installation. Also recall from our earlier discussion of authentication that, if you lack any substantial familiarity with security, you should probably leave the authentication at default settings.

The Firewall Configuration screen, like the two preceding screens, provides yet another way to configure a particular part of your system. We mentioned firewall

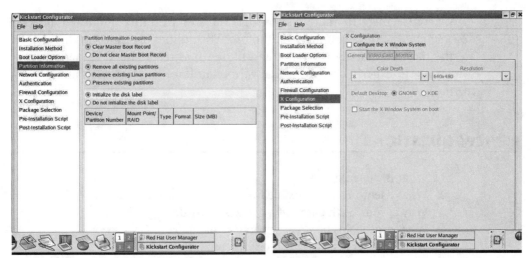

FIGURE 6.24 The Partition Information screen.   **FIGURE 6.25** The X Configuration screen.

configuration during the initial install and noted that you could always reconfigure the firewall settings at a later date, as you learned more about networks. The Kickstart Configurator is one of the vehicles you can use to reconfigure your firewall.

The X Configuration screen, shown in Figure 6.25, is quite interesting. With this screen you can reconfigure your system's screen resolution, video card, monitor, and default desktop. This screen is likely to be of interest even to casual users. One setting that people on any system (Windows, Macintosh, or Linux) seem inclined to change from time to time is their display settings.

The final three sections of Kickstart Configurator are used only to alter how an installation proceeds. Since we have already installed, these particular settings are not important to us at this time. If at some later date you want to install a new version of Red Hat, you can follow the installation instructions.

SUMMARY

This chapter has shown you the essentials of system administration via the KDE interface. There are certainly many more tasks you can do in KDE, but these are some of the most common. After studying this chapter, you should be able to add new users, manage groups, use the System Monitor, add and remove programs, use the KDE Control Center, and schedule tasks. Whether you are a casual home user or the system administrator for your office, these are common tasks that you will find yourself using with some frequency.

Of course, there are more system tools and administrative utilities in the KDE desktop interface that you may want to use. The utilities presented in this chapter are the most commonly encountered utilities. It is recommended that you take some time to experiment with these various utilities and become familiar with them.

REVIEW QUESTIONS

1. What is a daemon?
2. What daemon is responsible for scheduling tasks?
3. Why is your birth date not a good password?
4. What protocol is used for sending e-mail?
5. What protocol is used for receiving e-mail?
6. What KDE utility would you use to find out how much memory is being used by your system?
7. What is the purpose of the KDE Control Center?

7 The GNOME Interface

In This Chapter

- Getting Around in GNOME
- GNOME Graphics Applications
- GNOME Office Applications
- System Tools

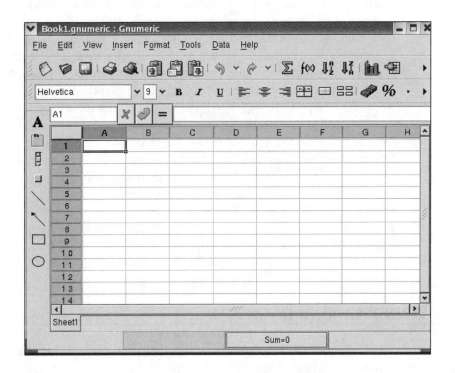

INTRODUCTION

As was previously mentioned, there are a number of different graphical interfaces you can use with Linux. Rather than have a single desktop environment choice as you have in Windows and Macintosh, you have several to choose from. Obviously, some of these are more commonly used than others. Some are rather obscure and rarely encountered. For the purposes of this book, we can ignore the more obscure desktop environments. KDE and GNOME are the two most commonly used desktop environments for Linux. Most of this book will focus on the KDE interface. This choice of KDE over alternative interfaces is strictly a matter of popularity. There is no technical reason to prefer KDE over GNOME. Both are very easy to use graphical interfaces and have several things in common. In fact, they even have many facets of their desktops in common. If you become proficient with one, learning the other should not be difficult. In fact, you can install both KDE and GNOME on your PC. At the login screen, simply click on Session at the bottom of the screen and select which interface you prefer to use during a session. Since GNOME and KDE can work side by side, and because it is so easy to switch back and forth between them, it seems prudent to examine GNOME, at least briefly. It should also be pointed out that GNOME is also quite popular, and many Linux users like it. If we at least look at both, then you might decide which interface you prefer. Remember that one of the cornerstones of the open source software philosophy is that you, the computer user, should have lots of choices. Even if you still prefer KDE, you will at least have a basic familiarity with GNOME. If you followed the instructions for installation in Chapter 2, "Installing Linux," then you should have both KDE and GNOME on your computer. If you did not, then skip to Chapter 14, "Miscellaneous Linux Applications," which has a section on adding new packages.

GNOME is part of the GNU project and is itself an open source application. GNOME is an acronym for GNU Network Object Model Environment. The GNOME project was officially started in August 1997, and the first release was in December of the same year. However, this release was just a barebones development release. It was intended for programmers to examine, improve upon, and submit changes, if they so desired. GNOME 1.0, the first version for the general public, was released in March 1999. GNOME is based on an underlying engine called GTX. This means that it can run on any Unix-like platform that uses GTX. You can find out more about GNOME at *www.GNOME.org/*.

GETTING AROUND IN GNOME

The first objective we must achieve is to help you get acclimated to GNOME. Before you can start using GNOME applications, you need to get used to moving around in the GNOME interface. You will need to know where to find things before you will be able to effectively use GNOME. Fortunately, the GNOME layout is not radically different from KDE, and by this point in this book, you should be comfortable with KDE. When you first launch GNOME, you will see a screen much like the one shown in Figure 7.1.

FIGURE 7.1   The GNOME interface.

As you can see, it is very similar to the KDE screen, and in fact it is almost identical. You also will find that the Start menu has almost identical options to those you saw in KDE. Still, there are several differences. The first is in some of the applications that ship with the interface. There are some applications that ship with KDE that do not ship with GNOME, and vice versa. For example, if you use Red Hat and KDE, then you have access to Image Magick. If you use Red Hat and GNOME, you do not. However, GNOME ships with Eye of GNOME Image Viewer, which KDE does not have. Both interfaces, however, ship with Gimp, which we will be exploring in some detail later in this book. You will probably also notice as you proceed through this book that when you install both GNOME and KDE, as we did in Chapter 2, you find applications mingled. If a KDE application can run in GNOME, and you have both GNOME and KDE installed, then you will see that KDE application when you run GNOME. The reverse is also true. If you have an application designed for GNOME, and both GNOME and KDE are installed, you will see that GNOME application even when you are using KDE.

Another difference between the two desktop environments is in how the interface itself behaves. With KDE, the Print Screen button on the keyboard does nothing. With GNOME, it works; in fact, it works better than it does in Windows. In Windows, the Print Scrn button simply copies the current screen to the Clipboard. You then would have to open some graphics program, such as Microsoft Paint, and paste that image into it before you could save it, alter it, or work with it in any way. With GNOME, when you click the Print Screen button, a small graphics program is launched containing the current screen.

You should be thrilled to know that the default Web browser and e-mail client in GNOME are the same as the ones in KDE. Mozilla is the default Web browser, and Evolution is the default e-mail client. There is absolutely no difference in how Mozilla works in KDE and how it works in GNOME. Incidentally, you also can get Mozilla for Windows; just go to *www.mozilla.org*. That allows you to use the same type of Web browser in GNOME, KDE, and Windows. This is probably more convenient than trying to keep current with two or more Web browsers. In a later chapter, we will look carefully at the things you can do with Mozilla. There are other applications available with GNOME. For example, GNOME also has a Web browser called Galleon, as well as an e-mail client named Balsa. But it still has Mozilla and Evolution, which you learned to use with KDE, so you may choose to continue to use those applications.

All the basic groups you found in KDE are still here in GNOME. You have Accessories, Games, Graphics, Internet, Office, Preferences, Programming, Sound and Video, System Settings, and System Tools. Many of the same applications and utilities are found in these groups. In short, if you are comfortable with KDE, you should be able to move around in GNOME without much difficulty. However, there are a few key differences, especially in regard to certain utilities or programs that exist with one interface but not the other. In this chapter we will look at some of these.

GNOME GRAPHICS APPLICATIONS

Now we will examine a few of the graphics applications that come with GNOME. Recall that many of the applications for KDE are also available in GNOME, but we will only be looking at those that are specific to GNOME.

The Paint Program

Just as with Windows and KDE, you will probably want to do some simple graphics manipulation with GNOME. GNOME's paint program can be found by selecting Graphics from the Start menu and then More Graphics Applications. This paint program, shown in Figure 7.2, is quite similar to the paint programs in KDE and Windows. All three applications offer very simple graphics editing and creating ca-

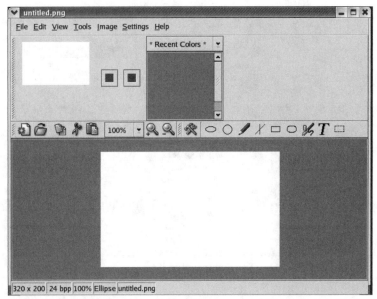

FIGURE 7.2 The GNOME paint program.

pabilities. However, it should be noted that none of these paint programs is a professional graphics program. They are basic home use graphics utilities.

Even though GNOME's paint program is very similar to KDE and Windows Paint, let's take a few moments to look at some basic functionality in GNOME's paint program. The applications, while similar, are not identical. When you click on the large block of color in the upper portion of the application's screen, you will be presented with a Color dialog, much like the one shown in Figure 7.3. This dialog lets you select from among a wide range of colors and shades. You may have noticed by now that the dialog boxes you saw in KDE and you now see in GNOME are almost identical to the dialog boxes you see in Windows. This is because the dialog box is a common way of getting input from the user and is not unique to any operating system.

When you click once on any of the tools in the toolbox, such as the Ellipse or Airbrush tool, you have selected that tool. You can then choose Tools from the drop-down menu and click on Tool Properties. This will allow you to change the behavior of a specific tool. For example, if you select one of the Shape tools, such as the Ellipse, you have several options as to how that shape should be filled, if you want it filled at all. The options are shown in Figure 7.4.

For example, you can choose to have a shape completely fill when drawn or fill to a certain percentage. You also can have it filled with horizontal, vertical, diagonal, or crossed lines. There are several other choices for how that shape can be filled. Figure 7.5 shows three circles, each filled in a different manner.

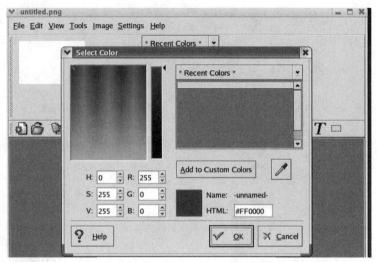

FIGURE 7.3 The Color dialog box.

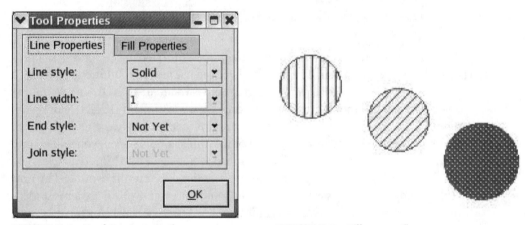

FIGURE 7.4 Tool Property options.   **FIGURE 7.5** Fill properties.

As you can see, the GNOME paint application is quite similar to the KDE and Windows paint applications. They all offer very similar functionality. The real difference between the three applications is not in what tools they offer, but in where the tools are found.

gThumb Image Viewer

This is an interesting graphics program. While it only has basic graphics manipulation tools, it has other interesting features that we will explore. This application does not have the very advanced graphics tools you might expect to find in commercial products like Adobe Photoshop, or CorelDRAW. For example, it has none of the special effects such as blur or oil paint we saw with Image Magick. You can find gThumb by going to Graphics and selecting gThumb Image Viewer. You will see something like what is shown in Figure 7.6.

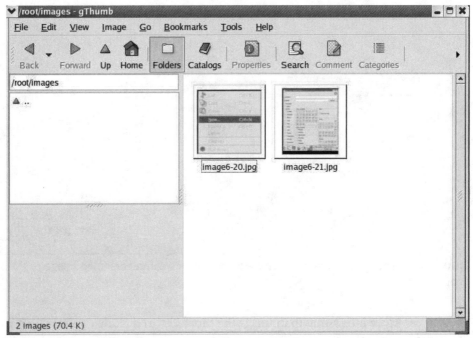

FIGURE 7.6   gThumb Image Viewer.

While gThumb does not have advanced graphics tools, it does have a few basic tools. If you look under the Image option on the drop-down menu, you will see that you can rotate, flip, mirror, or resize the image. You also can change the color balance and saturation, as well as create a negative of the image. These few options are rather basic, but they provide some simple graphics manipulation functionality. The real interesting thing about gThumb is found under Tools. If you go to the drop-down menu and select Tools, you will see several items of interest. One option that should catch your attention right away is the option to set the current image as the wallpaper. If you like the image you are viewing, you can make it the background/wallpaper for your current desktop. The options for using the currently selected image as the desktop wallpaper are shown in Figure 7.7.

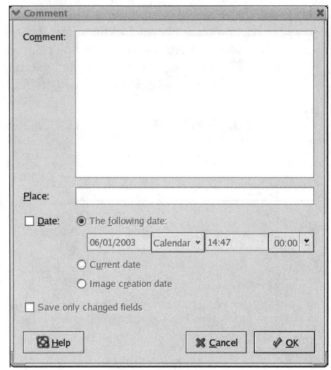

FIGURE 7.7 Setting the current image as wallpaper.

FIGURE 7.8 Adding comments to an image.

More interesting than this is the capability to include comments. If you select Edit from the drop-down menu, you should see the option to add comments, as shown in Figure 7.8.

You might wonder why you would add comments to a graphics file. There are several reasons. A professional photographer or journalist might want to add notes to a particular image. Since the comments are part of the image file, it is impossible to lose them. Even a casual home user might want to comment on certain images, noting the time, date, and occasion. The Comment option is probably the single most interesting aspect of gThumb. It is not the best package for graphics manipulation, but it is an excellent tool for cataloging your images.

GQView

GQView is a simple image viewing program. You find GQview by selecting Graphics from the Start menu and choosing More Graphics Applications. GQview, shown in Figure 7.9, is primarily for previewing images. It has very limited image manip-

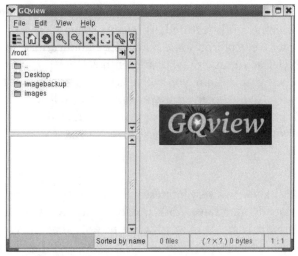

FIGURE 7.9   GQview.

ulation capabilities. You can rotate, mirror, or flip the image, and that is about the extent of its image editing functionality.

You might wonder, given its limited editing capabilities, why it is being mentioned at all. It is being mentioned because it has one very interesting feature. When you are viewing an image, if you look under Edit in the drop-down menu, you will see that you can choose to edit the image with one of several graphics programs, including GIMP, Electric Eye, and more. Although GQview is not ideal for editing images, it is great for previewing an image, and then, from inside GQview, you can then choose the appropriate graphics program to edit your image with.

These are just a few of the graphics-related programs that ship with the GNOME desktop environment. It also ships with a very powerful graphics tool called Gimp, which will be discussed later in this book. Also, if you will recall, when you install KDE and GNOME on the same machine, you will have access to some KDE programs in GNOME. You should note, however, that not all KDE and GNOME applications are compatible. Some applications written for one interface (KDE or GNOME) will not run in the other.

GNOME OFFICE APPLICATIONS

Office-type applications are among the most common programs for a computer user to work with. Word processing, spreadsheets, database management, and presentation software are elements of most office packages. Most Windows users are familiar with Microsoft Office and will need similar functionality in Linux. As was previously mentioned, later in this book we will give extensive coverage of Open Office, which is a full-featured office suite available free to Linux users. In a previous chapter we explored some other office applications such as KWord, KSpread, and GNU Cash that are available with KDE. If you installed both KDE and GNOME on your system, you will have access to many of these KDE applications, even under GNOME. Even if you did not install KDE and are strictly running GNOME, there are a few office applications that ship with GNOME that you can use. We will examine a few of these here.

AbiWord

GNOME ships with a very interesting word processor named AbiWord. If for some reason you do not have AbiWord on your PC, you can get it for free from *www.abisource.com/*. It is worthwhile to note that AbiWord is also available for Windows and Macintosh. This makes it a very useful word processor. Once you are comfortable with it, you can use the same word processor in a variety of operating systems. What makes AbiWord, shown in Figure 7.10a, so interesting for Windows users trying to make the transition to Linux is how similar the interface is to Microsoft Word. In fact, the AbiWord interface is virtually identical to some of the earlier versions of Microsoft Word. This means that learning to use AbiWord should be rather simple if you are already familiar with Microsoft Word.

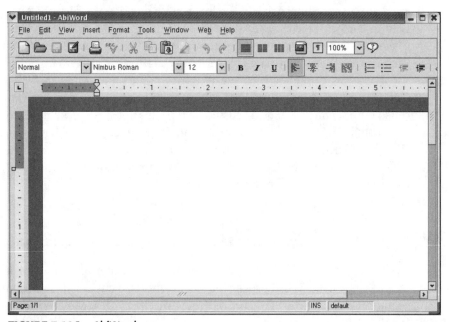

FIGURE 7.10A AbiWord.

If you compare this to Microsoft Word, shown in Figure 7.10b, you will see that the two have very similar layouts.

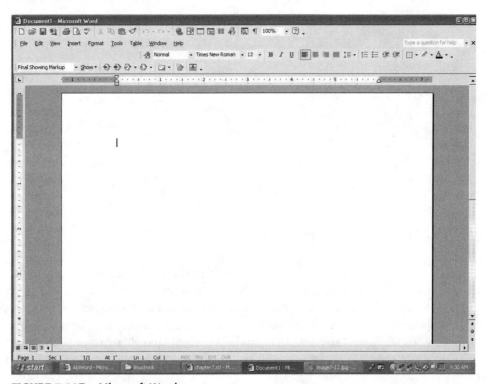

FIGURE 7.10B   Microsoft Word.

The toolbar and general layout of AbiWord should look quite familiar to Microsoft Word users. If you take a look at some of the more commonly used drop-down menus, you will find that they not only have many of the same options that Microsoft Word has, but in many cases they are found in the same place. For example, if you choose Format from the drop-down menu in Microsoft Word, as you see in Figure 7.10c, the first three options are Font, Paragraph, and Bullets. If you look under Format in AbiWord, you will see that its first three options are also Font, Paragraph, and Bullets.

This remains the case for many of the drop-down menus. In both Microsoft Word and AbiWord you will find that under Insert you have Page Number, Break, and Picture. With both software packages you will find the spell checker under Tools. Essentially, AbiWord's strength is that it is so similar to Microsoft Word that any competent Word user should have no problem changing to AbiWord.

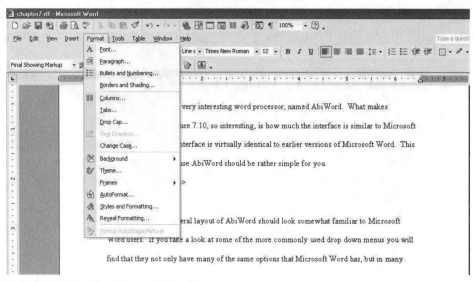

FIGURE 7.10C The Microsoft Word Format menu.

One of the most important features of AbiWord is its import capabilities. It can import documents that are in a Microsoft Word, Rich Text, HTML, or plain text format. This means that you can read documents that were written with other word processors. This is an invaluable feature because it is unlikely that all of your friends and colleagues are going to drop their current favorite word processors in favor of AbiWord.

GNumeric Worksheet

In addition to word processing, many people frequently find that they need to do some type of numeric calculation. Number crunching is a fact of life for everyone, not just bookkeepers and accountants. With GNOME, you have access to GNumeric Worksheet, a versatile and user-friendly spreadsheet program. This program is found by selecting Office from the Start menu and looking under More Office Applications. If for any reason your machine does not have GNumeric Worksheet, you can download it for free from *www.GNOME.org/projects/gnumeric/*. You can see GNumeric Worksheet in Figure 7.11. As you can see, it has a fairly standard interface, not much different from Microsoft Excel or KSpread.

We will look at a few of its key features, enough that you should be able to effectively use GNumeric Worksheet. The basic data entry is the same for all spreadsheets; simply type data directly into a given cell. If you want to put in new rows, columns, cells, or even graphs, you can do that from the Insert drop-down menu.

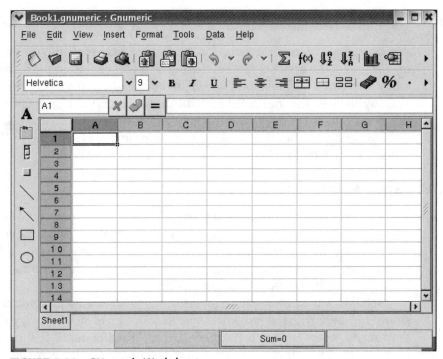

FIGURE 7.11   GNumeric Worksheet.

The Format drop-down menu is fairly standard. It allows you to change font, alignment, and related properties of columns, rows, or individual cells.

The most interesting thing about GNumeric Worksheet is under the Tools menu. Here you will find a rich assortment of very valuable tools. The first thing to direct your attention to is the Statistical Analysis option. Under this you have several categories that allow you to do a variety of statistical workups on your data, including an ANOVA (for readers not well versed in statistics, you will probably not find these statistical function options of particular interest). There also are options to generate standard descriptive statistics (mean, median, mode, standard deviation, and so on) and to do regression analysis. Math and physics aficionados will be thrilled to see that GNumeric Worksheet will even do a Fourier analysis.

What may be of even more interest to you is that GNumeric Worksheet can import files from Microsoft Excel, Lotus 1-2-3, and Quattro Pro. This ability to import files from other spreadsheet applications is a very important feature. Just because you have elected to move to Linux does not mean that all of your business colleagues have. For that reason, you will need to be able to read files they produce.

SYSTEM TOOLS

Any operating system, or desktop interface, must have some tools for administering the system. An entire chapter of this book was devoted to administering a Linux machine via the KDE interface. You will find that many of the same system tools are available in GNOME, and in the same place. However, there are a few tools either that come only with GNOME and do not come with KDE or that work with both GNOME and KDE, but that we did not examine in our exploration of KDE-based systems administration. Let's take a look at a few of these now.

GKrell System Monitor

In the preceding chapter we looked at one of KDE's system monitors. If you will recall, we found a great deal of information with this tool, including the current central processor use, memory use, and more. We also explored how this information could be very useful in diagnosing system problems and determining what if any hardware your system might need upgraded.

GNOME has its own system monitor, called GKrell system monitor. GKrell, shown in Figure 7.12, has its own unique features. To launch GKrell, you go to the Start menu, select System Tools, and choose GKrell System Monitor. Once you have launched it, you can see that it displays current CPU use, memory use, and date and time.

The first thing you probably notice about GKrell that differentiates it from either the KDE System Monitor or the Windows System Information screen is that it is a floating bar. This means that you can position it anywhere on the screen. You can even leave it open when you are working with other applications. This can be a wonderful asset when trying to diagnose what application is consuming the most resources. GKrell is meant to be a running system monitor. That means that it is meant to be left open and running during normal operations. That is why this tool is very popular with system administrators. They can keep an ongoing view of their system's performance, thus helping to diagnose problem areas.

If you right-click on GKrell, you can then select the Configure option. This brings you to the Configuration screen, shown in Figure 7.13. This screen allows you to configure many aspects of GKrell's appearance and performance. You can use the options on tab one to determine whether or not to display the hostname, system name, and more. The second tab allows you decide whether GKrell should be included on top of all other windows or not.

As you can see, GKrell provides the same information as the KDE System Monitor did. Its real advantages is that it is very easy to keep up and running on one portion of the screen, allowing you to keep a vigilant watch on system resources. This is often quite popular with system administrators.

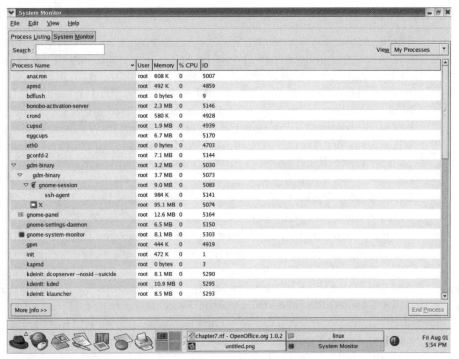

FIGURE 7.12 GKrell system monitor.

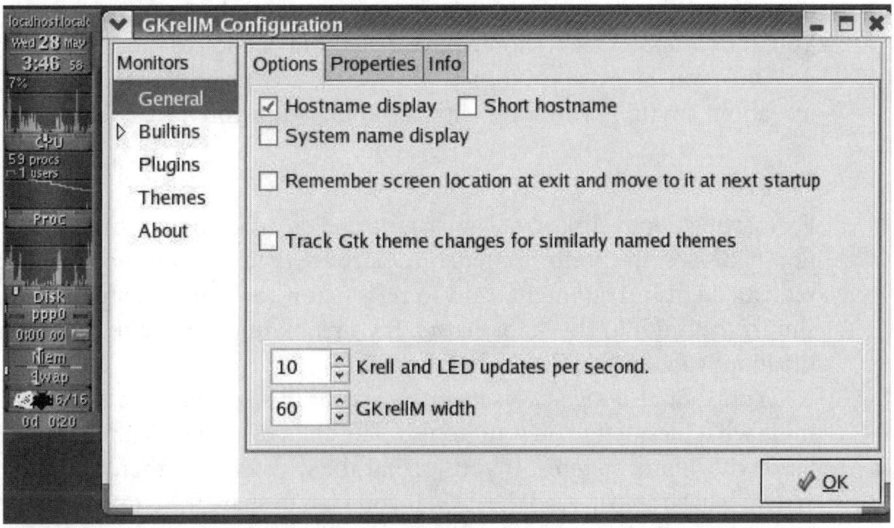

FIGURE 7.13 The GKrell Configuration screen.

Miscellaneous

There are several interesting utilities that are simple but interesting. A few of these will be examined here. You should be aware that under any of the major groups, such as System Tools or Accessories, there is a plethora of small but useful utilities. It would take a book several thousand pages in length to cover all of them. In this book we will try to touch on the more commonly used utilities, but you should not feel at all shy about exploring and experimenting. Most of these utilities are fairly self explanatory. You are very unlikely to do any harm to your system if you simply read whatever dialog boxes or instructions a utility presents you with.

Desktop Switching Tool

You already know by now that you can use either GNOME or KDE and that you can have both installed on the same system at the same time. You also know that you can log out of the system and, when you log back in, use the Session settings to change what desktop environment to use. What you don't know but are about to find out is that there is a quicker way to switch desktops. Under System Tools, you will see something called the Desktop Switcher, shown in Figure 7.14. When you click on this option, you can select any desktop environment installed on your machine and switch to it immediately. This is very convenient for users who like more than one desktop environment.

Consider that Linux gives you multiple desktop environments that you can easily switch back and forth between, as well as multiple desktops within a single environment. This should begin to impress upon you a theme that will be repeated throughout this book. The open source software philosophy is all about choice. You, the computer user, should have a plethora of choices for anything you want to do. Once you have made a choice, the open source licensing model allows you to do just about anything you want with the application you have chosen.

Floppy Formatter

Formatting floppy disks is still a task that needs to be done from time to time. Most floppy disks come preformatted, but there are many reasons why you may want to reformat a disk. You might want to reformat it to change the filesystem it uses, or simply to scan it to check for errors. If you look under System Tools, you will find the Floppy formatter, shown in Figure 7.15.

You should notice two separate areas of this screen. One area lets you determine what filesystem you want to use. The choices are FAT and ext2. ext2 is strictly used with Linux systems. If you format the disk as ext2, then no other operating system will be able to read the disk. If you plan to share the contents of the disk with anyone using Windows, then you should format the disk with FAT.

FIGURE 7.14   The Desktop Switcher.

FIGURE 7.15   The Floppy formatter.

It is also important to notice that you have three different formatting options. You can select to do a Quick format, which is really just a matter of completely erasing the disk. You also may select the Standard format. Finally, you have the Thorough format. This final option checks for any bad sectors on your disk. If you are concerned about disk errors, use the Thorough format option.

Desktop Sharing

The Desktop Sharing feature, found under Preferences, is truly an amazing utility. Have you ever wanted to show someone, a person not in the room with you, exactly what is on your computer screen? You might be calling a friend and asking him a technical question and want him to see exactly what is going on, or even have him fix the problem for you. You can do this with the Desktop Sharing tool. When you launch the Desktop Sharing tool, shown in Figure 7.16, you can e-mail an invitation to the person you want to log on to your system, or you can simply call him and give the settings the utility tells you to. The items the person will be given are your machine's IP address, a password, and the expiration date and time.

If you are connected to the Internet and the person you want to log on is connected and using Linux, he can log on to your system and take control of your desktop. The reason for the password is to ensure that only someone you authorize can log on to your system. The expiration date is to ensure that this person does not have indefinite carte blanche to hijack your system at his whim. While this tool can be dangerous because it gives another person control of your computer and should be used with care, it can be an incredible tool. If you are working remotely with someone, the ability for one of you to take control of the other's desktop and collaborate directly is invaluable.

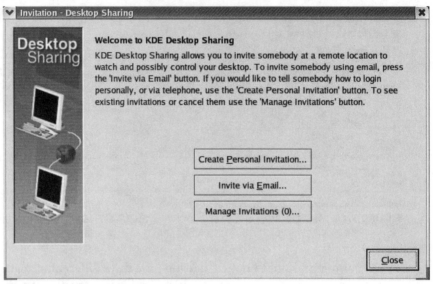

FIGURE 7.16 The Desktop Sharing tool.

SUMMARY

In this chapter we have examined the basics of the GNOME user interface. We have explored its similarities with KDE. We also have looked at a variety of applications available for GNOME. This is critical because the interface is not of much use without powerful applications to run in it. At this point you should be comfortable with the GNOME interface. However, keep in mind that throughout most of this book we will be focusing on KDE.

This chapter also introduced you to several system tools that either ship only with GNOME and not with KDE or ship with both but were not previously explored. We examined a new system monitor and several small but very useful utilities, and finally we looked at desktop sharing in GNOME.

REVIEW QUESTIONS

1. Which Linux word processor has an interface most like Microsoft Word?
2. What file types can GNumeric Worksheet import?
3. Which graphics program is ideal for cataloging images?
4. What does GNOME stand for?
5. When was GNOME 1.0 released?
6. Can GNOME run on non-Linux machines?
7. GNOME's equivalent of Microsoft Paint is called what?

SECTION

III

Moving from Microsoft Office to Open Office

For many readers, this will be the part of the book you have been waiting for. Many PC users are not too concerned with their system or how it works. What they really want to do is perform productive work. At some point, most people find basic office utilities such as word processors and spreadsheets to be quite useful. For many people that is the primary reason for purchasing a computer. The next several chapters of this book are devoted to showing you just how to do this.

Open Office® is an office suite that is distributed under an open source license. That means it is available as a free download. You can even get a Windows version of it. It comes with Red Hat and many other distributions of Linux. But you can also download a free version, as well as find out more about Open Office at *www.openoffice.org*.

We will start by examining word processing with Open Office in Chapter 8. Chapter 9 will show you how to work with spreadsheets using Open Office. Chapter 10 will introduce you to using Open Office for presentations you formerly did in Microsoft PowerPoint®. Finally, Chapter 11 will show you some of the extra utilities that are part of the Open Office suite.

8
Moving from Microsoft Word to Open Office

In This Chapter

- Open Office Address Book
- Essentials of Open Office Write
- Creating a Document
- Extra Features
- Formatting and Configuring

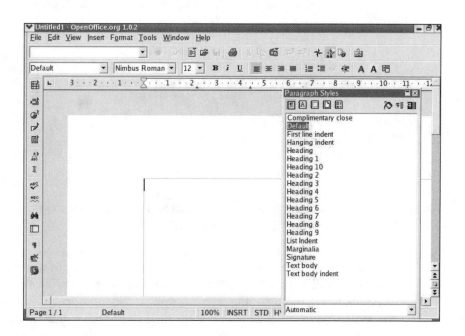

INTRODUCTION

Word processing, as we mentioned earlier, is a very common task, perhaps the most common task performed on a PC. At some point, virtually every computer user will need to do some type of word processing. For a home user this might mean writing a letter or composing a school report. For the business PC user this can mean creating business reports, keeping records, or generating memos. When you need to generate some type of text, of course you can use the limited capabilities of a standard text editor such as Microsoft's Notepad or WordPad, or perhaps the KWrite and Kate that come with KDE. We spent some time earlier in this book examining these text editors, and you should be basically competent with them by this point in the book. However, most people eventually find these applications to be inadequate and want something more. For most Windows users, that usually means using Microsoft Word. There are other word processors for Windows, such as Corel's WordPerfect, but most Windows users are familiar with Microsoft Word. You can see the familiar Microsoft Word interface in Figure 8.1.

FIGURE 8.1   Microsoft Word.

The chances are, even if you are only a novice Windows user, that you are probably familiar with the basics of Word. Even beginners usually have at least a cursory understanding of the essential toolbar functions found in Word. Right on the toolbar you can see buttons for saving, printing, changing the font, and aligning your text. In fact, you would have quite a time finding any word processor that did not have a toolbar that was very similar to this one. If you have used Microsoft

Word at all, you are probably aware of the plethora of other functions available to you from the various drop-down menus. This chapter is aimed at making you just as familiar and comfortable with Open Office's Writer program. It is a full-fledged and functional word processor.

As you progress through the material in this chapter, you will find that Writer has most of the features you are used to in Word. What makes the transition even easier is that many of these functions are found in the similar locations, with similar looking buttons to access them. This should come as no surprise. Both Open Office Writer and Microsoft Word are trying to accomplish the same goal, that of word processing, so it is no wonder that their functionality is quite similar. You will, however, find some instances where one word processor possesses some advantage over the other. Of course the primary advantage for Open Office will be price. It is a free download from *www.openoffice.org*. Perhaps more importantly, there are versions for both Linux and Microsoft Windows. That means that if you become enamored with Open Office on your Linux machine, you can also use the exact same product with a Windows machine!

OPEN OFFICE ADDRESS BOOK

Open Office, much like Microsoft Office, is not a single application. Rather, it is an integrated suite of applications. Each of these applications can be used separately, but there are functions that work with all of the applications. There are some utilities that are cross functional and work with all of the Open Office applications. The same is true with Microsoft Office, which has made a concerted effort over the years to tightly integrate all of the Microsoft Office applications into one cohesive unit.

When you first launch Open Office Writer or any of the Open Office applications for the first time, you will see one of the shared utilities in action. The very first thing that happens when you launch Open Office for the first time is that the Open Office Address Book Wizard appears. This wizard will set up a common address book that can be used in Open Office Writer as well as the various other Open Office applications. The first step of the wizard will ask you what type of existing address book you would like to use. This is shown in Figure 8.2.

The next phase of the wizard process is to select what address list from that address book you would prefer to use. You can see this step in Figure 8.3.

Many e-mail applications allow you to have multiple, separate address lists inside your address book. This is why you need to select a specific list from within an address book.

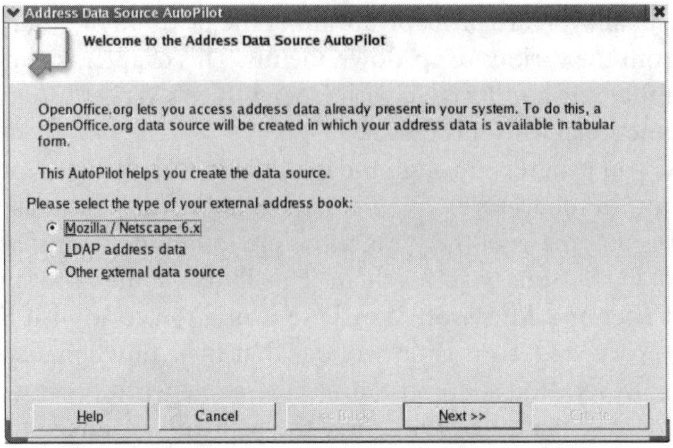

FIGURE 8.2   Selecting an address book type.

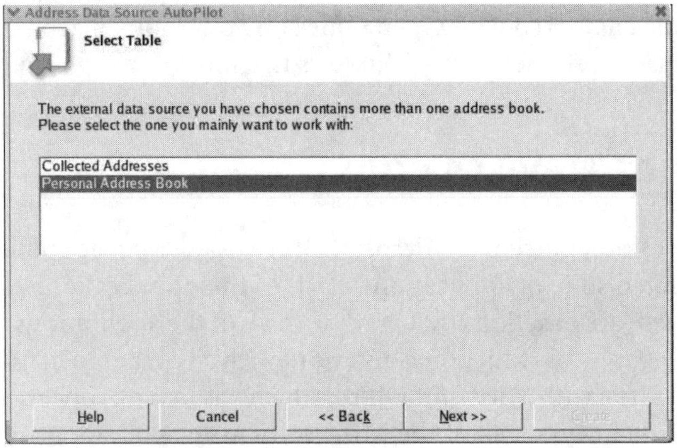

FIGURE 8.3   Selecting an address list.

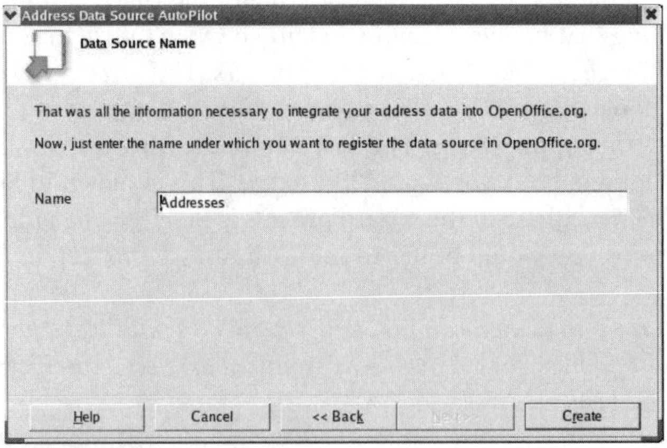

FIGURE 8.4   Choosing a name for your address book.

The last step is simply to give your address book a name. That name can be used in the future to access this address book. You can see this phase in Figure 8.4.

That's all there is to setting up your address book. We will return to the address book a bit later and examine how to use it. You will find that it can be a useful product with many different Open Office applications.

ESSENTIALS OF OPEN OFFICE WRITER

After you have finished setting up your address book, you will see a blank document waiting for you to start writing. This is also what you will see when you open Writer on subsequent occasions. The Address Book Setup Wizard runs only the very first time you launch an Open Office application. You can see the basic screen in Figure 8.5a.

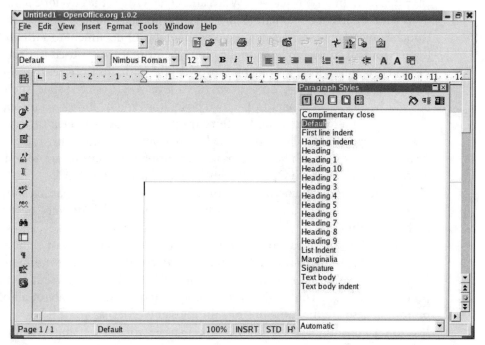

FIGURE 8.5A   The Open Office Writer screen.

This screen is not very different from the Microsoft Word screen shown in Figure 8.1. Both word processors' basic functions are in similar locations. What this means for you is that mastering the basics of Open Office Writer, if you already know your way around Microsoft Word, is not going to be particularly difficult.

The Top Toolbar

Let's take a moment to examine the toolbar at the top of the screen. You will note that it is divided into two toolbars. This is one very obvious difference between Open Office and Microsoft Word. That difference is that Microsoft Word condenses all the same buttons into a single toolbar.

When locations of toolbars and buttons are discussed, the default locations and buttons are what is being discussed. In many applications, including Microsoft Word, it is possible to drag a toolbar to a new location or customize the buttons displayed.

The top toolbar has an open folder icon that is used to open existing documents. You might notice that this is the same icon used in Microsoft Word for the same task. You will also notice a printer icon, obviously used to print, and a small envelope icon. In both Microsoft Word and Open Office, the envelope icon is used to attach the current document to an e-mail so you can send it. It will automatically launch your default e-mail client, so you can send your document to a friend or colleague. And, of course, in both applications the printer icon is used to print.

The second toolbar, the one on the lower half, contains the essential word processing functions. The first drop-down box allows you to select a style, such as text body or header. The second drop-down box allows you to choose your font. Then you can select a font size from the third drop-down box. The next three buttons, shown in Figure 8.5b, allow you to make whatever text is currently selected bold, italic, or underlined. These three basic text formatting buttons are found in the exact same order in both Open Office Writer and Microsoft Word.

Of course you can combine the functions of the three formatting buttons in order to make your text any combination, such as bold and underlined or bold, italicized, and underlined. The next three buttons, shown in Figure 8.5c, allow you to align text. You can make your text either left aligned, centered, or right aligned. Then we come to two buttons that allow you to create bulleted or numbered lists. Lists are very common in many documents and are therefore present in all word processors. Already you might notice something quite familiar about all of these buttons. These are the same buttons, in the same order, as you find in Microsoft Word. That means that maneuvering among basic word processing functions is not going to be difficult.

FIGURE 8.5B   The basic three text formatting buttons.

FIGURE 8.5C   Aligning text.

Just as the previous buttons were virtually identical to the buttons found on the Microsoft Word toolbar, so are the following buttons. You next come to two buttons that allow you to increase or decrease the indentation of a particular piece of text. Then you have a button that allows you to select font color. If you click on this button and hold it down for just a moment, you should see something much like what is shown in Figure 8.6a.

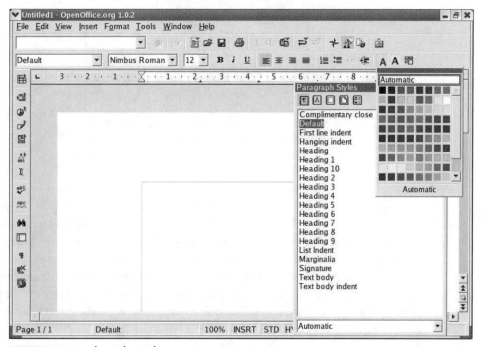

FIGURE 8.6A The color palette.

Unfortunately, this is one area in which Microsoft Word still has a slight edge over Open Office Writer. The number of colors you can choose from in Open Office is not as extensive as that found in Microsoft Word. When you select colors in Microsoft Word, you see a palette similar to the one shown in Figure 8.6a, but you can also select More Colors and see an additional palette, shown in Figure 8.6b. This is a small but significant difference between Microsoft Word and Open Office. There are other differences, which we shall explore as we encounter them. Next you come to a button that allows you to highlight text. This marks the end of the upper toolbar. As you can see, all the essential word processing functions you find in Microsoft Word are here. Many of these functions are found in the same or similar locations and with nearly identical functionality.

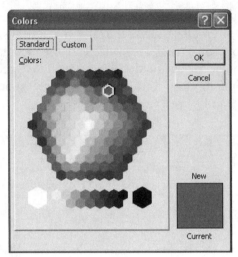

FIGURE 8.6B   Additional colors in
Microsoft Word.

Obviously this is just a quick overview of the toolbars at the top of Open Office Writer. You may be wondering why the cursory treatment of the upper toolbars. The reason is that since many of them offer functionality that is almost identical to Windows, you should have no trouble using these buttons. Also, the functionality of most of these buttons is self explanatory. It should be obvious that the bold button makes text bold. A long explanation is not only unnecessary but would probably be considered a bit pedantic. But don't worry, we will walk through an example later in this chapter that uses many of these basic functions, along with some more advanced functionality of Open Office Writer.

The Side Toolbar

In addition to the functions you will find along the top two toolbars, you should also notice a side toolbar that also offers functionality you will find quite useful. This toolbar, unlike the previous ones, is not found in Microsoft Word. However, Word does offer similar functionality; you just don't have a convenient toolbar along the side to help you find that functionality.

This toolbar is located along the left side and is seen in Figure 8.6c. We will examine this toolbar in the following paragraphs. Since at least some of these buttons offer functionality that is not exactly mirrored in Microsoft Word, a more extensive explanation will be afforded this toolbar than was given to the upper toolbars.

The uppermost button, if you hover your mouse over it, simply shows Insert. If you press and hold down the button just a moment, you will be presented with a

FIGURE 8.6C
The side toolbar.

series of choices, shown in Figure 8.7a. These choices include the option to insert tables, graphics, documents, footnotes, and header notes. Let's examine a few of the more common of these.

Tables are a very common tool used in documents to organize data in an easily read format. You have probably noticed a few tables in this book. Most word processors allow you to insert tables. With Microsoft Word, you insert a table by choosing the Table option from the drop-down menu and then selecting Insert and choosing Table. With Open Office Write, once you choose to insert a table you must set up the columns, rows, and other properties. You will be presented with a screen, shown in Figure 8.7b, where you can set up these properties.

Once you are satisfied with the settings you have chosen, you can press OK. If you have changed your mind about placing a table into your document, then just press Cancel. A table with properties like you saw in Figure 8.7b will appear, much like what you see in Figure 8.7c.

If you place your cursor in one of the cells of your table and press the Insert button again, you will be presented with the Table Format screen. This screen allows

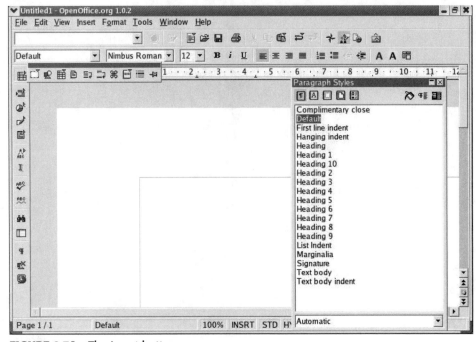

FIGURE 8.7A The Insert button.

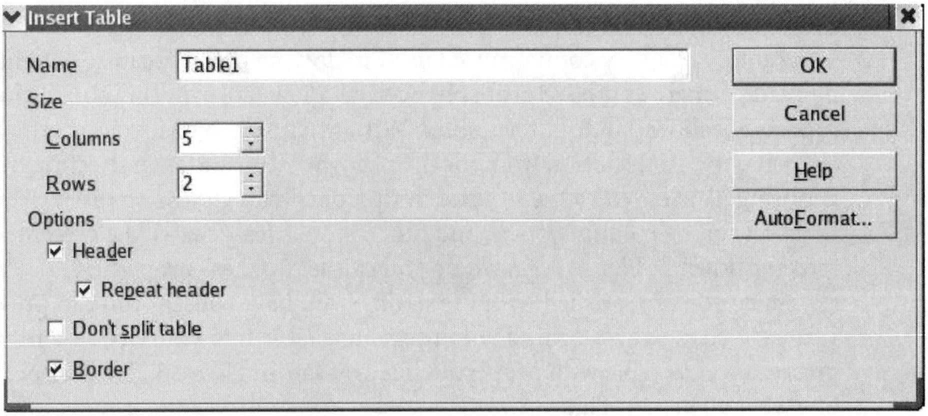

FIGURE 8.7B Setting a table's properties.

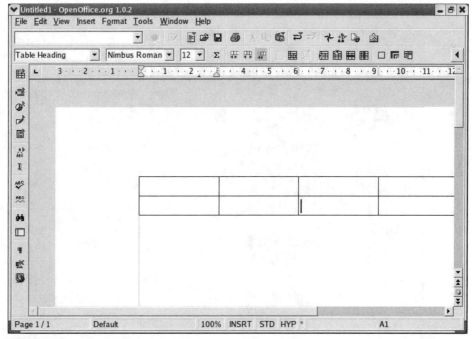

FIGURE 8.7C A table in a document.

you to reset previous table settings, as well as to format your table. This screen is shown in Figure 8.7d. This screen has several tabs. Each tab allows you to set something different about your table. In this picture the Background tab is shown. This tab allows you to change the background color. Note that in addition to selecting a color from the palette, you can also select whether that color is applied to a single cell, a row, or the entire table.

This is not that much different from inserting a table in Microsoft Word; it's really just where you find the functions that is different. Recall that in Microsoft Word you go to the Table drop-down menu and then choose Insert and Table. You would then be presented with the screen shown in Figure 8.7e. Here you would set the rows and columns of your table.

You could then place your cursor anywhere on the table and select Table from the drop-down menu and choose Table Properties. This would allow you to change many of your table's settings. You could also select Auto Format Table, also found under Table on the drop-down menu, to set up your table in a variety of predefined formatting schemes. You can see that option in Figure 8.7f.

You can see that inserting a table is not much different in Open Office than with Microsoft Office. There are a few subtle differences, such as where you find the functions to insert and manipulate tables. It is also a fact that Microsoft Word offers a few

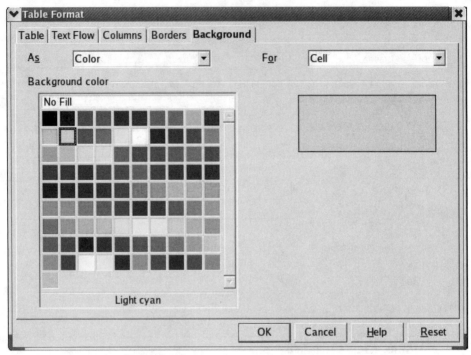

FIGURE 8.7D   Formatting the table.

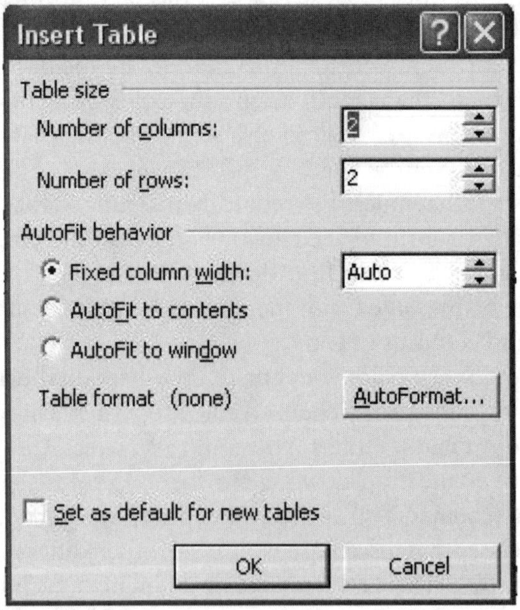

FIGURE 8.7E   Inserting a table in Microsoft Word.

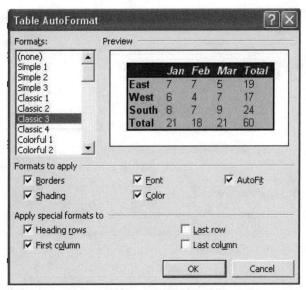

FIGURE 8.7F   Formatting a table in Microsoft Word.

table formatting options that are not available with Open Office, particularly the options shown in the preceding paragraph regarding the Autoformat option.

The next option under the Insert button is Insert Graphics. To insert graphics in Microsoft Word, you select Insert from the drop-down menu and choose Picture. You then select Word Art, Graphics from File, or Clip Art. When using Open Office Writer, you can still go to the drop-down menu, select Insert, and choose Graphics, or you can use the Insert button on the side toolbar and select Graphics. When you choose this option, you will be presented with a dialog box much like the one shown in Figure 8.8. This dialog will allow you to peruse your hard drive and find any image you might want to insert into your document.

You might notice that, by default, this dialog box starts in the gallery subdirectory of Open Office. This gallery is similar to the clip art option in Microsoft Word. Open Office Writer simply combines the clip art and graphics from file options, that are separate in Word. Although current versions of Open Office do not ship with as many graphics images as Microsoft Office does, they are not without a few images to display to the user.

Another option you will find under the Insert button is to insert a special character. From time to time you may require some character not present on your keyboard. Mathematical symbols such as the summation symbol Σ and various other symbols can be found by clicking the Insert button and choosing Special Characters. When you select this you will see something much like what is shown

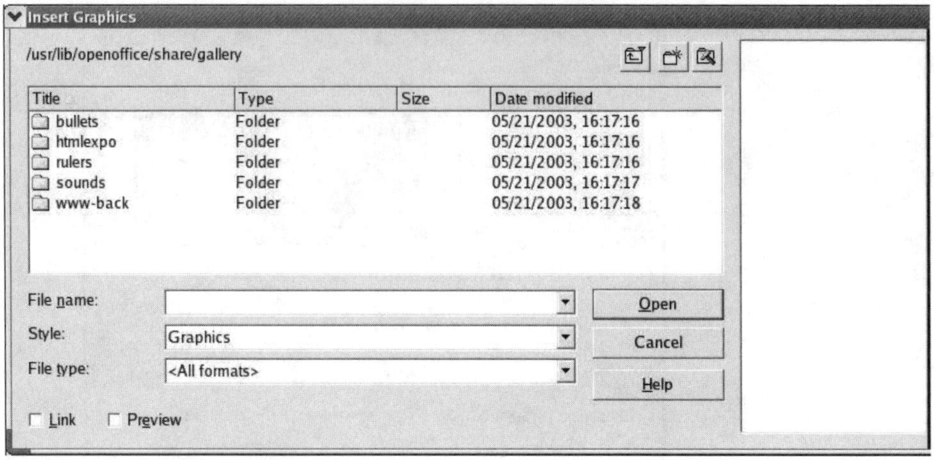

FIGURE 8.8 Inserting graphics.

in Figure 8.9. The same task can be accomplished in Microsoft Word by choosing Insert from the drop-down menu, and selecting Symbol.

The next item we find as we move down the toolbar on the left side of the screen is the button to insert fields. Fields include date fields, time fields, author's name, and more. When you click this button, you will see something very much like what is shown in Figure 8.10a.

This is a relatively straightforward option. You simply select the field that you want to insert, and it will be inserted at the point where you last had your cursor.

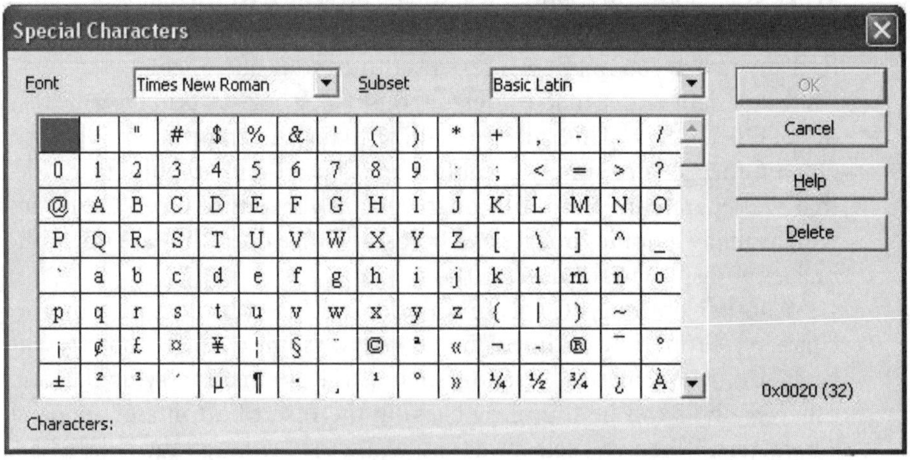

FIGURE 8.9 Inserting special characters.

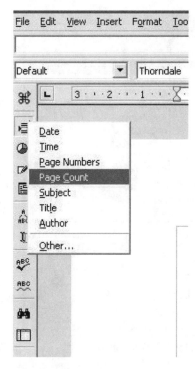

FIGURE 8.10A Inserting fields.

This can be quite convenient for inserting dates, times, and more. Microsoft Word has a similar function, found by selecting Insert from the drop-down menu and then going to Field. You are then presented with an image much like the one shown in Figure 8.10b. As you can see, Microsoft Word has more field options that the current version of Open Office Writer.

As we traverse the left toolbar going down, we next encounter the Insert Object button, seen in Figure 8.11. This option allows you to insert charts, plug-ins, and even Java applets.

Let's take a moment to examine the first of these options, inserting a chart. This can also be accomplished in Microsoft Word by selecting Insert from the drop-down menu, then choosing Object, and selecting the appropriate chart. With Writer, once you have selected Insert Object and Chart, you will see the screen in Figure 8.12.

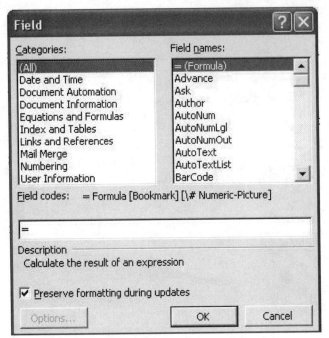

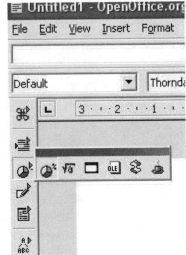

FIGURE 8.10B Inserting fields in Microsoft Word.

FIGURE 8.11 Inserting objects.

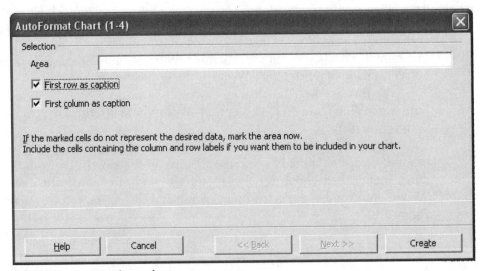

FIGURE 8.12 Inserting a chart.

If you press the Create button at this point, a basic chart will be inserted into your document. This is shown in Figure 8.13.

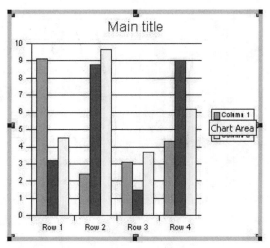

FIGURE 8.13 Configuring a chart.

If you then right-click on this chart, you will be presented with the option to change the chart type, data, and other factors about the chart. This is shown in Figure 8.14. Working with charts is very important for the business user of Open Office. For any presentation or report, you will probably be expected to show various charts and graphs that illustrate your data more clearly. It is highly recommended that you spend some time experimenting with charts in any word processor you choose. Make certain that you are completely comfortable with how to create a chart since it is such a valuable tool for adding impact to your presentation. In a later chapter you will also see that we can add charts to spreadsheets, and the technique is very similar. Therefore, if you learn how it works now, you will be ahead when we discuss that aspect of spreadsheets.

In addition to charts, you can draw basic lines and shapes. In Microsoft Word you can do this by selecting Insert from the drop-down menu and then choosing Picture, and finally selecting AutoShapes. With Writer, the next button down on the left side toolbar will accomplish this goal for you. Simply press this button and you are presented with several different choices for shapes and lines you can insert into your document. The choices are shown in Figure 8.15.

The next two buttons are a bit more complex and go beyond the scope of this chapter. They allow you to insert form-like items as you might see on a graphical program. Their use could occupy several chapters by itself. Remember that we are trying to ensure that you are a competent Open Office user who is comfortable with the essentials of the various Open Office products. We are not endeavoring to make you an expert on all of these issues. If you look in Appendix A, "Other Resources,"

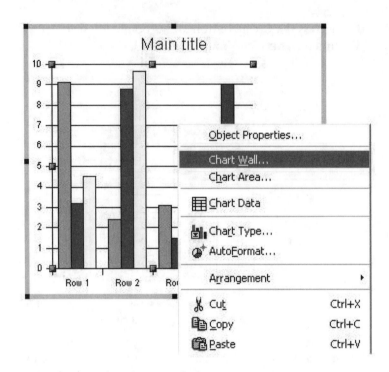

FIGURE 8.14   Changing your chart.

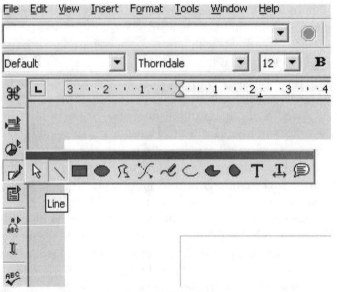

FIGURE 8.15   Inserting lines and shapes.

FIGURE 8.16
The spell check.

you will find a variety of resources to take you into a deeper study of many of the topics in this book. Some of these resources are Web pages, and others are books. We will move down a bit to the button with the checkmark and the letters abc above it, shown in Figure 8.16.

Clicking this button will initiate a spelling check on your document. You perform the same function in Microsoft Word by selecting Tools and then choosing Spelling and Grammar, or by pressing the F7 shortcut key. Just below the spell check button, you see another similar button. This button toggles automatic spell checking on and off in your document. This will cause the small red squiggly lines to appear under misspelled words as you type. Finally, we come to the binoculars. This enables you to search your document for a word or phrase. When you click this button, you are presented with something like what is shown in Figure 8.17.

You perform a search in Microsoft Word by selecting Edit and Find from the drop-down menu or using the shortcut keys Ctrl-F.

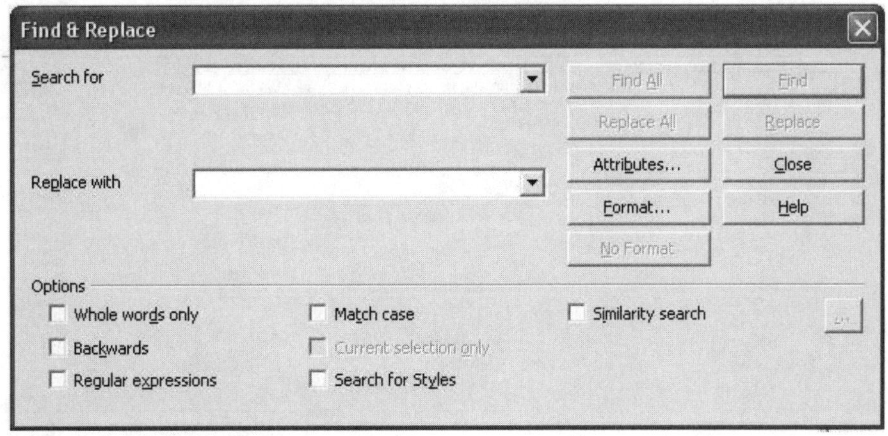

FIGURE 8.17 Searching the document.

CREATING A DOCUMENT

We have looked at various features and utilities within Open Office Writer (although certainly not all of its features). The best way to get you comfortable with Writer is to walk you through the process of creating a complex document that includes all of the various techniques we have seen so far, and perhaps a few more. We will use a fictitious company Lenny's Linux Widgets and create a report for that company.

Begin by opening up Writer and typing in the following paragraph:

```
Lenny's Linux Widgets
Quarterly Report for the first quarter of 2004.
```

Summary — This quarter we have met or exceeded all goals for both production and sales of Widgets for Linux. Our widgets work with either KDE, GNOME, or Ximian and are selling quite well.

Now we are going to highlight the first two lines and center them. You highlight text by dragging your mouse across it. You can then use the toolbar to make this text bold, font size 14, and centered. Your document should then look like what is seen in Figure 8.18.

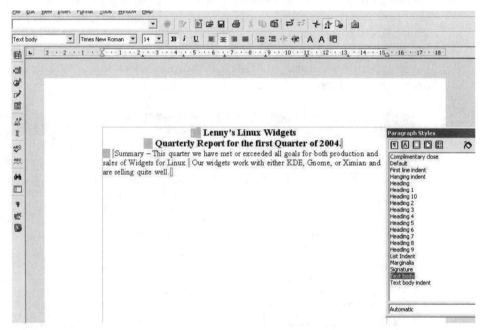

FIGURE 8.18 Creating a document.

Now skip down a few lines by pressing the Enter/Return key. You are going to insert an image from your hard drive. We previously discussed how to insert graphics using the toolbar on the side of the screen. You can also select Insert from the drop-down menu, then choose Graphics, and finally From File. Although some business- or Linux-oriented image would be best, you can select any image you want from your hard drive. For the example image you will see in just a bit, the image selected was a picture of the author.

Now we are going to add a graph. Again use the Enter key to skip down a few lines, and then you can add your graph. This was also discussed previously in the context of the toolbar at the right. Recall that you choose Insert Object and then choose the Chart option. Then, once you have a chart in your document, right-click on it and choose Chart Data. You can then alter the data and titles placed on your chart. This is shown in Figure 8.19. For our purposes, the columns should be months, and the rows should be any random business category you might think of. When you are done, press the checkmark button and then close the window.

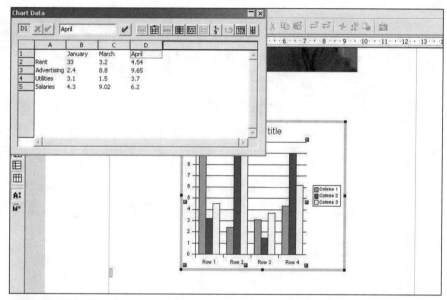

FIGURE 8.19   Creating a new chart.

Now for a few finishing touches. First we will go to the drop-down menu and select Insert. Then we will insert page numbers. Choose Insert and select Horizontal Line. You should see an image like the one in Figure 8.20.

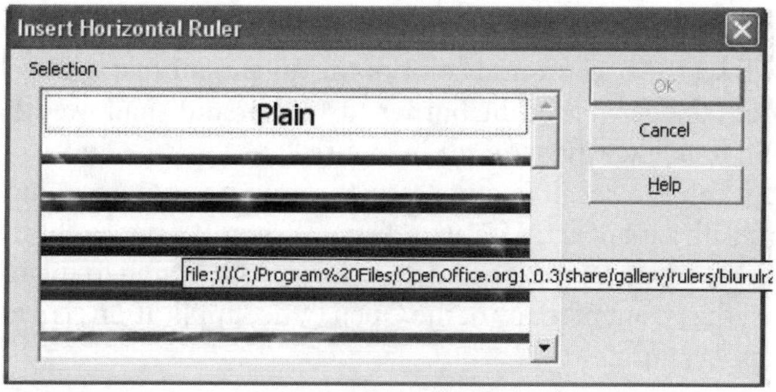

FIGURE 8.20   Inserting a horizontal line.

You can see that there are several types of lines you can select. You should select any line you find aesthetically pleasing. Now go to Format and choose Page.
You will see an image like the one shown in Figure 8.21. From this screen you can
format many things about the document's appearance.

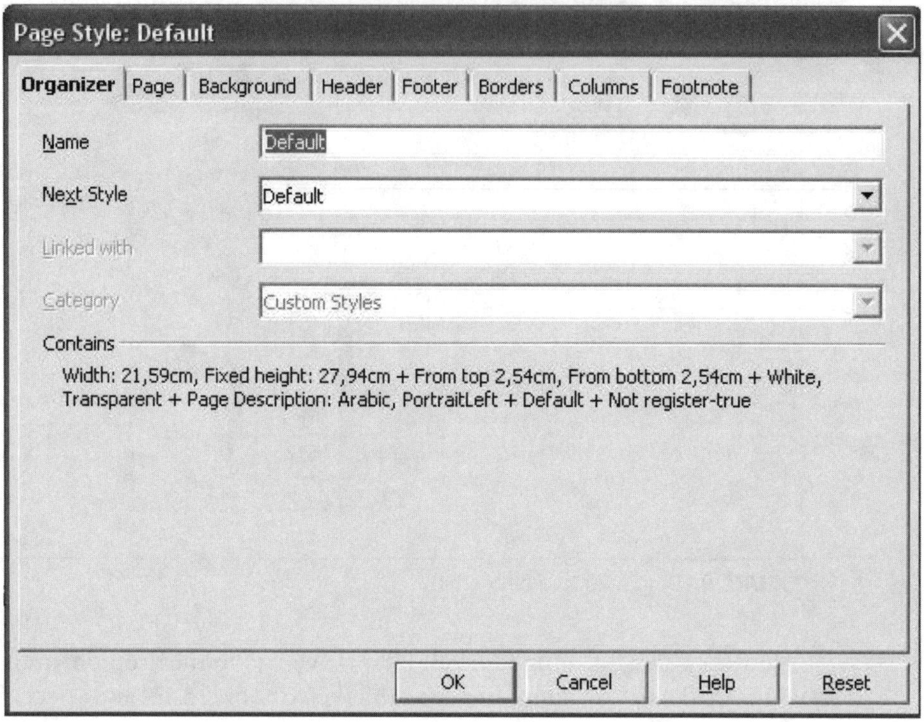

FIGURE 8.21   Formatting the document.

We are going to set only a few of the page properties. From the Background tab,
we will set the background color of the document to a light yellow color. From the
Border tab, we will set the border to 1.00 pt and shadowed. Now your document
should look like what you see in Figure 8.22.

As you can see, it is quite easy to set up a very interesting and dynamic document, with a lot of extra features, using Writer. It's not really any more difficult than
using Microsoft Word. Fortunately, for anyone trying to migrate from Windows to
Linux, the layout of many of the Open Office applications is similar to Microsoft Office applications.

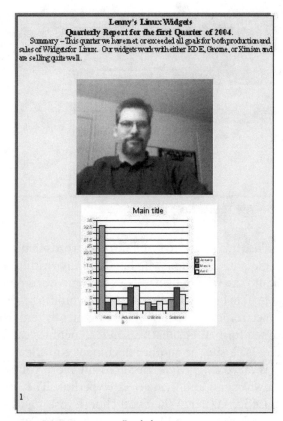

FIGURE 8.22 Your final document.

EXTRA FEATURES

What we have covered in this chapter, up to this point, is more than enough to enable you to create a variety of different documents for personal or business use. We have looked at all the basic text formatting, inserting images and charts, and more. However, much like Microsoft Word, Open Office Writer has a number of extra features. These extra features are not critical to creating documents but can be very helpful in enhancing your documents. We won't be covering all of the extra features available in Open Office Writer, but we will touch on a few and hopefully add something to your documents in the process.

Let's take a look at a simple, but very useful extra feature first—the Thesaurus. In Microsoft Word, you can right-click on a word and select Synonyms from the pop-up menu. In Open Office Writer you have the same functionality under the label of Thesaurus. If you highlight a word and then go to Tools in the drop-down menu and select Thesaurus, you will see the screen in Figure 8.23.

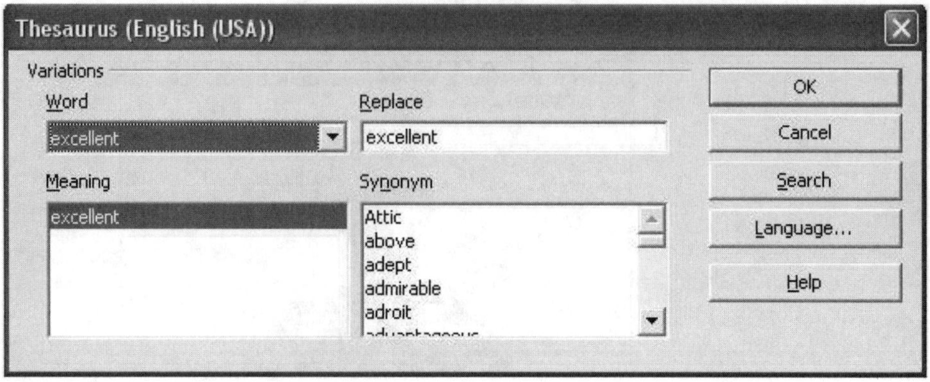

FIGURE 8.23   The Thesaurus.

You can use this screen to scroll through words that are synonyms for the word you have highlighted. Anyone who has done any writing at all is aware that it is too easy to fall into the trap of using the exact same word repeatedly. A thesaurus can be invaluable in helping you vary the words you use in any document.

In this electronic age, documents are frequently sent in electronic format rather than in printed format. For that reason it sometimes can be quite useful to have a link to a file, Web site, or another document embedded directly into your document. This is called a *hyperlink*. In Microsoft Word you would choose Insert from the drop-down menu and then select Hyperlink. The process is exactly the same with Open Office Writer. When you choose Insert and then select Hyperlink in Writer, you will see a screen like the one in Figure 8.24.

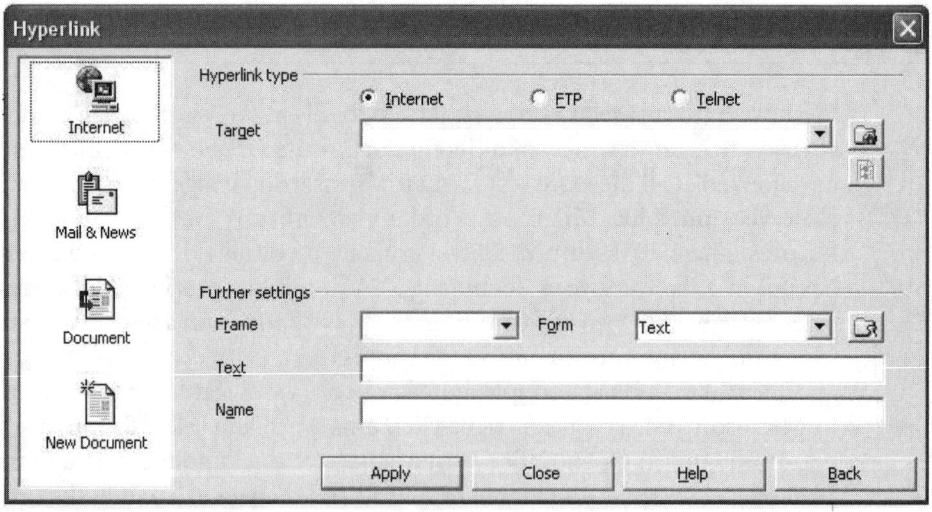

FIGURE 8.24   Inserting a hyperlink.

You then have a number of options for your link. If it is an Internet link, you must decide whether you want to link to a Web site, FTP site, or e-mail. You also can link to another document. For our purposes we will make a link to a Web site (the author's Web site). In the screen, select Internet, then type in *http://www.chuckeasttom.com*. You will note that this text appears below in the space marked Text. The text is what the readers of your document will see. We would like them to see something a bit more aesthetically pleasing than a Web address, so replace that text with **Chucks Web Page**. Then press the Apply button and the Close button. In your document you will now see a link with the text we gave it. This is shown in Figure 8.25 as it would appear in a document.

Chucks Web Page

FIGURE 8.25 A hyperlink in your document.

FORMATTING AND CONFIGURING

As with most professional applications, you can customize and configure Open Office Writer so that it suits your needs. In Microsoft Word you went to Tools on the drop-down menu and could select either Customize or Options. Each gave you access to slightly different aspects of the word processor you could alter. The good news is that the procedure is almost identical in Open Office Writer. If you select Tools from the drop-down menu, you will see both Configure and Options, as shown in Figure 8.26.

Let's examine Configuration first. When you choose this option you will see something like the image shown in Figure 8.27. The Toolbars tab happens to be the one that is initially showing. This is because it is probably the most commonly used. This tab allows you to select which toolbars will be visible. If you find that some toolbar is no longer showing, simply go here and add it. Conversely, if you find that you don't often use a toolbar, you can go here and remove it.

The Status Bar tab, shown in Figure 8.28, allows you to decide what items will be shown in the toolbar at the bottom of the Writer screen. By default, items such as Page Number and Insert Mode are shown. You can customize the status bar to show the elements that are important to you.

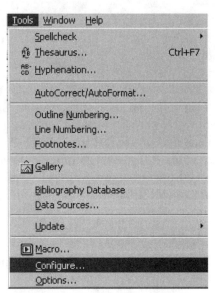

FIGURE 8.26   Configure and Options.

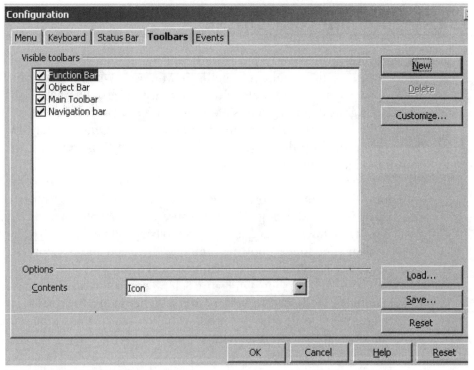

FIGURE 8.27   The Toolbars tab.

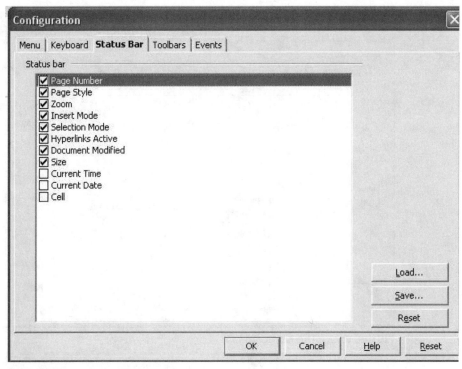

FIGURE 8.28 The Status Bar tab.

The Keyboard tab is shown in Figure 8.29. This tab allows you to alter the keyboard functionality. In Writer, as with many applications, you can access various functions via shortcut keys on the keyboard. One of the things you can do with this tab is to alter which shortcut keys work for which functions. This allows you to really customize Open Office Writer to suit your needs and preferences.

The Menu tab allows you to customize the drop-down menu. This tab is depicted in Figure 8.30. With this tab you can customize the current Writer menu and even add your own menu items to it.

The final tab of the Configuration screen is Events. This is an advanced setting that you should probably leave with its defaults, and we will not be delving into it. You can see that Open Office Writer offers you a lot of different configuration options.

This brings us to Options, also found under Tools. This screen, shown in Figure 8.31, allows you to customize other aspects of your application. By using the various options on the side of this screen you can alter the default colors, date format, printing behavior, and more. This screen combined with the Configuration

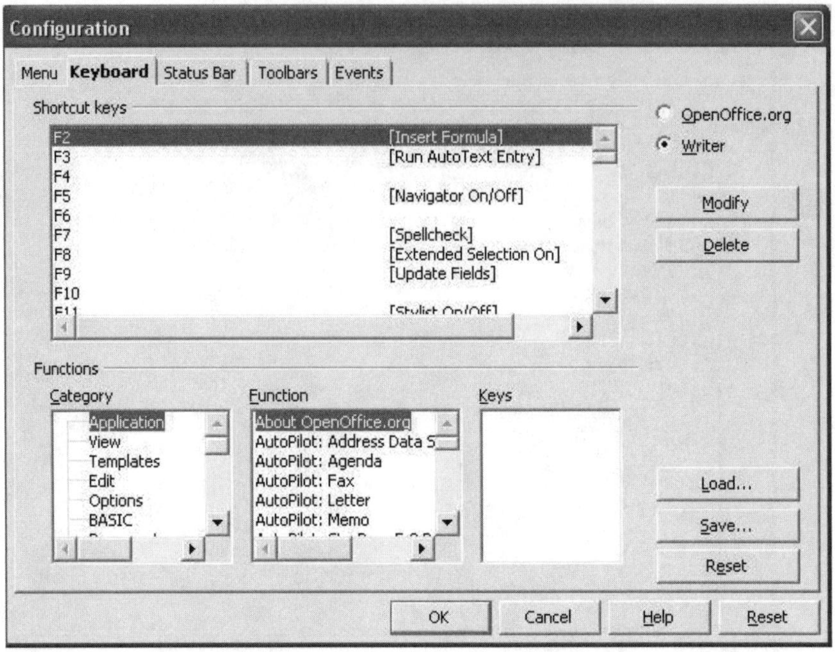

FIGURE 8.29 The Keyboard tab.

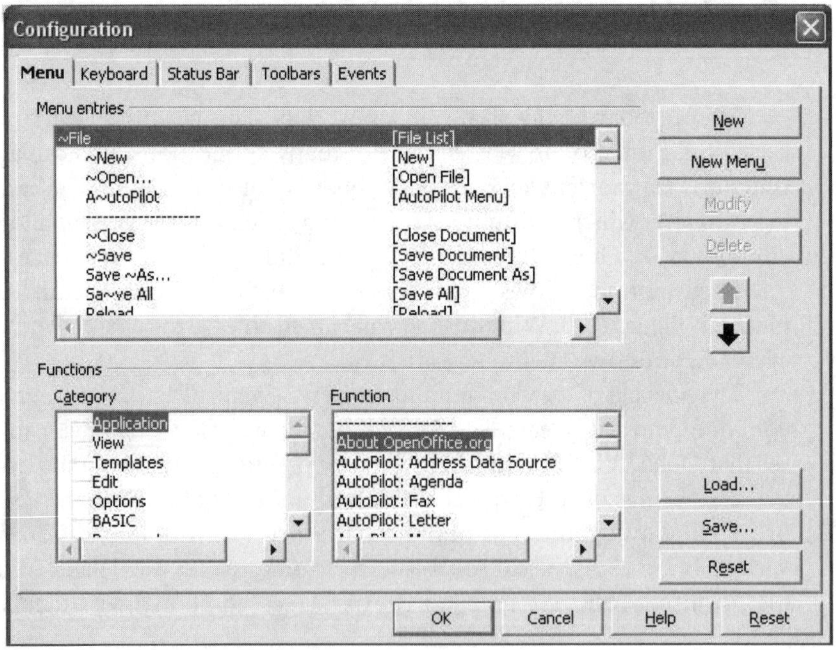

FIGURE 8.30 The Menu tab.

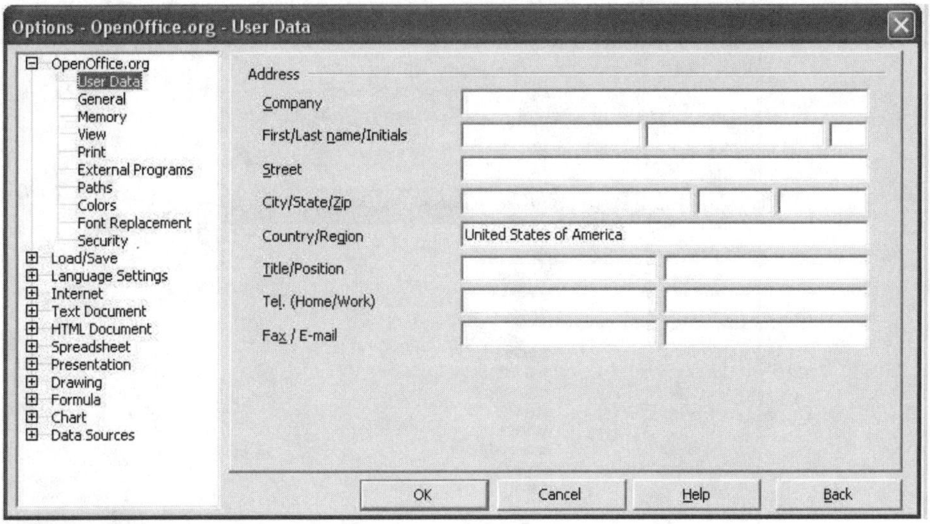

FIGURE 8.31 The Options screen.

screen should allow you to fully customize the behavior and appearance of Open Office Writer so that it suits your personal needs and preferences.

Also under the Tools menu you will find the Auto Correct/Auto Format screen shown in Figure 8.32. This screen allows you to change how Writer goes about correcting spelling and formatting.

The tab on this utility that is of most interest to us is the Word Completion tab. This is shown in Figure 8.33. Different people have very different views on any word processor performing word completion. Word completion simply means that as you are typing, as soon as the word processor recognizes that you are typing a word it knows, it will complete the word for you. Some people love this feature, others hate it. This tab will allow you to turn that feature on or off and customize how it behaves should you leave it on.

Obviously there are more features and details in Open Office Writer. An entire book could probably be written on just this one product. However, this chapter should be enough to give you a basic start using this word processor. If you read this chapter carefully and try the various techniques mentioned, you should be a competent user of Open Office Writer.

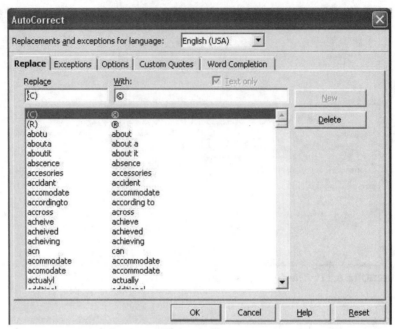

FIGURE 8.32   Auto Correct/Auto Format.

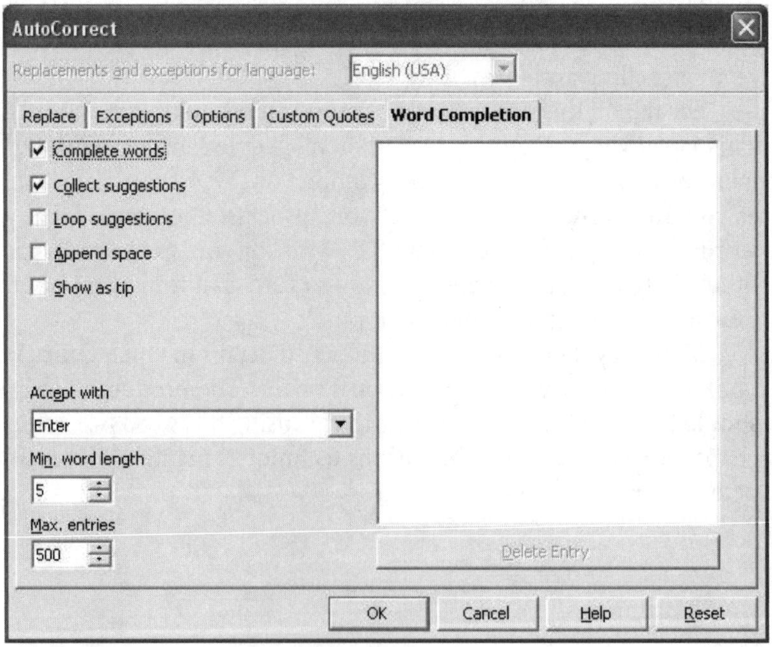

FIGURE 8.33   Word completion.

SUMMARY

In this chapter, we have seen the basics of how to use Open Office Writer. We have looked at the toolbars, text formatting, inserting objects, and more. You have seen how to create tables, insert charts, and format your document. After reading this chapter you should be basically proficient with Open Office Writer. You should also be aware of just how powerful this free word processor is.

REVIEW QUESTIONS

1. What three common text formatting buttons are found in the exact same order in both Microsoft Word and Open Office Writer?
2. What type of functions are found on the second toolbar in Writer?
3. Name an advantage that Microsoft Word has over Open Office Writer.
4. What is a common document tool used to organize data in an easily read format?
5. Inserting a symbol in Microsoft Word is duplicated in Open Office Writer by inserting a _____ _____.
6. Does Open Office Writer have more field options than Microsoft Word?

9 Spreadsheets with Open Office Calc

In This Chapter

- Basics of the Spreadsheet
- Working through a Spreadsheet
- Configuration

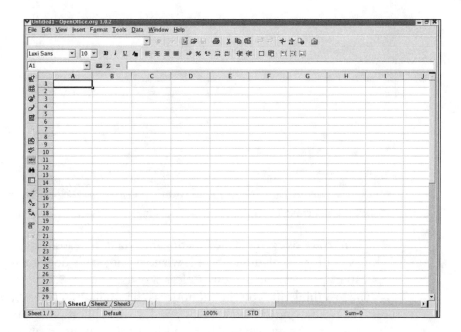

INTRODUCTION

Now that you have been given a tour of the Open Office Writer, you are ready to move on to the next application in the Open Office suite, the spreadsheet application, Calc. While word processing is probably the most common task performed on a PC by both home and business users, spreadsheets are by far the most commonly used business applications. Virtually any business of any size needs to keep financial records and perform financial calculations. For most Windows users, this means using Microsoft Excel, which is shown in Figure 9.1.

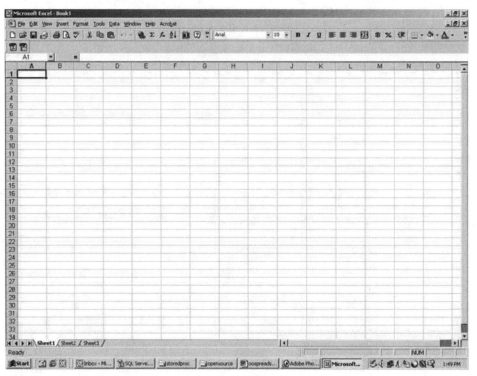

FIGURE 9.1 Microsoft Excel

Open Office offers the same functionality via its spreadsheet tool named Calc. Calc is short for calculation, which is what you normally do with any spreadsheet application, perform calculations. Calc is shown in Figure 9.2.

The first thing that you should notice is the similarities between these two figures. The basic layout and functionality of the two applications are nearly identical. This should not be surprising. All spreadsheet applications are an attempt to automate a bookkeeper's spreadsheet, so the general layout should be similar. As with the word processor, the spreadsheet tool in Open Office divides the toolbar into

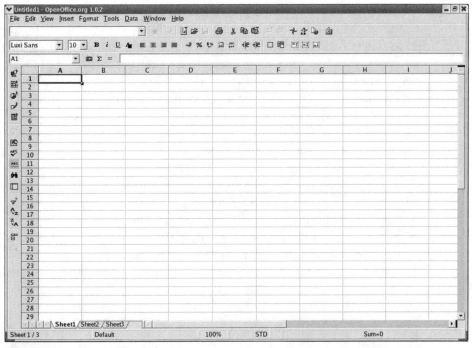

FIGURE 9.2   Open Office Calc.

rows. There will be some differences, but you still have essentially the same functionality with very similar icons in both Open Office and Excel. The buttons for opening files, saving files, printing, and formatting text are virtually identical. If you will note, even the drop-down menus have the same names and are in identical order in both Calc and Excel.

CALC BASICS

The toolbars in Open Office Calc are in a particular order with each toolbar containing specific tools for specific functions. The toolbars are listed here:

- A Menu toolbar
- A Function toolbar
- An Object toolbar
- A Calculation toolbar

The Menu toolbar contains Calc's main menus. The Menu toolbar provides user access to basic functions such as Open, Save, Copy, Cut, Paste, and so on. These functions are common to all Open Office applications. In fact, with almost any application, you will see the same or very similar items grouped under the File menu. The Object toolbar consists of a set of tools that are specific to calculation and cell formatting (number format, text alignment, borders). These are the buttons that are unique to Calc and will not be found in other Open Office applications. Finally, the Calculation toolbar enables a user to enter his own specific formulas for calculations. This toolbar also displays the current cursor position within the spreadsheet .

These toolbars can be customized. One way to do this is to right-click on any of the toolbars and select Visible Buttons, as shown in Figure 9.3. This enables you to choose what buttons are shown in the toolbar and which buttons are not shown.

When you right-click on any toolbar, all the toolbars are displayed in a list. The visible toolbars have a checkmark by their names on the list. You can choose to display or not display an entire toolbar by checking or unchecking it in the list. You

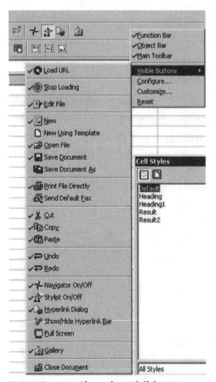

FIGURE 9.3 Choosing Visible Buttons.

FIGURE 9.4
The toolbar.

can also right-click on any toolbar and select Configure. This will enable you access to all of the configuration options in one convenient screen.

On the left of the screen you will see the toolbar, shown in Figure 9.4. This toolbar provides a number of specialized tools for use with a spreadsheet. We will explore these functions in more depth later in this chapter.

The spreadsheet is represented as a grid composed of rows and columns creating cells. A cell is referenced by its column (vertical reference), given as a letter such as A, B…Z, and its line (horizontal reference) is given as a number such as 1, 2…300. A particular cell might be identified as B10. This is the same as identifying a specific cell within Microsoft Excel. An individual cell contains some sort of data. You will usually place a number in a cell, as numeric data is usually used in a spreadsheet. However, you also can enter text directly into any cell. This is useful for labeling data.

Basic Calculations

Performing calculations is the reason for a spreadsheet program. Therefore, we should probably delve right into entering data and performing calculations. First we are going to create a simple spreadsheet for a small business. We will organize our spreadsheet in rows that designate types of expenses and columns that indicate months, as shown in Figure 9.5. Remember that you need to click inside a cell and then you can enter text or numbers. You should also note that if you enter January in the first month cell and then click on the lower-right corner of that cell and drag across, the subsequent cells will be filled automatically with the appropriate month, as you also see in Figure 9.5. This particular feature of Calc behaves in exactly the same manner as Excel. You can do the same thing with numeric values in a cell and drag your mouse. The values will be incremented by 1 in each cell. This works very much the same in Excel, but the actual values will be duplicated to subsequent cells rather than a steady increment of the value. In both Excel and Calc this function is called AutoFill, since it automatically fills in appropriate data.

Now enter some figures for the various cells. For our purposes, the actual numbers you enter are irrelevant, but of course those numbers would be very important in a real-world business situation. You can make your column headers a different font, perhaps bold. This will help them stand out from your actual data. You can accomplish this by highlighting an individual cell or an entire row and then selecting the formatting options you want to implement. This is how formatting cells is done in Excel, so you should have no problem with this task. Once you are done, your spreadsheet should look very much like the one in Figure 9.6.

Now we have our data in a very neat looking spreadsheet, but that is only the beginning of what anyone wants from spreadsheets. Simply typing in the data is not particularly exciting. We want to manipulate the data and produce statistics, answers,

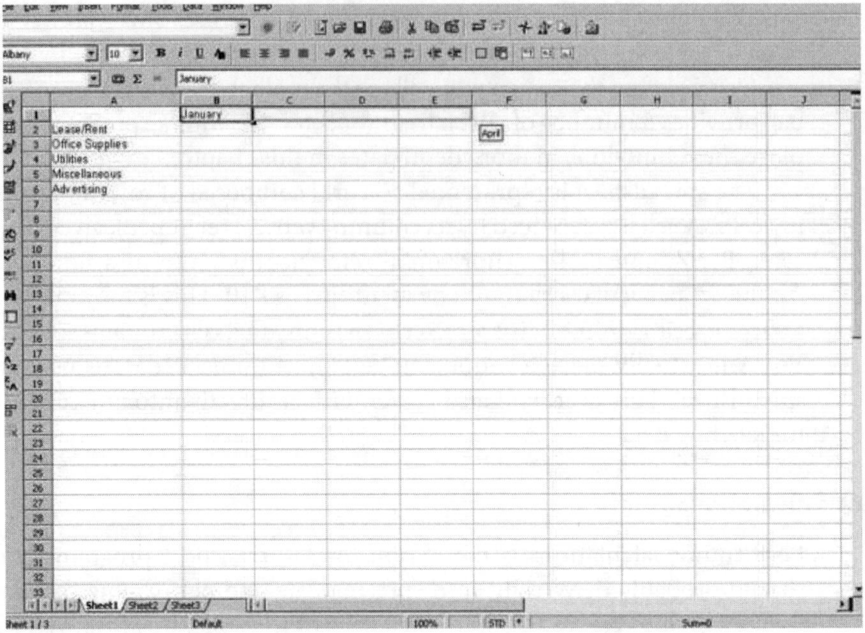

FIGURE 9.5 A simple spreadsheet.

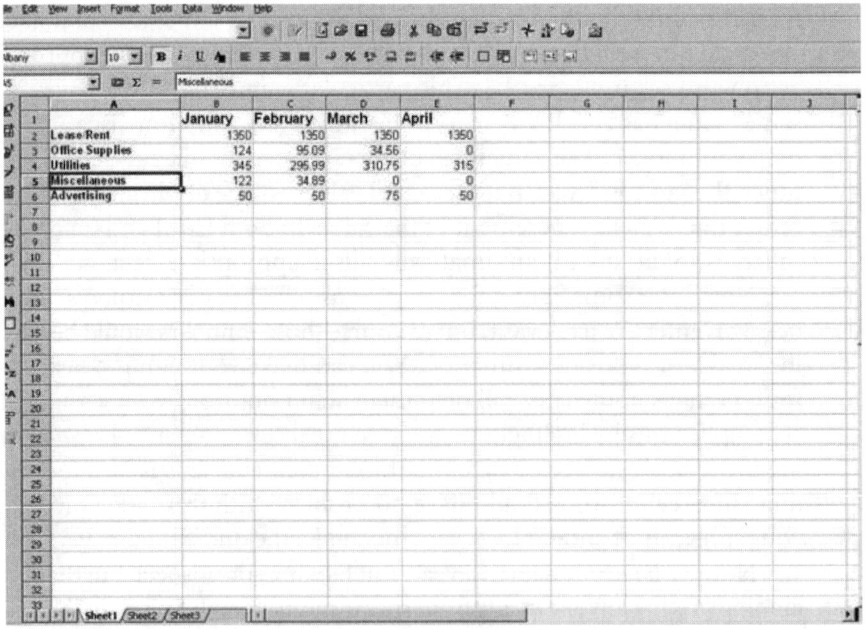

FIGURE 9.6 Sample data in your spreadsheet.

and such. In short, we want to do some number crunching. Now we will begin to manipulate the data in a variety of ways. The simplest calculation we can do is to total the values in a given row or column. If you click once in the first blank cell after a row or column of numbers, you can then go to the toolbar and click on the summation symbol, shown in Figure 9.7. Notice that we mentioned rows or columns. You can total up either a row or a column. In fact, all of the functions available in either Calc or Excel can be executed against data from either a row or a column.

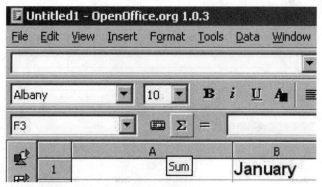

FIGURE 9.7   The summation button.

You will then be shown a formula in the formula bar, and you can choose to either accept it or reject it, as shown in Figure 9.8. If you choose to accept it, the answer to that formula will be displayed in the cell you initially clicked on.

This is very similar to how summation works in Excel. The buttons even look the same in both applications. The difference is that in Excel you don't have the option to accept or reject the choice you make. Once you click the summation button, the formula is inserted, and the calculation is done.

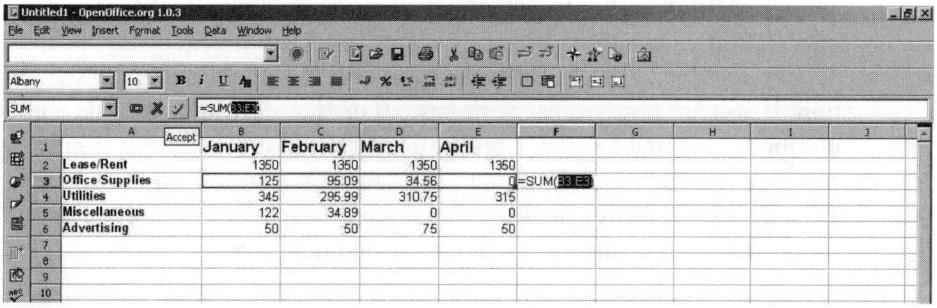

FIGURE 9.8   The summation formula.

This, however, is a rather simple calculation. You will probably require more advanced calculations. Before we move on to other calculations, we want to make sure we will remember what this column we just generated represents. Numbers without labels quickly become meaningless. For that reason, you probably want to label the column you put the sum in. You might give it some label such as Total. Once you have done that, you might notice the button to the left of the summation button. It is referred to as the Autopilot button. When you press it you will be shown a list of built-in functions you can insert into your spreadsheet, as shown in Figure 9.9.

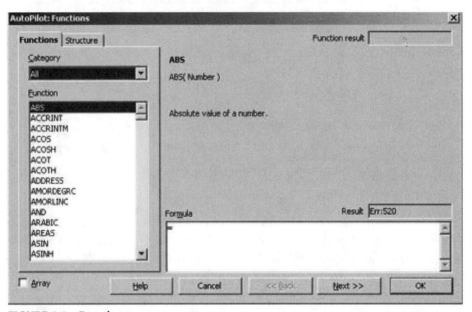

FIGURE 9.9   Functions.

There are literally dozens of calculations/functions listed here. Many, if not most, of the calculations you will require are listed here. For our purposes, scroll down the list until you find a function named STDEV. This is the standard deviation. If you are not familiar with basic statistics, don't worry. Calc will do all the number crunching for you. Conceptually, standard deviation is simply an average of how much each individual item in a sample deviates from the sample's average. This tells us whether or not the mean is a useful statistic. A high standard deviation means that there really was no norm for that data group.

When you have selected the STDEV function, press the next button and you will see a screen like the one in Figure 9.10, where you can enter the various cells you want to compute standard deviation for.

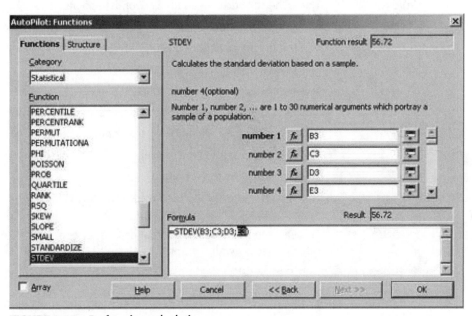

FIGURE 9.10   Performing calculations.

You should notice that on the right side, in the lower third of the screen, the result for the numbers you picked is already being displayed. When you click OK, this result will be put into the spreadsheet. If you should later change the value of any of the cells that you included in the standard deviation calculation, the calculation's total will automatically be revised to match the changed or new data. Also note that you can also get to these functions from the drop-down menu by selecting Insert and Functions. This is the way you get to similar functions in Microsoft Excel. In addition to average and standard deviation, you can see that there are dozens of other built-in functions you can use.

There is a large number of functions you can choose in Calc, some of which might be beyond some readers' mathematical understanding. However, Table 9.1 lists many of the commonly used functions and what they do.

TABLE 9.1 Calc Functions

Function	Purpose
AVERGE	This is the statistical mean for a set of data points.
CHITEST	This performs the Chi squared test, a common statistical function.
COS	This returns the trigonometric function cosine.
SIN	This returns the trigonometric function sine.
TAN	This returns the trigonometric function tangent.
COUNT	This returns the number of elements in a set of data points.
COVAR	This calculates the covariance for a set of data points.
EXP	This function calculates the exponent for a base number.
LOG	This function gives the logarithm.
PEARSON	This function returns the Pearson correlation coefficient. This is another common statistical function.
STDEV	This will return the standard deviation of a set of numbers. This is often presented with the mean.

This list is by no means exhaustive, but it does contain the more commonly used functions. Just as a point of information, there are two other ways you can get to the function list other than by using the Autopilot button. The first is to go to the drop-down menu, choose Insert, and select Functions. The second is to use the shortcut keys Ctrl-F2.

Drop-Down Menu

Everything we have done so far has been with the toolbars at the top of the screen. However, you have undoubtedly noticed the drop-down menus as well. Some people prefer to use drop-down menus rather than toolbars. Fortunately, you can accomplish most tasks with either approach, depending on your personal preferences.

The first drop-down menu, File, is much like the File menu in most Microsoft Office programs. When you click on the File drop-down menu, you are presented with a screen, like the one shown in Figure 9.11. You can see that you have the basic options you would expect. This includes options to create a new file, open an existing file, or save a file.

You can see that this is almost identical to the File drop-down menu in Microsoft Excel, shown in Figure 9.12. There is very little difference between these two

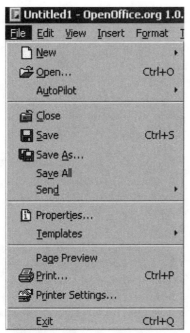

FIGURE 9.11 The File drop-down menu.

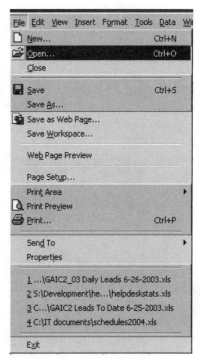

FIGURE 9.12 The File drop-down menu from Microsoft Excel.

menus. Remember that we had previously mentioned that in most applications you will find similar items under the File menu.

The biggest difference between the two is that Excel, like all Microsoft Office applications, lists your most recently opened files so that you can quickly access them. The current version of Open Office does not do this.

Next we come to the Edit menu, shown in Figure 9.9. This too is a standard drop-down menu, similar to what you might find in most Open Office or Microsoft Office applications. You can undo your last action, cut, copy, paste, select all, or find items. This is very close to what you see in Excel under the Edit menu.

The View drop-down menu, which we encounter next, is very important. This menu enables you to change various facets of the way you view the current worksheet. Of particular interest is the third option, Toolbar. This option enables you to select which toolbars will be displayed. You can remove any toolbar you don't want by unselecting it here. The last option is to choose to view Full Screen. This means without any toolbars, menus, or other items. The Microsoft Excel drop-down menu is nearly identical to this.

FIGURE 9.13 The Edit menu.

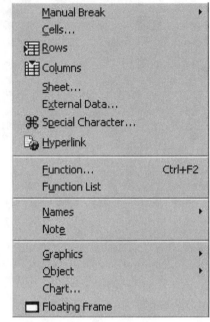

FIGURE 9.14 The Insert menu.

When we reach the Insert drop-down menu, we begin to get to some really interesting functionality. It is from this menu, shown in Figure 9.14, that you will be able to add new rows, columns, cells, graphics, and more. The addition of rows and columns is relatively straightforward and does not require much explanation. A row or column will be inserted at the spot where your cursor is.

You also can see the Insert Function option. This will insert the same built-in functions that we examined previously in this chapter. After that you can see the Graphics option. This option will present you with a dialog box, shown in Figure 9.15, where you can insert any standard image file on your machine.

Of even more interest is the Insert Object option. This option enables you to insert sounds, videos, OLE objects, Java applets, and more. This enables you to add a whole new dimension to your spreadsheets. For example, if you are doing a budget spreadsheet for a construction project, you could add a video of a building being built. You can do this in Microsoft Excel as well. You simply choose Insert and then select Object. You can then insert video clips, sound files, and more.

Inserting a chart, which you can do in Microsoft Excel, is a very common task in any spreadsheet tools. A spreadsheet is an excellent way to organize data and perform calculations. However, most people respond best to visual cues such as charts.

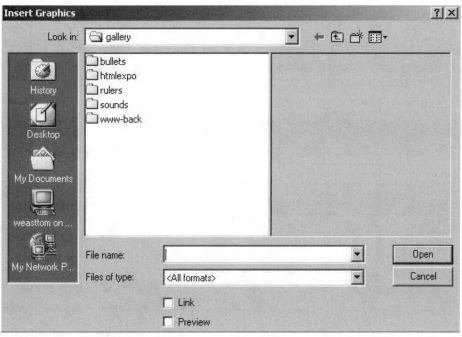

FIGURE 9.15 Inserting graphics.

If you select Insert and then choose Chart, you will see a screen, shown in Figure 9.16, that prompts you to choose what cells to include in your chart. You can also select which rows and columns you want to use as labels for your chart.

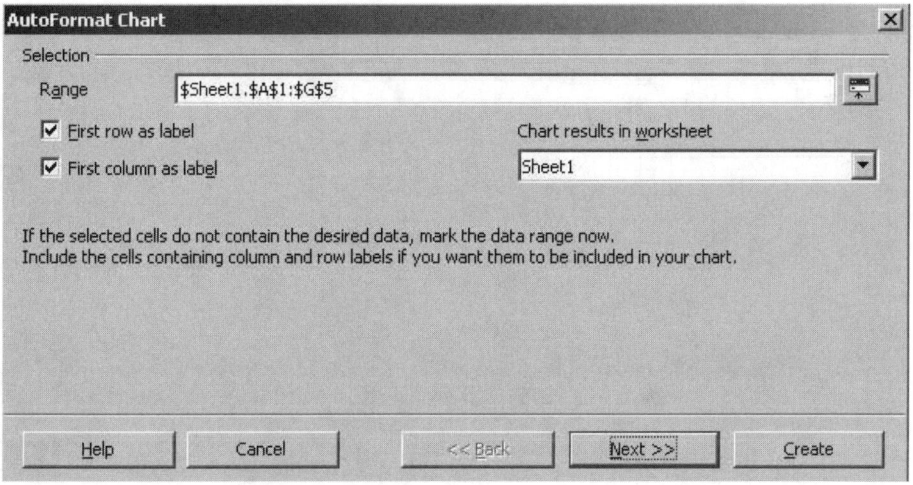

FIGURE 9.16 The Chart Wizard step one.

The next step, shown in Figure 9.17, enables you to select the various settings for your chart. You can select from bar charts, pie charts, line graphs, and 3D charts. There are a number of options at your disposal. You also can choose whether to display your data in rows or columns. For our purposes we will choose columns and a bar chart, then press Next.

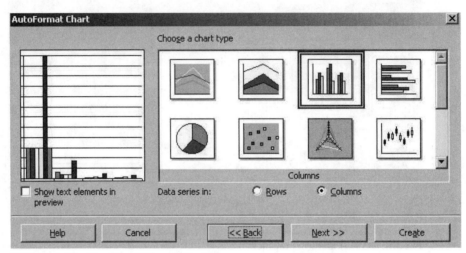

FIGURE 9.17 The Chart Wizard step two.

The next screen enables you to choose whether you want horizontal (X) and/or vertical (Y) grid lines. You then move to the next screen, shown in Figure 9.18, where you can enter a title for your chart and titles for the X and Y axes.

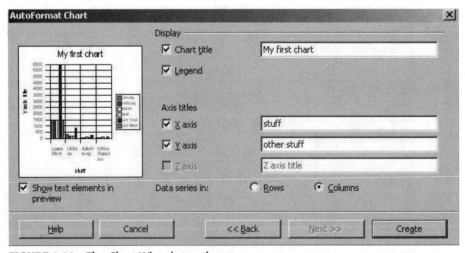

FIGURE 9.18 The Chart Wizard step three.

When you are done and press the Create button, you will have created a chart, much like the one shown in Figure 9.19. Charts are a very important addition to any spreadsheet. For most people, a chart is required to make the data really come alive.

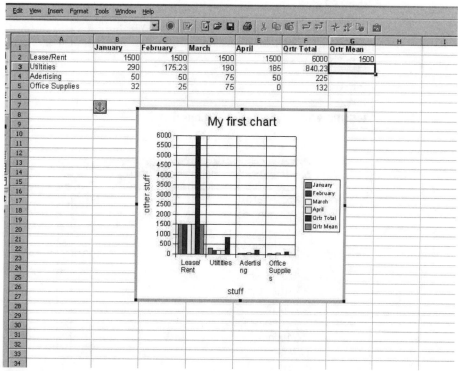

FIGURE 9.19   Your chart.

You can see that creating a chart is a relatively simple thing to do with Open Office Calc. Charts are a very important part of any spreadsheet application. Storing data, running calculations, and creating charts are the essential elements of any spreadsheet application.

The next button on this toolbar enables you to add simple drawings to your spreadsheet. This may seem like an unnecessary or even frivolous addition to a spreadsheet application, but that is not necessarily correct. The various drawing options, seen in Figure 9.20, enable you to add even more visual impact to your data presentation. When appropriately combined with a chart, this can make the presentation of your data far more compelling than it otherwise would be. Any graphical representation of your data has an important impact on the way others will receive and form conclusions based on that data.

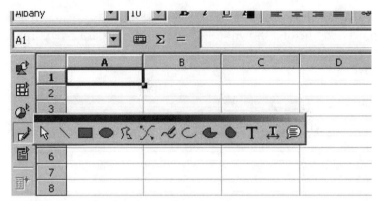

FIGURE 9.20 The drawing options.

FIGURE 9.21 Open Office Theme Selection.

Further down the toolbar we come to an option not present in Microsoft Excel. That option is themes. When you place your mouse over that button, the caption says Choosing Themes. When you click this button, you see the image in Figure 9.21. This enables you to select a theme for your spreadsheet.

For example, the Sun theme shown in Figure 9.22 is just one of the several themes you can select. Of course, these themes do not offer any new functionality to your spreadsheet, but just like charts and drawings, themes can add a new dimension to the presentation of your data.

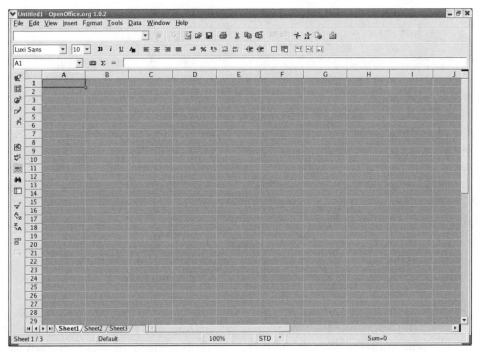

FIGURE 9.22 The Sun theme.

WORKING THROUGH A SPREADSHEET

Now that you have had several pages to examine the basic features of Calc, it is probably an appropriate time to work through the mechanics of creating a spreadsheet with all of the various features we have discussed so far. For the purposes of demonstrating the capabilities of Calc, we will create a spreadsheet for a basic home budget spreadsheet. We will begin by creating a simple spreadsheet with row headings of Rent, Food, Utilities, Credit Cards, and Miscellaneous. We will then have column headings for each month. You can then put in some sample data. Your spreadsheet should look like the one in Figure 9.23.

Now we have some basic data. To the right of the last month, June, we will create a Sub Total column. You do this by giving that column an appropriate label.

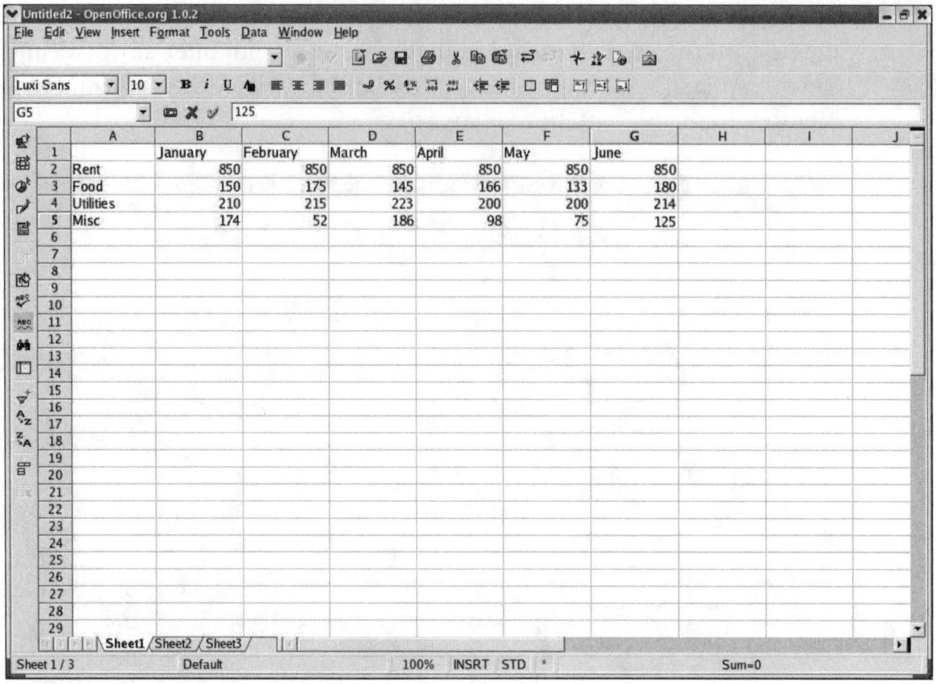

FIGURE 9.23 The basic spreadsheet with data.

Then you put your cursor in the first empty cell on the row for the first category, Rent, and press the summation symbol. If you then put your cursor on the bottom-right corner of this cell and drag it down, you will copy the summation formula to all the subsequent rows. They will automatically be incremented to fit the various rows. You will have something like what you see in Figure 9.24.

Now, just to demonstrate the various capabilities of Calc, we will add a column with average values for each row. Label the next available common average, then click in the first available cell. Then click on the button to the left of the summation button, as we saw earlier in this chapter. Then select the AVERAGE function. You then need to specify the cells you want to average, as is shown in Figure 9.25.

Now you can simply click and drag the corner of that cell down and repeat the function for all the subsequent rows, just as you did previously with the summation function. You should be aware that the capability to click in a corner of a cell and drag, thus replicating the value or the formula in the cell, is also available in Microsoft Excel. Your spreadsheet should now look like the one shown in Figure 9.26.

Now we can add some formatting to your spreadsheets. You should make the headings for the rows and columns bold. It is also important to add a chart. As we previously mentioned, the chart is a very important part of any spreadsheet because it adds a tremendous visual impact to your data. When you press the Insert Chart

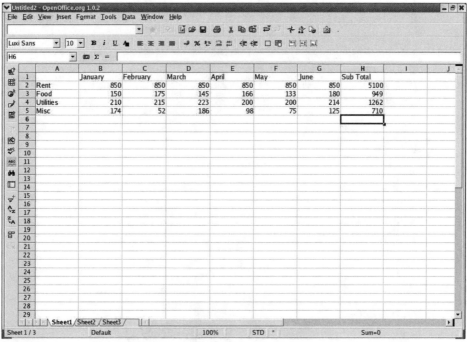

FIGURE 9.24   Adding subtotals to your spreadsheet.

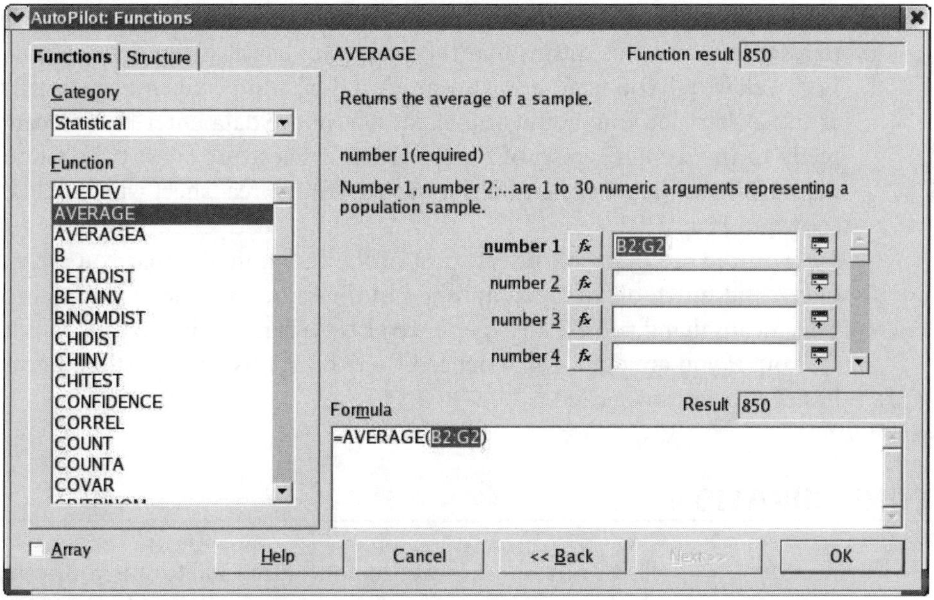

FIGURE 9.25   Adding an AVERAGE function.

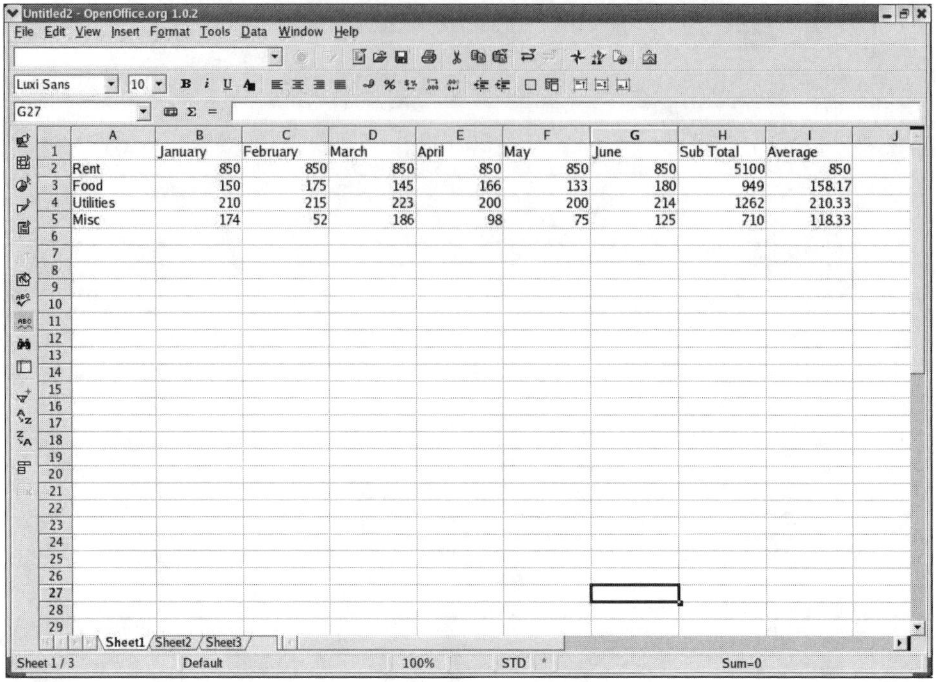

FIGURE 9.26 Replicating the AVERAGE function.

button, you will see your data highlighted automatically, and the cursor will change to a small chart. This means that the basic data has already been fed into a chart. Just click where you want it to appear. You then will be taken to a wizard that will create a chart for you, and it will already have the data entered. You can skip directly to the second screen of the wizard and select the chart type. Choose a bar graph. When you are done with the wizard, your spreadsheet will look like the one shown in Figure 9.27.

You can see that Calc offers most of the functionality that you are used to in Excel, and much of it is accomplished in the same, or at least a similar, manner. This means that if you are an experienced Excel user, moving to Calc should be easy for you. If you are not an experienced Excel user, this chapter should give you the basics and get you started.

CONFIGURATION

As with any application, you may want to configure Calc to suit your own preferences and needs. In Chapter 8, "Moving from Microsoft Word to Open Office," we

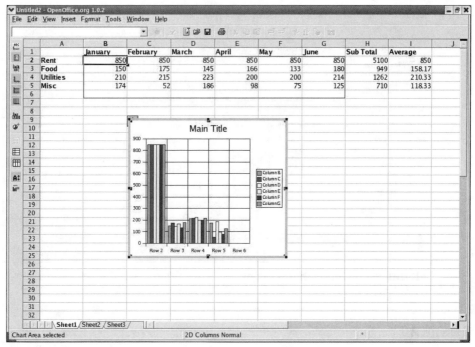

FIGURE 9.27   Adding a spreadsheet.

saw that configuring and customizing Writer was relatively easy, and you have a plethora of choices. You should not be surprised when you find a similar array of choices available to you in Calc. In fact, you have the same two options, Configure and Options, found under the Tools menu. If you look at these, they even offer nearly identical options to the configuration options you saw in Writer. There are really only two differences. When you go to Options in Calc, you have a set of options that are specifically for setting spreadsheet options. This is shown in Figure 9.28.

From this screen you can change the grid lines on your spreadsheet, set the default date format, and more. The other item that is different from Writer is the formula settings. With these settings you can change how formulas in your spreadsheet are formatted and sized.

As you can see, Calc, just like Writer, is pretty customizable. You can change configurations and options to make the application appear and perform in a manner that is most effective and most appealing to you.

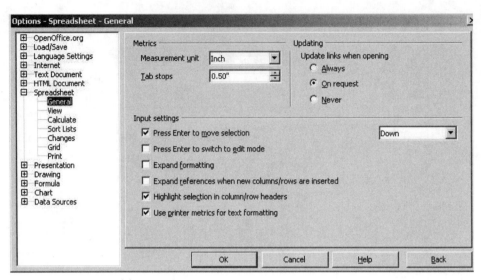

FIGURE 9.28 Spreadsheet options.

SUMMARY

In this chapter, we examined various aspects of using Open Office Calc. We looked at data entry, data formatting, performing calculations, creating charts, and a variety of other spreadsheet functions. After studying this chapter, you should be comfortable creating basic spreadsheets with Open Office Calc.

REVIEW QUESTIONS

1. Name one feature found in Calc that is not present in Microsoft Excel.
2. Why might you want to add a drawing to your spreadsheet?
3. What would you find on the Object toolbar?
4. What is one thing that Excel and all Microsoft Office products do that Calc does not?
5. How would you compute the standard deviation of a column or row?
6. How do you customize the toolbars in Calc?
7. What is the difference between using AutoFill on numbers versus using it on dates?

10 Moving from Microsoft PowerPoint to Open Office Impress

In This Chapter

- Getting Started with Impress
- Creating a Basic Slide Show
- Setting Up Your Slide Show
- Formatting and Configuring
- Templates

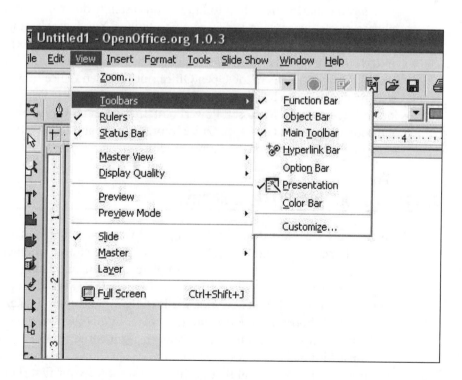

INTRODUCTION

In the preceding two chapters you were shown how to do word processing and how to work with spreadsheets using Open Office. Windows users are often quite familiar with both Microsoft Word and Microsoft Excel. You have now seen how to accomplish the same tasks in Linux using Open Office. Word processing and spreadsheets are core functions in any business and are even quite useful in a home computing environment. But they are not the whole story.

Another one of the Microsoft office applications that has been quite popular with Windows users is Microsoft PowerPoint. This application enables you to make dynamic multimedia presentations. This product originally was intended for business presentations and has become quite popular with salespeople and others who frequently need to capture an audience's attention with a powerful and dynamic presentation. Over the years, PowerPoint also has become quite popular with educators. Teachers, instructors, and college professors often found that PowerPoint presentations added an entirely new dimension to their classroom lectures. This eventually led to students, both college and secondary school, using PowerPoint for their classroom presentations. Now it is quite common to see anyone who makes a presentation, be it sales, classroom, or neighborhood watch, use PowerPoint.

As you make the transition to Linux, you certainly don't want to lose the capability to create dynamic and exciting presentations. You have already seen that the move to Linux won't cause you to lose the capability to create powerful documents or to work with spreadsheets. Neither will you be losing any presentation capabilities. One of the applications in the Open Office suite is Open Office Impress®. This very aptly named program helps you make the same sort of multimedia presentations you formerly created with Microsoft PowerPoint. In short, it is likely to impress both you and your audience. In fact, Open Office Impress even is able to open PowerPoint presentations. This means you can convert old presentations over to Linux.

GETTING STARTED WITH IMPRESS

The best place to start is to just dive right in. When you first launch Impress you will see the screen in Figure 10.1. You are prompted to choose whether you want to start with a blank presentation, use a template, or open an existing presentation.

This screen is strikingly similar to the Microsoft PowerPoint opening screen, shown in Figure 10.2. You have essentially the same choices to make. For our purposes we will choose a blank presentation. Later in this chapter we will revisit templates. Press the Create button in the bottom-right corner.

You are immediately presented with the screen shown in Figure 10.3. From this screen you can choose what sort of slide you want for your first slide. As you can

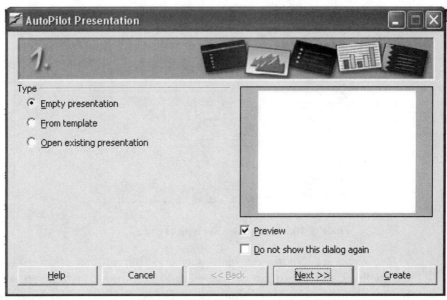

FIGURE 10.1   Getting started with Impress.

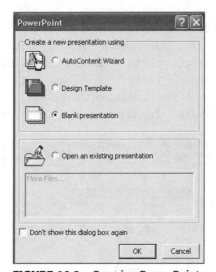

FIGURE 10.2   Opening PowerPoint.

see, there are a number of options. In fact, these are the same sort of options you are presented with when you start a new presentation with PowerPoint. To make certain that you are completely comfortable with Impress, we will select the completely blank slide.

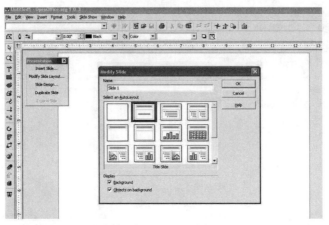

FIGURE 10.3 Selecting the type of slide.

Now you are looking at a blank screen with a number of drop-down menus and toolbars. The options under the File and Edit drop-down menus are the same options you have seen throughout Open Office. It has the basic opening, saving. closing, cutting, copying, and pasting options. In fact, in many applications, both Windows applications and Linux applications, you will find these same options in the same locations. As you have already noted and we have already discussed, File and Edit menus are pretty much the same in most applications.

Let's begin our examination with those options that are not common to all of Open Office applications. If you select View from the drop-down menu, you will see the image in Figure 10.4. You can see that there are several options here. The first that you should note is Toolbars. You can select which toolbars are visible and which are not.

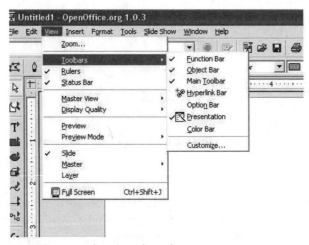

FIGURE 10.4 The View drop-down menu.

After that you can see that you can elect to have the ruler and the status bar visible or not. The next option is the Master View. This will enable you to select how your workspace appears to you. There are several options under this heading, including Drawing View, Outline View, Slides View, and Notes View. Each of these gives you a different view of your project. Usually, people use the Drawing or Outline view while working on a project. The Slides view enables you to see all of your slides in sequence and to drag and drop slides so that you can change their order. The Notes view shows the notes for your presentation.

The next item in the drop-down menu is the Insert menu, shown in Figure 10.5. This option enables you to insert a new slide into your presentation, a duplicate of the current slide, a field, a hyperlink, a spreadsheet, a graphic, or an object. Each of these can help make your presentation much more dynamic and informative.

Next is the Format menu, shown in Figure 10.6. This is a very extensive menu that offers you a number of options for altering the format of various elements in your presentation. You can format entire lines, text sections, characters, paragraphs, a slide's layout, or even add three-dimensional effects.

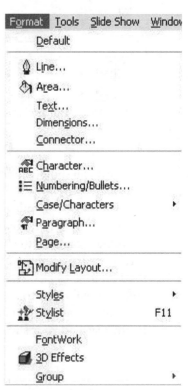

FIGURE 10.5 The Insert menu.

FIGURE 10.6 The Format menu.

The Tools menu, shown in Figure 10.7, is similar to the Tools menu in Open Office Writer or the one in Microsoft PowerPoint. It enables you to perform spell checking, set options for Impress, or configure your presentation. We will examine the options and configuration settings in more detail a little later in this chapter.

The next menu option, and the last that we will examine for now, is the Slide Show menu, seen in Figure 10.8. This menu is almost identical to the Slide Show menu found in Microsoft PowerPoint. This menu option enables you to set the various settings for your presentation. You can set timings, establish transitions between slides, and more. We will look at this option more extensively as we continue in this chapter.

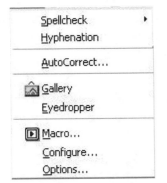

FIGURE 10.7   The Tools menu.

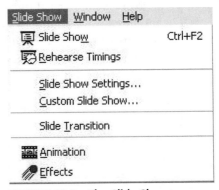

FIGURE 10.8   The Slide Show menu.

Next you should direct your attention to the toolbar at the left of the screen and shown in Figure 10.9. This toolbar has a number of interesting tools that enable you to create some dynamic features in your presentation.

The first tool on the toolbar that you should look closely at is the Text tool. It looks like a capital letter T. Even though Open Office Impress is not a word processor, you will probably want to add text to your presentations. You do this by using the Text tool. Click on it and a small box will appear on your slide. As you type text, your box will resize to accommodate the additional text. You will then have something like what is shown in Figure 10.10a. You can drag the box with your mouse to any place on your slide you would like it.

FIGURE 10.9   **FIGURE 10.10A**   The Text tool.
The toolbar.

The next three tools, shown in Figure 10.10b, enable you to make shapes. The first is for rectangular shapes, the second for circular shapes, and the third for three-dimensional shapes.

When you click and hold an any of these three tools, you are shown several options. For example, with the rectangular tool you can have your shape filled, unfilled, rounded, and so on. This is shown in Figure 10.11.

Once you have selected the shape you want, you drag your mouse across the slide, and that shape will be drawn. A few shapes from each of the three Shape tools are shown in Figure 10.12.

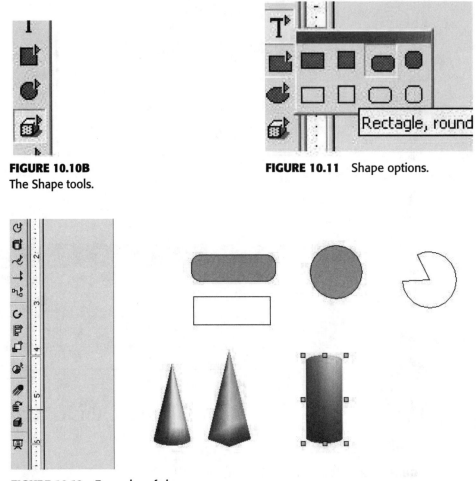

FIGURE 10.10B
The Shape tools.

FIGURE 10.11   Shape options.

Rectagle, round

FIGURE 10.12   Examples of shapes.

You can see that adding interesting shapes to your slide is a very easy task using Open Office Impress. Using Microsoft PowerPoint, you accomplish the same task by using either the Shape tools on the toolbar at the bottom of your screen, or by choosing Insert from the drop-down menu and selecting Pictures, then choosing AutoShapes. Both Open Office and Microsoft Office make creating shapes a very simple task.

The next two tools enable you to create curves and lines. With Microsoft PowerPoint this is accomplished either by using the AutoShape option found under Insert, Pictures, or by using the Line tool at the bottom of the screen. With Impress you use the two buttons on the left toolbar, shown in Figure 10.13.

Much like the shape tools previously described, the line and curve tools have a number of options for altering a line or curve. This enables you to make numerous lines and curves like the ones shown in Figure 10.14.

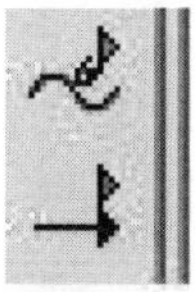

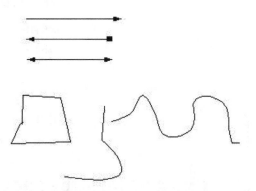

FIGURE 10.13
The line and
curve tools.

FIGURE 10.14   Types of lines and curves.

As you can see, there are a number of options you can use to enhance the appearance of your presentation. Of particular interest to business users might be the arrows. These can be crucial to creating organizational charts, flow charts, and other diagrams needed to demonstrate various concepts.

You can alter any of the shapes, lines, or curves after they have been placed on the slide. If you right-click on a shape, curve, or line, you will see a pop-up menu like the one shown in Figure 10.15.

With this menu, you can change the position, type, style, and more for any shape or line. You can even add effects. Effects determine how the item will appear on your slide when you run the slide show. Effects will be treated in some detail later in this chapter.

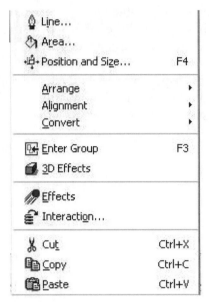

FIGURE 10.15 Pop-up menu.

CREATING A BASIC SLIDE SHOW

Now that we have spent several pages discussing the fundamentals of using Open Office Impress and comparing it to Microsoft PowerPoint, it is time to walk through an Impress presentation with a few slides. You are encouraged to follow along and do this exercise. We will be examining a fictitious company, Pete's Linux Widgets, and doing a sales presentation for that company. The same techniques could readily be applied to creating a presentation for a club, church, class assignment, or dozens of other applications.

We will begin by launching Impress and selecting the blank presentation. You will then be prompted to select your first slide. Earlier, when we were touring the fundamental functionality of Impress, we used a blank slide. This time we will use the second slide option, Title Slide, shown in Figure 10.16.

You can then click on one of the boxes on the slide and enter your text. For our example we will enter some information for our Linux Widget company. You can see this in Figure 10.17.

You can highlight any text and change its font, color, and other properties, just as you would in Microsoft Office. This enables you to create more interesting slides. As you can see in Figure 10.17, we used some different font properties. You can accomplish this by dragging your mouse across the text to highlight it and then se-

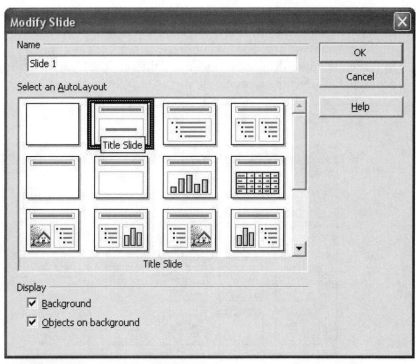

FIGURE 10.16   Inserting a title slide.

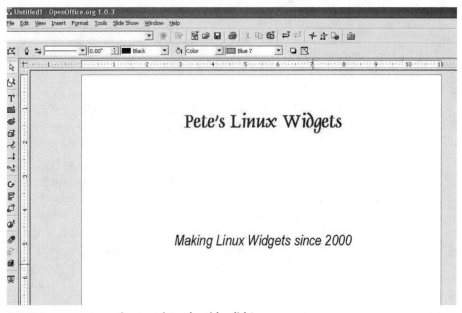

FIGURE 10.17   Inserting text into the title slide.

lecting Format from the drop-down menu. Then you will select Character, and you can then change the font, size, color, and more.

This makes the title slide for our presentation. Let's add another slide. If you select Insert from the drop-down menu and then choose New Slide, you will again be prompted to select the type of slide you want. We are going to select the slide that has a chart and a title, as you see in Figure 10.18.

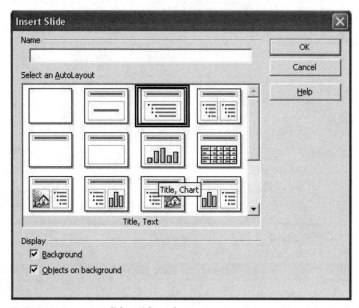

FIGURE 10.18 A slide with a chart.

You can then click on the title to add some text and click on the chart to start the Chart Wizard to create a chart. You have probably noticed by now that the Chart Wizard is much the same in all the various Open Office applications. In our case we are going to add a few simple pieces of data. Remember that once you have a chart, you right-click on it and choose Chart Data from the pop-up menu. When we are done, our chart looks something like what you see in Figure 10.19.

Now we are going to add the effects mentioned earlier in this chapter. To add an effect to any object, just click on it once to make certain it is the object with focus, then go to the drop-down menu and choose Slide Show, then Effects. In this case we are going to add effects to the chart. You will see a screen like the one shown in Figure 10.20 where you will select the effect you want to add.

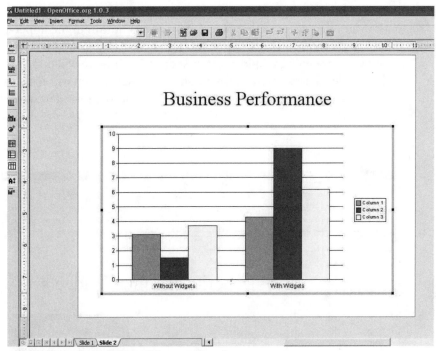

FIGURE 10.19   The chart slide completed.

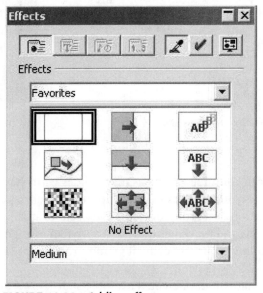

FIGURE 10.20   Adding effects.

You can select any effect you want. You then click the button with the check-mark to add that effect to that object. You have a button in the upper-right corner of the Effects window that will preview that effect for you.

Now we are going to add another slide. This time we will pick one with a title section, bulleted list section, and a graphic section. We then will click on each of the objects, adding text, items, or images until the slide looks similar to what you see in Figure 10.21.

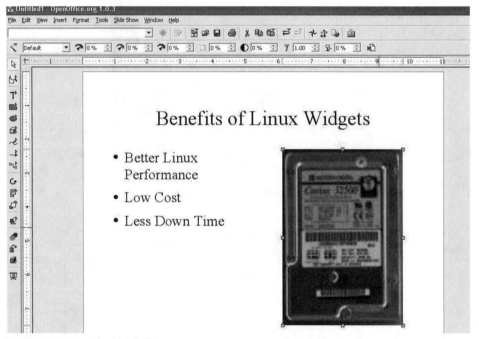

FIGURE 10.21   The third slide.

You can continue adding as many slides with charts, images, effects, and any-thing else as you want. As a design tip, remember to keep your audience in mind. A presentation to a group of elementary school students should probably contain lots of effects and movement. Make it as dynamic as possible. On the other hand, a presentation to your city council would probably need to be much more subdued but inundated with data.

Now that you have created a simple slide show, how do you show it? We will examine how to set up your slide show's presentation in the next section.

SETTING UP YOUR SLIDE SHOW

Once you have created your presentation, you will need to run it. A presentation is not much use unless you present it. If you have used Microsoft PowerPoint, you should have no trouble setting up your slide show with Impress. This is because Open Office Impress runs a slide show the same way that PowerPoint does. If you choose the Slide Show option from the drop-down menu, you will see a list of choices like the ones displayed in Figure 10.22.

FIGURE 10.22 Slide Show choices.

The first choice, labeled Slide Show, will run your slide show. Nothing will occur until you click your mouse. Each mouse click will cause the next action to occur. That action might be an effect on an object or perhaps a change to a new slide. Some people prefer to do their presentations in this manner. That way they don't have to time their speaking closely, since they will change the slide themselves whenever they reach an appropriate point in their presentation.

The second option, Rehearse Timings, works the same way, but a small timer shows at the bottom, enabling you to see exactly how long each action takes. It should be noted that in Microsoft PowerPoint, the Rehearse Timings option records the actions you take when walking through the presentation and will later play back the presentation automatically at that speed. Open Office Impress does not support this functionality.

The next option is Slide Show Settings. When you select this, you will be presented with the Settings screen, seen in Figure 10.23, and you can set various settings. You can change the mouse pointer, decide whether or not the Navigator should be visible, and choose whether or not to make the presentation show on top of all other application windows that might be open at that time.

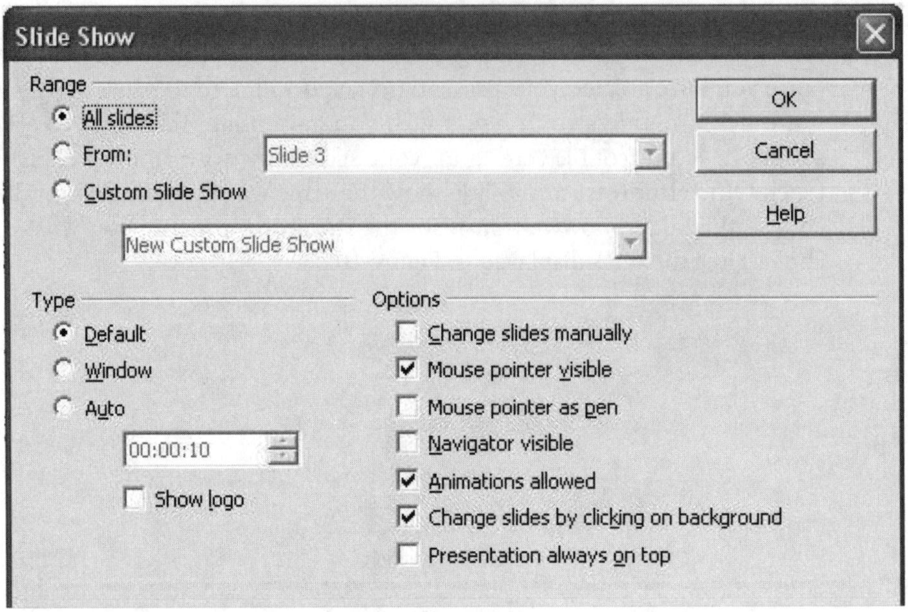

FIGURE 10.23 The Slide Show Settings window.

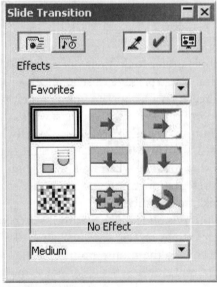

FIGURE 10.24 Slide transitions.

The Animation and Custom Slide Show options are somewhat advanced and a bit beyond the scope of an introductory text, so we will be skipping them here. However, the *www.openoffice.org* Web site has resources on these and other Open Office options. We have already worked with the Effects option.

The last option we will look at is Slide Transitions. When you choose this you will be presented with the window shown in Figure 10.24. This is quite similar to the Effects screen. Here you can decide how one slide will transition into the next. Instead of just having one disappear and the next appear, you can have slide-ins, fade-ins, and such. Essentially, you have all the slide transition options you are used to in Microsoft PowerPoint.

FORMATTING AND CONFIGURING

Just as with Microsoft Office and other Open Office applications you have worked with, you can configure and change Open Office Impress to suit your needs and preferences. If you choose Tools from the drop-down menu and select Configure, you will see an image much like that shown in Figure 10.25.

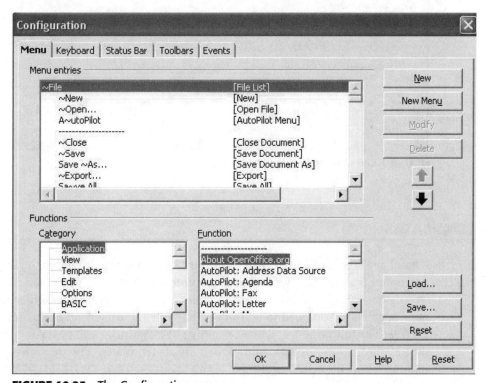

FIGURE 10.25   The Configuration screen.

This screen, as you can see, has several tabs that enable you to customize what menu items you see, what shortcut keys there are, what toolbars are displayed, and more. This screen is useful in helping you to reconfigure Open Office Impress to meet your individual preferences.

The other option we are going to examine is Options, also found under the Tools drop-down menu. This screen, shown in Figure 10.26, is replete with numerous options that enable you to set the behavior of Open Office Impress. For most readers, leaving the defaults will be adequate. The author works with default settings, but people often have different tastes, and you might find you want to change certain things. Any configuration options will be found within these two menu choices in the Tools menu.

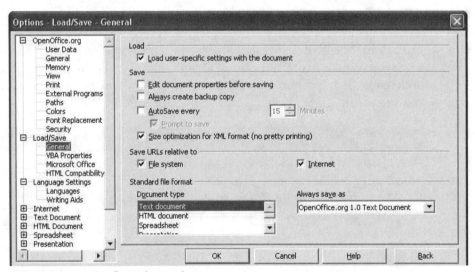

FIGURE 10.26 Configuration options.

TEMPLATES

If you have ever used Microsoft PowerPoint, then you are familiar with templates. A template is a preset layout for a presentation. The layout, graphics, and design are already done, and you have to put in your text and images. Open Office has this same capability. You need to go out on the Web and download templates, which are free. The following list, while certainly not exhaustive, will give you a place to start in finding and downloading Open Office templates. The directory you installed Open Office into will have a subdirectory, \share\template, where you should place all templates.

- *http://csip.ece.gatech.edu/Information/StarOffice_Templates/index.shtml*
- *http://whiteboard.openoffice.org/doc/Samples_Templates/User/template/*
- *www.getopenoffice.org/templates.html*
- *www.ex.ac.uk/~knackaer/ooo.htm*

NOTE

Some of these templates will be in compressed files, TAR for Linux, ZIP for Windows. You will need to uncompress them.

After you have downloaded these templates, you will need to use an Open Office utility to include them in your applications. If you look under Open Office in the Start menu, you will see an application named Global. We will discuss this application a bit more in Chapter 11, "Other Open Office Applications," but for now you need to know that this is the appropriate utility for incorporating templates. Once you launch that utility, go to File, choose Templates, and select Organize. You will see a screen like the one shown in Figure 10.27.

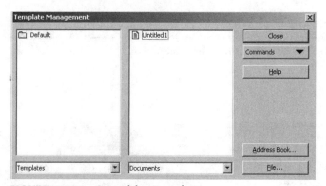

FIGURE 10.27   Organizing templates.

Now click on the Default folder in the window on the left side of the screen. This will cause this folder to be selected. Then find the Command button on the right side of the screen and click it. You will see several options; choose Import Template. If you did not properly select the Default folder first, the Import option will be disabled. You can go through a standard dialog box and select any templates you want to include. Now you are ready to use templates.

If you return to Open Office Impress, on the beginning screen select the button marked From Template, and you will see all of the templates you imported, as shown in Figure 10.28. Just select the one you want to use and click the Next button.

Once you move to the next screen, you can select any design you like for your slides. As you click on each design, it will be previewed in a small window, as you see in Figure 10.29. This should help you to decide which template design is most appropriate for your presentation.

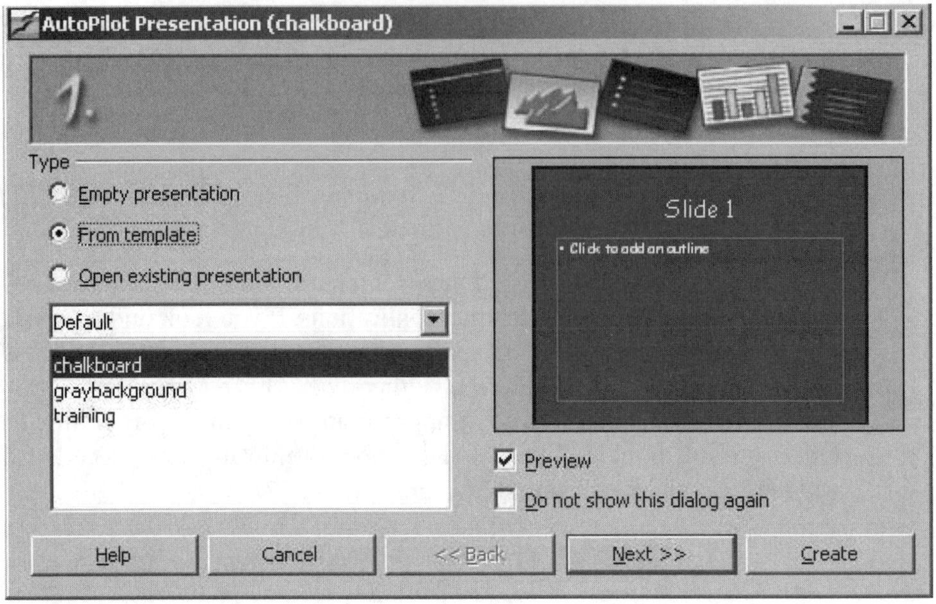

FIGURE 10.28 Selecting a template.

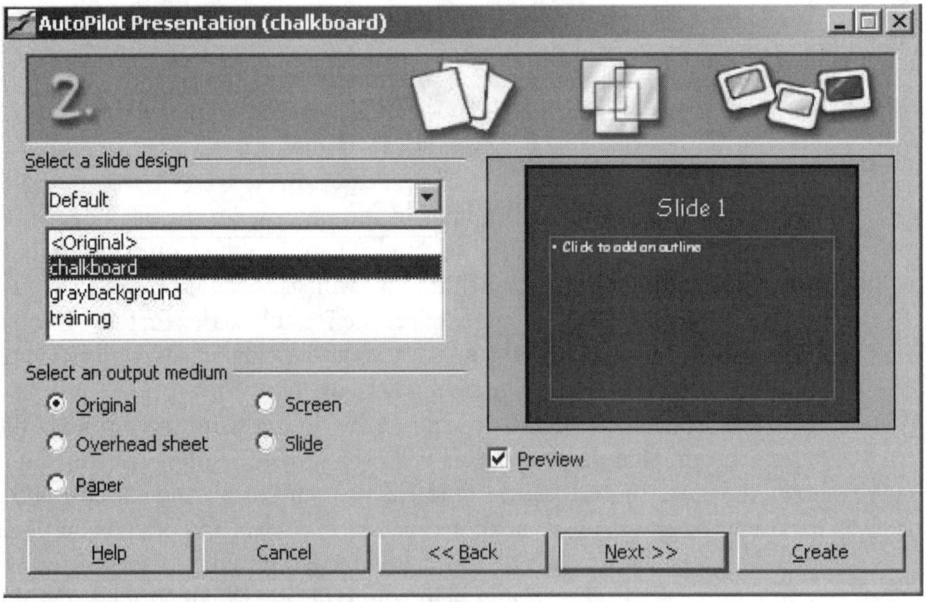

FIGURE 10.29 Selecting a design.

Now you should click the Next button again. On this screen you can choose what type of transitions should occur between slides in your presentation. You also can select the speed of the transitions and even whether or not to have the slides progress automatically. If you choose automatic progression, you can then select the time to wait between slides. The fourth screen asks for some company information; then you click the Create button on the last screen, and you have a basic presentation. Figure 10.30 shows the basic presentation we have created. Of course, yours might look different if you selected a different template.

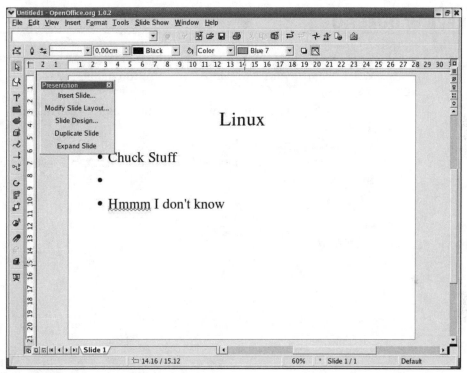

FIGURE 10.30   Basic template presentation.

You can see that Impress offers you the use of templates, just like Microsoft PowerPoint, but it has a few disadvantages. PowerPoint comes with a lot of templates already loaded. Impress comes with none. You have to scour the Internet looking for templates. Also, Microsoft PowerPoint has even more templates on the Web.

SUMMARY

In this chapter you were introduced to Open Office Impress. We began with a quick tour of essential functions and then walked through a simple presentation. We then moved on to exploring briefly how to set up and run a slide show. Finally, we finished with an examination of where to go in order to customize Impress. After studying this chapter, you should be able to create and run dynamic and exciting presentations using Open Office Impress.

REVIEW QUESTIONS

1. Does Open Office Impress support automatic slide show presentation?
2. What drop-down menu would you use to change the toolbars that are displayed?
3. What drop-down menu would you use to add three-dimensional effects to text?
4. What is the purpose of the Slides view?
5. What is the difference between Rehearse Timings in PowerPoint and in Impress?

11

Other Open Office Applications

In This Chapter

- Draw
- HTML Editor
- Open Office Setup
- Math
- Global

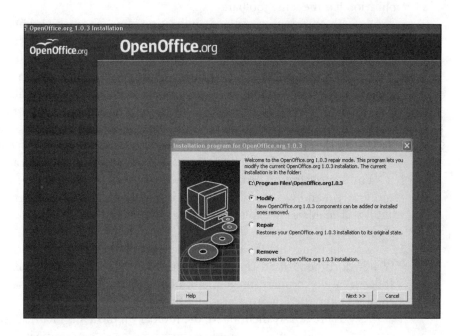

INTRODUCTION

Throughout this section we have been discussing the three most commonly used Open Office applications. You have seen how to create documents, spreadsheets, and presentations. These applications closely parallel the functions of Microsoft Word, Microsoft Excel, and Microsoft PowerPoint. However, Writer, Calc, and Impress are not the only things that Open Office has to offer.

There are several less commonly used applications. These applications form part of the Open Office suite and can be quite useful. In this chapter we will briefly examine each of these and explore their basic functionality. After this chapter you should be able to use these applications with relative ease.

DRAW

Open Office Draw® is a very useful application. With this application you can create your own drawings. When you first launch Draw, you might notice that the toolbar on the left is identical to the one found in Impress. If you recall, that toolbar contained various graphical elements, so it should be no surprise that this application has the same toolbar.

As with any graphics-related application, you can open various graphics files and then edit or alter them as you see fit. When you go to File on the drop-down menu and select Open, you will see something like what is shown in Figure 11.1.

Notice that there is a plethora of graphics types that Draw can open. You can open GIFs, JPEG, BMP, WMF, ICO, and even Kodak Photo CD files. This means that you have a number of graphics types you can work with. For our purposes we will open any image file on your PC and begin altering it using the Draw program. The images in this book might use a different image than you have on your machine. That is not important as long as you have some image you can work with.

For demonstration purposes this book is using a rather simple image, a black and gray yin and yang symbol, shown in Figure 11.2. This figure is rather simple, but it will enable us to explore the things you can do with the image once you have it opened in Draw.

Keep in mind that the images you create in Draw will often be used later in a Writer document or an Impress slide show presentation. This means that, while you cannot do complex image manipulation, you can create logos and the sort of graphics often used in brochures and fliers.

As was previously mentioned, the toolbar on the left is identical to the one you were introduced to with Impress, so there is no need to examine it again. However,

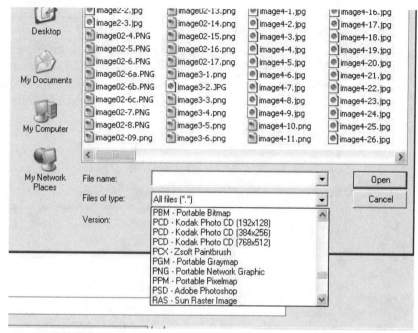

FIGURE 11.1   The Open menu.

FIGURE 11.2   The sample picture.

the toolbar at the top is not identical to the toolbars you have previously seen. You get a new set of options when you have an image selected.

Let's examine some of its functionality with our sample image. The first item of interest on the upper toolbar is the first drop-down box. If you click on it you see that it has four options: default, grayscale, black and white, and watermark. Each of these changes your image. For example, the black and white option, when applied to our yin and yang symbol, is shown in Figure 11.3.

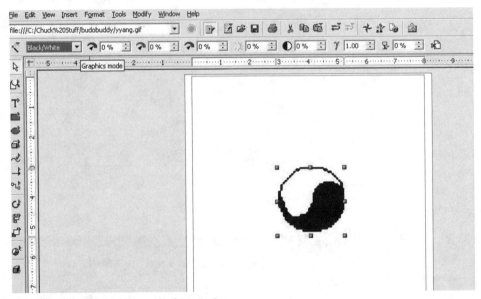

FIGURE 11.3 The black and white option.

The next three buttons are not of much use with a black and white image or with the grayscale images used in most books. These three buttons enable you to alter the amount of red, green, and blue in an image. Most computer graphics colors are created by mixing reds, greens, and blues. Therefore, altering the levels of these colors in your image will enable you to alter the image's overall color. These buttons are shown in Figure 11.4.

The next two buttons, shown in Figure 11.5, enable you to alter the brightness and contrast of a picture. Careful alteration of both brightness and contrast can help clear up an otherwise difficult picture.

FIGURE 11.4 The red, green, and blue buttons.

FIGURE 11.5 Brightness and contrast buttons.

The next two buttons, shown in Figure 11.6, enable you to alter the gamma and the transparency of an image. The transparency setting is the one that we will be taking a closer look at.

There are times when you might want an image to have varying degrees of opaqueness. You may want the image to be at least partially transparent. That is where the transparency setting comes in. A setting of zero indicates that your image is completely opaque with no transparency at all. A setting of 100 indicates that your image is completely transparent and in fact not visible. Figure 11.7 shows a few different transparency settings for our yin and yang symbol.

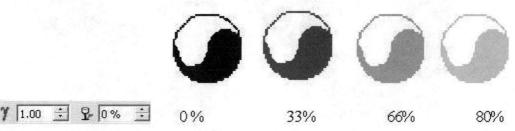

FIGURE 11.6 Gamma and transparency settings.

FIGURE 11.7 Transparency settings.

As we learned earlier, many of the tools and settings in this application are identical to the ones found in Impress, which is why we don't need an entire chapter for this application. Let's examine a few drop-down menu items that Draw does not share with Impress. In Figure 11.8 you can see the drop-down menu for flipping an image. This is found by going to the Modify drop-down menu and selecting Flip. You can completely flip an image, either horizontally or vertically.

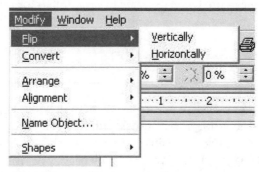

FIGURE 11.8 Flipping an image.

There are some other interesting options under the Modify menu. For example, you will find the Arrange menu item. If you have more than one object on your drawing, you can use the Arrange options to alter the positioning of the objects. For example, in Figure 11.9 there is a cube in front of our image. If you go to Modify on the drop-down menu, select Arrange, and choose Bring to Front, the image you have selected will be brought to the front. If you click once on our yin and yang emblem, you can then bring it back to the front, as it is in Figure 11.10.

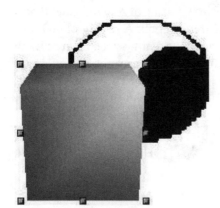

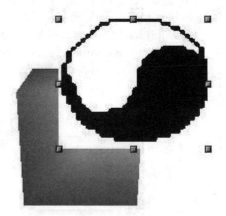

FIGURE 11.9   An image blocking our image.

FIGURE 11.10   Bringing our image back to the front.

The next option under Modify is Alignment. This menu item is self-explanatory. It enables you to align the image you have selected. You can give it a horizontal alignment of left, right, or center. You also can give it a vertical alignment of top, bottom, or center.

This is not everything you can do with the Draw application, of course. Combining what we have covered here with what you learned about Impress, you should be able to use Draw to create basic graphics for purposes such as brochures, fliers, and more.

HTML EDITOR

Most computer users like to surf the Web. In previous chapters you were briefly introduced to the browser that comes with Red Hat Linux 9.0. You probably already have a lot of experience visiting Web sites using Microsoft Internet Explorer or Netscape Navigator. What are those Web pages you visit, and how would you make one of your own? Eventually, most avid computer users and even many novice users ask themselves these questions. A Web site is one or more documents written in a language called HTML (HyperText Markup Language). This language is something Web browsers understand. When they go to a Web address and see HTML documents, the browsers can interpret those documents and display the contents to you in your browser.

This leaves the question of how you might make your own Web pages. You could take a course at a local community college and learn how to use HTML. You also could purchase several HTML books and study them. Fortunately, if you have neither the time nor the inclination for such an in-depth study of HTML, Open Office has an alternative. One of the applications in Open Office is HTML Editor. That editor, depicted in Figure 11.11, looks much like a standard word processor.

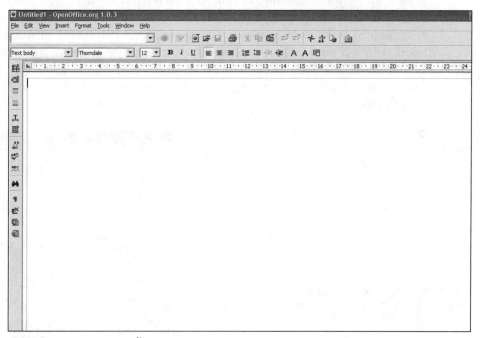

FIGURE 11.11   HTML Editor.

You can insert text, change fonts, insert pictures, and do many of the things you have always done in word processors like Open Office Writer and Microsoft Word. However, the HTML Editor takes what you are writing and inserting and generates the HTML language code for you. You then have a Web page without actually knowing anything at all about HTML! This probably has your interest, so let's jump right in.

HTML Editor Basics

When you first open the HTML Editor, you will notice that the toolbar at the top looks very much like the toolbar from Open Office Writer. This should be expected.

Web pages often include text. That text might be bold, italicized, centered, or formatted in some other way. You will need the same text manipulation tools that you would in any word processor. Even the toolbar at the side is very similar to what you saw in Open Office Writer. It enables you to insert tables, images, and other items.

The first button on the side toolbar enables you to insert many common items. This button is shown in Figure 11.12.

Some of these options should be familiar to you. Inserting graphics or a table works in exactly the same way as it did with Open Office Writer. However, inserting a frame may sound strange to you. A frame is a way to organize elements in any document into logical groupings. When you choose this option, you then drag your mouse on the document to create the frame. If you then right-click on the frame, you will see a pop-up menu with several options. The most important is about midway down the list and says Frame. If you click on this option you will see a screen, much like the one in Figure 11.13, where you can alter a number of your frame's properties.

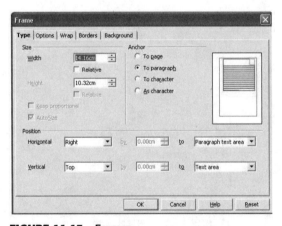

FIGURE 11.12   The first insert button.   **FIGURE 11.13**   Frames.

Under that is a button for inserting various fields. This button's options are shown in Figure 11.14. You can insert date fields, page number, author, and more. This is a rather simple but useful item to add to any Web page.

The rest of the buttons on this left toolbar, except for the very last button, have been discussed in previous chapters. These buttons are identical to the ones you find in Open Office Writer. However, the last button is quite different. You have already learned that one way to create HTML pages for the Web is to learn the HTML language and type in all that code. The last button on this toolbar enables you to view the HTML code you have generated with this HTML Editor. That code will look similar to what you see in Figure 11.15.

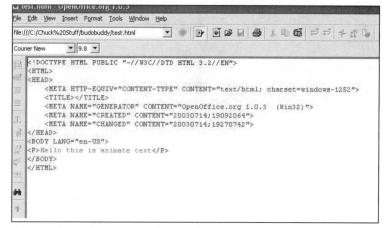

FIGURE 11.14
Inserting special fields.

FIGURE 11.15 HTML source code.

Some of the HTML code should make sense to you because it is very close to plain English. Other elements of it will seem peculiar. However, the real point here is that you don't have to know anything at all about HTML code to create some pretty decent Web pages using the Open Office HTML Editor.

Next you should turn your attention to the drop-down menu at the top of the screen. Take a moment to examine the Insert menu shown in Figure 11.16. The first few items duplicate options you have seen in the toolbar buttons, either on the left or at the top. It is common practice in many applications, including both Open Office and Microsoft Office, to duplicate functions. This way you can use whatever method you prefer, a toolbar or a drop-down menu.

The third option down, however, is not duplicated in the toolbar. It enables you to insert a hyperlink. A hyperlink is a link to an e-mail address, a file, or another Web site. It is certain that you have at some point clicked your mouse on a link on some Web page and been taken to another Web page. This is a hyperlink. When you click on that option in the drop-down menu, you will see a screen like the one in Figure 11.17.

The buttons on the left enable you to determine what type of link this is. It might be an Internet link to a Web site or perhaps a link to an e-mail address, or even a link to a document. For our purposes we will stick with Internet links. You then need only to type in the Web address in the Target text field. Then in the Text field you can put whatever text you want the reader of your Web page to see. For our purposes we will put in the Web site of this book's author, *www.chuckeasttom.com* in Target, and for the text we will put click here to visit Chuck's web page. This is all shown in Figure 11.18.

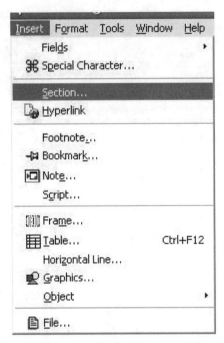

FIGURE 11.16 The Insert menu.

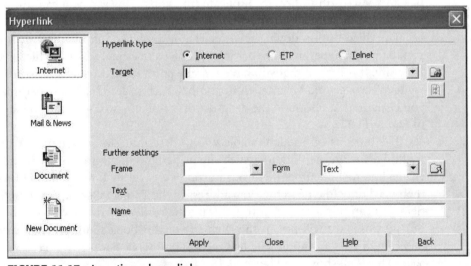

FIGURE 11.17 Inserting a hyperlink.

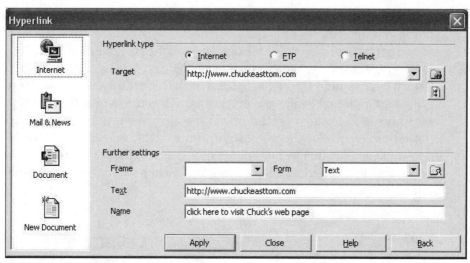

FIGURE 11.18   Setting up a hyperlink.

You click the Apply button and then the Close button, and this link will be inserted into your HTML document. Inserting links is rather important. Most Web pages have links of one sort or another. When you are done, your link will look much like the one you see in Figure 11.19.

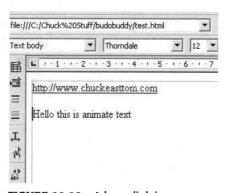

FIGURE 11.19   A hyperlink in your Web page.

A Basic Web Page

With all of the basics out of the way, let's create a very basic Web site. So that all readers are on the same page, so to speak, we will create a Web page about Linux. The only image we will use will be the Linux penguin Tux. You can do a Web search using Google™ or Yahoo!™ and easily find this image. With most Web browsers you right-click on an image in a Web page and select Save As from the drop-down menu.

Starting with a blank HTML document in the HTML Editor, we will type in the phrase *Linux is Cool*. We will then make that text centered, bold, italicized, and a much larger font using the toolbar at the top (remember the common text formatting buttons found in all word processors). Then use the Enter key to skip down a few lines. You can then use the drop-down menu to select Insert and Graphics and insert an image. For the purposes of this example we will insert the previously downloaded Tux image. You should note that your image is surrounded by small dots, enabling you to resize it if you want. Right now your Web page should look much like what is shown in Figure 11.20.

FIGURE 11.20   The basic Web page.

Now we are going to add a table. Recall that the toolbar on the left side of your screen is where you will go to do this. Click on the uppermost button and then select the button that looks like a table. You then drag your mouse over the same number of cells you want your table to have, as depicted in Figure 11.21.

Now we are going to practice creating links. Each of these cells is going to have a link to some Linux-related Web site. In case you have forgotten, put your mouse

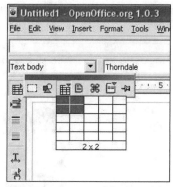

FIGURE 11.21   Adding a table.

in one of the cells, click once, then go to the drop-down menu and select Insert and Hyperlink. Each of our cells will have a different link. The links are listed here:

Linux Online: *www.linux.org/*

Linux.Com: *www.linux.com/*

Red Hat: *www.redhat.com/*

Open Office: *www.openoffice.org/*

We now have a relatively simple Web page, but one that shows the basics of developing a Web page. Obviously there is a lot more you can do with the HTML Editor, but this gives you enough to create a basic résumé Web page or personal Web page. You can see the Web page we created in Figure 11.22.

Once you have created a Web page, you might want to make it available on the Web. To do that you will need to have some Web server host your Web site. Fortunately, Web hosting, much like Linux and Open Office, can be obtained at little or no charge. Two very popular free Web hosting services are *www.geocities.com* and *www.angelfire.com*. For business sites, *www.netfirms.com* is very popular. If you visit any of these sites you will find complete instructions for obtaining free Web space and uploading your Web page.

Obviously this short segment will not make you a professional Web developer. It would be virtually impossible for you to do that without some extensive knowledge of HTML and at least one scripting language such as JavaScript. However, it is not the purpose of the Open Office HTML Editor or this book to make you a professional Web developer. The purpose is to make you competent enough to put up a simple Web page with very little difficulty. It is recommended that you spend some time experimenting with the HTML Editor.

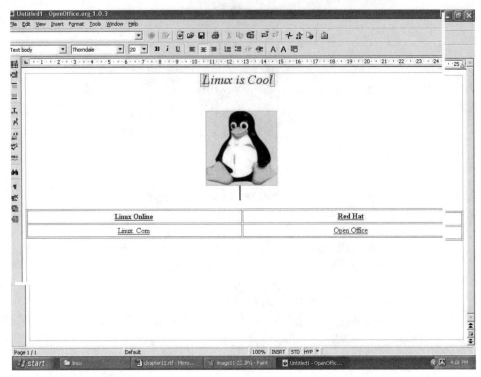

FIGURE 11.22 Our sample Web page.

Some Advanced Features

For some of you, the previous elements of a Web page are not enough. You want more. Let's explore just a few additional items you can use in your Web pages. First let's examine using images for links. You have probably been to Web sites where you clicked on a link in order to visit some other Web page. If you will right-click on any image, such as our Tux image, and choose Graphics, you will see a screen that enables you to alter almost any facet of that image. We are interested in the fourth tab, labeled Hyperlink. Enter your Web address, as you see in Figure 11.23, and your picture is now a link to a Web site.

An even more interesting option can be found by right-clicking on your picture and selecting Image Map. An image map is when one picture links to more than one Web site. Different regions of the image are linked to different sites. When you select the Image Map option, you are presented with the Image Map Editor shown in Figure 11.24.

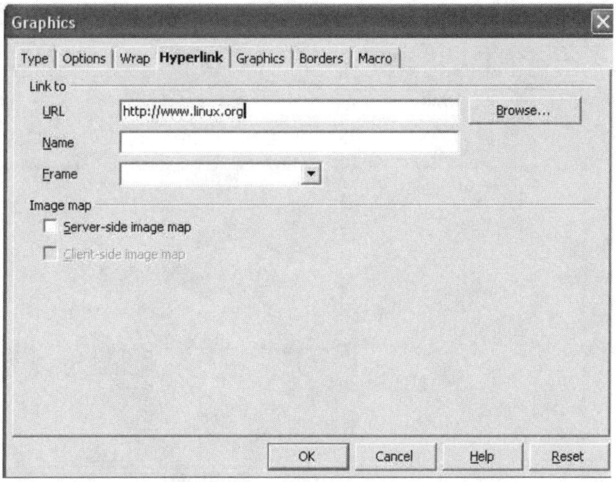

FIGURE 11.23   Making a picture a Web link.

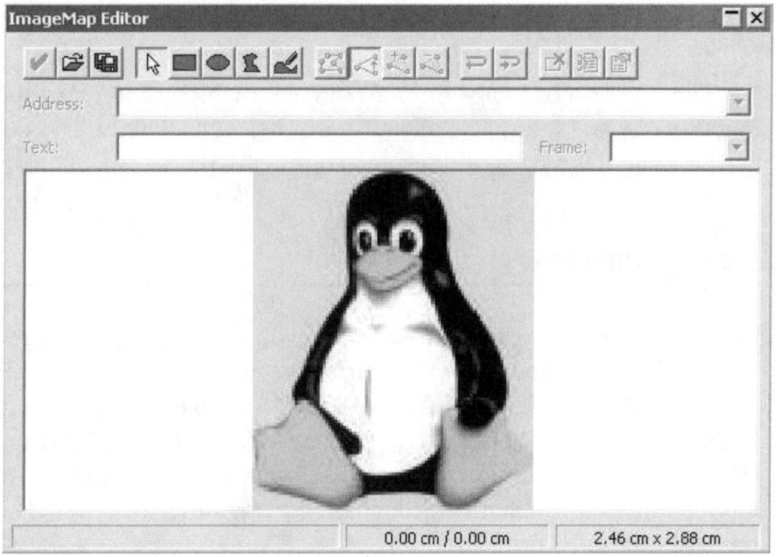

FIGURE 11.24   The Image Map Editor.

Now you can select any of the shape tools in the toolbar and drag your mouse across an area. That area will be highlighted with that shape. You then assign that area a Web address, as you see in Figure 11.25. Just remember not to have any overlap in your regions.

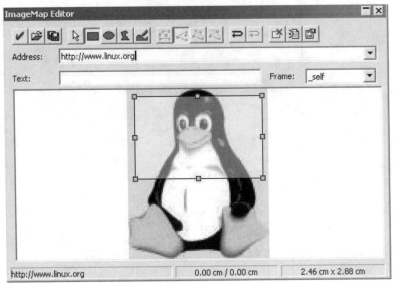

FIGURE 11.25 Creating an image map.

The addition of image links and image maps should really increase both the functionality and the appeal of your Web site. And all of this was done without any need for you to know anything at all about HTML.

OPEN OFFICE SETUP

When you first run Open Office or when you first install it, you get an opportunity to set the various parameters and settings of the Open Office suite. However, if you are anything at all like most people, you may have forgotten some settings or changed your mind. Fortunately, you can select Open Office Setup from the Open Office Setup menu option, in the same location all Open Office applications are found, and go through a wizard, changing anything you want. The first screen of this is shown in Figure 11.26.

This utility will enable you to modify any of the settings you would normally set during installation. This can be very valuable, as you may not know how to change those settings without reinstalling.

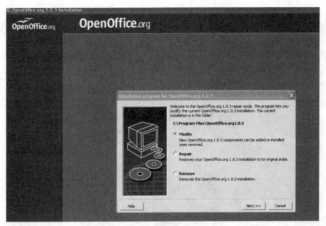

FIGURE 11.26   The Open Office setup.

MATH

If you have ever needed to create a document that contained mathematical equations, then you know it is not easy to find an application that combines the required formatting and printing of word processing and the representation of mathematical equations. Most word processors have very limited capability in this regard. Even Microsoft Word and its companion Math Equation Editor do not fully accomplish this goal. This is another area in which Open Office has a superior performance. Open Office Math is essentially a mathematical word processor. You can use it to create documents that contain mathematical equations. This is very useful for mathematicians, engineers, astronomers, chemists, physicists, or students taking courses in any of these disciplines. You can see the basic Open Office Math screen shown in Figure 11.27.

Notice the small box in the upper-right corner with various mathematical symbols in it. In this box you can select various types of symbols. The top row contains the types. As you pass your mouse over them, as shown in Figure 11.28, a tool will show you what type it is. If you click on that type, you will see a different set of symbols in the main window.

You can then use a combination of those symbols and your own typing to create mathematical formula documents that you can save, edit, open, or print just like any standard text document. So with Open Office Math, you have a word processor for mathematics.

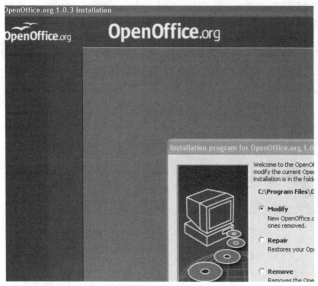

FIGURE 11.27   Open Office Math.

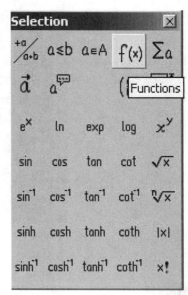

FIGURE 11.28   The symbol types.

GLOBAL

You may well be wondering what this option is for. When you launch the Global application, you see something much like what is shown in Figure 11.29. It looks quite a bit like a word processor, but it is not. This application is for storing and organizing global data, data that can be shared among your various Open Office applications. The document you are looking at is the master document for your word processor, but many functions in it are common to all of your Open Office applications. You can alter this document and save it. It will then be the template for new word processing documents you create.

You already saw this application used a bit in the last chapter to import templates. That is just the beginning of what you can do with this application. Recall that we went to File and then Templates and chose Import. You also can alter your Address Book. When you look under File and Templates, you should see Address Book. When you select this you are taken to the screen shown in Figure 11.30, and you can adjust the format of your Address Book.

You can see that Global is exactly what its name implies. It is a utility that gives you access to the Global shared elements of Open Office. It is here that you can create the basic template for new documents, as well as import templates for use in Excel and Impress.

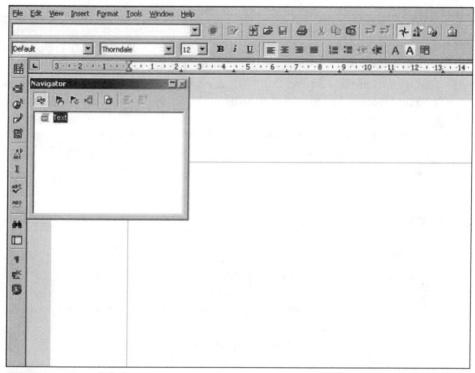

FIGURE 11.29   Global.

FIGURE 11.30   The Address Book.

SUMMARY

In this chapter, we examined some of the extra applications that ship with Open Office. Perhaps the most important is the HTML Editor. We examined the basics of how to use this application to develop your own Web pages and discussed how to find free or low-cost Web hosting for your Web page. This information is of use to virtually any computer user.

We also took a look at how to change the Open Office settings using the Open Office Setup utility. It has a very user-friendly wizard that will enable you to change any settings you would normally set during installation.

REVIEW QUESTIONS

1. What is an image map?
2. How would you make a picture into a link to a Web site?
3. Name at least one free Web hosting site.
4. List three graphics types that you can insert into your Web page.
5. What is the purpose of the Open Office Setup utility?
6. What is the purpose of Open Office Math?
7. What is the purpose of Open Office Global?

IV Important Linux Applications

This section will show you how to use several applications. There are a number of common tasks that you may have done in Windows and will probably want to continuing doing in Linux. The chapters in this section will show you the basics of a wide range of Linux applications. The section begins with an entire chapter on GIMP. GIMP is a very powerful graphics tool that will enable you to do professional digital image manipulation. The next chapter in this section shows you around various Internet utilities. You will learn how to use Linux Web browsers, chat clients, e-mail, and more.

Chapter 14 is a sort of smorgasbord. Many of the small applications and utilities that did not seem to fit anywhere else are covered here. Chapters 15 and 16 will show you how to set up your own Web server or FTP server. Finally, Chapter 17 shows you around the world of gamming in Linux. We will look at some of the games that install with Red Hat Linux, and we will discuss where to go on the Internet to find more Linux games.

12

Moving from Adobe Photoshop to GIMP

In This Chapter

- What Is GIMP
- GIMP Basics
- The Toolbox

INTRODUCTION

Like many Windows users, you probably have come to expect a lot of powerful graphics capability on your PC. Some Windows users are satisfied with the Paint and Photo Editor applications that come with Windows and are found under Accessories in the Programs menu. However, neither of these applications is a full-featured, robust, graphics package. Neither of these packages is of professional caliber. They are quite limited in what they enable you to do with an image. This of course leads to the question of what graphics application is of professional caliber? Many Windows users, as well as Macintosh users, turn to Adobe Photoshop as their choice for graphics applications. Adobe Photoshop is one of the most widely used graphics applications on the market today. It is hard to imagine anyone involved in graphics design, digital photography, or a related field who has not used Adobe Photoshop. However, there is no version of Photoshop available for Unix or Linux machines. It should also be pointed out that Adobe Photoshop is a commercial product and can cost several hundred dollars. Even if there were a version of Adobe Photoshop released for Linux (and as of this writing there are not even any hints or rumors to that effect), there is still another reason why you might want to search for an alternative product. If you are a home user, not a graphic artist, who wants a professional caliber program for your own use, it may seem unreasonable for you to pay several hundred dollars for a graphics application.

This is where GIMP comes in. GIMP is a graphics application that can do virtually everything that Adobe Photoshop can do. In fact, if you are experienced with Photoshop, you will probably be able to master GIMP within a matter of a few hours. The two applications are that similar. There are two real advantages to GIMP. The first is price. GIMP is open source and is available as a free download from *www.gimp.org*. The second advantage is the platforms that GIMP is available for. GIMP was designed for Unix and Linux, but there is also a Windows version available. Much like Open Office, you can get GIMP for free and use it on both Windows and Linux machines.

WHAT IS GIMP?

GIMP is an acronym for General Image Manipulation Program. As we already mentioned, GIMP is an open source software application and is available free of charge. It was originally a project of Spencer Kimball and Peter Mattis, two students who were undergraduates at the University of California, Berkeley, when they created GIMP. It began as a project for one of their classes. They actually started out to write a LISP compiler. Frustration with the project caused the two students to move in a new direction. They decided to write an image manipulation project in C. The result has quickly grown into a full-fledged image editing program. As of this writing, GIMP releases are being orchestrated by Manish Singh. You can find out more on the history, current status, and future of GIMP by going to *www.gimp.org*. You can also download your own copy of GIMP for Linux or for Windows from this Web site.

GIMP is a complete, fully functional graphics program. It is on a par with Adobe Photoshop and shares many features with that product. GIMP enables you to do professional-level graphics manipulation. It is ideal for a graphic artist, advertising professional, or any person that needs top-quality graphics. In this chapter we will examine using GIMP and walk you through the basics. If you followed the installation instruction in Chapter 2, "Installing Linux," then GIMP is already on your PC. If you did not, you can use the Packages option to add GIMP, or you can download it from the GIMP site.

GIMP BASICS

When you first launch GIMP, you will see a splash screen, shown in Figure 12.1. This screen is there to let you know the progress of GIMP in loading its various components and tools. How long this process takes depends on your computer.

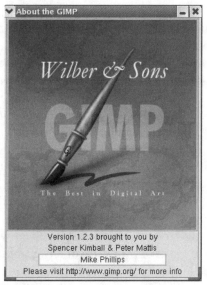

FIGURE 12.1 The GIMP splash screen.

However, even on slow computers it is usually less than one minute. Of course, if you have several applications running simultaneously, this will slow things down quite a bit.

Once the splash screen is done, you are shown a tip screen, depicted in Figure 12.2. There is a small check box on the bottom of this screen where you can elect to have tips show up at startup all the time. As a beginner it is probably a good idea to keep these tips showing. You will probably learn a lot about GIMP by reading these tips when learning GIMP. After you are more comfortable with GIMP, you can then decide to stop the tips from showing up every time you start GIMP.

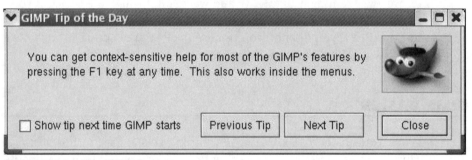

FIGURE 12.2   The GIMP tip screen.

Once GIMP is running and you have made it past the splash screen and tip screen, you should immediately notice one major difference between GIMP and Adobe Photoshop. Photoshop, shown in Figure 12.3, has all the various tools together on one screen.

GIMP has each set of tools in a separate window, shown in Figure 12.4. These windows can be moved or even closed in any manner you want. Some people find this layout a little confusing, but once you get used to it, you may come to realize that it provides you with a great deal of flexibility. You will find that many professional graphics programs choose this sort of layout. This is due to its flexibility. It enables the software user to place things in any way that he finds convenient.

In a single chapter we will not be able to make you a master of GIMP, and no book will be able to give you creativity or artistic talent if you happen to be lacking in that area. However, this chapter can provide you with a basic understanding of the tools available to you in GIMP. Even without artistic inclinations, a person with a firm grasp of the basics of any graphics tool can create some interesting and compelling images. The author is lacking in artistic talent but has been able to create interesting and exciting Web graphics using both Adobe Photoshop

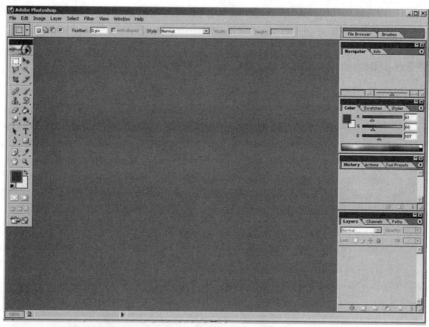

FIGURE 12.3   Adobe Photoshop.

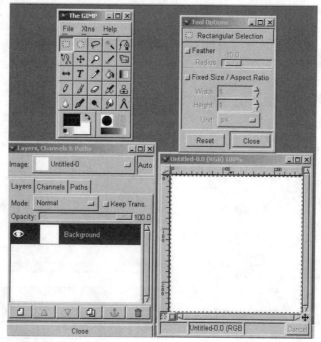

FIGURE 12.4   GIMP.

and GIMP. This means that even if you are not an artist, don't give up; you might find that GIMP gives you the right tools so you can at least fake it!

GIMP Drop-Down Menu

Let's begin our exploration of GIMP by examining the drop-down menu at the top. This is actually a good place to begin examining any software package you are new to. Usually the drop-down menu provides access to an application's core functionality. You will find many useful menu items here. Start with the File menu, shown in Figure 12.5a. As you can see, this menu offers some basics you probably expected, such as Open, Close, New, and Exit.

Most of these are standard menu options that you have undoubtably seen in countless applications, with both Microsoft Windows applications and Linux. The Open menu, however, will present a dialog box that looks just a little different from the one you may be used to in Microsoft Windows. This dialog box, shown in Figure 12.5b, works just like any other dialog box but has a slightly different look and feel than the standard Windows dialog box.

FIGURE 12.5A   The File menu.

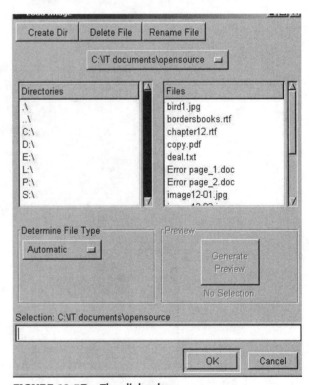

FIGURE 12.5B   The dialog box.

This menu also has a few items you might not be familiar with. The first is the Acquire menu, shown in Figure 12.6. This menu item is for acquiring images directly from some source, usually a device attached to your computer such as a scanner, Web cam, or digital camera. The sources include a screen shot of your current screen, the clipboard (items that were previously copied from some source), and a scanner you might have connected to your PC.

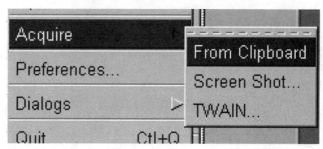

FIGURE 12.6   The Acquire menu.

After you start GIMP you will be working with either a new image or an existing image. The most common choice is to modify an existing image. Working with an existing image, you can alter and enhance that image, and very little artistic ability is required. To create an image completely from scratch requires a certain level of artistic competence. In this chapter we will concentrate on how you can alter existing images, with only moderate coverage of creating new images. This emphasis is because many readers lack the artistic skills to create images from scratch; as was previously mentioned, it is certain that the author is lacking in that regard!

To follow along with this chapter, you can open any image you like. In the figures in this book, you will see that we will be working with a picture of an eagle. But it should be stressed that for our purposes, any image will do. Our eagle image is shown in Figure 12.7.

Before we jump into all of those interesting-looking tools you see in your toolbox, we want to find out what we can do with this image by clicking a few options (without any artistic acumen at all). Don't worry, we will be experimenting with them in due course. But first, let's examine what you can do with a few quick clicks of your mouse. If you will right-click your mouse on the image, you will see a popup menu like the one shown in Figure 12.8. This pop-up menu gives you access to a lot of options that we will explore.

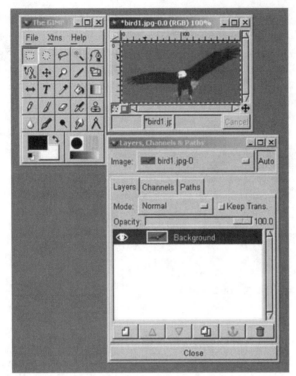

FIGURE 12.7 The sample image.

FIGURE 12.8
The pop-up menu.

As you can see, there are several options, and most of them have submenu items under them. That means that there is a lot to explore in this pop-up menu. The same functions you see in the pop-up menu are also available in Adobe Photoshop. However, in Photoshop they are available from the drop-down menu at the top of the screen. You will find that in many cases the menu items even have the same names. They are just in a different location. The first option, File, repeats what you found under the File menu. Once again we see an application giving you multiple avenues to the same functionality. This is common practice in any application whose aim is to be user friendly. The second option, Edit, shown in Figure 12.9, should also be familiar to you. Most of its options are standard to all Edit menus. You can cut, copy, paste, undo, and so on. There are only a few items that you may not have seen before, and their functions are obvious. For example, Fill with BG Color fills the entire image with whatever color it has in its background.

The next item on this pop-up menu may be quite new to you. It is the Select menu, shown in Figure 12.10. This menu enables you to take a selected portion of the image and invert it, grow it, and more. You also can choose to select the entire

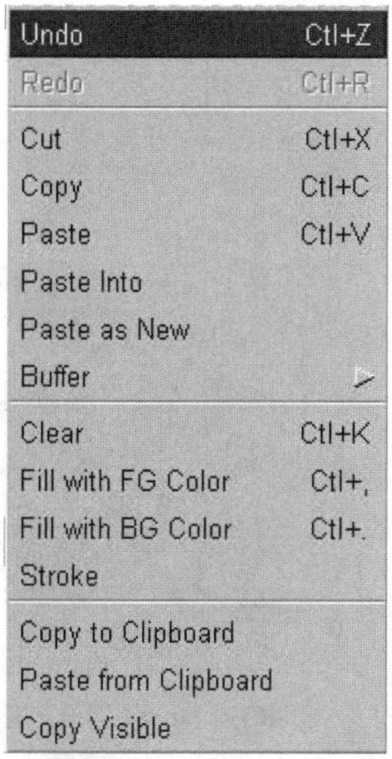

Undo	Ctl+Z
Redo	Ctl+R
Cut	Ctl+X
Copy	Ctl+C
Paste	Ctl+V
Paste Into	
Paste as New	
Buffer	▸
Clear	Ctl+K
Fill with FG Color	Ctl+,
Fill with BG Color	Ctl+.
Stroke	
Copy to Clipboard	
Paste from Clipboard	
Copy Visible	

FIGURE 12.9   The Edit menu.

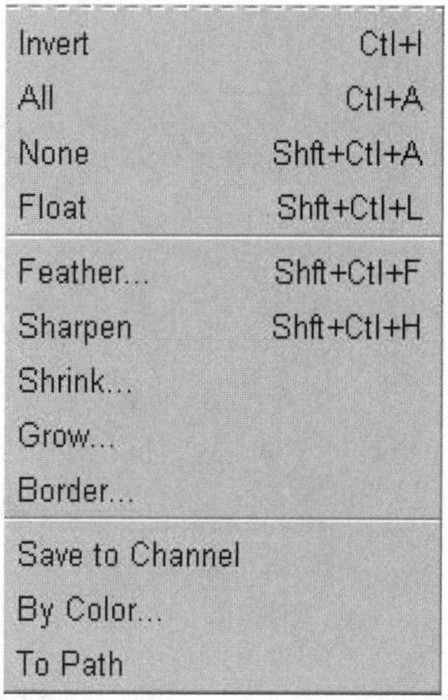

Invert	Ctl+I
All	Ctl+A
None	Shft+Ctl+A
Float	Shft+Ctl+L
Feather...	Shft+Ctl+F
Sharpen	Shft+Ctl+H
Shrink...	
Grow...	
Border...	
Save to Channel	
By Color...	
To Path	

FIGURE 12.10   The Select menu.

image or none of the image or invert your selection (select the area you did NOT drag your mouse around). In case you are wondering how to select an area of an image, the default tool for GIMP (and for Photoshop) is the Selection tool. Just drag your mouse anywhere around the image and it will draw a dotted-line rectangle. The area inside the rectangle is selected.

The View menu, shown in Figure 12.11, is also quite important. You can zoom in or out, turn the toolbars on or off, toggle the status bar on or off, and more. Often, people using a graphics application—GIMP, Photoshop, or some other program—find that zooming in enables them to make changes easier. They can then zoom back out to normal size when done making those changes.

Next we come to the Image menu, shown in Figure 12.12. This menu enables you to change the image itself in a number of interesting ways. The Image Mode, the first option you have, determines if this image is RGB (Red Green Blue), which is how JPEG and bitmap images are, or indexed, which is how GIF images are. This is actually quite important. It is not at all uncommon for people using graphics applications to want to change an image from one type to another. This can be done for many reasons. It is common on Web pages to want the smallest image possible. That is usually a JPEG. Any image that is a GIF or BMP file, when converted to a JPEG, will be significantly smaller. In order to change an image, you must first make certain that its mode is correct. You cannot save an image as a JPEG if its mode is not RGB. In many cases you can change the mode of the image, thus enabling you to save the image as a different file format. The

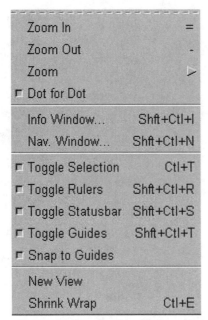

FIGURE 12.11   The View menu.

FIGURE 12.12   The Image menu.

Decompose option enables you to extract layers from the image. A layer is when you have sections that were pasted into your current image. These different sections are layers. This is a task that the casual user will not likely perform, but one a graphics designer might use quite frequently.

Next we come to the Layers menu, seen in Figure 12.13. This menu enables you to work with the various layers in your image. As we previously mentioned, when you copy and paste image fragments from different images into a single image, you have layers. Each image that is brought in is in its own layer. The Layers menu enables you to work with these layers.

The Tools menu, shown in Figure 12.14, gives you access to the same tools found in the Toolbox. After we have worked with the Toolbox, if you find you prefer using the drop-down menu, you can use this menu item to accomplish most of the tasks you would otherwise use the Toolbox for. We will skip examining the use of tools for now and return to that topic when we examine the Toolbox.

The Dialogs menu enables you to select patterns, gradients, and brushes. For example, when you look under Dialog and select Brushes, you see the screen in Figure 12.15. You have quite a range of options in selecting your Brush settings before you begin painting. We will examine brushes in more detail when we get to the Toolbox.

FIGURE 12.13   The Layers menu.

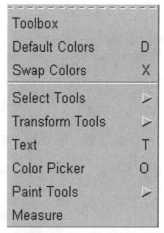

FIGURE 12.14   The Tools menu.

Now to the Filters menu. This menu, shown in Figure 12.16, is full of very interesting filters you can apply to your images. These filters enable you to alter the appearance of your image completely and radically. You have access to everything from blur effects to artistic effects. We will examine a few of them here, but it is highly recommended that you take some time to see what each of the filters looks like. That way you can become more familiar with the images and discover which ones you find particularly attractive.

These filters provide a very easy to use method to add an artistic flair to any image. With the simple click of a mouse, you can add very interesting effects to your images. Filters are also used frequently with Adobe Photoshop. In Photoshop you will find them on the drop-down menu under Filters.

Let's take a look at a few of the filters and see what they can do for our eagle image. Let's begin with one of the artistic filters, cubism. You go to Filters, select Artistic, and choose Cubism. You are presented with a screen, shown in Figure 12.17, enabling you to alter the parameters of this filter. For our example, we will use the default settings, and we produce the image shown in Figure 12.18.

As you can see, an artistic filter makes it quite easy to add a very interesting flair to any image. There are other artistic filters, including the Van Goh filter and the Oilify filter. The Oilify filter changes your image so that it looks like an oil painting. Figure 12.19 shows our image after the Oilify filter has been applied.

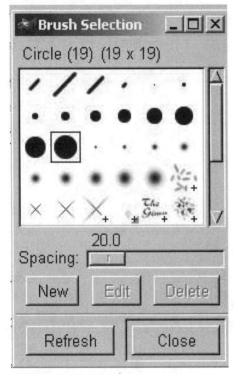

FIGURE 12.15 Brushes.

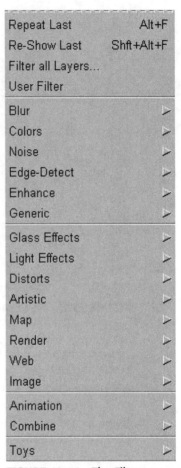

FIGURE 12.16 The Filters menu.

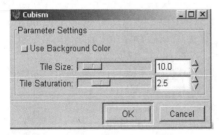

FIGURE 12.17 The Cubism filter settings.

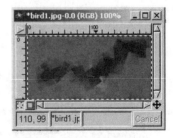

FIGURE 12.18 The Cubism filter applied to our eagle.

FIGURE 12.19   The Oilify filter.

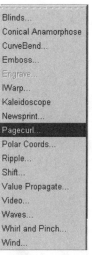

FIGURE 12.20   The Distort menu.

FIGURE 12.21   The Ripple effect.

Another interesting set of filters is found under the Distort menu, shown in Figure 12.20. You can add some pretty dramatic effects to any image. Some of your choices are the Ripple, IWarp, and Emboss effects. Figure 12.21 shows our image, this time with the Ripple effect.

It should be clear that filters are a very powerful way to alter any image. You can create some startling effects in your pictures with the filter effects. One popular way to use these is to scan in a photo of some person and render it as an Oil Painting or some other effect. You can really jazz up old family photos with a scanner and GIMP. The filters we mentioned are just a few of those available with GIMP. Even a cursory glance at the toolbar will show you several other filters. Which filters should be used is purely a matter of personal taste.

THE TOOLBOX

One problem with the effects we have examined is that they apply to the entire image. They don't enable you to pick and choose what you want to alter. For this or for the creation of new images, we need to take a look at the GIMP Toolbox, shown in Figure 12.22. You can see that it is not very different from the Photoshop toolbox shown in Figure 12.23.

The first two tools, shown in Figure 12.24, are Selection tools. They enable you to select a portion of your image. You can then cut that portion, copy it, fill it in, or

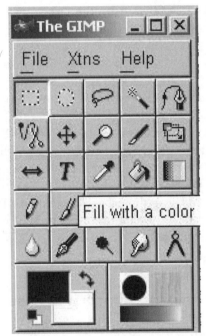

FIGURE 12.22 The GIMP Toolbox.

FIGURE 12.23 The Photoshop toolbox.

in some cases apply a filter to just that portion. The first Selection tool selects rectangular sections, and the second tool selects elliptical sections. You click on the tool you want, then drag your mouse across the image to select a region.

FIGURE 12.24
Selection tools.

FIGURE 12.25 More
selection tools.

FIGURE 12.26 The
Move, Zoom, and
Crop tools.

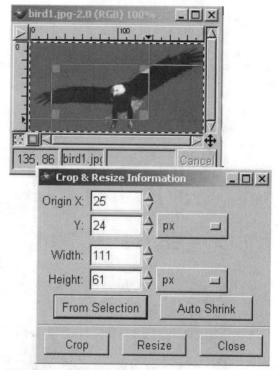

FIGURE 12.27 Cropping an image.

The third tool is also a Selection tool. However, it does freehand selection. You click on the tool and then draw with your mouse around the region you want to select. This tool is very useful for those with an artistic leaning, but perhaps not as useful for those of us who have some difficulty drawing.

The next three tools are all also selection tools. These three, shown in Figure 12.25, are quite a bit more complicated. They enable you to select contiguous regions, regions defined by curves, and shapes. These tools are probably not for the beginner.

The next three tools, shown in Figure 12.26, are very interesting. These enable you to move, zoom, or crop your image. The Move tool is rather simple. If you have pasted in an image, perhaps one cut or copied from another image, you can move it around until it is where you want. The second tool enables you to zoom in on an area of your image. If you are touching up an image, it is often a good idea to zoom in to do so.

The third tool, the Crop tool, is a little more complex. After you select this tool and drag across a region of your image, you will see something like what is shown in Figure 12.27. You can now choose to crop the image so that only the area that is selected remains. You also can resize your image. Then the entire image will remain, but it will shrink to the size of the region you have selected.

The next tool enables you to rotate your image in any fashion you wish. Our image is shown with the Rotation tool in Figure 12.28.

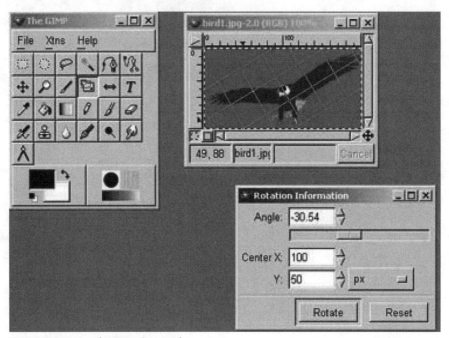

FIGURE 12.28 The Rotation tool.

The next tool, shown in Figure 12.29 is the Flip tool. It enables you to flip your image.

FIGURE 12.29
The Flip tool.

The next tool is very useful. It is the Text tool. This tool is used to add text to your image. When you use this tool and click on your image, you will be presented with a screen much like the one shown in Figure 12.30. The Font tab on this screen

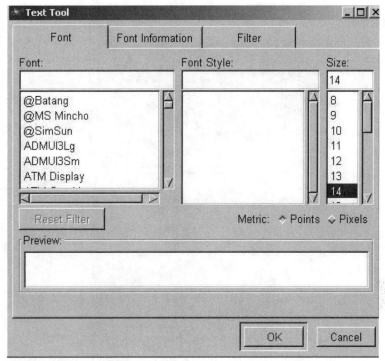

FIGURE 12.30 Using the Text tool.

enables you to select the font and font size. The Font Information tab gives information about the font. This may seem a bit odd, but graphics professionals often want rather in-depth information about the fonts they use. Remember that GIMP is designed to be a useful tool for the graphics professional as well as the casual home user. The Filter tab enables you to make the font bold, italic, and so on.

Once you have chosen your settings, you enter the text you want. This brings us to the next tool, which is a very important tool. It is the Eyedropper tool. Anyone who has used Photoshop has probably used this tool. When you use the Eyedropper, you place it over a portion of the image and click, as shown in Figure 12.31. You will have the exact color of that portion of the image and can use that color with any paint tools. Basically this tool enables you to match the exact color of some portion of your image so that you can do touchups with a matching color.

The next two tools, shown in Figure 12.32, enable you to use the currently selected color (perhaps one you got with the Eyedropper) and either splash an entire area with that color (using the Paint Bucket tool) or paint a background that color.

FIGURE 12.31 The Eyedropper tool.

FIGURE 12.32
The Paint Bucket and
Background tools.

While we are on the topic of color selection, it is a good time to point out that you can select the color for any painting tool by using the squares at the bottom-left side. Click on the square, and you are presented with the Color Selection screen shown in Figure 12.33, where you can select the color for that tool to paint with. This is exactly the same way Adobe Photoshop does color selection.

Selecting colors brings us to painting and drawing with those colors, and the next four tools, shown in Figure 12.34, enable us to do this. Each of these tools is used freehand. Drag your mouse, and you are drawing. The first is the Pencil tool and draws a thin line. The Paint tool will make strokes in the same manner as a paint brush would.

It is important to remember that you can change the settings for the pencil, paint brush, or eraser. If you go to File, select Dialogs, and choose Brushes, you will

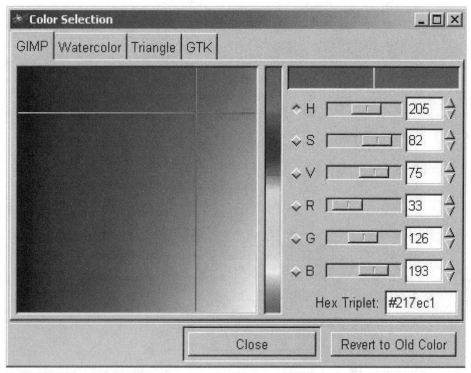

FIGURE 12.33 Selecting colors.

FIGURE 12.34 The Pencil,
Paint, Erase, and Airbrush tools.

be presented with a screen like the one shown in Figure 12.35, where you can select the type of strokes you want your tool to make.

The third tool is the Erase tool. It erases something you have previously drawn. Then we come to the Airbrush tool. The Airbrush tool acts like a conventional airbrush, appearing to blow the paint onto the image. You can set it by going to File, selecting Dialogs, and choosing Tool Options, after selecting the Airbrush, of course. This dialog box is shown in Figure 12.36. As you can see, it is easy to change the pressure and the opacity of the airbrush. These are probably the two most important properties when airbrushing.

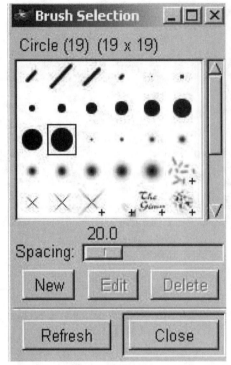

FIGURE 12.35 Brush stroke settings.

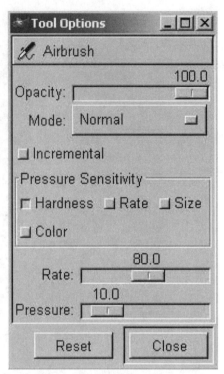

FIGURE 12.36 The Airbrush properties.

The Tool Options window is one that works with any tool. You will get different settings for different tools.

Next is the Clone tool. It appears as a rubber stamp in the Toolbox. This tool works exactly the same as the Clone tool found in Adobe Photoshop. You use it to copy a section of an image to another place. You clone a portion of an image. This is very useful for restoring old photographs .

Next we come to the Blur tool. This tool can be used to blur or sharpen an image or a section of an image. The Tool Options for this tool are shown in Figure 12.37.

The last four tools, shown in Figure 12.38, are pretty simple. The first draws in ink. It is much like the Pencil, Paintbrush, and Airbrush tools. The next tool, the Burn tool, is used to burn off shaded or dark areas. This can be especially useful in restoring scanned photographs. The Smudge tool does exactly what its name suggests, it smudges an area of a picture. The Measure tool is used to measure the distance between points on your image.

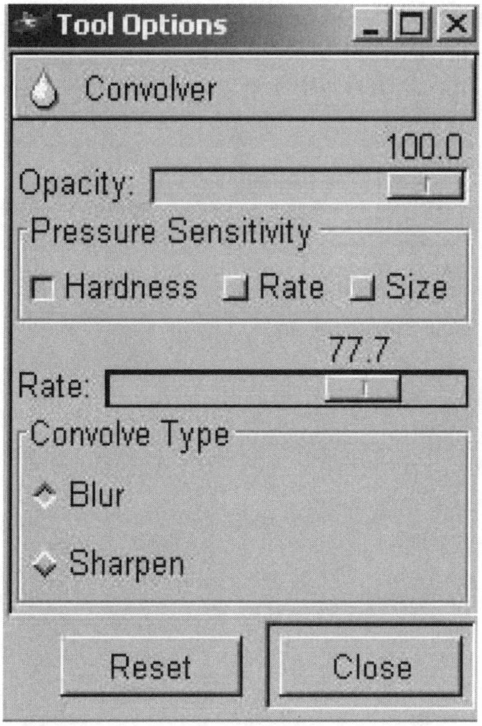

FIGURE 12.37 The Blur tool.

FIGURE 12.38 The Ink, Burn, Smudge, and Measure tools.

As you can see, GIMP offers you a full range of functional and artistic graphics tools. It gives you virtually every option that Photoshop does, but it is free of charge. One area that Photoshop does surpass GIMP in is add-ons. You can find a number of add-on utilities for Photoshop that enable you to do even more with it. Unfortunately, there are almost no such add-ons for GIMP.

SUMMARY

In this chapter, we examined the GIMP software packages. If you are an experienced Adobe Photoshop user, then you should master GIMP in very little time. Even if you are not experienced with packages like Photoshop, this chapter should provide you with the essential skills you need to perform significant graphic manipulation on any image. We have discussed the use of the various drop-down menus, tools, and the Toolbox. Each of these tools has been shown and its basic use explained. At this point you should be comfortable working with GIMP. The only thing you need now is some practice with GIMP and a bit of creative flair.

REVIEW QUESTIONS

1. What does GIMP stand for?
2. What does the Oilify filter do?
3. What does the Freehand selection tool do?
4. What does the Eyedropper do?
5. How do you change settings for the Airbrush tool?
6. What tools does the Tool Options dialog work with?
7. What are the two most important properties when airbrushing?
8. What is the purpose of the Clone tool?

13

Web Browsers, E-Mail, and Internet Applications

In This Chapter

- IP Addresses and the Web
- Web Browsers
- E-Mail
- FTP Client
- Chat

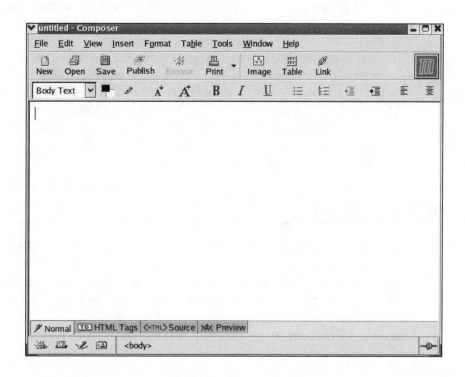

INTRODUCTION

In an earlier chapter we discussed briefly the basics of using Mozilla and Evolution for Web browsing and e-mail, respectively. In this chapter we are going to examine several different Web utilities in depth. It is hoped that after completing this chapter, you will be comfortable using the various Linux Web utilities you have available to you. The Internet is one of the primary reasons why many people get a home computer. Fortunately, Linux ships with all the applications needed to use all aspects of the Internet.

IP ADDRESSES AND THE WEB

As we delve into Web-based applications in this and subsequent chapters, you will need to understand how things are organized and located on the Internet. Everything on the Internet must eventually be located via what is called an IP address. To quote from Webopedia, a very popular online resource at *www.Webopedia.com/ TERM/I/IP_address.html*, "An identifier for a computer or device on a TCP/IP network. Networks using the TCP/IP protocol route messages based on the IP address of the destination. The format of an IP address is a 32-bit numeric address written as four numbers separated by periods. Each number can be 0 to 255. For example, 1.160.10.240 could be an IP address."

An IP address is a way of locating a particular machine. There are four numbers separated by periods. Each of the four numbers can be from zero to 255. When you type in a Web address such as *www.chuckeasttom.com*, that name is translated into the appropriate IP address. This is important to realize because as we discuss Web applications in this chapter, and then in later chapters we discuss various network utilities, Web servers, and more, you will need to know what is meant by an IP address.

WEB BROWSERS

Let's face it, most people want to surf the Web! It is a fact of modern life. Whether for entertainment, education, research, or commerce, the Web is where it is at. Your computer would not be worth much to you if you couldn't get on the Internet. We will first take a look at some commonly used Linux browsers. We will spend a little more time going into more depth with the Mozilla browser and also look at a few others.

Mozilla

First you may want a little background about Mozilla. Obviously it is a Web browser, but how did it start, what is its purpose, etc.? Mozilla is an outgrowth of development on the Netscape Communicator browser, which you may have used in Windows. This explains why so much of Mozilla is strikingly similar to Netscape. Mozilla is essentially a project to continue Netscape Communicator as an open source browser. The project has been continued by employees of Netscape, Red Hat, other companies, and contributors from the open source developer community. Since some Red Hat employees actually devote some time to Mozilla, you can see why it figures so prominently in the Red Hat Linux distribution.

The Mozilla project began when the Netscape Navigator 4.x series of browsers was coming to an end. The original plan was to stabilize the code and release version 5.0. This plan changed when it was decided that more ambitious changes were ready for release. This led to a divergence between Netscape and the Mozilla browser. They still have very strong similarities. Netscape 6.0 and above are based on the same source code as the Mozilla browser.

Now that you have a little background, let's take a look at the Mozilla browser. If you will recall, you need to go the Start menu and select Internet. You should see a menu much like what is shown in Figure 13.1. We will be examining many of these applications in this chapter, including some under the Other Internet Applications option. But we will start with Mozilla.

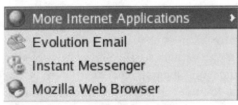

FIGURE 13.1 Internet applications.

Once you have launched Mozilla, you will see the familiar Mozilla opening screen shown in Figure 13.2. You should notice that when you install Mozilla as part of the Red Hat Linux distribution, the default home page of Mozilla is the Red Hat information page. It might be a good idea to review this page a little.

If you will recall, we discussed Mozilla earlier in this book. However, at that time you were given just enough information to get you up and running. In this chapter we will systematically examine Mozilla, giving you a much more in-depth look at it. We will begin by taking a look at each of the drop-down menus

FIGURE 13.2 Mozilla.

and examining their menu items. Let's get started looking at the File menu, shown in Figure 13.3.

The first menu item under the File menu is New. The submenu is shown in Figure 13.4. As the name suggests, this menu item is for creating new things. The first thing you can do under this menu is to create a new Navigator window. Remember that Mozilla and Netscape Navigator are very closely related. With that fact in mind, you can probably guess that a new Navigator window means a new browser window. That way you can look at more than one Web site at a time. You can do the same thing with Internet Explorer by going to File and selecting New, then choosing New Window.

The other options under New enable you to create a new message, address card, or composer page. A message means an e-mail message. Mozilla, like Netscape Navigator, incorporates e-mail functionality. If you select this option, you can create and send e-mail messages from inside Mozilla. The first time you try this option, you will start a wizard that will walk you through the steps of setting up an e-mail account. We will walk through that now, setting up the e-mail account for the author (without the real password of course!). The first page of the wizard,

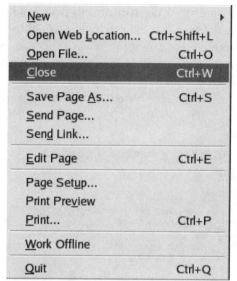

New	▶
Open Web Location...	Ctrl+Shift+L
Open File...	Ctrl+O
Close	Ctrl+W
Save Page As...	Ctrl+S
Send Page...	
Send Link...	
Edit Page	Ctrl+E
Page Setup...	
Print Preview	
Print...	Ctrl+P
Work Offline	
Quit	Ctrl+Q

FIGURE 13.3   The File menu.

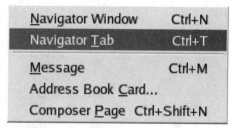

Navigator Window	Ctrl+N
Navigator Tab	Ctrl+T
Message	Ctrl+M
Address Book Card...	
Composer Page	Ctrl+Shift+N

FIGURE 13.4   The New menu.

shown in Figure 13.5, asks whether you are setting up an e-mail account or a newsgroup account. Since newsgroups are less commonly used, we will concentrate on the e-mail account setup.

However, many readers may not know what a newsgroup is. A newsgroup is basically a worldwide bulletin board. Before the Web was popular, newsgroups

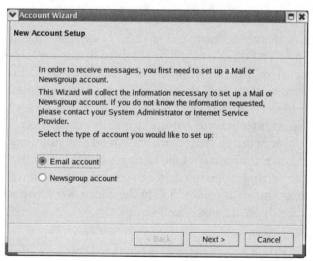

FIGURE 13.5   Screen one of Mozilla's e-mail setup wizard.

were used by people at universities and research institutes to post, read, and respond to messages. Today there are thousands of newsgroups devoted to virtually every topic imaginable. You can access these newsgroups via your Web browser through various sites that act as portals to the newsgroups. Perhaps the most widely known such portal is *www.dejanews.com*.

The next screen, shown in Figure 13.6, has you enter your name and e-mail address.

FIGURE 13.6   Name and e-mail address.

The next screen, shown in Figure 13.7, asks you to enter the server names for your e-mail servers. This would be obtained from your Internet service provider or e-mail provider. Remember that POP is short for Post Office Protocol, and it is the protocol used to retrieve e-mail. SMTP stands for Simple Mail Transfer Protocol and is used to send e-mail.

The next three screens require very little explanation. They simply ask you to confirm your name, the name you wish to refer to this e-mail account by, and then you are shown a summary of the settings you have chosen and you can go forward or back and change something. When you are done, you will be taken to the new e-mail screen, shown in Figure 13.8. In the future, when you select New Message, you will go directly to the new e-mail screen.

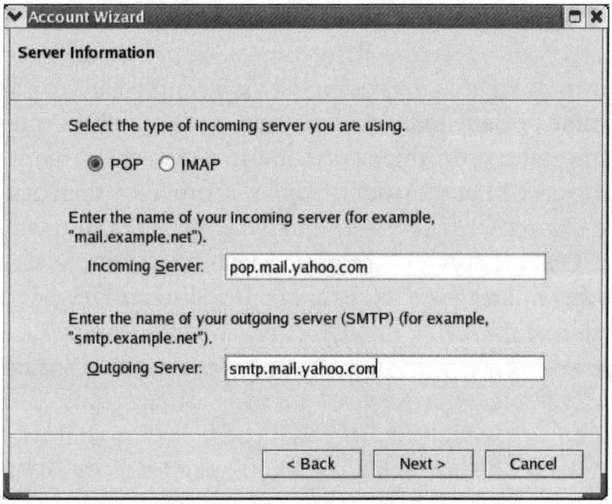

FIGURE 13.7   Setting up your e-mail servers.

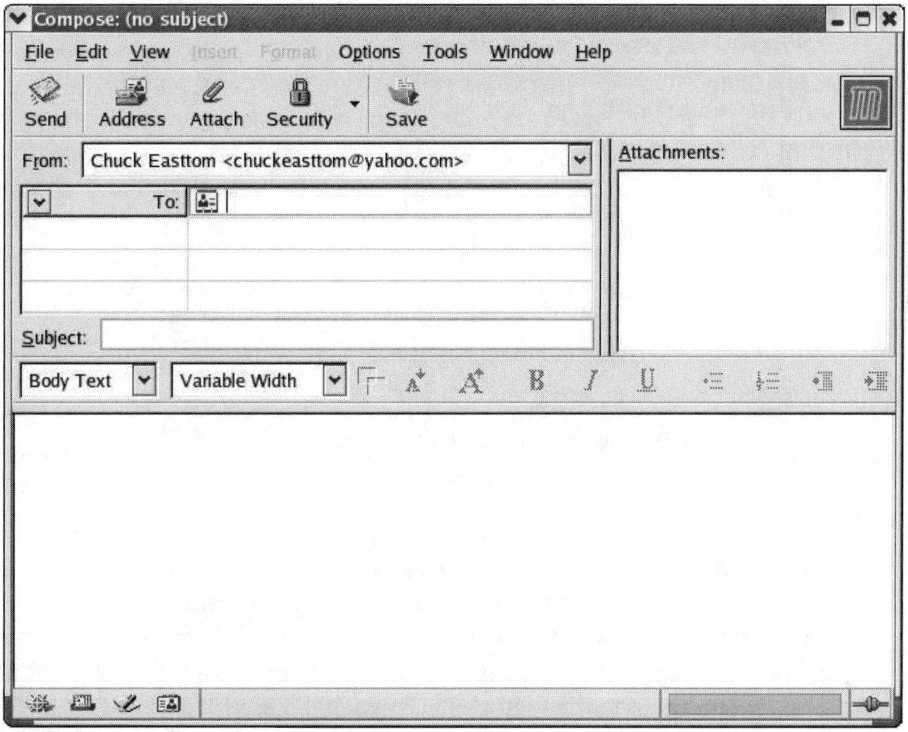

FIGURE 13.8   A new e-mail message.

Also under New you will see New Composer Page. This item is very interesting. When you choose this item you will be presented with a screen much like the one shown in Figure 13.9. Composer is a simple HTML editor, much like the one we examined briefly just a few chapters ago. It enables you to place text, graphics, links, and more onto the document, in much the same way as you would place them into a word processor document. Composer then generates the HTML code for you. Composer is also found in Netscape Communicator. While it will not do advanced HTML for you, it will do most of the basic Web page items such as text formatting, links, tables, and images. It is also remarkably easy to use.

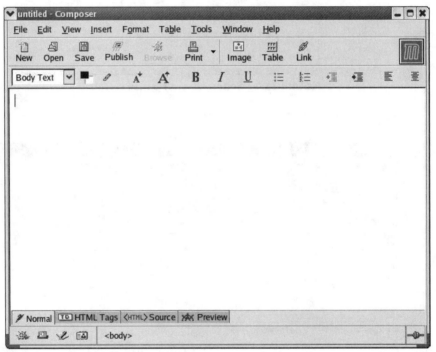

FIGURE 13.9   The Composer screen.

The rest of the options you see under File are fairly standard. There are options to save, open, close, or print Web page documents. Save, open, close, and print are common items found under the File menu in a great many applications. Their functionality is rather obvious and does not require in-depth explanation. Of course, the Exit option is common to all applications, and also has a rather obvious function.

This brings us to the Edit menu, shown in Figure 13.10. The Edit menu is much like any other Edit menu you might find in any other application. It enables you to copy, paste, cut, select, and so on. Some of these functions will not work on many

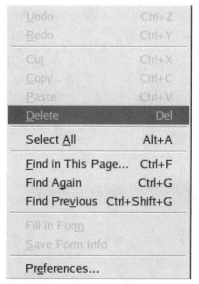

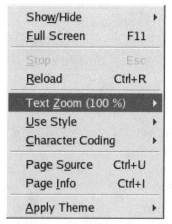

FIGURE 13.10   The Edit menu.   **FIGURE 13.11**   The View menu.

Web pages. For example, you cannot cut something from a Web site unless it is a value in Web form.

Remember that in an earlier chapter we discussed the Preferences option found under the Edit menu. This is one area that we examined when you were first introduced to Mozilla. These preferences enable you to set items such as the proxy server that you are using, if you are using one. You can also set up your home page here, which is the starting page that will appear when the browser launches.

The next menu is the View menu, shown in Figure 13.11. This menu enables you to zoom in or out on portions of a Web site, and it also enables you to choose which toolbars you want to be visible. If, later in this chapter we mention a toolbar that you do not see on your Mozilla browser, go to View and choose Show/Hide; you will be able to bring that toolbar back into view.

One option under this menu that might not be self explanatory is the Reload option. This behaves exactly like the Refresh option found in Internet Explorer. The purpose of this button is to query the Web site and make sure we have loaded the most recent version of the Web page. There are several different reasons why your browser might display an earlier version of a Web page rather than the latest. One reason is caching. Many browsers can be set up to cache Web pages. This means that when you visit a Web site, the pages are downloaded to your computer. Next time you visit that site, you will see the cached version. The browser only periodically checks to see if there is a newer version. This causes Web pages that you visit frequently to load much faster. However, it can mean that you are not seeing the very latest version of that Web page, particularly with Web pages that are changed frequently.

Now we come to the Go menu, shown in Figure 13.12. This menu is used to direct your browser to go to some other site. The first option is Home, which will cause your browser to go to the home site designated for your browser. You can also go to the Red Hat welcome page. This is very useful because that page has a lot of information that can be quite helpful to a novice Linux user.

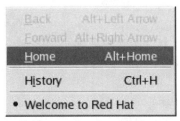

FIGURE 13.12 The Go menu.

We have not yet discussed the other option under the Go menu, the option of History. History is a list of the last several Web sites you have visited. This can be quite useful if you remember finding an interesting Web page a few days ago but did not bookmark the page and don't remember how you got to that site initially. When you select History, you will be presented with a screen much like the one shown in Figure 13.13. Of course, yours will probably have several sites you have visited; this one does not, since it is a fresh install of Mozilla specifically for the purpose of writing this book.

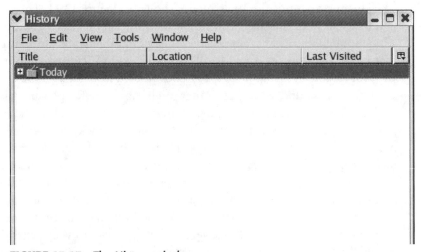

FIGURE 13.13 The History window.

Notice that the history is divided into the actual days when the Web site was visited. This can be extremely helpful in retracing your steps to an interesting Web page. This brings us to the Bookmark menu, shown in Figure 13.14. This menu is essentially the same thing as Favorites in Microsoft's Internet Explorer. It enables your Web browser to remember the address of any Web site you visit. When you visit a Web site you like, go to the Bookmark menu and select Add Bookmark.

FIGURE 13.14 The Bookmark menu.

After surfing the Net a while, you could end up with lot of bookmarks. It can become quite difficult to find one when you want it. If you go to the Manage Bookmark option, you will see a screen much like the one shown in Figure 13.15. This screen enables you to organize your bookmarks. You can create new folders and organize your bookmarks by subject matter. You also can delete bookmarks from here.

FIGURE 13.15 Managing bookmarks.

The next menu may be the most important one in Mozilla. It is certainly the most complex. This is the Tools menu, shown in Figure 13.16. There is a similar menu found in Internet Explorer. The first option does not require any explanation because it searches the Web as its title suggests.

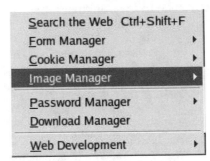

FIGURE 13.16   The Tools menu.

The rest of the options under Tools are managers for various functions you may encounter when visiting a particular Web site. For example, on some Web pages you will fill out forms with some sort of information. Form Manager enables you to customize that experience.

The next option, Cookie Manager, is of far more importance to the average user. First let's define exactly what a cookie is. When you visit some Web pages, they will gather information about you. It could be information you fill out on a form or information that can be gathered by your connection to that Web site. Information in the latter category would include the operating system you are using, type of Web browser, your IP address, e-mail address, and more. That information is then stored on a small file on your computer. When you visit that Web site again or another Web site that is designed to work with the first Web site, that information is read back. This means that information about your activities on the Web can be tracked, and a small amount of personal data about you can be tracked. This all occurs behind the scenes, so you don't see it happen. If you have ever been to a Web site that remembers you, you have been to a site that uses cookies. The Cookie Manager enables you to alter the way your browser works with cookies.

You can choose the option of Block Cookies From This Site, and your machine will no longer accept cookies from the Web site you are currently viewing. Of more use is the Cookie Manager, shown in Figure 13.17. With this utility you can view what is stored in cookies already on your machine. You can then block further cookies from that site, delete the cookies, or leave them. In short, Mozilla puts you in control of the cookies your machine accepts and how it processes them.

The Image Manager enables you to do almost the same things with images that you do with cookies using the Cookie Manager. The Download Manager, the next

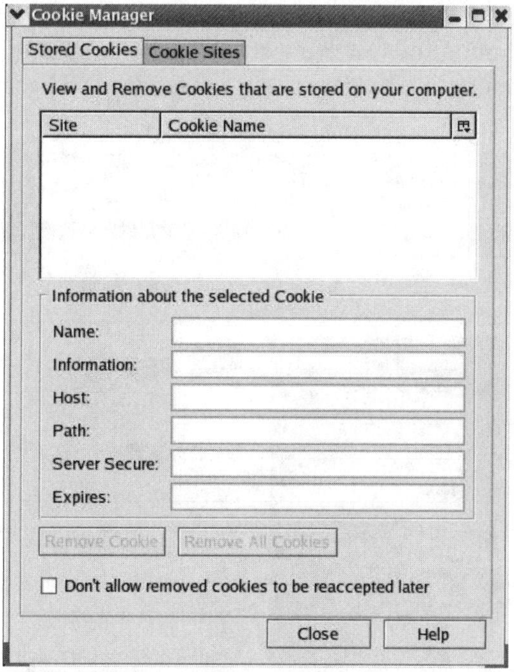

FIGURE 13.17   Cookie Manager.

tool, is quite useful because it enables you to see a list of everything the browser has downloaded from the Web, when they were downloaded, and from what site. This can be very important, especially if you find you have downloaded something that has harmed your computer.

In essence, this is Mozilla. The various buttons on the toolbar enable you to move forward and backward, reload the current page, and accomplish the most basic Web browsing functions. You can see that Mozilla is a full-featured Web browser that should meet all of your needs.

Konqueror

If you look under the Other Internet Applications submenu, you will find yet another browser, the Konqueror browser, shown in Figure 13.18. This browser's drop-down menu is almost identical to the one in Mozilla, with just a few exceptions. The first is that what Mozilla and Internet Explorer refer to as the File menu, Konqueror refers to as the Location menu. The name is different but the functionality is the same. The Edit, Go, View, and Bookmark menus are essentially the same as the ones found in Mozilla.

Where we begin to notice real differences between Konqueror and Mozilla is under the Tool menu, shown in Figure 13.19. Before we explore these differences, recall that we have seen several applications, including the File Manager, that behave much like a Web browser. They have browser-like navigation, bookmarks, and other things common to Web browsers. All these applications used the Konqueror Web browser interface. That is why they all looked and behaved so similarly.

FIGURE 13.18   The Konqueror Web browser.

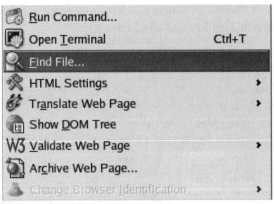

FIGURE 13.19   The Tools menu.

Some of these Tools options might look a bit confusing. That is to be expected because several of them are not really related to Web browsing. Remember that Konqueror can be used to browse the directories and files on your machine as well. The first option under Tools, the Run Command option, enables you to literally execute any shell command you might want. Type it in, and it will execute. If you are used to Windows 2000 or Windows XP, you may have seen something similar when you launch the Start menu and see the Run option.

The next option, Open Terminal, does just that. It opens a terminal or shell. If you need to access a shell quickly, it's right there for you. The Find option, next, is probably of more common use. This screen is much like the Search option in Windows 2000 or Windows XP. The other options past this, such as HTML Settings and Validate Web, are of use to Web developers who want to either fine-tune their Web surfing or check out the validity of Web code on a particular Web site. The basic functionality of Konqueror is much like any other Web browser.

E-MAIL

In a previous chapter we took a brief look at the Evolution e-mail client. In this chapter we will look a little deeper at exactly what e-mail is, take a second look at Evolution, and briefly look at KMail. Our previous examination of Evolution was designed to get you up and running quickly and was not overly thorough.

First we should define what e-mail is. It is actually older than Web pages. E-mail was originally meant to send plain text messages asynchronously. Asynchronously simply means that the two users do not need to be online at the same time, as they do with chatting. One person sends a text message to another, and the recipient can view it at his leisure. In time, e-mail grew and incorporated the kind of word processing features you might expect in KWrite or Word. You could also send pictures and attachments. Now e-mail is a major form of communication for many people, including the author (who welcomes e-mail from readers at *chuckeasttom@yahoo.com*)!

E-mail, like all computer communication, is accomplished via the use of specific communication protocols. These protocols determine how computers will communicate in order to transmit the data. We have already discussed that e-mail is sent using Simple Mail Transfer Protocol, or SMTP, and received using POP3, or Post Office Protocol Version 3. The items you might attach to an e-mail, such as documents and pictures, are handled by yet another protocol. That protocol is MIME, or Multipurpose Internet Mail Extension.

You need a few things to use e-mail. First you must have an e-mail server. That is usually set up by your Internet service provider or at the company where you work. Next, just as with regular mail, you need a valid e-mail address to send it to, and a valid return address. Finally, you need a properly configured e-mail client.

Evolution

In an earlier chapter, we took a brief look at the Evolution e-mail client, shown in Figure 13.20. We went through the initial wizard to set up your e-mail connection and got you ready to send and receive e-mail. In this chapter we will explore this topic in a bit more depth, as we did with Mozilla. We will not walk through the wizard again. It is relatively self explanatory, and we covered it earlier.

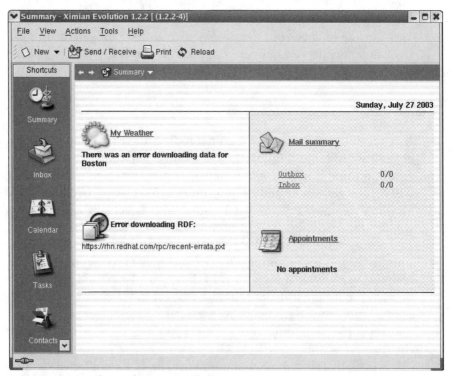

FIGURE 13.20 The Evolution e-mail client.

If you look on the toolbar at the left side, you will see Inbox, Calendar, and Contact List. This is the same basic functionality you find with Microsoft Outlook. The Inbox contains your incoming mail. It is relatively simple. Messages are in the box, and you can double-click one to open it, and you can reply to it, close it, or delete.

The Calendar, shown in Figure 13.21, is a very interesting tool. It is something that both Outlook and Evolution share, but many other e-mail applications may lack. In the main window you see the schedule for a given day. In the upper-right corner you see a monthly calendar that you can alter. If you use the arrow keys at the top of the calendar, you can change months and then double-click on any day to bring that day's schedule into the main window.

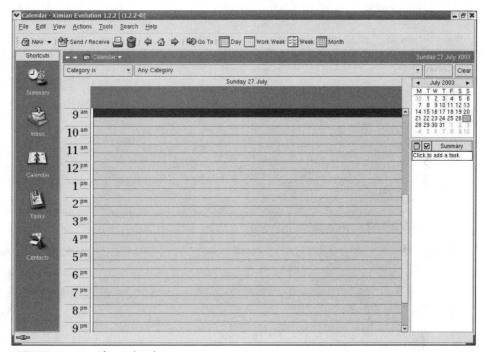

FIGURE 13.21   The Calendar screen.

When you find a timeslot where you want to schedule something, you double-click on it. You will be presented with the screen you see in Figure 13.22. Here you can enter details about the appointment and even schedule Evolution to give you a reminder when the time for that appointment is approaching. This functionality is virtually identical to the calendar in Outlook, so longtime Microsoft Office users should have no trouble adjusting to the Evolution calendar.

Next we will direct our attention to the Contact Manager option, shown in Figure 13.23. This operates very much like Microsoft Outlook. When you open it, all of your contacts are displayed in a vertical list. You also can use the small drop-down box to select only contacts who meet some criteria. This is especially useful if you have a lot of contacts in your list.

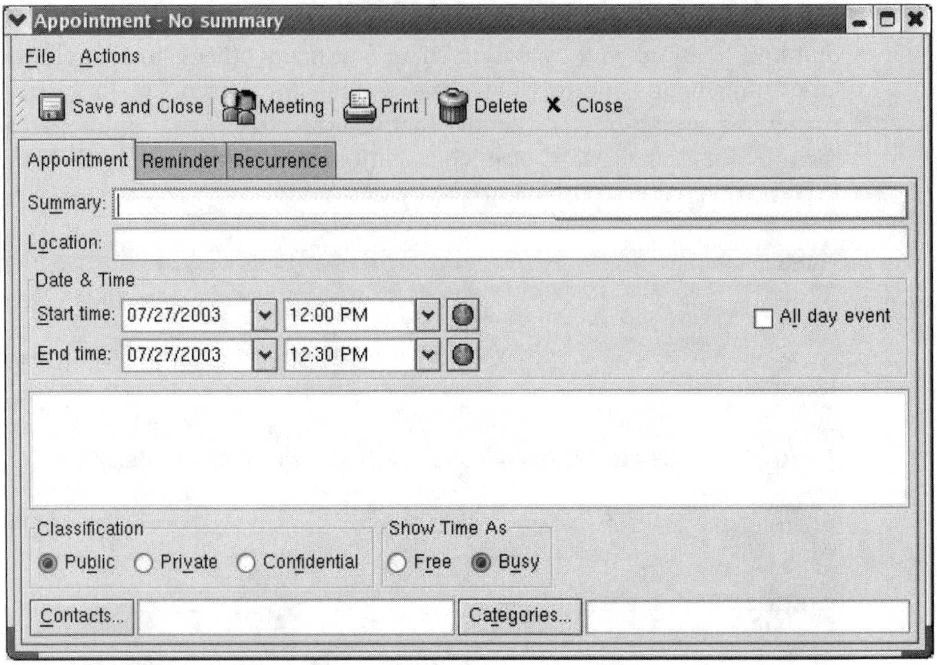

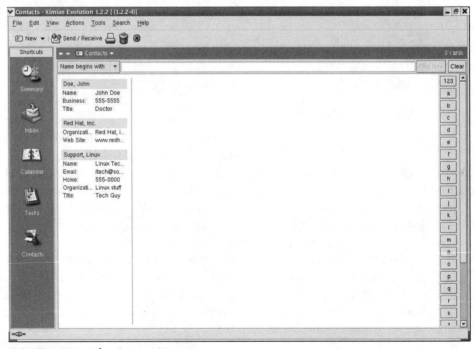

FIGURE 13.22 The Calendar.

FIGURE 13.23 The Contact Manager.

Now let's direct our attention back to some of the various functions you find in the drop-down menu and toolbar of Evolution. You may want to change back to the Inbox to do this. First let's talk about making new items. You can either use the File menu and choose New or you can click on the button labeled New in the toolbar. In either case you will end up at a screen much like the one shown in Figure 13.24.

From here you can create a new e-mail message, a new contact item for your Contact List, a new appointment, or even a new folder. The folder is really important. After a time your Inbox might become quite full. There may be e-mail messages you don't want to discard, but which are crowding your Inbox. You can create folders and move your messages into these folders, thus keeping them organized.

The Edit menu, shown in Figure 13.25, enables you to do the basic text editing functions you have become accustomed to. This includes Select All, Copy, Cut, Paste, and so on. It also has a few options for actions that are strictly e-mail related. You can mark your messages. You can mark them as having been read, unread, important, and others. This is another function that is virtually identical to Microsoft Outlook.

FIGURE 13.24 The New menu.

FIGURE 13.25 The Edit menu.

The View menu is relatively straightforward. It enables you to select what you want to view in the main window. The next really interesting menu is the Action menu, shown in Figure 13.26. The very first action shown is quite important. It enables you to direct Evolution to send any messages waiting to go out and to contact

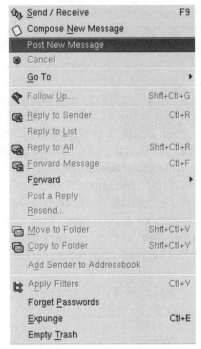

FIGURE 13.26 The Action menu.

your e-mail server to retrieve any incoming messages. You can also accomplish this by using the Send/Receive button on the toolbar. Of equal importance is the Empty Trash option at the bottom. This will empty Trash, which is the folder that contains all messages you have deleted. Conversely if you have deleted a message you wish you had not, it will be in Trash until you empty Trash.

The last aspect of Evolution that we will examine is found under Tools by selecting Settings. You are then presented with the screen shown in Figure 13.27. Here you can set up the e-mail accounts to use, what servers to connect to and more.

For example, under the Mail Preferences option, you can decide whether to have Trash automatically deleted when you exit Evolution or to have some sound play when new mail arrives. Essentially, this screen enables you to customize your entire e-mail experience.

KMail

The KMail e-mail client is a very interesting and useful application and is shown in Figure 13.28. However, it is strictly an e-mail client. It does not have a contact manager or calendar like Evolution and Outlook. When you first look at KMail, you can see the basic mail boxes: Inbox, Outbox, Sent, Trash, and so on.

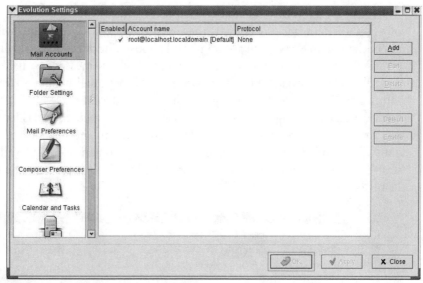

FIGURE 13.27   The Settings screen.

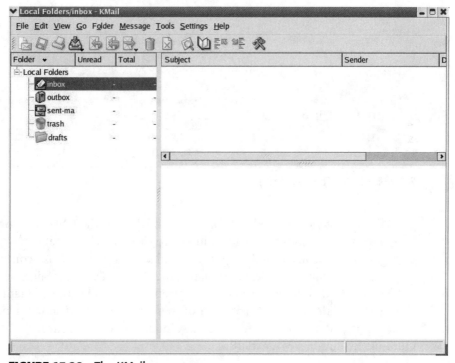

FIGURE 13.28   The KMail program.

There are a few differences between KMail and Evolution, besides the absence of a contact manager or calendar, that we should explore. To begin with, in order to check mail, in KMail you go to File and choose Check Mail. This will query your e-mail server for any e-mail you have. To create a new message, you go to Message and select New Message. All of the basic e-mail functionality that you found in Evolution and Outlook is still present, it is just in a different place.

One real advantage that KMail has over many e-mail clients is its filtering capability. If you go to Settings on the drop-down menu and select Configure Filters, you will see the screen shown in Figure 13.29. You can use this to filter out unwanted messages based on any number of criteria. This is perhaps the most useful feature of KMail.

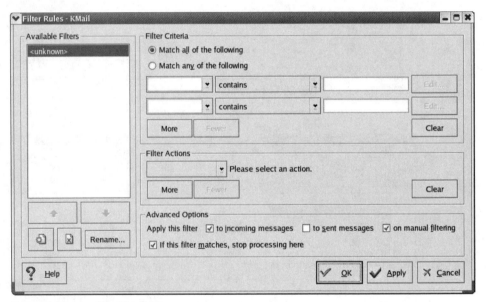

FIGURE 13.29 The KMail Filter.

The other item you need to be aware of in KMail is the KMail Settings screen, also found under Settings and shown in Figure 13.30. It is here that you would go to configure your incoming and outgoing e-mail servers. You can also configure how your outgoing mail will appear and many other facets of your KMail experience.

You can find even more e-mail applications that install with Red Hat Linux, including Mozilla Mail and Korn. Each of these has certain advantages and disadvantages. If you are looking for a Linux e-mail client that is most like Microsoft Outlook, Evolution is your solution.

FIGURE 13.30   KMail settings.

FTP CLIENTS

FTP (File Transfer Protocol) is how you get files across the Internet. If you have ever downloaded something from a Web page, you were using FTP from within the Web browser. You can also use FTP client applications that are for connecting to a specific Web site and uploading or downloading files. If you decide to put up your own Web site, it is likely that the Internet service provider or Web hosting company will give you an FTP address. You would then use your FTP client application to upload new Web pages, change names, alter files, and so on. With Linux you have several options for FTP clients, and we will look at one such option, gFTP, shown in Figure 13.31.

On the left side you see a list of all the directories and files on your computer. Once you connect, the right side will show those directories and files on the FTP host computer that you have access to. You can then drag and drop files from one side to another. How do you get connected in the first place? Notice at the top of

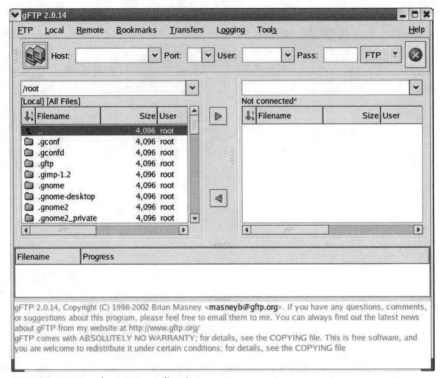

FIGURE 13.31 The gFTP application.

the screen the boxes labeled Host, Port, User, and Pass. In the Host box you will enter the address of the FTP host computer. This could be a URL, much like a standard Web address, or it could be an IP address like 10.10.10.x. You then type in the port.

Throughout this book you will see IP addresses much like this one. Real IP addresses on the Web are not generally 10.10.10.x. *However, there are a lot of IP addresses in use, and it was necessary to make certain that a real IP address for a real server on the Web was not used.*

The host and port information will have to be given to you by whomever is giving you access to the FTP server. However, if no port information is given, the default port for FTP is 21. The Username and Password fields are rather self explanatory. Once you have filled these in, click on the Computer icon to the left of Host, and it will attempt to connect.

For those readers who have an interest in developing Web pages, the FTP client will be very important. Without it, you may have trouble accessing your Web server to upload your Web pages. Many Web hosting services give you a login name and password and ask you to use FTP to upload files to their Web server. Also, in a later chapter, we will be exploring the use of FTP servers in Linux.

CHAT

A lot of people like to go into chat rooms on the Internet, and it would be a gross oversight if we did not at least give this topic a cursory overview. The idea of chat software is simple. You connect to some chat server, and everyone connected can participate in a live conversation via the Internet. To chat you must have access to a chat server and a chat client. (Just do a Web search for chat room on Google or Yahoo!. You should find quite a few.) Linux comes with one called IRC Chat, shown in Figure 13.32.

FIGURE 13.32   The IRC Chat program.

Once you have located a chat server you want to use, you will need to enter that server's information into the Chat application. If you click on the New Server button at the bottom of the screen, you will be presented with a screen like the one shown in Figure 13.33, where you can enter all the server's particulars.

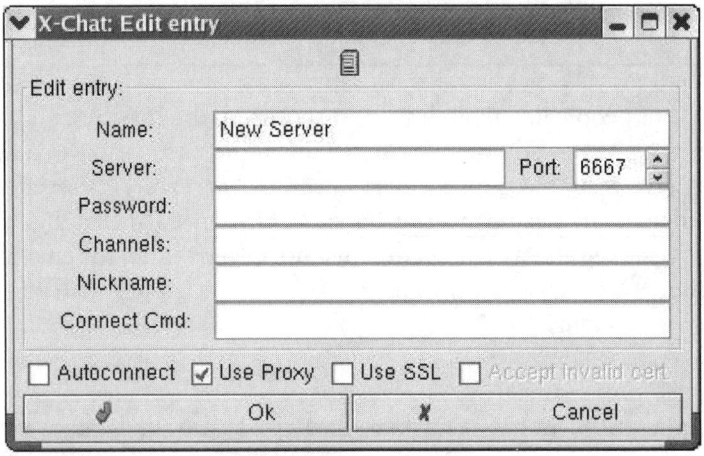

FIGURE 13.33   Server information.

You should notice that many popular chat servers are already listed in the software. At the top of the screen you list your real name and any nickname you may want to use. When you are ready to chat, click the server you want to use and click the Connect button. You will be ready to chat away the hours!

On a more technical note, a chat room actually uses channels, not unlike your television, in order to accommodate the various chats going on. A typical chat server will host multiple channels, each dedicated to a particular topic. You will find a channel dedicated to virtually any topic you might like. A simple place to start would be to go to any search engine you like and type in your topic and the words "IRC channel." For example, you could type in "Linux IRC channel," and you would find a plethora of chat channels ready for you to use.

SUMMARY

This chapter has been a very important one. Most people spend much of their computer time on the Internet. In this chapter we have taken a rather close look at

Web browsers, e-mail clients, FTP clients, and chat software. You should now be ready to effectively use Linux to accomplish all the Web activities you previously accomplished in Windows.

REVIEW QUESTIONS

1. What Microsoft product is Evolution most like?
2. What is POP3?
3. A bookmark in Mozilla is most like_____ in Internet Explorer.
4. Mozilla is most like the _____ browser.
5. What is the most useful feature of KMail?
6. What is the default port for FTP?
6. What is the process to retrieve your e-mail in KMail?

14

Miscellaneous Linux Applications

In This Chapter

- Sound Utilities
- GNOME Pilot
- KDEPrintFax
- Configure Panel
- GNOME Toastmaster
- Kandalf's Tips
- Digital Camera Tool
- Adding Packages
- Utilities

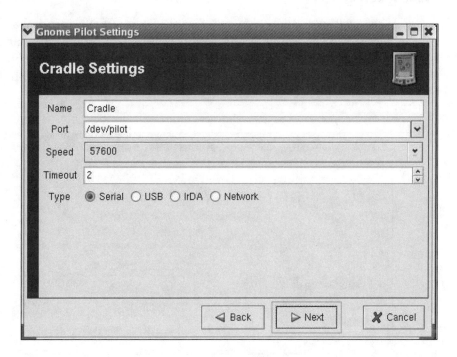

INTRODUCTION

The purpose of this chapter is to bring to your attention several Linux applications that have not been previously covered. Some of these may not have fit neatly into a preceding category, or were omitted to keep from making certain chapters much too long. Whatever the reason, there are still a few interesting Linux applications that we have not examined, but will examine now. There are several of these applications, each with its own purpose. Hopefully this chapter will not only expose you to them but will also encourage you to look deeper into Linux at other facets that we cannot cover in the space of a single book.

Sound Utilities

In Windows you probably became used to having access to a variety of sound and video applications, each with its own unique purpose. Linux has several of these as well. In fact, in the Start menu you will see an entire category called Sound and Video. Obviously these applications depend on the presence of a sound card, speakers, and in some cases a microphone.

Sound Recorder

This small application, shown in Figure 14.1, is virtually identical to the Windows Sound Recorder. If you press Record, it begins recording any sound that is currently playing on your computer or coming in through the microphone. When you are done recording, you press Stop and then select Save As from the File menu to save the file. That's how easy it is to make a WAV file.

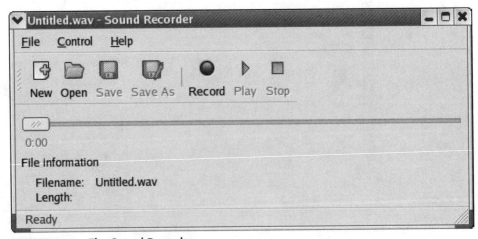

FIGURE 14.1 The Sound Recorder.

One of the most common sound file types is the WAV file. These files end in the extension `.wav`.

KsCD

This application, shown in Figure 14.2, is a CD player. It is used to play music from any standard CD. Many people find playing their favorite music while working on their computer to be quite relaxing. You might notice that the interface is very similar to the Windows Media Player or RealPlayer. This is because all of these applications require the same functionality you might find on a conventional CD player in your home. They need to be able to play, skip a track, stop, pause, and eject.

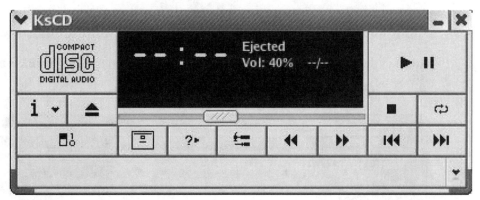

FIGURE 14.2   KsCD.

Volume Control

No discussion of sound and video would be complete without discussing the Volume Control application shown in Figure 14.3. This application allows you to control the

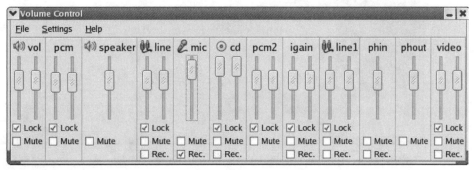

FIGURE 14.3   Volume Control.

way sound is played and recorded on your Linux PC. Very similar functionality is also available in Windows.

GNOME PILOT

This is an application that was designed for GNOME. However, if you installed both GNOME and KDE, as was suggested in Chapter 2 "Installing Linux," you will have access to it in KDE as well. Many people these days use personal digital assistants (PDAs), and GNOME Pilot is a neat little application that will help you synchronize your PDA with your PC, allowing the transfer of data between the two. Of course this application will not be of much use to you if you do not have a PDA, and you might consider skipping this part. If you are continuing, it will be important that you have your PDA connected before launching this wizard.

When you launch GNOME Pilot for the first time, a wizard will walk you through the process of setting up your PDA-Linux connection. The first screen of this wizard is shown in Figure 14.4.

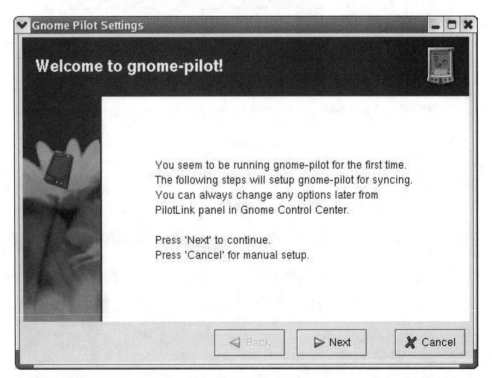

FIGURE 14.4   The GNOME Pilot Wizard, screen one.

The second screen of the wizard, shown in Figure 14.5, begins gathering important information about your PDA and its cradle. In case you are not aware, *cradle* is the term for the stand you mount your PDA in. This screen will ask you what you want to name that cradle, what type of connection you have, and what speed you connect at.

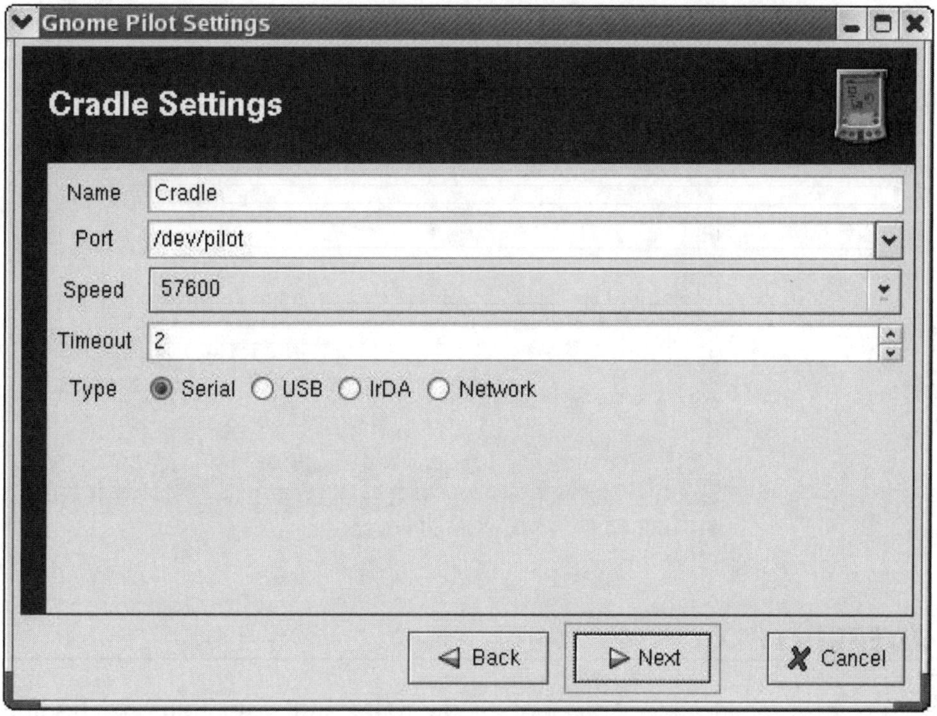

FIGURE 14.5 The GNOME Pilot Wizard Cradle Settings.

The next two screens inquire as to whether or not you have ever used the sync software to synchronize your PDA with GNOME and then starts the process of querying your PDA, via the connection you have defined. This is why it is critical to have your PDA connected when you run this wizard.

Once you are done you will be taken to the main screen for GNOME Pilot, shown in Figure 14.6. This screen displays the various PDAs you have set up and their current status. You can set up GNOME Pilot to handle more than one PDA. You also can add new PDAs and edit existing ones from this screen without using the wizard. The wizard will launch only the first time you start GNOME Pilot.

FIGURE 14.6 The GNOME Pilot screen.

KDEPRINTFAX

Also found under Accessories is the KDEPrintFax application. This application, shown in Figure 14.7, allows you to send faxes from your computer. Of course this is dependent upon you having a fax modem installed. However, this should not be any great concern. Most personal computers made in the last several years have included a fax modem as standard equipment.

Let's begin with the Personal Settings screen, shown in Figure 14.8 and found under Settings and Configure KDEPrintFax. The setup is relatively easy. On this screen you put in information about yourself and your company. The Page Setup and System settings under that are there to help you configure how your fax modem will work. The settings for the fax modem itself are dependent upon the manufacturer's specifications. The settings for how to format the fax are a matter of your personal preference.

When you are ready to send a fax, the process is actually quite simple. You first click on the Add File button. You will then be able to browse your machine's hard

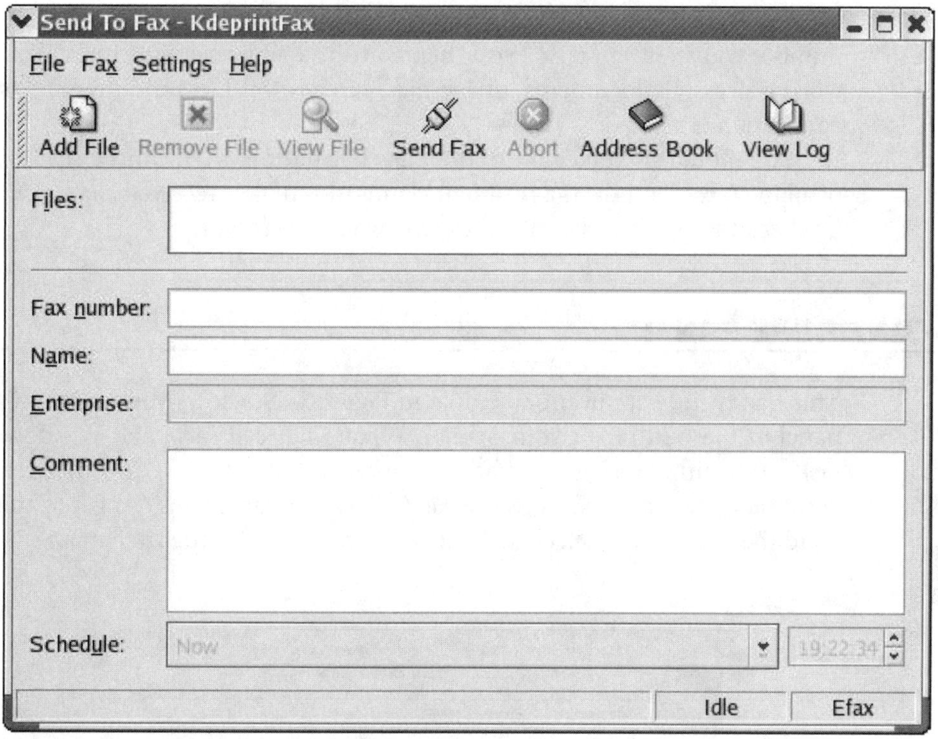

FIGURE 14.7   The KDEPrintFax application.

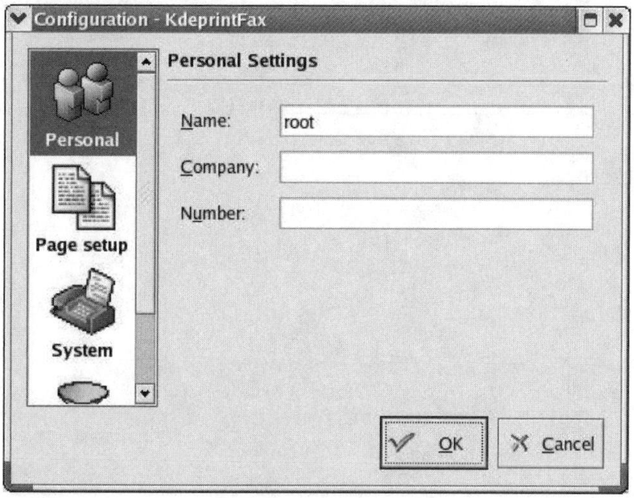

FIGURE 14.8   Configuring KDEPrintFax.

drive and attach any file you want. In the field marked Fax Number, type in the number you want to fax to. You then go to Fax and select Send Fax. You can fax word processing documents, image files, spreadsheet files, and more through this application.

You should also take note of the View Log button. KDEPrintFax keeps a record of all the faxes it sends. If a recipient claims not to have received a fax, you can easily check to see if it was sent and exactly when it was sent.

CONFIGURE PANEL

This handy little application, shown in Figure 14.9, allows you to reconfigure the panel at the bottom of your screen. What KDE calls a panel, Windows calls a taskbar. In either case it is the background bar at the bottom of your screen where you find certain application icons, as well as the Start menu. To get to this utility, go to the Start menu, select Preferences, and choose Configure Panel.

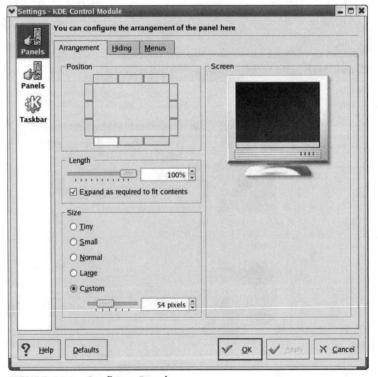

FIGURE 14.9   Configure Panel.

The Position section in the upper-left part of the screen allows you to decide where on your screen the panel will be. It does not have to appear at the bottom if you don't want it to. Just below this is a place where you can set the length of the panel. By default it stretches across the entire bottom of the screen, but you can certainly change that if you wish .

The second tab on this screen allows you to decide whether or not the panel should hide when not in use, and if so, allows you to set the parameter for hiding. This screen is shown in Figure 14.10. Notice that you can set how fast the panel will hide, whether or not other applications can appear over it, and other settings.

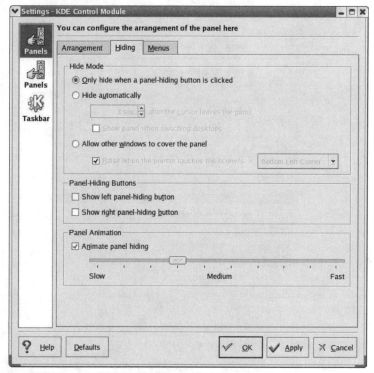

FIGURE 14.10 The Panel Hide configuration.

The third tab is even more interesting and is shown in Figure 14.11. This tab allows you to set what if any submenus your panel will have. You also can decide how long the History will be. The History in any application is a list of the most recently used files. For most applications in Linux and Windows the default is four. But you can set that to whatever you want.

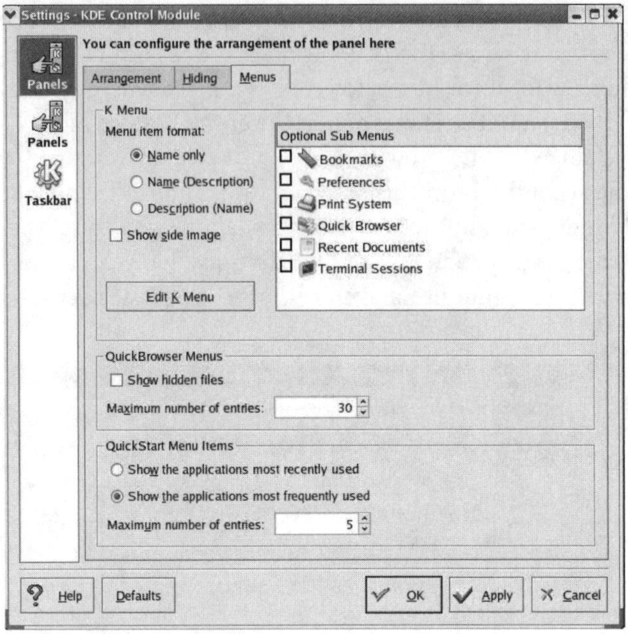

FIGURE 14.11 Menus.

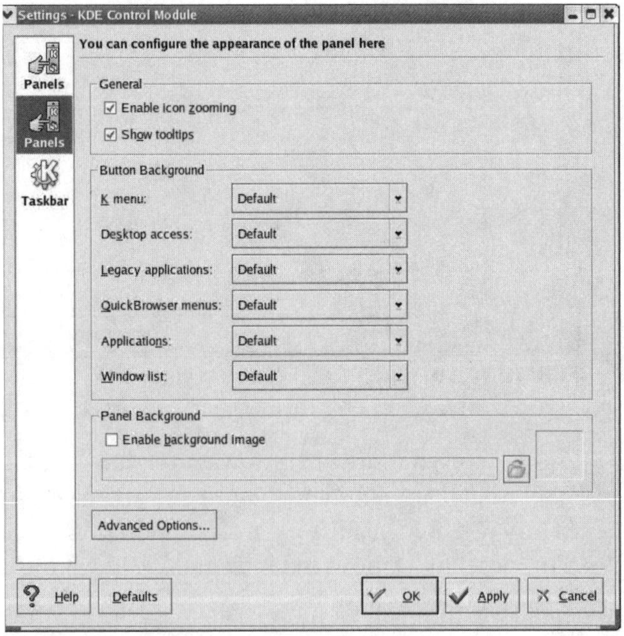

FIGURE 14.12 The second panel screen.

The second tab, shown in Figure 14.12, allows you to take panel configuration to a much deeper level. You can select to have tooltips on your panel, a background image for your panel, and many other exciting things. You can even change the way the Start menu looks.

The final section of this application, Taskbar, shown in Figure 14.13, allows you to configure a few more settings in your panel. You can decide what mouse clicks on the panel will do, as well as how items will be grouped on the panel.

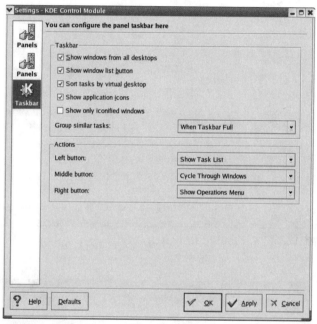

FIGURE 14.13 The Taskbar configuration.

GNOME TOASTMASTER

In this modern day of computing, many people have a CD writer, also often called a CD burner, on their PC. They often want to save files and even back up important information by burning it to a CD. To do this you will need two things. The first is the appropriate CD writer hardware installed on your computer. The second is some sort of CD writer software. GNOME Toastmaster is a CD writing application, and it is shown in Figure 14.14.

You drag files from the directory at the top to the small box at the bottom right. When all the files you want to write to a CD are collected, you are ready to create your CD. You click the Record button on the toolbar at the top. As with

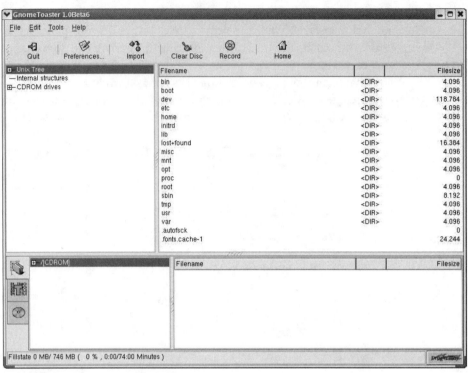

FIGURE 14.14 GNOME Toastmaster.

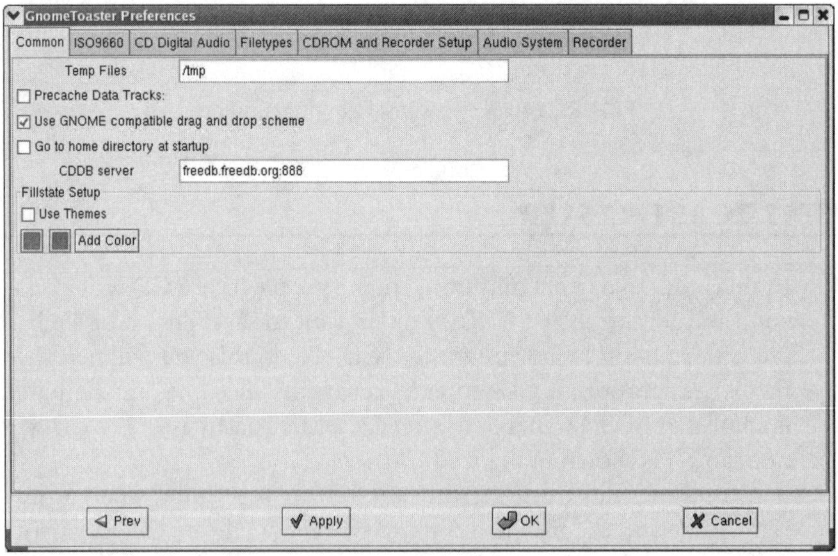

FIGURE 14.15 Configuring GNOME Toastmaster.

many applications, you can alter the way this one behaves in order to suit your individual needs or preferences. The configuration screen is found by going to Edit and Preferences and is shown in Figure 14.15.

The various tabs allow you to configure several different types of settings. There are a number of settings you can change here, but most of them are rather complicated and you are probably better off leaving the default settings.

VIDEO AND MULTIMEDIA

We previously talked about some sound applications that come with Red Hat Linux, and we just recently discussed how to create your own CDs. Now we will go into video and multimedia applications. It is very common today to be able to download and view movie clips from the Internet. Often movie producers will release short clips of an upcoming movie as a way of generating excitement about the movie. You will also occasionally find manufacturers that will put out how-to videos on the Internet. For that reason, being able to play video files is very important if you truly want to get the maximum efficiency out of your Internet experience.

Under the Sound and Video category, in the subcategory Other Sound and Video Applications, you will see an item entitled Multimedia Player. This is much like Windows Media Player or QuickTime. It allows you to open and play a variety of video formats. This application is shown in Figure 14.16.

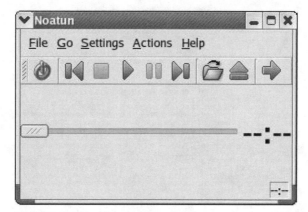

FIGURE 14.16   The Multimedia Player.

This application will allow you to play WAV sound files, MPEG3 video files as well as other multimedia file formats. Like all the applications we have looked at, this one can be configured to your personal tastes. Go to Settings and select Configure, and you will be looking at a screen very similar to the one you see in Figure 14.17.

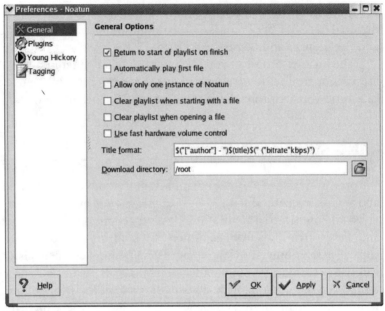

FIGURE 14.17   Configuring the Multimedia Player.

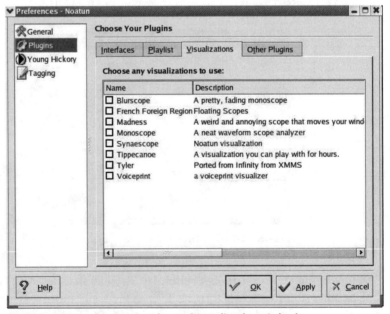

FIGURE 14.18   Configuring the Multimedia Player's look.

From this screen you can configure the default directory for downloading and playing files, you can set up plug-ins that allow you to play other multimedia formats, and more. The third tab of the Plugins screen, shown in Figure 14.18, shows some sample multimedia effects.

KANDALF'S TIPS

This is a very useful application for the Linux beginner. Kandalf's Tips, shown in Figure 14.19, will show you all of the various tips that you might normally see when the system starts up. You can peruse these tips and learn many interesting things about Linux. For any beginner, it is a very good idea to spend a bit of time perusing these tips.

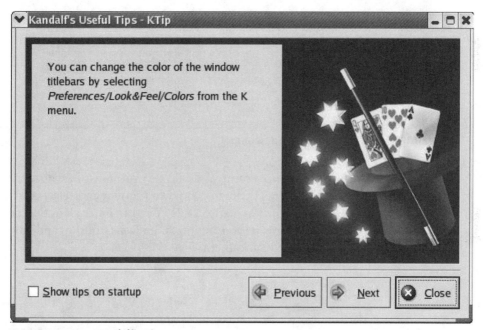

FIGURE 14.19 Kandalf's Tips.

DIGITAL CAMERA TOOL

If you look under the Graphics category, you will find a Digital Camera tool. This tool can interface with a digital camera, including a Web camera, that you might have attached to your computer. This application, shown in Figure 14.20, is relatively easy to use.

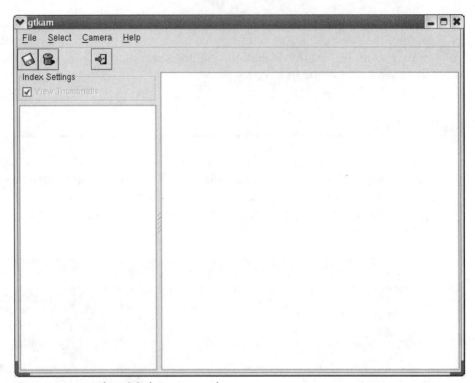

FIGURE 14.20 The Digital Camera tool.

The first step is to set up a camera. To do this you must first have the camera attached to your computer. Then you can go to Camera and select Add Camera. You will see the screen shown in Figure 14.21. You can enter all of the specific details about your camera here, or you can press the Detect button and have the application attempt to detect your camera.

FIGURE 14.21 Configuring your camera.

Once your camera is connected and configured, when you take shots with it, they will appear in this application, and you can then choose to save or delete them. And of course if you do save them on your PC, you can use one of the other applications we have covered in this book to either e-mail or fax the picture to any interested parties.

ADDING PACKAGES

This process was briefly discussed in Chapter 6, "Linux Administration from KDE," but will be discussed again here, in more depth this time. Adding and removing packages is a critical skill that you will absolutely need in order to able work with Linux successfully. It is entirely possible that you might find that there were applications you need but did not install. Conversely, you may have installed applications you find you no longer need. Fortunately, in KDE you can easily add or remove packages. Go to the Start menu, select System Settings, and choose Package Management. The computer will then take a little time determining what is already installed on your computer. How long this takes will depend on how fast your computer is. You will then see something much like what is depicted in Figure 14.22.

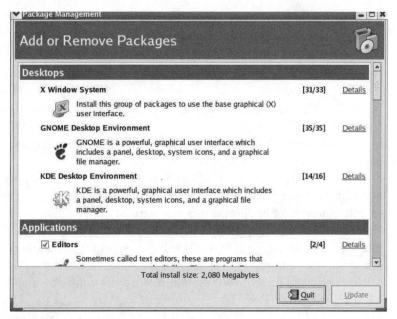

FIGURE 14.22 Adding packages.

You scroll up and down to see what packages you have installed. If there is an entire group you want to add, then click the checkmark beside it. If you want to add only one application in a group, click on the word *Details* to the right of that package and you will see a screen like the one shown in Figure 14.23 that shows all the applications in that package. Check the check box beside the application you want to add.

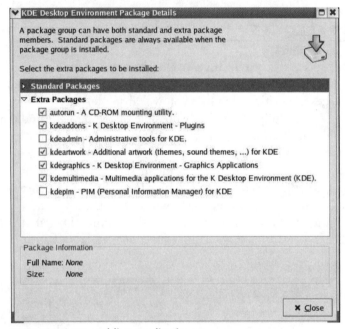

FIGURE 14.23   Adding applications.

Now click the Update button and you will see a screen like the one shown in Figure 14.24. The utility is seeing how many packages and applications you selected and how much space they will take up. When it's done, it will give you a summary of what you selected and you click OK.

After a few moments you will be prompted to insert the appropriate installation disk, and your packages will be added. As you can see, adding new applications or entire groups of applications is not hard at all. Deleting them is just as easy. Uncheck the group or application you want to remove, then press the Update button. The only difference is that you will not be prompted to insert any disks when removing applications.

You also can enable your system to automatically download and install the latest updates from Red Hat (assuming you are using the Red Hat distribution). This is a really useful feature of Red Hat and will keep your system up to date. This requires you to register your system with Red Hat (and that process is free).

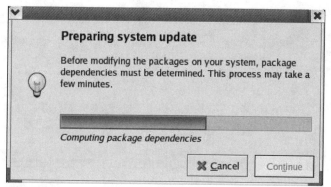

FIGURE 14.24   Preparing to install.

The Red Hat page on this subject, with complete instructions, can be found at *www.redhat.com/docs/manuals/RHNetwork/ref-guide/3.2/intro.html.*

UTILITIES

There are a number of small but useful utilities you will find in Linux. Let's take a moment to look at just a few of them here. Hopefully, after reading this, you will have found at least one that will prove useful to you.

KFind

In Windows 2000 and Windows XP you have probably seen the Search option under the Start menu. This option is used to search the drives and folders for files matching given criteria. Linux has a very similar option called KFind. The KFind utility, shown in Figure 14.25, works in much the same way.

As you can see, you enter the filename, select the directory you want to look in, and click Find. However, you can customize your search by using some of the options on the other tabs. For example, on the Contents tab, shown in Figure 14.26, you can look only in certain types of files containing the provided text.

There are several ways you can continue to refine your search in a variety of interesting ways. This tool can be very valuable. If you are anything like the author, you will periodically forget where you have placed a file! You could then benefit from this search utility.

GDM Setup

Throughout this book the login screen has been referred to several times. You have been admonished to go to the Session section to alter what desktop environment

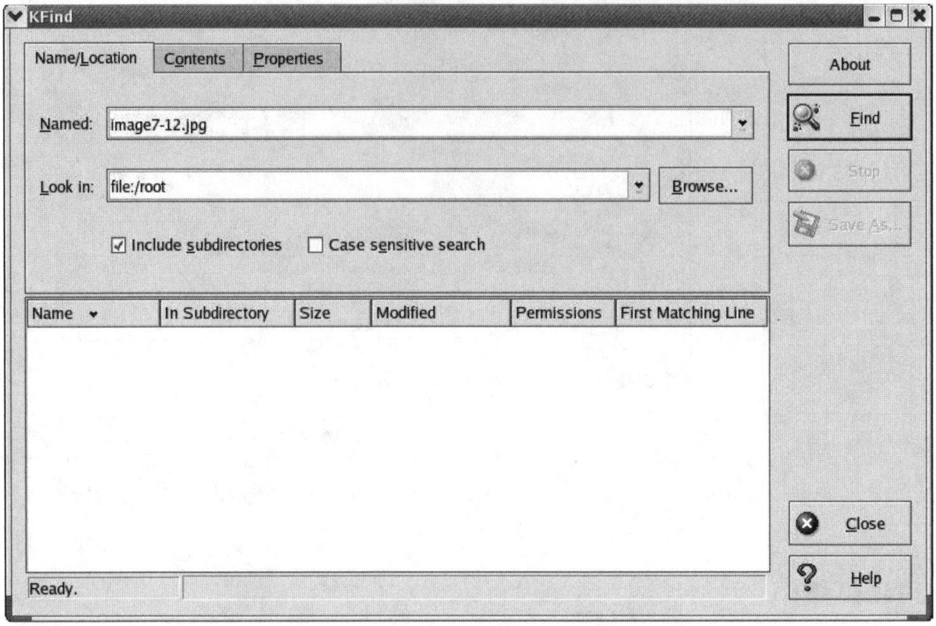

FIGURE 14.25   The KFind utility.

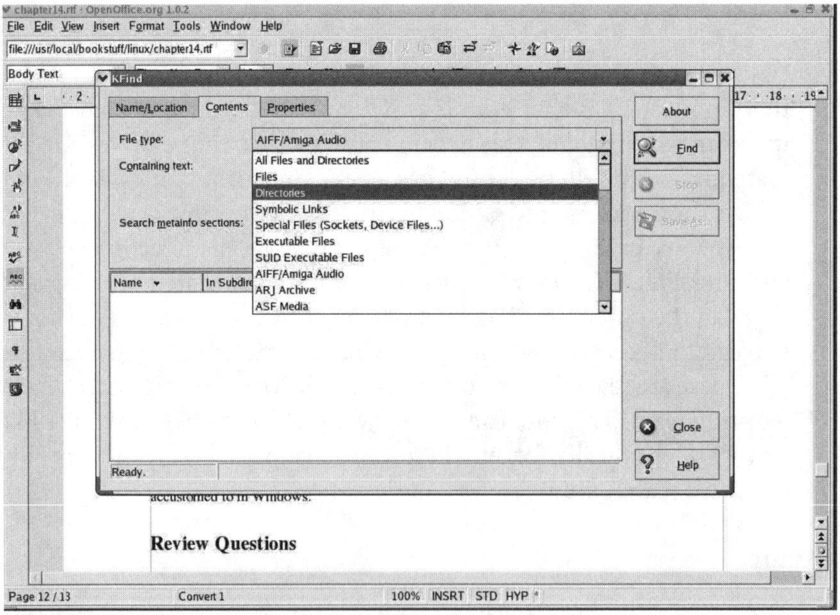

FIGURE 14.26   Refining your search.

you are using. But you may not have realized that you can even customize this login screen to suit your individual tastes and preferences. To accomplish this, you go to the Start menu, choose System Settings, and select Login Screen. You will then be looking at a screen much like the one shown in Figure 14.27.

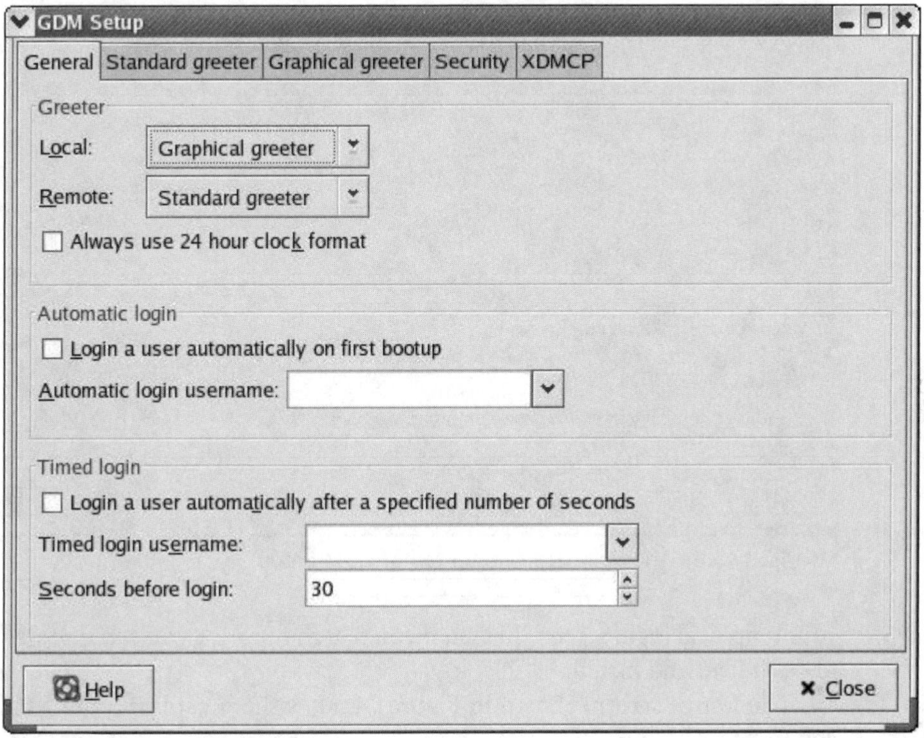

FIGURE 14.27   GDM Setup.

As you can see, there are a number of settings you can alter even on this first tab. You can select whether or not to have a graphical screen for login. Most users will probably prefer this. You can then select to have the system automatically log on after a certain waiting period. You can even choose whether or not to use the 24-hour clock.

The second tab allows you to configure the Standard Greeter. You can see this tab in Figure 14.28. On this screen you can select to have the Standard Greeter use a solid color background, an image background, or no background at all. You also can select what greeting to use.

The third tab, shown in Figure 14.29, allows you to configure the graphical greeting the way you configured the standard greeting. You can select a theme for

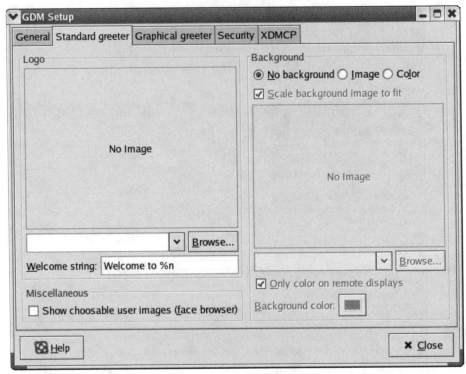

FIGURE 14.28   The Standard Greeter tab of GDM Setup.

your graphical login screen. In fact, if you search the Web you can find new themes to download and install.

The fourth screen, shown in Figure 14.30, is the most important. This allows you to set up various security settings. You can choose whether or not to even show the System menu, whether or not to allow root logins, and other important settings.

The final tab is rather advanced. The settings there should be left alone. However, with just the first three tabs it is pretty easy to configure your login screen to meet your preferences and your security needs.

SUMMARY

This chapter has been a smorgasbord of interesting applications and utilities. Each of the applications covered in this chapter has been nonessential but interesting. You can use your Linux system without using these applications, but they add a dimension to your Linux experience and allow you to do more of the things you may have become accustomed to in Windows.

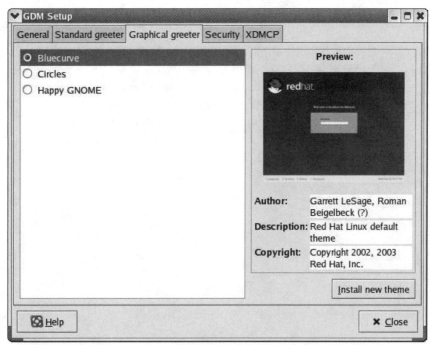

FIGURE 14.29   The Graphical Greeter tab of GDM Setup.

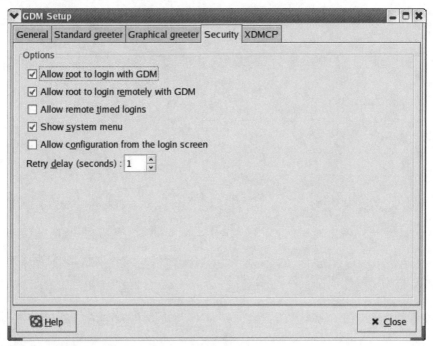

FIGURE 14.30   The third tab of GDM Setup.

REVIEW QUESTIONS

1. Which Linux application is most like RealPlayer or QuickTime?
2. What is GNOME Pilot for?
3. The Sound Recorder uses what type of file by default?
4. What is GNOME Toastmaster?
5. What application do you use to send a fax from KDE?
6. How do you send a document using that application?

15   Web Servers in Linux

In This Chapter

- How Do Web Servers Work?
- The Apache Web Server
- Configuring Apache from KDE
- Other Web Servers for Linux

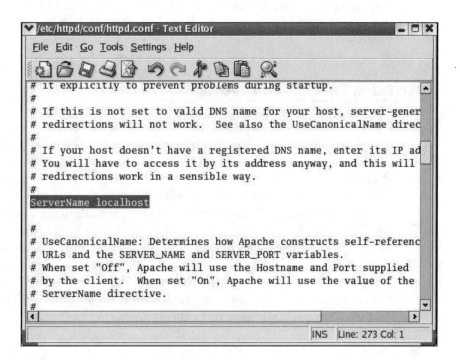

INTRODUCTION

A Web server is a computer that runs software that serves up Web pages. When you visit a Web site such as that for this book's publisher, *www.charlesriver.com/,* your browser connects to that machine, probably after connecting to your Internet service provider and a veritable host of intermediate sites or routers, and requests an HTML document from that machine. That machine then serves up that HTML document, and thus we have a Web server. That explains what a Web server is, but not why you might want one. In earlier chapters we discussed briefly how to develop your own Web pages, using some of the tools that come with Red Hat Linux 9.0. You can then use a commercial or free Web hosting service. But what if you want to host those Web pages from your home machine? Or what if you are administering a small network in an office and want to provide a Web site for the office, or just an internal Web site for people in that office to use? In any of these scenarios you might want your own Web server. Fortunately for you, Linux provides such Web servers.

Red Hat ships with a very popular Web server, the Apache server, which we will examine in detail in this chapter. There are also several free or low-cost Web servers you can download from the Internet. We will briefly discuss some of these later in this chapter. At the end of this chapter you should have a basic understanding of what Web servers are, how they work, and how to set up the Apache Web server.

HOW DO WEB SERVERS WORK?

It is possible that you could set up and run the Apache Web server and not really understand how it is working. Such a course of action is bound to be fraught with problems. Anytime you are operating technology and have no idea how or why it works, you are asking for problems. For this reason we will take a few moments to discuss how Web servers work and communicate.

To begin with, recall that every type of communication that a computer does is handled by some sort of protocol. You have already learned that e-mail is sent using SMTP (Simple Mail Transfer Protocol) on port 25 and received using POP3 (Post Office Protocol Version 3) on port 110. You also learned that files are uploaded or downloaded on the Internet using FTP (File Transfer Protocol), and it works on port 21. Web communication is no different. It uses HTTP (Hypertext Transfer Protocol) and works on port 80.

HTTP works by requests and responses. A Web browser sends a specific request to an address. That address can be either an IP address such as 10.10.10.01 or a URL such as *www.chuckeasttom.com.* The Web server that is at that address then sends back a specific response. In essence a Web server is any computer that has some program on it that can listen to port 80 and respond to the HTTP requests it receives.

Just for your information, IP stands for Internet Protocol, and URL stands for Uniform Resource Locator. It is basically just a technical way of saying Web address.

How does a Web server respond when it gets this request? It begins by sending back a numeric code to the Web browser that sent the request. That code tells the browser what is happening on the server side. Have you ever seen a Web page response like "HTTP 404 - File Not Found," as shown in Figure 15.1a? The number

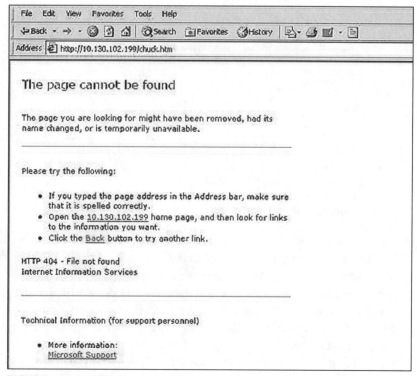

FIGURE 15.1A   Error message 404.

404 is the error code that all Web servers send to browsers if they cannot find the Web page that the browser requested.

If the response is that the request was OK and the server is processing it, then the server will respond by sending the appropriate HTML document to the Web browser that was requesting that document. The browser then loads that document into memory and displays it in the browser. The basic process of sending and receiving requests between a Web browser, your ISP, and a Web server is diagrammed in Figure 15.1b.

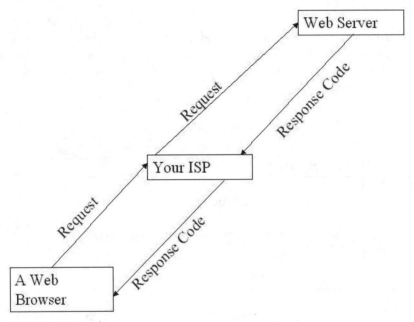

FIGURE 15.1B The process.

There are a number of codes that a Web server can send back to a browser. Some of the more common codes are listed in Table 15.1. It is important that you remember two facts. The first is that these error codes are the same regardless of the browser making the request or the Web server answering the request. An Internet Explorer browser connecting to a Microsoft Internet Information Server® Web server will get the same codes that a Mozilla browser connecting to an Apache Web server will get. The second fact to keep in mind is that the browser will not display some codes to you. For example, if the code indicates that the Web page was found and is being sent, then that code will not be displayed. Usually your browser will only display those codes that indicate an error of some type has occurred.

TABLE 15.1   HTTP Return Codes

Code	Meaning
101	This is an indication that the browser has asked to switch protocols (maybe to download a file, so it is switching to FTP) and the server is agreeing.
200	This is just an OK message.
202	The request has been accepted.
301	The page has been moved and you are being redirected to the new address.
401	The browser is not authorized to do whatever it is attempting.
404	The requested file could not be found.
504	Server timed out.

Some of these response codes you would never see. The browser would process them. Some, like 401, 404, and 504, you will probably see at some point in your Web surfing. It is not necessary for you to commit this list to memory. What is important is that you understand what is going on in the background when you use your Web browser to visit some Web site. Messages are being sent from your browser to the server. On the server end, some software is listening in to port 80 for standard browser requests and then responding. That is the essence of a Web server. Now keep in mind that commercial Web servers are generally run on very high-end computers with backup hard drives, lots of memory, and lots of processor power. However, you can certainly run a Web site from your personal computer. It just won't be able to handle thousands of visitors every day.

This leads us to the Web server software. There are several programs available that will listen on port 80 and respond to HTTP requests. Some are easier to use than others. Also, some work on one operating system but not another. The two most commonly used are Microsoft's Internet Information Server, commonly called IIS, and the Apache Web Server from *www.apache.org*. Since IIS is strictly for Windows, we will devote much of this chapter to Apache.

You can go to www.netcraft.org *and type in any Web site's address. It will then tell you what kind of Web server that Web site is using.*

THE APACHE WEB SERVER

Apache is a full-featured robust Web server that is available, free of charge, for Unix, Linux, and even for Windows. This software is completely open source and is free to download from *www.apache.org*. It also ships with Red Hat Linux. The fact that it is included in the Red Hat installation makes it ideal for our purposes. The Apache Project is a collaborative software development project whose aim is to produce a robust, professional-level, full-featured HTTP (Web) server. The project is managed by a group of volunteers located around the world, using the Internet and the Web to communicate. These volunteers are known as the Apache Group. It is important to realize that the entire process is done by volunteers donating their time and expertise. In addition, hundreds of Apache users have contributed ideas to the project.

Apache History

Before we delve into the intricacies of working with Apache, it might be a good idea to explore its history just a little. In February 1995, the most popular server software on the Web was an HTTP daemon developed by Rob McCool at the National Center for Supercomputing Applications, University of Illinois, Urbana-Champaign. Recall that a daemon is just a program that runs in the background without interaction from the user sitting at the computer. In Windows these are called services. Unfortunately, development of that Web server stalled after Mr. McCool left NCSA in 1994. However, since it was open source, many Webmasters developed their own extensions to the Web server as they were needed. A small group of these Webmasters decided that they should coordinate their efforts into a standard release of the software. Brian Behlendorf and Cliff Skolnick put together a mailing list and set up a server to hold extensions written by the core development team. At that point these eight core contributors formed the foundation of the original Apache Group. The names of these individuals are

Brian Behlendorf
Roy T. Fielding
Rob Hartill
David Robinson
Cliff Skolnick
Randy Terbush
Robert S. Thau
Andrew Wilson

They started with Version 1.3 of the NCSA Web server as a base and then added all of the published bug fixes and enhancements they could find. Apache was an immediate success. Webmasters loved the price: free! And developers loved the open source concept. This enabled any competent programmer to make modifications and submit them for release as part of the next version of Apache.

Apache exists today for a few rather simple reasons. It is a robust, professional-grade Web server that is free of charge. Apache was originally available only for Unix-based systems, but has since been ported to Windows. This brings us to one last but very humorous point in the history of Apache, the name. Some people seem to think the name is derived from the Native American tribe, but this is not true. Since this Web server was originally the work of several different developers patched together, it was called A-Patchy-Server. This name eventually morphed into Apache Server.

HOW TO SET UP APACHE

If you have Red Hat Linux, then Apache comes with it. And if you followed the instructions in Chapter 2, then it is already installed on your system. However, in case you are not sure, remember that you can go to the Start menu, select System Tools, and choose Packages to see if it is installed. You can add it if it's not already installed.

Now we are going to need to modify a few files. To find them it would be best to use the File Manager, so your next step is to launch that application. If you will recall, when we first discussed File Manager, you where admonished to spend some time getting comfortable with it, as it would be used later in this book. If you still don't feel comfortable with the File Manager, take the following steps slowly, consulting the images provided in this chapter to ensure that you are on the right track.

You will need to first find the /etc/httpd/conf directory. Use the File Manager to locate the etc directory, then open it. Within that directory you will find a subdirectory named httpd. Then you look under that directory for yet another subdirectory named conf. Browse through this until you find the httpd.conf file. When you find it, right-click on it and open it with Text Editor. This directory and file are shown in Figure 15.2.

Do not double-click on the file. If you do that, the document will be opened in a read-only mode, and you won't be able to make any changes. Recall that many applications, including the File Manager, work like a Web browser. If you double-click on a file, it will open like a Web page, for viewing only.

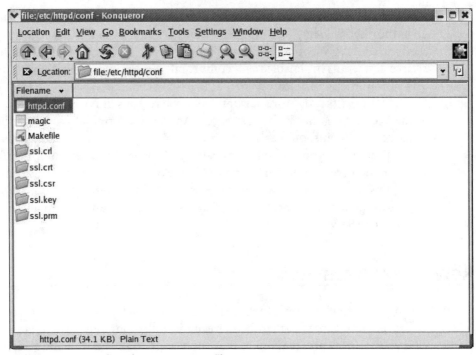

FIGURE 15.2 Finding the `httpd.conf` file.

You will see that this is a large text file with a lot of information in it. You may even feel a bit overwhelmed. There are dozens of settings available in this file. However, most of them are not required for basic Web server operation. These settings are important for advanced Web server operations that are beyond the scope of this book. Entire books have been written on Apache, and you would need to consult such a book to go deeper into Apache. There are only a few settings in this that you even care about. The most important is ServerName. Follow these steps and you can have your server running.

It will only be accessible from your machine. This is a test mode to see if the Apache server itself works properly. If all goes well, we will go back and change a few things to make it accessible from the entire Internet. Also note that the ServerName setting is sometimes commented out with a pound symbol in front of it. Delete the pound symbol.

1. Set the `ServerName = localhost`. This is shown in Figure 15.3.
2. Save the file.

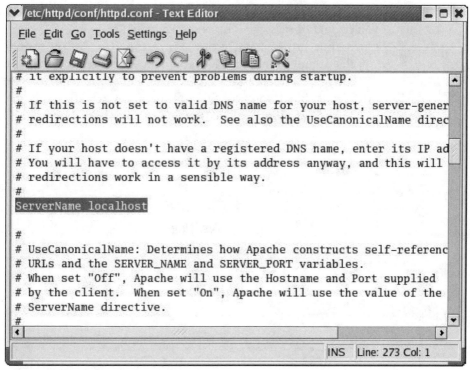

FIGURE 15.3   The ServerName setting.

FIGURE 15.4   Starting the HTTPD service.

3. From a shell, type /etc/init.d/httpd start. The server should start and you get an OK message. This is shown in Figure 15.4.
4. Open your browser and go to http://localhost/. You should see the Apache default Web site. The screen you should see is depicted in Figure 15.5. If you do not see this screen, then one of the steps was executed in error; most likely your changing of the httpd.conf file. Common errors and their resolutions are discussed in just a few paragraphs.

FIGURE 15.5   The default Web page.

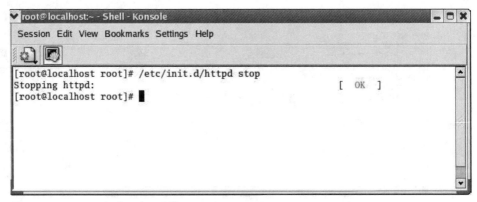

FIGURE 15.6   Stopping the HTTPD service.

If your test worked and you can see the basic Apache default page, it is time to make your server go live. To do this, there are just a few steps to follow.

1. First stop the server. You do this by going to a shell and typing in `/etc/init.d/httpd` stop. This is shown in Figure 15.6.
2. In the `/etc/httpd/conf/httpd.conf` file, change the following settings:
   a. Change `servername` to your registered URL or to your IP port such as `10.10.10.117:80`. If you don't remember your IP address, don't worry. Just go to the shell and type in `ifconfig`. This will give you your IP address.
   b. Change `listen` to reflect the IP and port you want.
3. Check the `documentroot` directory to make certain that is where you want your Web pages to be served from. The default is `/var/www/html`. Whatever directory you put as your `documentroot` is where Apache will look for Web pages.
4. From a shell, type `/etc/init.d/httpd` start.

You should now be running a Web server. Go to any other machine that is connected to the Internet and point the browser to *http://yourserverurlorip*. For example, you might point the browser to *http://10.10.10.01* if that is the IP of your machine.

If you are running this from your home, then the chances are that you use an Internet service provider to get to your machine. For this to work all of the time, you will have to do two things:

1. Leave your Internet connection running. If you are not connected to the Internet, no one can reach your Web server.
2. Ask your ISP for a static IP address. Recall from our previous discussions of network configuration that this means you have the same IP address every time you log on. Without this, your IP may change, and then people trying to visit your Web site won't find it.

Any time you change the configuration file, you must stop the Web server and restart it.

NOTE

If you want to use a URL rather than an IP address, you will need to go through the appropriate company to register a domain name. For example, the author has his Web site registered as *www.chuckeasttom.com*. There are several companies that will perform this service for you for a small fee. A list of a few of the more widely known companies is provided here:

■ *www.networksolutions.com*
■ *www.register.com/*
■ *www.cheap-domainregistration.com/*
■ *www.nic.us/*
■ *www.easyspace.com/*
■ *www.aitdomains.com/*

You also can do a Web search using a search engine such as Yahoo! or Google to find other places to register your domain. This list is not an endorsement of any of these sites, it is only a starting point in case you don't know where to go to register a domain name.

At this point your Apache Web server is almost ready to go. There is only one small hurdle to overcome. When you first installed Linux, you probably left the firewall settings at their default values. With many distributions, this blocks HTTP and FTP, and that will keep your Web server from being able to communicate. It is probably a good idea to go to your firewall settings (recall from earlier chapters that we explored where to find this) and make certain that HTTP and FTP packets are not being blocked.

In a perfect world, every reader would follow these steps and have his Web server up and running. However, we all know that we don't live in a perfect world, and things do go wrong sometimes. It is possible that you typed in something incorrectly. It is also possible that something else went wrong. While there may be a seemingly endless number of possibilities, there are a few common problems and their resolution. For your convenience, they are listed in Table 15.2. Of course, the very first step in troubleshooting is to check the basics. The following are the four basic Apache troubleshooting steps. Check these before checking anything else:

1. Is your Web server running?
2. Is it connected to the Internet?
3. Did you type in the address correctly without misspelling it?
4. Have you checked the error log for error messages?

If these steps don't uncover your problem, then consider the options in Table 15.2.

TABLE 15.2   Common Problems

Problem	Resolution
When connecting to the IP address, the browser says Cannot Resolve IP Address, Already in Use.	If you have `ServerName` and `Listen` set to the same IP address, this error will occur. Either change `Listen` to another IP or comment it out altogether.
Apache fails to start	When you changed `ServerName`, you probably messed up the spelling, such as forgetting a space between `ServerName` and the name: `ServerNameLocalHost` instead of `ServerName LocalHost`, or `ServerName=LocalHost` instead of `ServernameLocalHost`.
Unknown errors	If you are having problems that you cannot otherwise diagnose, then you should check the error log. The default location for that is `/usr/local/apache/logs/error_log`. However, if you check the error setting in the `httpd.conf` file, you can find out exactly where your error log is. If none of that helps, try the online Apache Frequently Asked Questions at *httpd.apache.org/docs/misc/FAQ.html*. The four troubleshooting steps, the items in this table, or even the Apache documentation cannot solve every problem. However, the overwhelming majority of problems are configuration issues and can be solved by trying out these few steps.

THE APACHE CONFIGURATION FILE

We have changed a few items in the `httpd.conf` file, but we offered no explanation of what those items meant. Let's take just a moment to examine this file closer. Also keep in mind that this file is heavily commented. Reading through the comments after you are finished with this chapter might be helpful for some readers. For now let's take a look at a few items and what they mean. Table 15.3 will also mention some settings we have not worked with. Recall that the `httpd.conf` file has dozens of settings, many of them unnecessary for basic Web server operation.

TABLE 15.3 The `httpd.conf` file

Item	Purpose
`DocumentRoot`	This is the root Web folder. It is here that Apache will look for Web pages.
`ServerRoot`	This is the root folder for log files. Apache keeps various log files of what is occurring.
`Port`	This is what port to listen in on. Normally this will be set to 80.
`Listen`	This is an alternative IP address and port to listen to. This is important if you have more than one NIC with different IP addresses and you want both to respond to connections.
`MaxClients`	The maximum number of Web browsers that can simultaneously connect to your Web server.
`ServerName`	The name of your server.
`ServerAdmin`	This is the e-mail address for the Webmaster.

In this case that would be you. This is a very exciting topic. Not only can you create your own Web pages with Linux, but you can put them up for the entire world to see. You should now be able to set up and run Apache. If you wish to delve deeper into the intricacies of the Apache Web server, then it is suggested that you begin with *www.apache.org*. After that you might consider looking into books explicitly about Apache.

A few points about Web pages and Web servers. All Web servers by default look for the Web page `index.html` or `index.htm`. In other words, if you were to register www.*mydomain.com*, when someone typed in *www.mydomain.com*, your Web server would look in the document root directory for a file named either `index.htm` or `index.html`. This is what you should always name your starting page. That page can then have links to any other pages. Also remember that the most common error on the Internet is misspelled Web addresses. Always check that before spending time checking to see if your server is configured and running properly.

CONFIGURING APACHE FROM WITHIN KDE

Like many things in Linux, you can configure your Apache Web server manually, as we have already discussed, or you can use a convenient graphical utility to configure and start your Apache Web server. To do this, you go to the Start menu, choose System Settings, then More System Settings, and then select HTTP Settings. You will then be looking at a screen like the one in Figure 15.7.

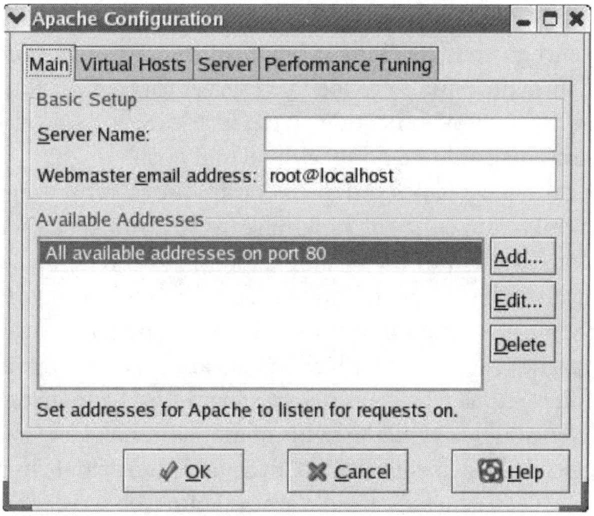

FIGURE 15.7   Configuring Apache from KDE.

The first tab is where you would set the Server Name and server admin settings. This utility will then write the values you select into the httpd.conf file. If you were trying to test this server for local connection, you would put localhost into the text field labeled Server Name. If you were trying to prepare the server to go live, you would, of course, put your machine's actual IP address or URL here.

The second tab, shown in Figure 15.8, is for setting up virtual hosts. A virtual host is an advanced feature of many Web servers, and configuring one is beyond the

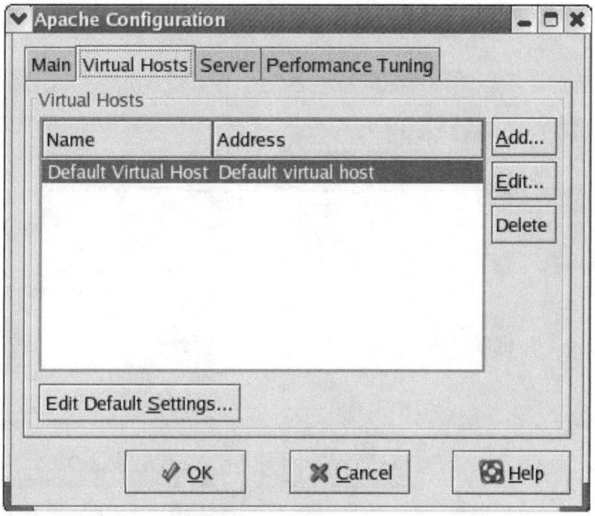

FIGURE 15.8   The Virtual Hosts tab.

scope of this book. However, a simple definition is in order. A virtual host is what you have when your machine is host to more than one Web address. For example, if your Linux machine were the Web server for an ISP, you might find several customers who want Web hosting space and want to register domains for their Web addresses. This could be done with virtual hosts.

The third tab enables you to customize the server settings and is shown in Figure 15.9. Several of these may be unfamiliar to you and are a bit advanced. You probably should leave these with the default settings. However, you should note the User and Group fields at the bottom of this tab. Your Web server must run as some user with the rights given to that user. In this case there is a special user called Apache and a group called Apache. The reason for having a separate user and group for your Web server is that if you ran it as whatever user was logged in, then anyone who hacked into your Web server would have all the rights of that user. If you are logged in as root, then they would essentially own your system. Even with the separate user and group, it is recommended that you generally avoid running your Web server as root. It is important to realize that Apache will start as root no matter what settings you have. However, it will then change to the user/group you defined before it begins responding to requests.

The Performance Tuning tab, shown in Figure 15.10, enables you to adjust items such as the maximum number of connections and the maximum requests per connection. These settings are not so important in a Web server being used for a very small group or by an individual as a hobby. However, if the number of visits to your Web server grows and begins to tax the resources of your machine, you might consider adjusting these settings.

The specifics of how to adjust performance settings are a bit advanced. If you begin to get that much traffic to your Web site, then it is probably time to do some more advanced study on the topic of Apache Web server. This chapter is interested

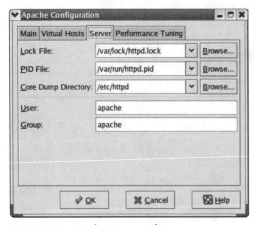

FIGURE 15.9 The Server tab.

FIGURE 15.10 The Performance Tuning tab.

only in getting a basic Web server up and running, not in equipping you to be a Web hosting service!

OTHER WEB SERVERS FOR LINUX

Apache is, by far, the most commonly used Web server for Linux. It also has a Windows version, and it is not uncommon to find Windows machines running Apache Web server. If you were to choose a single Web server to study, Apache would be the one. However, it is not the only Web server available for Linux. Table 15.4 lists some other Web servers and tells you a bit about them, including where you might download them from the Internet. We will not be examining any of these in depth because they do not come with the Red Hat installation. However, it is important that you be aware that there are alternatives to Apache and know where to look for them.

TABLE 15.4   Alternative Web Servers

Web Server	Address to Download	Features
Essentia Web	www.essencomp.com/	High-performance HTTP/1.1 1–compliant multithreaded server. Supports thousands of virtual servers. Browser-based server management. Access control on each directory, based on users or groups. Built-in Java servlet and JSP engine
Abyss	www.aprelium.com/ abyssws/	Abyss Web Server X1 is a free personal Web server available for Windows and Linux operating systems. It supports HTTP/1.1, CGI, Server Side Includes (SSI), custom error pages, and user access control. It also has a remote Web management interface that makes its configuration as easy as browsing a Web site.
Dune	ftp://metalab.unc.edu/pub/ Linux/apps/www/servers/	This is a small, easy to use Web server designed for personal use, not commercial use. The server itself is less than 300 bytes, which means it is quite small and takes up virtually no appreciable amount of hard drive space.

As you can see, you have a number of choices when it comes to setting up a Web server on your Linux machine. While Apache is the most common choice, it is not the only one. By this point in this book you should begin to realize that this is what the open source movement is all about, choice. The idea is that you should have several choices, and you pick the one you like the best.

SUMMARY

In this chapter, we have covered a lot of very technical information. You have seen the basics of how Web servers work and how they communicate with the Web browser. You have also found out about Apache Web server. You should now be familiar with its history as well as the basic setup for Apache. After reading this chapter you should be basically competent with the essentials of setting up a Web server on a Linux machine.

REVIEW QUESTIONS

1. What protocol do Web browsers use?
2. What is the default port for Web servers to listen on?
3. In simple terms, what is a Web server?
4. What is HTTP return code 301?
5. How did Apache server get its name?
6. What is the name of the Apache configuration file?
7. What is the Server Admin setting in the configuration file?
8. What are four basic troubleshooting steps you should first take when having an Apache problem?

16

Linux FTP Servers

In This Chapter

- What Is an FTP Server?
- VSFTP
- ProFTPD
- PureFTPd
- WU-FTP

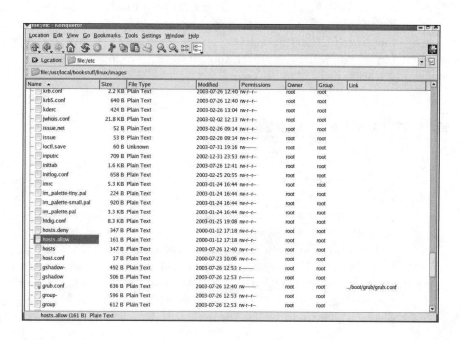

INTRODUCTION

In an earlier chapter we introduced you to an FTP client application for Linux. You could use this client to connect to any FTP server, regardless of the operating system the FTP server was running on, and upload or download files. Linux doesn't just supply you with FTP client software, it also provides you with the server software as well. In this chapter we will explore some FTP server options for Linux.

You might be wondering why you want an FTP server. Some readers won't need one. However, if you had an FTP server running on your home machine, you could upload and download files from anywhere with an Internet connection. If, for example, you are on a business trip and forgot to bring along some documents on your home computer, you could log on to your home PC's FTP server and download them.

Another reason to run an FTP server is to do so in conjunction with the Web server described in the preceding chapter. For example, if you set up a Web server for a club, organization, church group, or perhaps neighborhood association that you are a member of, you would need to have some method for letting members of that group upload their own Web pages. You could simply have them hand you a disk with the files on it, then you would upload them. However, this is not very efficient. With an FTP server running on your machine, you could give each member of your group a login ID and password, and they could then log on and upload their own files. In this chapter you will learn how to set up your own FTP server in Linux. You will also be given some information on what an FTP server is and how it works.

WHAT IS AN FTP SERVER?

An FTP server is simply software that can respond to FTP requests, just as a Web server is a computer that has an application listening to and responding to HTTP requests on port 80. With FTP servers, the software must listen for FTP requests on port 21. Microsoft's Internet Information Server package includes an FTP server. It basically allows users to upload files to your computer. Bear in mind that this can be the source of significant security risks. If you allow users to upload any file they like to your Web site, then someone could upload harmful software to your system. It is best to go to the Web site for the FTP server you prefer and read all of the documentation they have before trying to run an FTP server. This chapter is meant to give you an introduction to the topic and show you how to set up the basic configuration options.

VSFTP

We will start with one of the easiest FTP servers to configure. VSFTP is very easy to configure, and it ships with Red Hat 9.0. That means that you should already have it. Recall from Chapter 14, "Miscellaneous Linux Applications," how to look under packages and ensure that this application is properly installed on your computer. Once it is installed, you are ready to configure and run it. There are just a few simple steps to follow.

1. Find the file /etc/vsftp/vsftp.conf. This is shown in Figure 16.1.
2. Check to ensure that it has the following properties set:
   a. disabled is set to no.
   b. Make sure it has local_enabled = yes.
   c. Make sure that allow_anonymous = yes.
      This is shown in Figure 16.2.
3. Find the /etc/hosts.allow file. You can see it in Figure 16.3. It should have the setting vsftp: ALL . That is shown in Figure 16.4.
4. From a shell, type chkconfig –add xinetd. Then type /etc/init.d/xinetd start. This is shown in Figure 16.5.

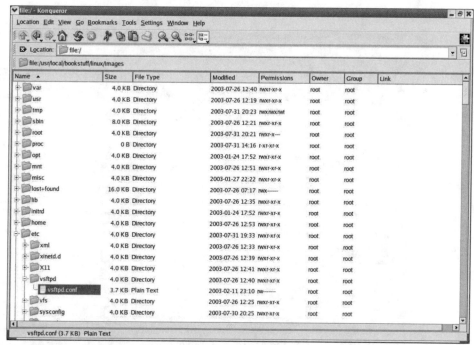

FIGURE 16.1   Finding the configuration file for VSFTP.

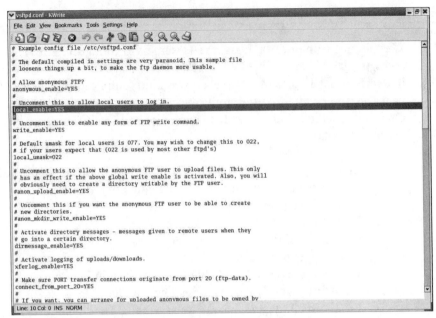

FIGURE 16.2 The configuration settings.

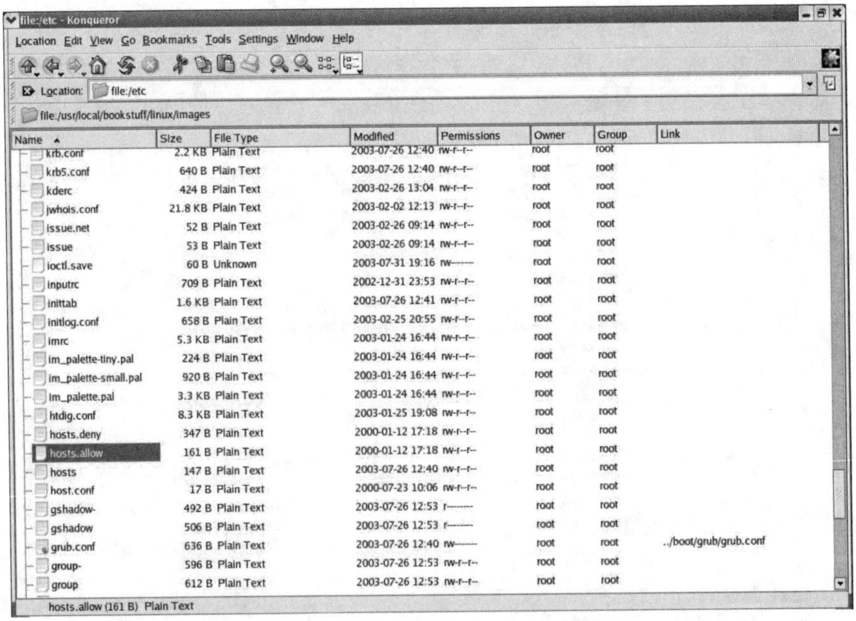

FIGURE 16.3 Finding the hosts.allow file.

FIGURE 16.4   `hosts.allow` settings.

FIGURE 16.5   Starting your FTP server.

What your shell command did was add your VSFTP server to the xinetd process. That process governs Internet and network connections. The second line started your FTP server. Your FTP server is now running. You should be able to go to any other machine and log in using any FTP client. Bear in mind that the FTP protocol is not dependent upon the operating system. You can go to a Windows machine and use FTP to connect to your Linux FTP server. The easiest way to log on would be anonymously:

```
username = anonymous
password = anye-mail@anywhere.com
```

If you assign any usernames and passwords to VSFTP, then you could use those to log on. If you examined the configuration file for VSFTP, you probably noted that there were several additional settings you could alter. The basic settings for VSFTP are shown in Table 16.1, along with a brief explanation.

TABLE 16.1   VSFTP Settings

Setting	Purpose
anonymous_enable	Determines whether or not anonymous users are allowed to log in.
local_enable	Determines if a local user can log in.
write_enable	Can a connected user perform write operations?
dirmessage_enable	Do you want messages to display when the user connects to certain directories?
ascii_upload_enable	Do you want to allow the upload of ASCII files?
ascii_download_enable	Do you want to allow the download of ASCII files?
ftpd_banner	Do you want a banner to display when a user first logs on?

There is another file that you may want to consider examining. This file is /etc/vsftpusers, and it contains a list of users who are not allowed to log in to the FTP server under any circumstances. Adding a username to this list will block that user from ever logging in to your FTP server. If you have a particular user who is unable to log in, you might consider checking this file to see if he is there for some reason. There are several users that are listed by default. The default listing for this file is shown in Figure 16.6.

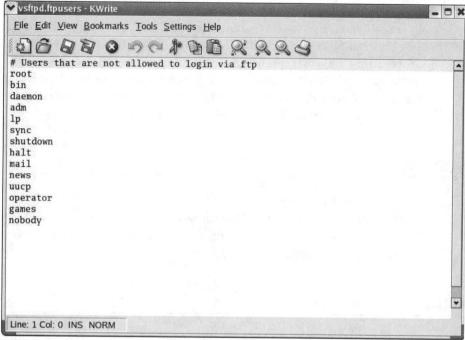

FIGURE 16.6 The vsftpusers file.

This is just a basic setup for VSFTP. It will run and allow people to upload and download. It is recommended that after you finish this chapter you pick one FTP server that seems to be your favorite and spend some time learning it in more depth. A good place to start is a simple Web search for that FTP server.

PROFTPD

ProFTPD does not come with the Red Hat installation CD-ROM, but it is a very popular FTP server, and for that reason it would be a mistake not to discuss it here. It can be obtained from *http://proftpd.linux.co.uk/*.

The most commonly used server is WU-FTPD. However, the designers of ProFTPD thought that, while WU-FTPD provides excellent performance and is generally a good product, it lacked certain features found in newer Win32 FTP. With this in mind, they set out to create an FTP server for Unix and Linux systems that had the features they felt should be there.

Installing ProFTPD is relatively simple. After you have downloaded the package from a Web site (the one previously mentioned would be a good place to start), you can go to a shell, change to the directory where the package is located, and type in `rpm —install proftpd-{version}.rpm`.

This will place the configuration file for ProFTPD in either `/usr/local/etc/proftpd.conf` or `/etc/proftpd.conf`. With this and any other software that does not come with Red Hat, your best place to look for more information is the documentation of that vendor. We are listing FTP servers here that are not included in the Red Hat installation to give you an idea of what alternatives are available.

PUREFTPD

PureFTPd does not ship with Red Hat, but it is a very useful and popular FTP server. You can find it at the Web address *www.pureftpd.org/*. You can then download and install it on your machine. One of the biggest advantages of this FTP server is that it is quite easy to set up.

WU-FTP

WU-FTP (Washington University FTP Server) ships with Red Hat Linux 9.0. It is one of the most commonly used FTP servers in the world of Linux. If you followed the instructions in Chapter 2, it should be installed on your machine. You can check your packages, and if it is not installed, you can add it. Your first step in configuring this FTP server will be to find the configuration file. That can be found at `/etc/xinetd.d/wu-ftpd`. Change `disable = yes` to `disable = no`.

To change the permissions so that various users can access your FTP server, you will need to go to the access permission file found at `/etc/ftpaccess directory`. To allow a given user access you must make the following settings: `allow-uid ftp` (uid is the user ID) `allow-gid ftp` (gid is the group ID).

It is imperative that you make certain that users you have added match actual users on your system. Then make certain that the users' home directories are the ones where you want them to put their uploads. When you manage users and groups, you set each user's home directory. This will be the directory that he will first see when he connects with FTP. If you are using FTP to allow customers of a Web server to upload pages, then user `jdoe` would probably have a home directory something like `/var/www/html/users/jdoe/`.

The following entries in the configuration file are not critical, but it might be a good idea to take a look at them:

- `readme`: This setting in the `config` file identifies a readme file that users have access to.
- `e-mail root@localhost`: This is the admin's e-mail address.
- `loginfails 5`: How many login attempts before failure?
- `message`: This is the welcome message file you want to display.

Now you can start WU-FTP by typing `>/etc/init.d/xinetd restart` at the shell. To stop the FTP server, type `ftpshut now`.

The configuration you have just seen is very basic. You would be well advised to spend some time reading the documentation on the WU-FTP Web site.

As a final word of caution, you should bear in mind what was stated at the beginning of this chapter. FTP servers can be a significant security risk. If this chapter is your first introduction to FTP servers, then you are advised to not set one up on a commercial or business server without first reviewing all of the documentation for that Web server. Go to that Web server's home page and read the online documentation, with particular attention to the security notes.

SUMMARY

In this chapter, you saw the essentials of three different FTP servers. You saw where to get an FTP server and in some cases how to configure and start it. All of these FTP servers are open source and can be found on the Internet and downloaded free of charge. With each of the FTP servers that we actually configured, we did a basic configuration. It would be advisable for you to spend some time studying any FTP server you want to use in more detail. This chapter was meant to get you started with FTP servers. Also, you should note that you should have only one FTP server running at a time. If you have more than one running, they will conflict with each other and neither will work.

REVIEW QUESTIONS

1. What port do FTP servers work on?
2. What does FTP stand for?
3. What is the main configuration file for VSFTP?
4. What is the most commonly used FTP server?
5. What happens to a user who is added to the vsftpusers file?
6. In VSFTP, what does the `ftpd_bannerG` setting do?

17

Fun and Games in Linux

In This Chapter

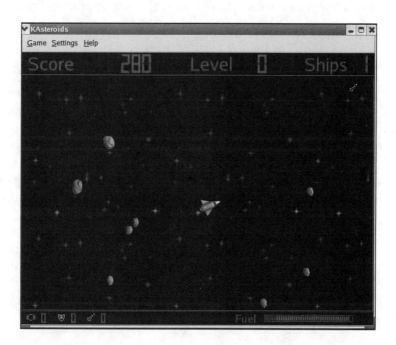

INTRODUCTION

Throughout this book we have focused on solid, practical Linux features and Linux-related applications. The final section of the book, which follows this chapter, is one of very intense and serious Linux shell manipulation that is certainly not for the faint of heart. Now seems like an appropriate time to relax a bit and find out how we can have some fun with Linux.

It is a fact that many, if not most, PC users spend at least some of their time playing games on their computers. Some users, like the author, spend far too much time playing games! Before you can truly embrace Linux, you will probably want to know what games Linux has for you. The unfortunate fact is that many of the major commercial PC games are not available for Linux. However, the good news is that some are, and Linux ships with several games already installed. In this chapter we will first look at the games Linux comes with, and then we will explore where you can find other games.

When you go to the Start menu, you will find a section for games. This includes a few obvious games like KPoker and KBackgammon. These are simply KDE versions of Poker and Backgammon. If you know how to play the traditional versions of those games, you should have no problem with the Linux versions. We want to explore a few games that might not be so obvious, but that can be quite fun!

KOLF

What would the world of PCs be without computerized golf? Even people who don't enjoy playing real golf on a golf course can find playing computer golf a relaxing diversion. The KDE interface has such a game, called Kolf, and its main screen is shown in Figure 17.1.

To start a new game, select the Game menu and choose New Game. You will see the screen that is shown in Figure 17.2. Here is where you set up your new game. Obviously you have to pick your players' names, but there is a lot more here for you to do.

On the Course tab of this screen, shown in Figure 17.3, you can set up the parameters of your course. You can select the type of course, create a new course, and set the par for that course. For our example we will choose the Really Easy course.

You are then taken to the game screen. Here you move your mouse to where you want your club and press the mouse button. The longer you hold down the

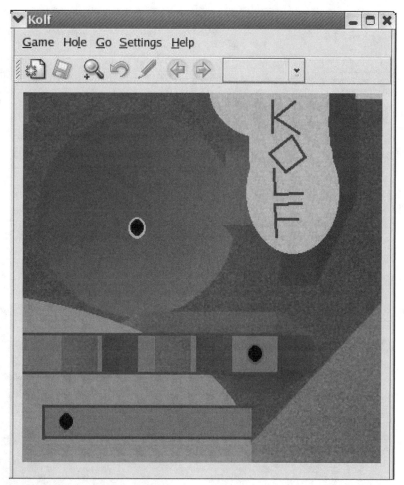

FIGURE 17.1 The Kolf game.

mouse button, the more power will be in your swing. This is shown in Figure 17.4. When you let go, you will swing and hit the ball. You can use the arrow keys at the top of the screen to move on to the next hole if you wish to skip the current hole. Kolf probably won't improve your real golf score, but it could certainly be a fun way to spend a little time.

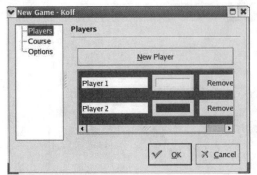

FIGURE 17.2   Starting a new game.

FIGURE 17.3   Setting up a course.

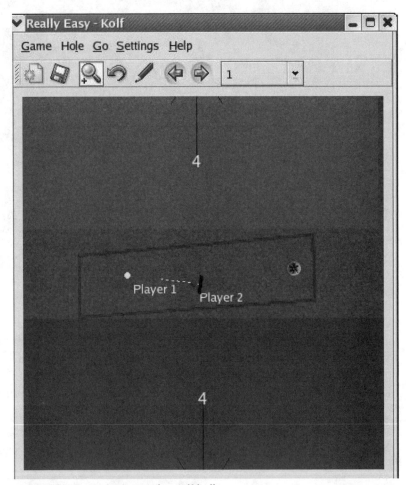

FIGURE 17.4   Swinging at the golf ball.

KBATTLESHIP

This is a fun one for you military simulation lovers. The KBattleship game, shown in Figure 17.5, allows you to battle it out in a naval campaign. In this game, one player is the server, the other player connects to that server, and you match wits on the simulated high seas.

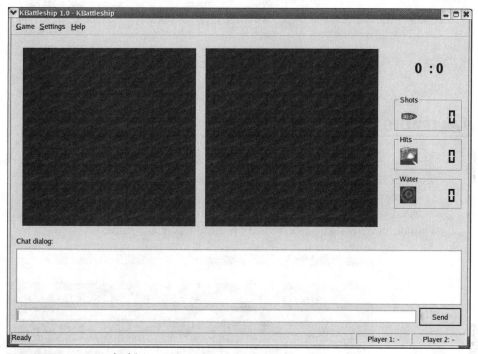

FIGURE 17.5   KBattleship.

When you choose the Game menu, shown in Figure 17.6, you have the option to make your game the server or to connect to another server. To connect to another server, you must both be on some sort of network or connected via the Internet.

When you first choose to start your machine as the server, you will be asked to provide a nickname for yourself in the game and to pick a port for the other player to connect to. This is shown in Figure 17.7. The other player connects to the server. He also must pick a nickname and then enter the IP address and port number of your machine.

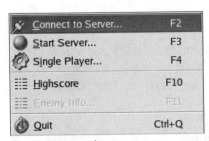

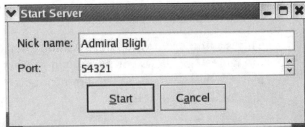

FIGURE 17.6 The Game menu.   **FIGURE 17.7** Starting you PC as a game server.

Under the Help menu, you will also find documentation and further help and hints regarding the KBattleship game.

KASTEROIDS

This one is an oldy but a goody. Asteroids was a very popular arcade game in the early 1980s. KAsteroids is a Linux version of this game. You can see the KAsteroids screen in Figure 17.8. The goal of KAsteroids is to use your spaceship to destroy asteroids and not get smashed by any asteroids. The KAsteroids game actually has much more realistic asteroids than did the original game.

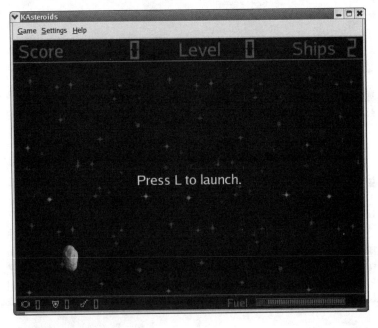

FIGURE 17.8 KAsteroids.

The game itself is very simple. You use the L key to launch the game, then you maneuver your ship using the arrow keys. You fire at asteroids with the spacebar. Destroy as many asteroids as you can without getting smashed by one yourself. Figure 17.9 shows KAsteroids in action. This game may not prepare you for NASA, but it can be a lot of fun.

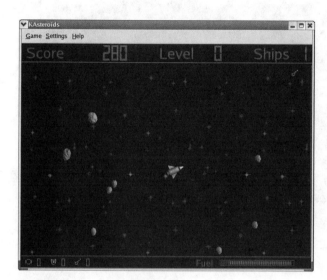

FIGURE 17.9   Playing KAsteroids.

FIGURE 17.10   KMines.

KMINES

This game is essentially a replica of the ever-popular Microsoft Minesweeper® game. The board, shown in Figure 17.10, even looks much the same. You try to guess where flags are while not picking a square with a mine. This game will make you feel like you were back on a Windows machine.

KWIN4

A very popular game among children and therefore parents of children is Connect Four®. If you happen to be a fan of this particular game, you will be pleased to know that an analog of it exists in the world of Linux. This game is KWin4, shown in Figure 17.11. This game works exactly like the traditional game. The idea is to connect four of your pieces in a row before your opponent does. In this case, your opponent is the computer.

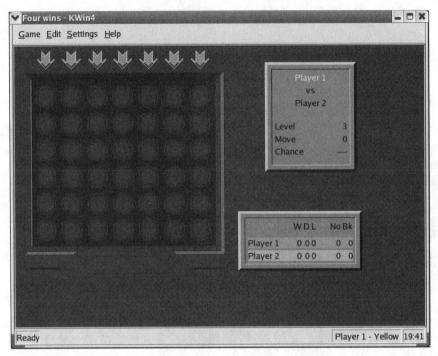

FIGURE 17.11 KWin4.

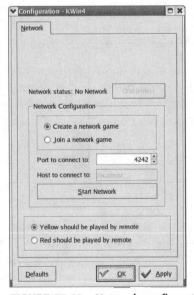

FIGURE 17.12 Network configuration.

This game also can be played over the Internet or a network connection with another person as your opponent. To set this up, go to the File menu and select Network Configuration. You will be taken to the screen shown in Figure 17.12. Here you can set up yourself as the game server or connect to someone else's server.

There are several other interesting games that ship with Red Hat Linux. For example, there is the KSpaceDuel, shown in Figure 17.13, and chess, shown in Figure 17.14. The important thing to keep in mind is that there are a lot of games available for Linux. While some commercial hits might not be available for Linux, you should keep in mind that Red Hat Linux installs with far more games than any version of Windows.

FIGURE 17.13   KSpaceDuel.

FIGURE 17.14 Chess.

FINDING OTHER LINUX GAMES

What you are probably most interested in is finding the big-name commercial games in a Linux format. While many are not available for Linux, some certainly are, and in this section we want to make certain that you can find them. The following list has some wonderful Web sites where you can obtain lots of Linux games, including Linux versions of major commercial games such as Quake III and Castle Wolfenstien, two names that are likely to be etched in the mind of any avid gamer. The site *www.lokigames* specializes in Linux versions of mainstream games.

www.linuxgames.com/
www.lokigames.com/
games.linux.sk/
www.tuxgames.com/
www.happypenguin.org/

Although you can get some of the major game releases for Linux, there are several you cannot. As of this writing you cannot get Everquest, SimLife, Command and Conquer, Grand Theft Auto, and many other mainstream games. However, the following lists some of the big hits that are available for Linux.

- Never Winter Nights
- Quake III Descent
- SimCity 3000
- Return to Castle Wolfenstein
- Sid Meier's Alpha Centauri
- Civilization Call to Power
- Soldier of Fortune
- Heretic II
- Tycoon II

Of course, if you cannot find your favorite games for Linux, one solution to your problem might be to go with a Linux PC and take the money you save from not purchasing a Windows license or Microsoft Office and use it to buy a Sony PlayStation® or Nintendo® system for games.

SUMMARY

This chapter could have been called the lighter side of Linux. In it we examined the world of Linux games. We looked at some of the games that come with Red Hat 9.0 and examined how to play them. We also looked at what major commercial games are available for Linux. Given Linux's growing popularity, it seems likely that the future will bring even more games for Linux.

REVIEW QUESTIONS

1. What is the name of the Linux golf game described in this chapter?
2. Which operating system ships with more games, Windows or Linux?
3. What Web site specializes in Linux versions of popular commercial games?
4. KMine is most like what Windows game?
5. List three major game hits that are available in Linux.

V Advanced Linux

Much of this section is concerned with how to use a Linux shell. Although you can use Linux with a very slick-looking graphical interface, in fact there are several graphical interfaces to choose from, and many Linux aficionados feel more at home with command-line interfaces. The various command-line interfaces, or shells, available for Linux have far more functionality than the Windows command prompt. The reason for this is quite simple. Windows was designed to be used via a graphical interface. It was not meant to be used via a command-line interface. The graphical interface and the operating system are one. With Linux, the exact opposite is true. It was meant to be used through a command-line interface. The graphical interface is simply a tool that many Linux users find convenient.

In the next several chapters we will examine various aspects of using the shell. We will look at many shell commands, explore administering a Linux machine via shell commands, and even look into the basics of writing your own shell scripts. This section should provide you with the tools you need to be competent at using the shell to perform most tasks in Linux.

It should be noted that the following section is rather advanced. Some readers may want to skip it altogether. If you are a casual computer user who just wants basic Internet and word processing, it is perfectly okay for you to skip this section. However, if you want to use Linux to manage your small office as a server or you want to understand Linux on a deeper level, this section is for you.

The section also will show you some advanced features of Linux that can be used through the KDE desktop. This includes file sharing with Windows and running the Linux machine as a network server.

18

Linux Shell Commands

In This Chapter

- The Shell Itself
- File and Directory Management
- System Commands
- Network Utilities
- Miscellaneous Commands

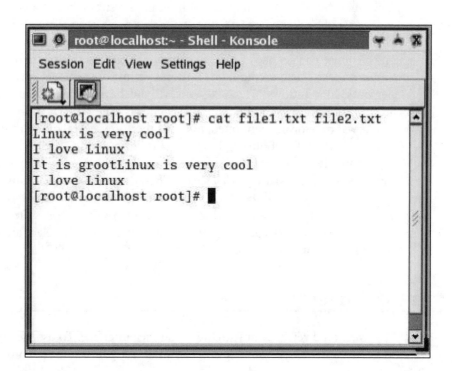

INTRODUCTION

Shells were briefly introduced in Chapter 3, "Basics of the Linux Operating System," and we examined a few very basic shell commands in that chapter. However, we did not delve deeply into how to work within a shell. In this chapter we will explore shells in more depth. Some of the previous commands may be covered briefly again, and you will be introduced to a number of new shell commands.

Using the shell is an important part of working with a Linux machine. Before there were graphical interfaces such as KDE and GNOME, shell commands were the only way to use Linux or Unix. Many Linux aficionados still find the shell to be the most efficient way to perform many tasks.

In this chapter we will examine a variety of shell tasks, grouped together by functionality. That way we can look at a series of shell commands that all have similar operations. At the end of this chapter, if you follow along and execute these commands on your own Linux machine, you should be familiar with Linux shell commands. It is highly recommended that you use each of the commands mentioned in this chapter. Reading them without any experience using them will not help you to learn them.

It has been 15 chapters since we discussed shells, and it might be prudent to review what a shell is. A shell, if you will recall, is a simple text-based interface with your computer. You enter text, and it appears in a screen. That screen usually has a simple mono color background (often blue or black), and the text is a simple font. The response you get back from the computer is also in this plain font on the same simple screen. There are no fancy buttons, drop-down menus, or other graphical elements. In Windows NT, 2000, and XP you have a shell called the command prompt. In Windows 95 and Windows 98 it was called the DOS prompt.

As was previously mentioned, in Linux there are several different shells you can work with, including Bourne, Bourne-again (bash), and C shell. The vast majority of commands are common to all shells. In this chapter we will explore only those commands that are shared by all shells. Therefore, you can select any shell as your default shell. If you will recall, when you establish a user account, you can set that user's default shell. That is the shell he will get when he invokes the terminal window. However, unless you have some compelling reason to select one of the other shells, it is probably best to leave the default as the bash shell.

THE SHELL ITSELF

First we should get familiar with the actual shell interface. To use the shell, you need to go to System Tools and select Terminal. As you get more comfortable with

Linux, you will discover alternate ways to invoke the shell, but for now we can use this route. When you start a shell, you will see something much like what is shown in Figure 18.1. Notice that the cursor prompt you see is actually the username of the user who is currently logged on. There are shell commands to change even that, but for our purposes it's just fine.

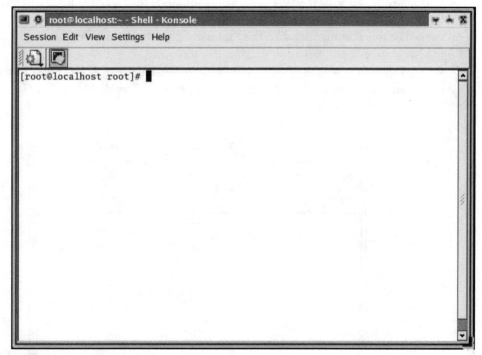

FIGURE 18.1 The terminal.

The drop-down menu at the top should look familiar to you. It is quite similar to the drop-down menu of many Web browsers and is the common interface you have seen in almost all KDE applications. Two particular menu items are of special importance. The first is the File menu. Under this you can see options to start a new session. A session is an individual instance of a shell. You can have multiple sessions running at one time, all controlled from this single terminal window. This enables you to work with several different shell commands at the same time if you want. You should also note the Settings menu. Under this you see a number of options for customizing the terminal window. You can change the size, color combination, and other aspects of the terminal.

The first commands we will look at involve the shell itself and how it behaves. All shells have an interesting feature called History. The history command enables you to see the commands that have been entered previously. By default, this command will return the last 500 shell commands. This may be far more than you want to view. This brings us to a related command, HISTSIZE. Before we continue discussing this command, you should note that it is typed in all capital letters, intentionally. It is one of the very few shell commands that is typed in all uppercase. By typing in HISTSIZE=5, as shown in Figure 18.2, you are telling the shell to only return the last five commands when the history shell command is executed.

Technically speaking, HISTSIZE is not a command per se. It is actually an environmental variable. However, for our purposes here it works like and can be used like other commands.

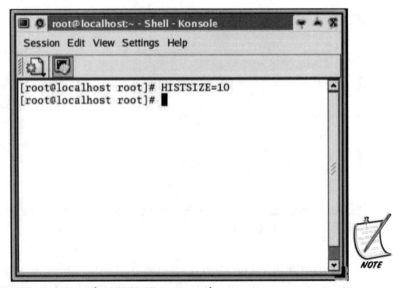

FIGURE 18.2 The HISTSIZE command.

You must type in the shell commands exactly as you see them in this text or they will not work. For example, HISTSIZE=5 is all uppercase letters with no spaces. Typing it in any other way will not work. Most shell commands are all lowercase. These commands are case sensitive.

The history and HISTSIZE commands can be very useful. There may be occasions when you need to know what was done a few commands back. Another useful command is `clear`. Enter the word `clear` and press Return and it will clear the current view of the shell. This can be useful when you have to run several commands and the shell is appearing a bit cluttered.

While we will be working with the bash shell, you may be curious as to how you would go about invoking the other shells that we have mentioned. One obvious way is to set up that shell as the default shell for that user. However, there should be some way to change what shell you are using while the terminal is open. Fortunately, there is a way to do that very thing. You enter the abbreviation for that shell, and you will then be using that shell. For example, if you want to use the C shell, type in `csh` and then press Enter. You will not see any dramatic change in the appearance of the shell itself. In fact, you will see very little change. The cursor prompt will change slightly, indicating that you are using a different shell. In fact, that will be the only immediate indication that you have invoked a different shell. All the shell commands we will work with in this book will work in any shell. However, if you switch to C shell, you can do all the commands that are unique to that shell. When you are ready to switch back to bash, just enter `bash`. You can invoke the various other shells with just as much ease. Typing in `ksh` will invoke the Korn shell, and `sh` will invoke the Bourne shell. Changing between shells is a very easy thing to do.

There are two other very important shell commands you need to be aware of. Both of these will provide valuable information about other commands. The first is the `man` command, which was discussed briefly earlier in this book. Linux has a built-in manual. When you enter `man` followed by a particular command, you will display the manual page for that command.

For example, if you want to know about the `ls` command, enter `man ls`. You will immediately discover that most commands have several flags you can pass to them to make them behave differently. A flag is a character such as a letter that tells the command to modify its behavior in some way. You also will need to know how to exit the manual page when you are done reading it. That is simple; just enter the letter *q*, and you will quit the manual page.

Another useful command is `help`. If you enter a command followed by two dashes and the word `help`, you will see a brief list of flags you can pass to that command. `help` is sort of like an abbreviated manual page. An example of using `help` is shown here:

```
ls—help
```

FILE AND DIRECTORY MANAGEMENT

In Chapter 3 you were briefly introduced to some file and directory management commands. You were shown how to create directories, copy files, list contents of a directory, and remove files and directories. Several of the commands explored in Chapter 3, and a few new ones that we will examine now, are shown in Table 18.1.

TABLE 18.1 File and Directory Management Commands

Linux Command	Explanation and Example	Windows Command Prompt Equivalent
ls	This lists the contents of the current directory. Example: ls	The dir command is equivalent to the ls command. Example: dir
cp	This copies one file to another directory. Example: Cp filename.txt directoryname	The copy command is equivalent to the ls command. Example: copy filename.txt directoryname
mkdir	The mkdir command creates a new directory. Example: mkdir directoryname	The md command is the equivalent of the mkdir. Its syntax is identical to mkdir. Example: md directoryname
cd	The cd command is used to change directories. Example: cd directory name	The cd command is also used in Windows, and its syntax is identical. Example: cd directoryname
rm	The rm command is used to delete or remove a file. Example: rm filename	The del command is the equivalent to the rm command. Example: del filename
rmdir	The rmdir command is used to remove or delete entire directories. Example: rmdir directoryname	The rd command is the equivalent of the rmdir command. Example: rd directoryname
mv	This command is used to move a file. Example: mv myfile.txt myfolder	The equivalent command in Windows is move. Example: move myfile.txt myfolder
diff	This command performs a byte by byte comparison of two files and tells you what is different about them. Example: diff myfile.txt myfile2.txt	The comp command will perform a binary comparison of two files.
cmp	This command performs a textual comparison of two files and tells you the difference between the two. Example: cmp myfile.txt myfile2.txt	There is no equivalent command in Windows.
spell	This command performs a spell check on a target file and tells you if any words are misspelled. Example: spell myfile.txt	There is no equivalent command in Windows.

continues

TABLE 18.1   Continued

Linux Command	Explanation and Example	Windows Command Prompt Equivalent
head	This command returns just the first few lines of a file. This is useful when searching for a particular file. Rather than opening the entire file, just view the first few lines to see if it is the one you want. Example: `head myfile.txt`	There is no Windows equivalent.
cat	This command will concatenate two files. The two files are put into one, one file being appended to the end of the other. Example: `cat myfile.text myfile2.text`	There is no Windows equivalent.
>	This is the redirect command. Instead of displaying the output of a command such as `ls` to the screen, it redirects it to a file. Example: `ls > file1.txt`	This works in the Windows command prompt in much the same way.

diff and cmp

These two commands are used to compare two files and determine what differences the two files have. In order to demonstrate these commands, we will have to create two sample text files. For demonstration purposes you can open up any Linux text editor (Kate or KWrite, for example) and type in the following three lines:

```
Linux is very cool
I love Linux
It is awesome
```

Save that as `file1.txt`. Start a new text file and enter these three lines:

```
Linux is very cool
I love Linux
It is great
```

Save that as `file2.txt`. You should notice that, except for the last line, these two files are identical. This is intentional, as it gives us a chance to explore the `diff` and `cmp` commands and find the differences between these two files. Now we can use both the `diff` command and the `cmp` command and see what they tell us about these two files. Figure 18.3 shows the output from running the `cmp` command. Figure 18.4 shows the output from running the `diff` command.

FIGURE 18.3 The `cmp` command.

FIGURE 18.4 The `diff` command.

You are probably thinking that the `diff` command gives you more information than the `cmp` command, but that is not exactly accurate. The two commands give different output because they compare the files differently. The `cmp` command compares the files byte by byte in their binary format. Remember that ultimately everything in your computer is stored as ones or zeros (binary format). Therefore, it reports the specific bytes that are different. The `diff` command performs a textual comparison and returns what line or lines of text are different. Both of these commands can be quite useful. For example, if you have two versions of the same file and want to know exactly what is different between the two, either the `diff` or the `cmp` command can tell you.

spell, head, cat, and redirect

The next four commands we will look at are very useful when you are working with text files. The first of these commands, the `spell` command, is used frequently by most Linux users. You use this command to find any misspelled words in a file. When you run the `spell` command, it will return all words in that file that are misspelled. The misspelled words will be listed vertically as they are in Figure 18.5.

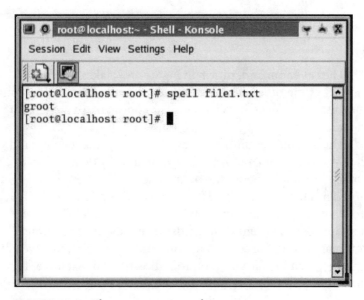

FIGURE 18.5 The `spell` command.

The head command is very useful for searching through files. If you are seeking a particular file and do not recall what the filename is, in Windows you would have to open each file that you think might be it and scan it to see if it is indeed the file you are looking for. The head command will return just the first few lines of a file, and that is usually enough to determine if it is the file you are seeking. This is shown in Figure 18.6.

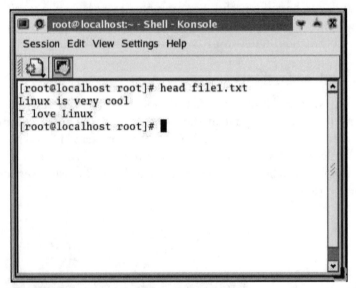

FIGURE 18.6 The head command.

The cat command, shown in Figure 18.7, takes two files and appends one onto the end of the other. This is a very commonly used shell command. There is no equivalent command in Windows. The concatenated contents are then displayed to the screen.

The last, but certainly not least, file management command we will examine is the redirect command. All shell commands by default display their output to the screen. However, there may be instances when you would prefer the output be stored in a file. That is where the redirect command comes in. It causes the output from some other command to be redirected to a file. This is very useful, particularly for some of the system commands we are about to examine. To use the redirect command, enter the command you want to redirect, followed by the greater than sign (>), then the file you want to redirect to. For example, ls > myfile.txt takes the output from the ls command and places it in a file named myfile.txt.

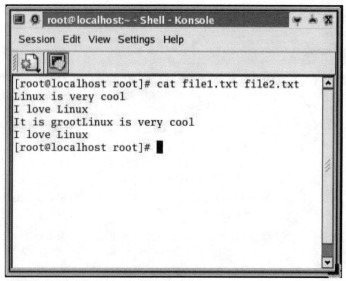

FIGURE 18.7 The cat command.

SYSTEM COMMANDS

There are a number of very useful shell commands that will give you a wealth of information about your system. These commands are useful for either a system administrator monitoring a system or any Linux user wanting to examine what is happening on his machine. The more commonly used system commands are shown in Table 18.2 and will be explained in this chapter. Many if not most of these commands have no Windows equivalent because Windows is meant to be run from the graphical interface, and not all functionality is supported from the command line. In Windows there is no real separation between the operating system and the graphical interface. This is different from Linux, where the graphical interface is completely separate from the operating system, and the operating system can be run without the graphical interface.

TABLE 18.2 System Commands

Command	Purpose	Windows Equivalent
ps	This command will list all currently running processes. Any program or daemon is a process.	No Windows equivalent.
top	This command lists all currently running processes, whether the user started them or not. It also lists more detail on the processes.	No Windows equivalent.
ifconfig	This will list information about your network card.	The Windows equivalent is ipconfig.
ping	This command is used to see if you can reach a specific IP address.	The same command works in Windows.
traceroute	This command will trace the route to a specific IP address.	The Windows equivalent is tracert.
finger	This command is used to get information about a user.	The same command works in Windows.
who	This command will tell you all the users currently logged in to your system. This is useful if your Linux machine is being used as a server for an office.	There is no Windows equivalent.
date	This command will display the current date and time.	The same command works in Windows.
uname	This command displays the name of the current system.	There is no Windows equivalent.
whois	This command is similar to finger and gives information about a targeted user.	There is no Windows equivalent.
env	This command will list all environmental variables.	There is no Windows equivalent.
kill	This command is used to stop a currently running process.	There is no Windows equivalent.

ps, top, kill, and env

Three of these commands, ps, top, and env, are all related to each other in that they provide valuable information about how your system is currently functioning. The fourth command, kill, is used to stop running processes. The commands ps and top both show the processes that are currently running. Every program, utility, or daemon on your PC is a process. The ps command, shown in Figure 18.8, shows only those processes that you, the current user, initiated.

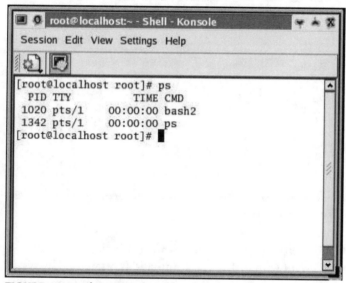

FIGURE 18.8   The ps command.

The top command shows all the processes, even those you did not initiate. Your system starts a number of processes for you. The top command also tells you what user started a process, what the process ID is, how much CPU time the process is using, how much memory it is using, and more. The top command is shown in Figure 18.9.

The PID is a unique identifier for each running process. It stands for Process Identifier. In Windows, every running process is assigned a Windows handle. The Windows handle and the PID are essentially the same things.

The top command provides a lot of information—perhaps too much. It certainly fills up the screen quickly. This is one instance where the redirect command would be very useful. You can dump the output of the top command to a text file and read it at your leisure. Recall that you do this by typing in:

```
top > somefile.txt
```

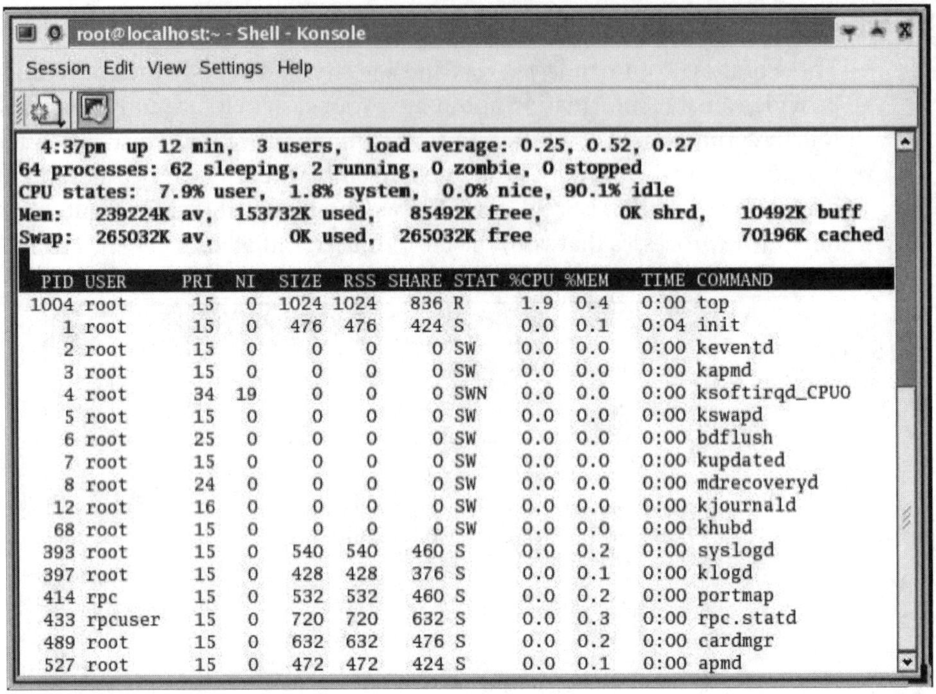

FIGURE 18.9   The top command.

Then you can open that file in any text editor and read it, search it, or do whatever you want with it. The top command is often used by system administrators either to identify processes that are consuming too much system resources or to search for telltale signs of hackers or viruses.

The env command provides you with all the current environmental variables. Environmental variables will be specific to a given user. This means that if you run the env command while a different user is logged in, you may get different results. Environmental variables cover many aspects of the user's environment. The home directory, current user, and current history size are all environmental variables.

The path statement is also a very important environmental variable. The path statement lists all the paths in which the operating system will look for a command when you type it in the shell. All the commands we study are actually programs somewhere on your machine. The path statement tells the shell where to look for commands you enter. This is important because there are some software packages you may install, particularly programming tools such as Java, that ask you to add one of their directories to the path. The env command's display is shown in Figure 18.10.

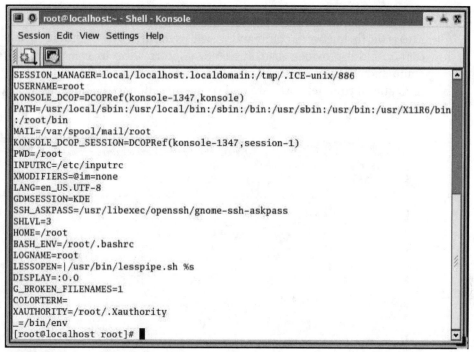

FIGURE 18.10 The env command.

The kill command is perhaps the simplest command of all. You enter the word kill followed by the process ID (PID). An example is kill 1045. Be very careful with this command. If you kill a process the system requires, you could cause the system to function improperly or even crash. This is one reason why you don't want people to log in as root. Only root can kill a system process. If a user is logged in under a user account, he cannot kill a system process.

NETWORK UTILITIES

Whether your computer is on a local network or using the Internet, there are several network commands that you may find quite useful. There are several basic network-oriented commands you probably need to be familiar with. Each of these can provide very useful information about your connection to a network or the Internet, as well as help diagnose specific connectivity problems.

ifconfig

This is the first network command we will examine. The Windows equivalent is ip-config, and it provides virtually identical information to ifconfig. The ifconfig command just gives a little extra data. Basically, the information it supplies regards the status of your network card and your connection to the Internet. The output of this command is shown in Figure 18.11.

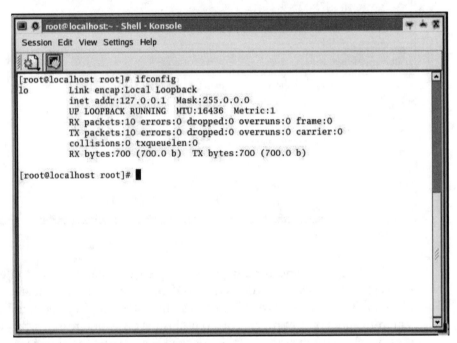

FIGURE 18.11   The ifconfig command.

The ifconfig command will tell you if your network card is up and running. If you are currently connected to a local network or the Internet, it will send out packets periodically to ensure that you still are connected. This command also will display the IP address of your computer's network card. ifconfig is discussed in more detail in Chapter 19, "Linux Administration from the Shell."

ping

The ping utility is much like a SONAR ping on a submarine. It sends out packets to a given IP address, as shown in Figure 18.12, and tells you whether or not they were received. One of the first things to check if you are having trouble getting on a net-

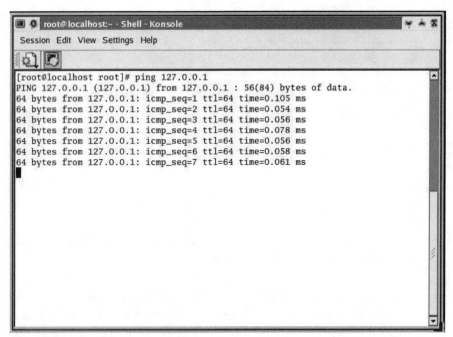

FIGURE 18.12   The ping command.

work or the Internet is to try and ping a known IP address. You also can ping Internet sites by their names. For example, you can try to ping *www.chuckeasttom.com*. If you find that you cannot get a response from any site you ping, then you are probably not connected to the Internet. If you can get some sites to respond and not others, then the problem most likely lies with those sites. The ping command works exactly the same from a Windows command prompt as it does in a Linux or Unix shell.

traceroute

This command is essentially an improved ping. Instead of just telling you if it got to a given IP address, it will tell you how it got there. When you go to an Internet Web site, the odds are that your package goes through several intermediary sites. The traceroute command will tell you where it's going and how long each hop takes. This is very important diagnostic information. If you are having slow response time from Web sites and find that the slowest hop is from your Internet service provider to the next hop, your ISP might be having a problem. You can see an example of traceroute in Figure 18.13.

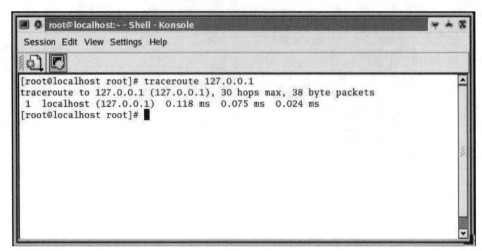

FIGURE 18.13   The `traceroute` command.

The `traceroute` command is not unique to Linux and Unix. Windows provides the same functionality via its `tracert` command. It is called in the exact same manner, by typing in `tracert` followed by the IP address, and it returns the same information.

In the figures for the preceding examples, you may have noticed the address 127.0.0.1 to `ping` *or* `traceroute` *to. This is called the loopback address. It is used to check your own machine. It is often viewed as being a way to address your own network interface card; however, you should realize that you will have a loopback address even if no NIC is found in your machine. It is commonly used to diagnose network problems. If you cannot successfully ping your network card, then you may have a bad network card.*

MISCELLANEOUS COMMANDS

There are several useful commands that do not fit neatly into any one category. We will examine several of these commands here. These commands include `finger`, `who`, `whois`, and `date`. The `date` command is the simplest, as it returns the current date and time. Enter `date` in all lowercase letters at the shell, and you should see something like what is shown in Figure 18.14.

The `finger` command is used to get back information regarding a specific user. This often is useful for a system administrator. For example, if you run `top` and see that one specific user is spawning several processes on your server and those

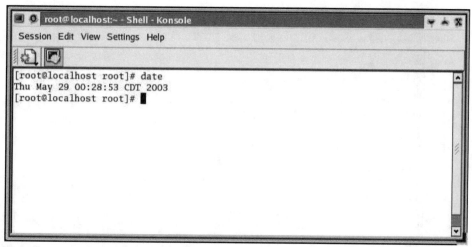

FIGURE 18.14 The date command.

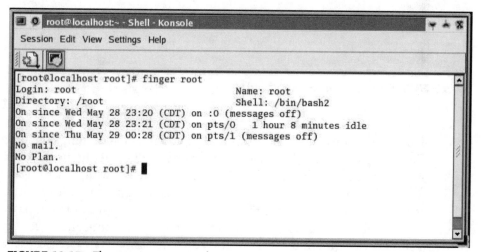

FIGURE 18.15 The finger command.

processes are consuming resources, you may want to find out about that user. In Figure 18.15, you can see the finger command used on the root user.

The who command is also quite useful for a system administrator. It will give you a list of all the users currently logged on to your system. This can be very important. You will want to know who is on your system. You can see the output of the who command in Figure 18.16.

One common trick used by hackers is to log on to a system after hours using a valid user account. Some administrators create a script (we will discuss scripts in

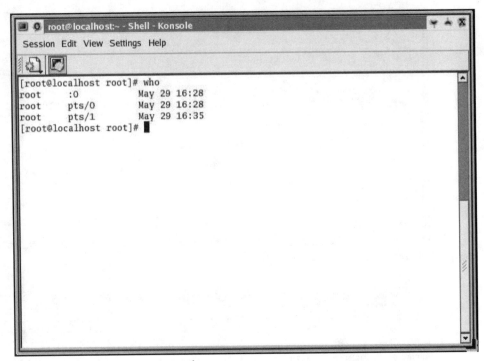

FIGURE 18.16   The who command.

detail later in this book) that runs the who command and dumps the output to a file. You can then schedule that script to run at night, after hours. If you find that at 2 A.M. a user was shown to be logged in, and you know that user was not in the building, then you should suspect a hacker is using that user account. You can delete that account and issue the user a new account with a different password.

The whois command is quite similar to the finger command, except that normally it is used with Internet addresses. You might ask whois www.chuckeasttom.com. If the information is available, this command will return information about the party that registered that domain name. You may not be aware, but when you register a domain, the information you provide is public domain. Anyone can look up the registration information about any domain.

There is another very simple command. It is the uname command. When you enter uname at the shell, it will tell you what operating system you are using. This may seem like an entirely useless command until you consider that these shells can be used with Linux or Unix. You may not be sure whether you are sitting at a Unix machine or a Linux machine.

SUMMARY

This chapter has been a sort of whirlwind tour of shell commands. We have examined file manipulation commands, system commands, network utilities, and even the shell itself. This information, coupled with the shell commands you were introduced to in Chapter 3, should make you basically comfortable with using the shell.

The commands we covered are just a few of the many shell commands available to you with Linux. These are the most commonly used commands, and a knowledge of them is enough to make you a very technically savvy user—a Linux power user, if you will. Some of the commands we covered are also quite useful to system administrators.

REVIEW QUESTIONS

1. What is the primary difference between `ping` and `traceroute`?
2. What does the `finger` command do?
3. What is the Windows equivalent for the `diff` command?
4. What is the difference between the `diff` command and the `cmp` command?
5. What is the difference between the `ps` command and the `top` command?
6. What does the `head` command do?
7. What is the loopback address?

19

System Administration from the Shell

In This Chapter

- Run Levels and `init`
- The Filesystem
- Managing Users and Groups
- Configuring and Activating Network Cards
- Miscellaneous Shell Commands
- File Compression from the Shell

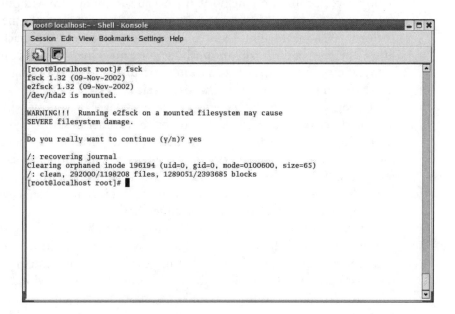

INTRODUCTION

In one of the previous chapters we examined Linux system administration from within the KDE interface. While it is true that administering your Linux machine from a graphical desktop environment is easy and quite convenient, it is important for you to be aware that many Linux administrators prefer using shell commands for system administration. There are several reasons for this. The first being that, once you become comfortable working with the shell, you often can accomplish tasks much faster than you can through a graphical interface. Another reason is that there are occasions when you may want to run your Linux machine without any graphical interface at all, and that would necessitate administering it via shell commands. Although most people, especially those coming from a Windows background, prefer the graphical interface, you should be aware that it is quite possible, and in some instances even desirable, to run Linux without any graphical interface. If, for example, your Linux machine is used as a Web server, mail server, or file server, there may be no need for any of the features present in a graphical user interface like KDE or GNOME. You should bear in mind that any program, including a desktop environment, uses resources. Therefore, running a graphical desktop environment will use some of your system's processor time and memory. If you can run the system without the desktop environment, you will free more of those resources for the tasks the server must perform. This means that if you are working with a very old machine that has limited resources or if you are pushing your machine to its maximum performance, you can improve that machine's performance by working entirely from the shell and foregoing the graphical interface.

Of course there are some significant disadvantages to working without a graphical interface. Without KDE, GNOME, or some other desktop environment, you would not have access to any of the interesting applications we have explored in previous chapters. You would normally want to use a desktop interface for any system that will be an individual's home computer or business workstation. Working purely from the shell with no desktop environment is generally appropriate only for machines that will be used as specialized servers.

In this chapter we will examine how to perform basic Linux system administration from the shell. This will include activities ranging from managing users and groups to configuring and activating your network interface card. What this means is that we will expand on the shell commands you previously learned. We will add several new commands and explore some previous commands in more depth.

RUN LEVELS AND INIT

This chapter is about Linux administration from the shell, and the most fundamental administrative task would be to shut down or reboot the machine. As even a casual Windows user, you realize that turning the power off repeatedly is not very good for your system. With Windows XP you would go to the Start menu and choose Turn Off the Computer, and you would be presented with a screen like what you see in Figure 19.1.

FIGURE 19.1   Shutting down Windows.

Before the advent of Windows 95, Windows 3.1 was a desktop environment separate from the underlying operating system, DOS, and you could invoke Windows from DOS by typing in win. With a shell in Linux, you will still need a way to shut down the machine, reboot the machine, or invoke the desktop environment. In the shell you accomplish all of this with run levels.

Run Levels

A run level is the level at which your system is currently running or operating. You can change the run level any time you like from the shell by typing in init followed by the number designating the run level you want to use. There are six run levels in all. Each designates that progressively more of the system is functioning. Run level 0 designates that the system is shut down. Run level 1 indicates the system is running in shell mode only, no graphical interface and no network support. This moves progressively to run level 5, which means that full network support and a graphical desktop environment such as KDE or GNOME is running. The last run level is 6, which designates a reboot. All of the run levels are summarized in Table 19.1.

TABLE 19.1   Run Levels

Run Level	Purpose
0	This is a complete system shutdown. You invoke this run level by typing `init 0` at the shell. In Windows you can accomplish the same thing by clicking on the Start button and then clicking on Shut Down.
1	This is single-user mode. There is no support for any network or Internet connection and no support for any graphical desktop environment. This is similar to the Safe Mode in Windows. You invoke this run level by typing `init 1` at the shell.
2	This is multiuser mode without any graphical interface and without network support. You invoke this run level by typing `init 2` at the shell.
3	This is full multiuser mode with all functionality except a graphical desktop. This run level is often used for servers that do not require a graphical interface. You invoke this run level by typing `init 3` at the shell.
4	This run level is unused at this time.
5	This run level is a complete system with multiuser capability, full network support, and a graphical desktop environment. This is most often used for personal workstations. You invoke this run level by typing `init 5` at the shell.
6	This is a system reboot. You invoke this run level by typing `init 6` at the shell.

What all of this means is that if you type `init 0` from the shell, the machine will commence its shutdown process. However, if you type `init 6`, the machine will reboot. This may lead you to ask, what is this `init`? The `init` command, like all shell commands, is a program built into Linux shells. The `init` program is very important. In fact, it is absolutely essential to the operation of a Linux system. The `init` program literally initializes your system. When used as a shell command, it initializes your system to the specified run level. This is why it is also used to invoke certain specified run levels. When you type in `init 6`, you are saying to initialize the machine to run level 6. You can see this in Figure 19.2.

init

It is important that you recall that all shell commands are actually programs. As was previously mentioned, the `init` program just happens to be a very important one.

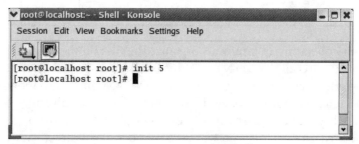

FIGURE 19.2   The init command at the shell.

What is it that init does that is so important and how does it work? Some readers may not want this level of detail about init and should feel free to skip the following paragraphs. However, for the curious reader who wants to understand what is happening in the background, the following few paragraphs will explain quite a bit. The init program works to initialize the machine. It takes over the boot process as soon as the Linux kernel is done loading into memory. The Linux kernel finishes its part of the boot process by starting the init program. This means that init is always the first process on your machine, and that is why its process number is always 1. init, like all commands is really a program, and can be found in the directory /sbin/init. If the kernel can't find init, it tries to run /bin/sh, and if that also fails, the startup of the system fails.

When init starts, it completes the boot process by performing a number of administrative tasks. The init program will start by checking filesystems, starting various services, and starting they getty process. The getty process handles input from the keyboard. You might not have thought about it before, but there must be a process on your machine to handle everything your computer needs to do. With operating systems such as Windows, all of that is transparent to you. You cannot access background system processes, and even system administrators are often unaware of their existence. However, Linux and all Unix-like systems allow you to access many fundamental system processes.

Most university computer science programs include coursework on Unix or Linux. It often is either required or highly recommended. The reason for this emphasis on Unix-like systems is the aforementioned access to the underlying processes. For a computer science student, even one who may never professionally work with Linux or Unix, the ability to look into the fundamental mechanisms of the operating system is crucial to his learning process.

THE FILESYSTEM

Every operating system must organize the files on the computer in some fashion. You may recall that early on in this book we discussed filesystems. Every operating system has certain directories that are of paramount importance. In Windows, the actual operating system is stored in the windows directory on your root drive, usually your C drive. In most cases, you will find Windows in c:\windows. Beneath the windows directory you will see a number of subdirectories, such as system and system32. The entire windows directory, with its subdirectories, contains files that are critical to your computer functioning. Unless you have some advanced knowledge of the Windows operating system, you should not tamper with anything in these directories.

Other important directories include Program Files shown in Figure 19.3. This is where most programs will be installed by default. This is also generally on the root drive. You also have probably noticed a default document directory on Windows machines. This is a directory that the operating system creates for you. It is meant to contain items that are considered crucial or fundamental to the system's normal operation.

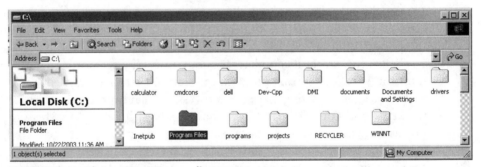

FIGURE 19.3   The Program Files directory.

It was mentioned briefly earlier in this book but must be emphasized again that Windows refers to a directory as a folder. They are the same things. In this book we will use the terms interchangeably.

Since we are using the phrase *root drive*, it might be prudent to define that term. Do not confuse the root drive of any operating system with the root user. The root user, in Unix and Unix-like systems, is the system administrator. In Windows the root user is referred to as the administrator. The root drive or director, for any operating system, is the main directory. For example, if you have three hard drives in your system, or one hard drive divided into three partitions, the one that contains the operating system is the root drive.

As was mentioned previously, in any operating system there are certain key directories. These directories hold certain types of files. This is true in Linux as well as Windows. Let's examine some of those directories and what they contain. There are several directories in Linux, each with its own particular purpose. The File Manager, shown in Figure 19.4, is showing all the top-level directories. We will examine several of these in the following pages.

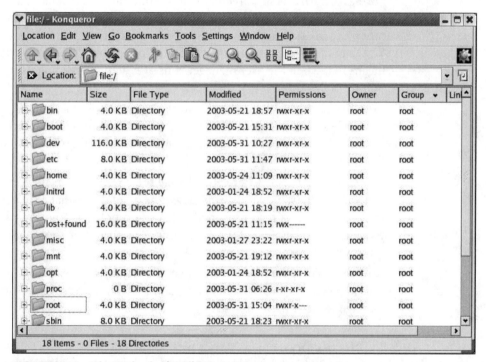

FIGURE 19.4　Directories in the File Manager.

/root: The /root directory is the home directory for the root user. It usually is not accessible to other users on the system.

/bin: The /bin directory holds binary files. Compiled programs are binary files. You will find a number of programs/applications in this directory. In fact, many shell commands are stored in this directory.

/sbin: This directory is very much like /bin, but the commands are not intended for the average computer user. For that reason, /sbin is not usually in the default path of normal users but will be in root's default path. That means that most users who log on cannot access /sbin or any commands stored there.

/etc: The /etc folder contains configuration files. Most applications require some configuration when they start up. All of those configuration files can be found in this directory. This directory has several subdirectories, each containing a different type of configuration file. Let's look at a few of those subdirectories:

etc/passwd: In this subdirectory you will find the user database, with fields giving the username, real name, home directory, encrypted password, and other information about each user. Note that the password is encrypted. You cannot go to this directory and read other people's passwords. That means that when the user manager runs, it is actually reading its information from this directory.

/etc/group: This subdirectory is quite similar to /etc/passwd, except that it describes groups instead of users. All the information about a group, including a list of user accounts that are members of that group, are stored in this directory.

/etc/inittab: This is where you change the configuration file for init. If you will recall, we previously discussed the pivotal role that init plays in a Linux system. It is recommended that you do not reconfigure this unless you are very sure of what you are doing. A novice user should not touch this directory.

/etc/motd: You may have noticed that after logon you get a brief message. This is called the message of the day, and it is found in this directory. This message is often used by system administrators to send information to all users.

/dev: This directory contains device files. Remember that Linux treats all the drives as files. All hard drives start with hd, and floppy drives start with fd. The main hard drive might be named /dev/hd0. The floppy drive would be called /dev/fd0.

/mnt: Although you may not be aware of it, any drive must be mounted prior to its use. The process of mounting a drive involves the operating system accessing it and loading it into memory. In Windows, this is all completely transparent. In modern versions of Linux, it is almost transparent. Most temporary storage drives, such as CD-ROMs and floppy drives, are mounted. The operating system does this for you, however. In older Linux/Unix systems, you had to use shell commands to mount the floppy drive before you could access it. This is no longer the case. However, you will find your floppy in a subdirectory of the /mnt directory, where all mounted temporary storage devices are found.

/boot: This directory contains those files that are used by the bootstrap loader. This means that LILO will look here for files it needs, as will GRUB (remember that with Linux 9.0, GRUB is the default boot loader instead of LILO). Kernel images are often kept here instead of in the root directory. This directory is critical to the boot process. It is another area that the novice user should leave alone.

/usr: Some commands are in /bin or in /usr/local/bin. This directory also contains /usr/share/man, /usr/share/info, and /usr/share/doc, where you will find documentation. This is where you will find all of those manual pages accessed by the man command.

It is not important that you memorize all of these directories. However, a basic familiarity with what is in the directories would be useful. This also leads us to the topic of maneuvering around the directories from the shell. There are a few rather simple commands that you can use to maneuver in the shell. You have seen the cd command. You can type in cd followed by the name of the directory and you will change to that directory. If you then type in just cd and press Enter, you will go to your home directory. Both of these commands are shown in Figure 19.5.

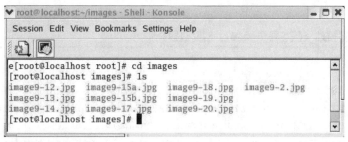

FIGURE 19.5 The cd command.

If you want to use the shell to get to any of the directories we have mentioned, you must first be at the root directory. You then type in cd /mnt (or whatever directory you want to change to). In Figure 19.6 you can see a change to the /mnt directory followed by the ls command being used to list files and subdirectories.

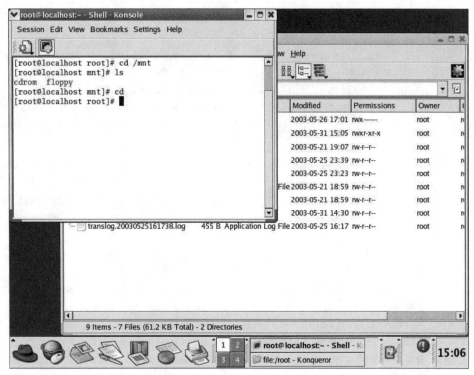

FIGURE 19.6 Using cd to peruse directories.

MANAGING USERS AND GROUPS

Windows provides only very limited capability to manage users or groups from the command line. This is due the fact, previously mentioned, that Windows is designed to be used from the graphical interface. Linux, however, can be used just as effectively from the shell as it can from the graphical desktop environments. In fact, some Linux enthusiasts might argue that it is better to use Linux from the shell. Whether you are using a desktop environment such as KDE or GNOME or are working from the shell, you will still need to manage users and groups.

logname

Though it may seem odd, the first shell command we need to examine is the logname command. This command will tell you what user is currently logged on to a terminal. This might sound odd, but it is necessary. Especially in multiuser environments, you may not know what username was used to log on to a system. This means you will not know what privileges he has. The `logname` command is typed in just as you see in Figure 19.7, and it tells you the username that is currently logged on to that system.

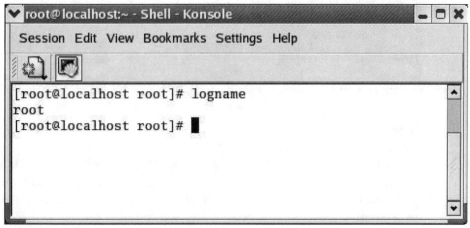

FIGURE 19.7 The `logname` command.

Useradd and groupadd

Another command you need to be familiar with is `useradd`. This command is used to add users from the shell. This command also has a number of flags you can use with it. In Figure 19.8 you can see the display for `useradd –help`. As you can see, there are several flags you can pass to it.

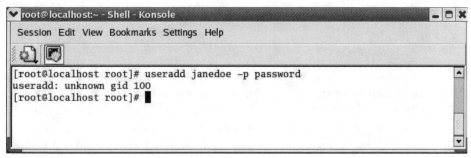

FIGURE 19.8 The `useradd` flags.

You can specify a group for the user to belong to, expiration date, password, and everything you might specify through KDE's user and group manager. However, in many cases you will just specify a username and password. Figure 19.9

root@localhost:~ - Shell - Konsole
Session Edit View Bookmarks Settings Help
usage: useradd [-u uid [-o]] [-g group] [-G group,...]
[-d home] [-s shell] [-c comment] [-m [-k template]]
[-f inactive] [-e expire] [-p passwd] [-M] [-n] [-r] name
useradd -D [-g group] [-b base] [-s shell]
[-f inactive] [-e expire]
[root@localhost root]#

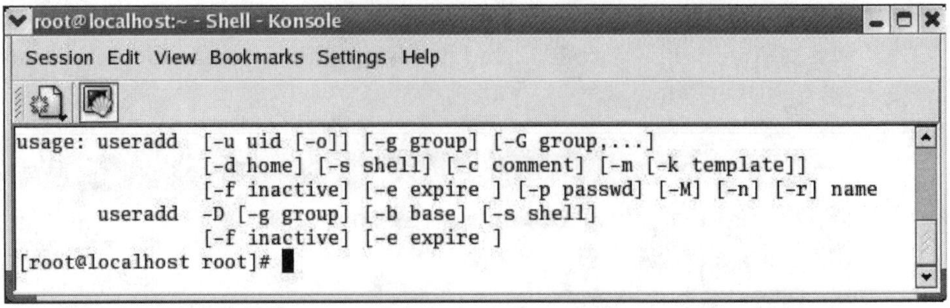

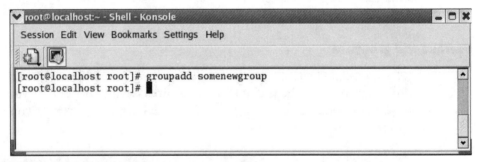

FIGURE 19.9 Adding a user with `useradd`.

shows a new user, named `someusername`, with the password of `password`, being added with the `useradd` command.

As you may have guessed, you also can add groups with a very similar command, `groupadd`. This command has fewer flags. You can essentially specify the group name and group ID and very little else. Figure 19.10a shows a new group named `somenewgroup` being added.

root@localhost:~ - Shell - Konsole
Session Edit View Bookmarks Settings Help
[root@localhost root]# groupadd somenewgroup
[root@localhost root]#

FIGURE 19.10A Using the `groupadd` command.

Once you have executed this command, you have a new user account with a home directory and the capability to log on to and use the system. You can verify this by using File Manager to look in the home directory and see if a subdirectory has been created for this new user. This would be a sure sign that the user was added successfully. As Figure 19.10b shows, the user has been added successfully.

Another interesting command that is closely related to `useradd` and `groupadd` is the `groups` command. This command will tell you what groups the currently logged-on user is a member of. You can see this command used on the root user in Figure 19.11.

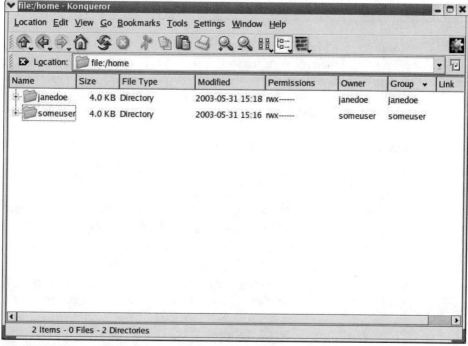

FIGURE 19.10B The new user's home directory.

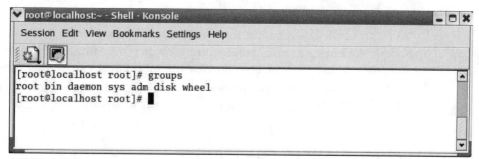

FIGURE 19.11 The groups command.

As you can see, managing users and groups from the shell is not really any more difficult than from the graphical desktop environments. It may be a little less visually appealing, but you can still perform the required functions.

CONFIGURING AND ACTIVATING NETWORK CARDS

In addition to adding users and groups, it is likely that you will need to activate, configure, and manage your network cards. A lot of this can be done by giving the `ifconfig` command, previously introduced, a more thorough examination. There are several flags that you can pass to `ifconfig` that alter the behavior of the network interface card. The most commonly used flags are discussed in Table 19.2.

TABLE 19.2 `ifconfig` Flags

Flag	Purpose
`-a`	This flag is used to display all the information about your IP addresses, including the loopback address.
`add <address>`	This allows you to add additional IP addresses to your card. The syntax is `ipconfig add 10.10.10.55`.
`delete <address>`	This does just the opposite of the `add` command. It deletes one of the addresses you have added. An example is `ipconfig delete 10.10.10.55`.
`up`	This command turns the network card on. An example is `ifconfig -up`.
`down`	This command, as you might guess, turns a network card off. An example is `ifconfig -down`.

As with all shell commands, there are plenty of flags you can pass to `ifconfig` to make it work in the manner you require. However, the commands listed in Table 19.2 are the essential flags for `ifconfig` that you must know. Combining a thorough knowledge of `ifconfig` with `who`, `ping`, `whois`, `finger`, and `traceroute` will enable you to do basic network operations and troubleshooting from the shell.

MISCELLANEOUS SHELL COMMANDS

There are a number of shell commands that do not neatly fit into any category but may prove useful for any Linux system administrator. The commands can provide you with useful information about your system or assist you in performing certain tasks. In the next few paragraphs we will take look at some of these commands.

du and free

It can be quite important for you to find out information about your machine's current state. In KDE or GNOME you would use the System Information utility to view the use of memory and free diskspace. From the shell we have a few commands we can use. The du command, short for disk usage, will tell you how many bytes of disk space the current directory is occupying. You can see this command in Figure 19.12.

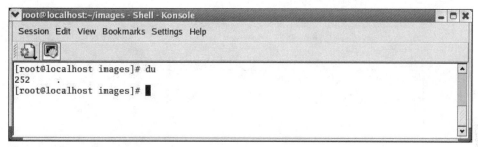

FIGURE 19.12   The du command.

You can also use shell commands to determine how much free memory your system has available. The free command, shown in Figure 19.13, will display the total memory, memory in use, and free memory in bytes. This is quite useful in diagnosing slow or inadequate performance on your machine, which is often caused by too little memory.

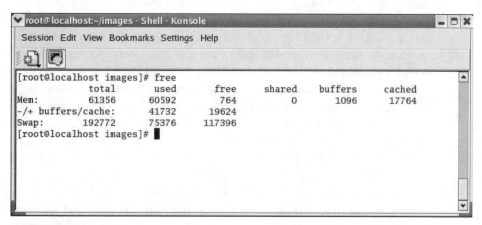

FIGURE 19.13   The free command.

pwd

When you are looking at your prompt, it usually lists the name of the current directory and the current user. It does not list the complete path to your directory. If you are in a directory that is a subdirectory of yet another subdirectory, it can get quite easy to forget where you actually are. The pwd command, shown in Figure 19.14, will display the complete path to your current location. It is the shell equivalent of leaving a trail of bread crumbs so you can find your way back home.

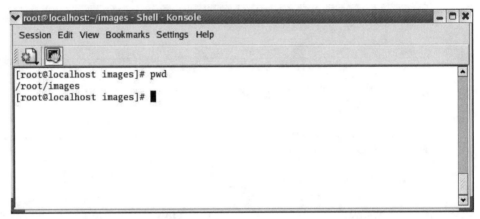

FIGURE 19.14 The pwd command.

dmesg

This is a very interesting command and may prove quite useful if you need to diagnose system problems. When your system boots up, you see a lot of information telling you what processes are starting, what processes failed, what hardware is being initialized, and more. Unfortunately, you may not have watched the bootup process carefully, or you may not remember what you saw. If, for example, your sound card is not working, it would be a good idea to know if it was properly initialized during bootup. You can use the dmesg command, shown in Figures 19.15a and 19.15b, to view all the messages that were displayed during bootup.

As you can see, this command produces a tremendous amount of output. It can be quite daunting to read through this entire series of screens searching for a single item. This is where the redirect command can be quite helpful. If you type in dmesg > boot.txt, the dmesg output will be redirected to a file. You can then use any text editor you like to open that file and search for the items you need to check. This is just one example of how, using various shell commands together, you can make the system easy to manage.

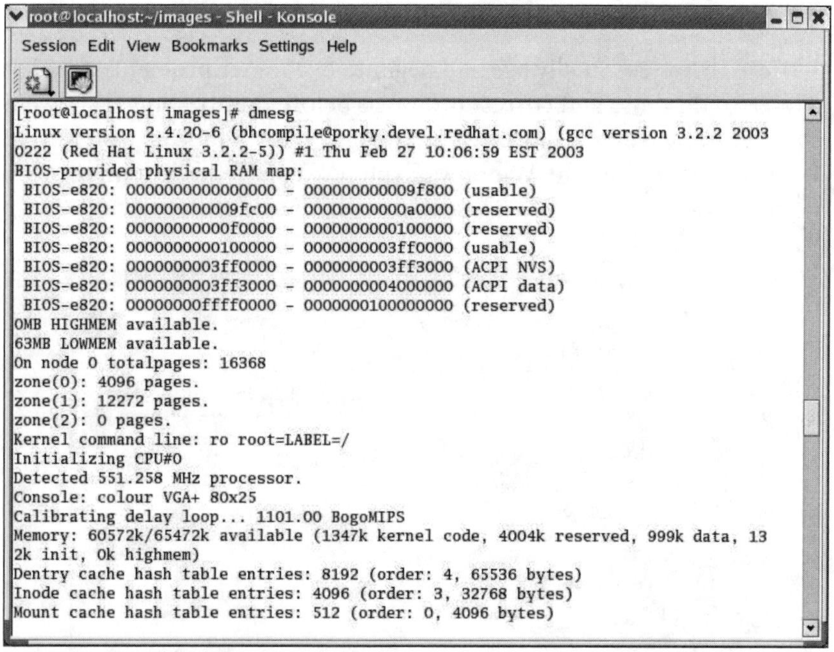

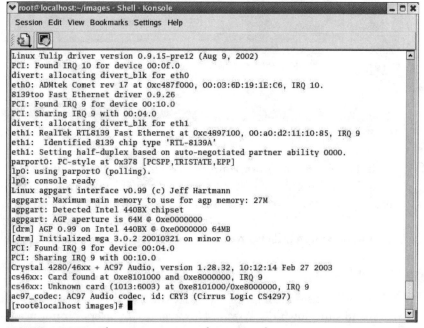

FIGURE 19.15A   The dmesg command.

FIGURE 19.15B   The dmesg command, continued.

fsck

Hard drives eventually age and begin to encounter problems. It is important to be able to diagnose and correct problems before they become too severe. Every computer needs a process to check the system. With Windows, you can run a Scan Disk on any drive from the Windows Explorer. You right-click on the drive, and under Properties choose Tools. This is shown in Figure 19.16.

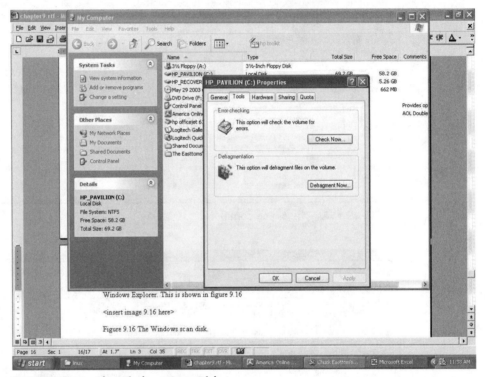

FIGURE 19.16   The Windows Scan Disk.

In Linux you can run `fsck` on any drive from the shell. This is short for filesystem check. It will check the integrity of the filesystem. This command can be quite useful in ensuring that your computer is optimized to perform its best. You can see this command in Figure 19.17. However, with later versions of Linux using ext3 as the filesystem, optimization is rarely if ever required, so you may not use this command very often.

logout and shutdown

When we discussed run levels and `init`, you saw that you could use the command `init 0` to shut down the system. However, many users cannot use the `init` com-

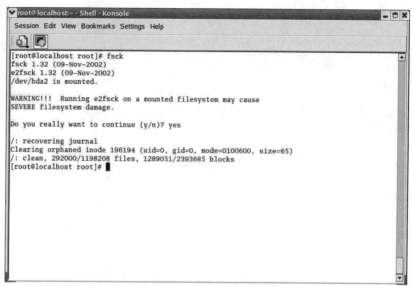

FIGURE 19.17   The fsck command.

mand. It is meant to be the tool of the root user, not all users. How do you reboot or shut down the system from the shell if you are not logged on as the root user? The answer is to go to KDE and choose the Logout option from the Start menu. However, if you are logged on as root or use the su command for superuser mode, there are other commands that also will work for shutting down the system. The shutdown command does exactly what init 6 does. Just type in shutdown at the shell, and the system will shut down. You can also log out using the command logout typed in at the shell. logout works for any user, but remember that shutdown will work only for root.

passwd and su

You also may need to change the password of the user currently logged on. This can be done with the passwd command. If you type in the command passwd, as shown in Figure 19.18, you will be prompted to enter a new password. If the system feels that this password is too easy to crack, because either it is a standard dictionary word or too short, the system will tell you that it is a bad password. You then retype the password to confirm it.

There will be times when you may go to a Linux machine where someone has logged on, and you want to do some task that requires the privileges of the root user. Logging out, then logging back in as the root, can be tedious. Fortunately, you don't have to do that. You can invoke the superuser mode. If you type in su at the

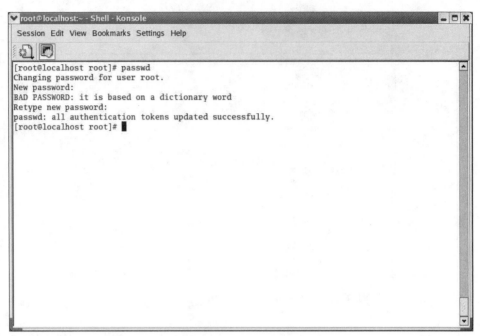

FIGURE 19.18 The passwd command.

shell, you will be asked for the root password. If you supply it, you will have root privileges.

FILE COMPRESSION FROM THE SHELL

Many people find that from time to time they need to compress several files into one archived file. There can be many reasons for doing this. One reason is to archive old files that you don't use but do not want to destroy. Most archiving tools also compress the files, so that the archived file takes up less disk space than the original file did. However, you should be aware that compression is not always part of compiling files into an archive file. With some archive tools, compression is an option that you choose to add or not to add. Another reason to archive files is to send them over the Internet. If you have five files to send, compressing them into a single archive would make it easier to send them.

There are several programs available for Windows that do this sort of archiving. Perhaps the most popular is WinZip®. WinZip is a shareware program, which means you can download a free trial version. It has a very user-friendly graphical interface that enables you to compress files into an archive and extract them from that archive with ease.

Just as Windows users need the capability to archive and extract files, so do Linux users. There is a very interesting Linux utility that works from the shell called tar. The tar program can be used to compress files and to extract them. It comes with all Linux distributions, so if you send a tar file to a friend or colleague who is using Linux, you can rest assured that he will have the necessary tools to extract the files. Since tar is a shell command, you might have guessed that there are several flags you can pass to it to make it do what you require. Table 19.3 illustrates the most important of these flags. You can get a complete list at the shell by typing in tar —help.

TABLE 19.3 The tar Flags

The Flag	The Flag's Purpose
-c	This flag is used to create a new archive file.
-x	This flag is used to extract files from an archive.
-r	This flag is used to append new files to an existing archive.
-f	This is used in working with a file.
-t	This is used simply to list the contents of an archive file.
-t	This is used to list the contents of an archive file.
-v	This is often used with —t. It designates a verbose response.
-z	This flag directs the tar to use gzip compression.

Let's take a look at these files in action. In Figure 19.19 you can see that an ls command was executed to see what files were in the current directory. Then the tar command was used to create a new archive file. This was done by typing tar, followed by the flags for create (c) and file (f) and the new archive file's name, then the files to add to this archive were listed.

If you want to view the content of an existing file, you would again use the tar command, only with different flags. This is shown in Figure 19.20, where we first use ls to list the directory's contents, then use tar with the flags to list (t), file (f), and verbose output (v).

Tar is a very commonly used utility in all Unix-like operating systems. You will find that many software packages that are distributed for Unix or Linux on the Internet come as tar files, frequently called tarballs. This means that you can get a lot

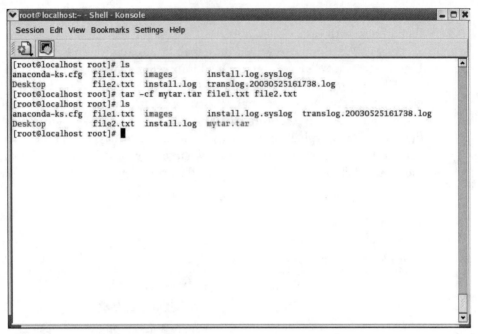

FIGURE 19.19   Creating a tar file.

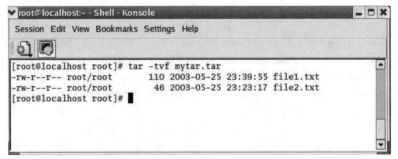

FIGURE 19.20   Listing the contents of a tar file.

of useful programs for Linux, most of which are free, from the Internet. But it also means you will need to know how to use tar to decompress those files.

SUMMARY

In this chapter, we examined system administration from the shell. Several important concepts about the Linux operating system, such as the structure of the filesystem, important directories, and the init command also were explored. In addition to the shell commands mentioned in this chapter, the commands mentioned in previous chapters can be useful to the system administrator. In essence, any system administrator will need to be at least somewhat familiar with shell commands.

REVIEW QUESTIONS

1. What is found in the /bin directory?
2. What does the command init 6 do?
3. What is the shell command to activate your network card?
4. What is in the /mnt directory?
5. What is /dev/fp0/?
6. Where would you look to change the message of the day?
7. Why should an inexperienced person never alter anything in /etc/inittab?
8. What is the purpose of the pwd command?
9. What command is used to see how much free memory you have on your system?

20 Basic Shell Scripting

In This Chapter

- Script Basics
- Variables in Shell Scripts
- Getting Input from the User
- Math in Scripts
- `if` Statements in Scripts
- Loops in Scripts

```
[root@localhost root]# bash scriptten.sh
Count down
1
2
3
4
5
blast off!
[root@localhost root]#
```

INTRODUCTION

The previous chapter discussed administering your computer via shell commands. You will find that frequently multiple commands are used together to accomplish some tasks. For example, if you really want to get a picture of your computer's performance, you might use several different shell commands to get a complete view of your system. Normally, shells are interactive. This means that a shell will accept a command from you via your keyboard and execute that command. If you use certain commands on a routine basis, it can be tedious to retype the same series of commands each time you need them. You can store this sequence of commands to a text file and instruct the shell to execute this text file instead of entering the commands. This is what is known as a *shell script*.

Windows has something quite similar to this, although it is not used much anymore. In Windows you can use a standard text editor to create what is called a *batch file* and execute that file from the command prompt. Batch files were very popular when DOS and Windows 3.1 were the current operating systems, but they have fallen out of use in recent years. So that you understand the concept, let's examine how to write a simple batch file in Windows.

The first step is to open Notepad and enter the following lines:

```
cd\windows
 dir *.log
cd\
```

These are the commands to change directories to the windows directory, list all files that end with .log, and then change back to the root directory (c:\). Then choose File and Save As, and save the file to the root directory with the name test.bat. Make certain that you change the file type to All Files, rather than Text, as you see in Figure 20.1.

Now open a command prompt and change to the c:\ directory (you can do this by typing in cd\ and pressing the Enter key). Then enter test.bat and then press the Enter key. You should see something very much like what is shown in Figure 20.2.

You can see that in essence a batch file is simply a way to execute a number of commands by typing in only a single command at the prompt. Batch files are sometimes used if there is a series of commands that is routinely executed in sequence. The Linux script performs just about the same purpose as the batch file, except that Linux scripts have more versatility and can be used in much the same manner as many standard programming languages.

Shell scripts, in essence, are miniature programs. They can do many of the things that traditional programming languages such as C, C++, BASIC, and others do. This makes them very powerful and versatile. There are entire books written just on

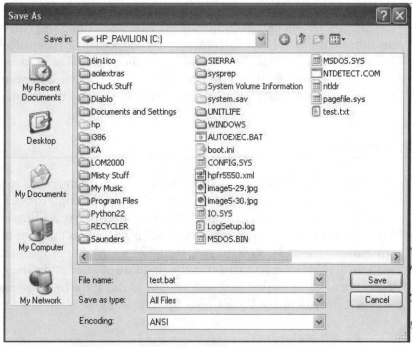

FIGURE 20.1 Saving your batch file.

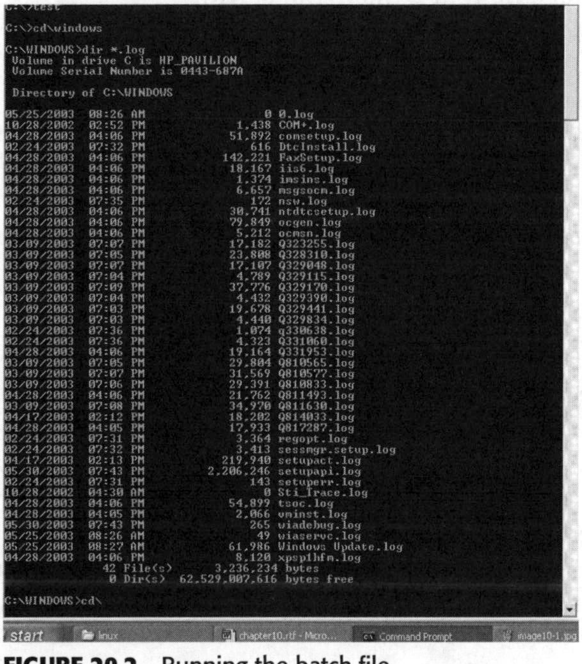

FIGURE 20.2 Running the batch file.

shell scripting, and that should give you some idea of how deep this topic can be. In this chapter we will be exploring only the basics of writing shell scripts. If you are planning to use your Linux machine for a server, perhaps for a small office, or if you want to delve deeper into the world of Linux, then you will want to study this chapter carefully. However, if you are a casual Linux user who just wants to surf the Internet and use the Office tools, you should feel free to skip this chapter.

SCRIPT BASICS

As we have already mentioned, if you have a series of commands you want to automate, the most efficient way to do that is via a script. Scripts can be written in any basic text editor. You can use Kate, KWrite, or any other text editor that you want. The only problem to keep in mind when writing a script is that scripts are generally written for a particular shell (bash, C shell, Korn, etc.). For this reason, all the shells have an agreed upon standard that the first line of a script declares what type of shell it runs in. Then that shell will be used to run the script. For example, if you want a script run by the C shell, your first line would be this:

```
#!/bin/chsh
```

If you want your script to run in bash:

```
#! /bin/sh
```

Keep in mind that any line, other than the first line of the script, that has a # is considered a comment and is ignored. In case you are unfamiliar with this use of the word comments, they are used by programmers to leave notes for any other programmer who might look at their code. A comment is not executed and has no effect on the workings of the program or script. It is just an explanatory note for other programmers.

What this first line of the script is saying is that the subsequent lines should be executed with the designated shell. The ! symbol, in this case, means to execute, so this line literally says execute the following lines in the designated shell.

It might be helpful to see a few scripts in action. Let's take a look at a couple of simple scripts. While these scripts are quite simple, they illustrate the basics of script writing and should help you begin to get comfortable with the concept of scripts. You can use any text editor you like. When you are done typing your script, read through it carefully for spelling errors or typos. Beginners often miss basic errors that will cause a script to behave in unpredicted ways or not run at all. Here is a sample script, seen in Figure 20.3:

```
#!/bin/sh
hostname
who
exit 0
```

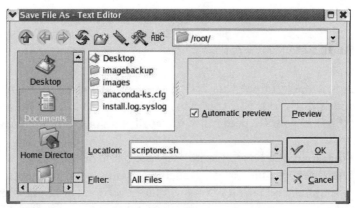

FIGURE 20.3   Saving your script file.

If you save this with the name `scriptone.sh`, you can then go to the shell, change to whatever directory you saved your script to, and run the `ls` command. You should see `scriptone.sh` in green print among the other contents of that directory, as you see in Figure 20.4. You can now enter `bash scriptone.sh` and see output similar to what is shown in Figure 20.5.

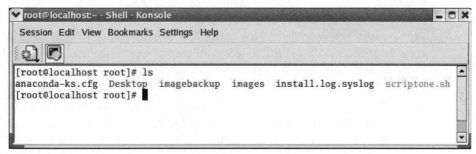

FIGURE 20.4   Script files in green print.

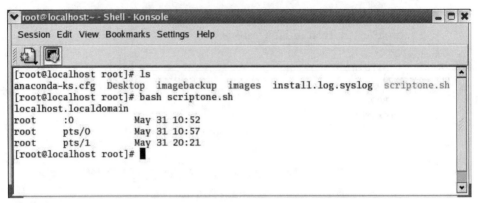

FIGURE 20.5   Running script one.

Notice the last line of the script. It is not one of the shell commands we have previously discussed. This command tells a script that it is done and to exit. If you omit this line, your script may not run at all; if it does run, it will have unpredictable results.

You might also be wondering why the name of your script was in green. This indicates an executable script. All such scripts appear in green, just as all directories appear in blue, and tar files in red. In older versions of Linux a script file was not immediately executable. You had to first use the chmod command (an abbreviation for *change mode*) to change the file's mode to an executable one. For example, after saving your script you would have had to enter the following at the shell:

```
chmod 777 scriptone.sh
```

If you are using an older version of Linux you may still have to do this. If you try typing in the name of your script and an error occurs, try using chmod, as shown above, to change the mode to an executable script. That was not too difficult, was it?

Let's try one more script. In this script we will introduce some interesting new additions to your repertoire of shell commands. As you know, you can run an ls command and list everything in a directory. However, if you use the command prompt in Windows very much, you might be wondering if you can filter the results. In Windows, for example, you could enter dir *.exe and get only files ending with an .exe extension. Can you do the same thing in Linux? Yes, you certainly can. In fact, the asterisk wildcard works the same way. There is also another wildcard character you can use, the question mark. A question mark indicates a single character. So for example if you type ls *.txt at the shell, you will see all text files. If you enter ?.txt, you will see only text files with a one-character name. There are several wildcards, and we will use them in our next script. Several of the commonly used wildcards are summarized in Table 20.1.

TABLE 20.1 Wildcards

Wildcard	Purpose
*	This means any character and any number of characters. For example, `*.sh` means any shell, any file that ends in the `.sh` extension, regardless of how many characters are in the name.
?	This denotes one character. For example, `????.txt` means all text files that have a four-character name.
!	This means *not*, or negation.
[abc]	This means containing any of the characters listed. `[abc]???.txt` means all text files that start with an a, b, or c followed by three characters.
[a-m]	This means any character in the range shown. `[a-l]??.txt` means any file starting with some letter from a to e, followed by two characters.

Let's put some of these wildcards you just learned to good use and put them in a script. Open your favorite text editor and enter the following text:

```
#!/bin/sh
ls *.txt
ls [a-m]???.txt
ls ??.txt
exit 0
```

Now save this script in the same manner as you did the previous script. Make sure the file type is set to All Files and save it with the name scripttwo.sh. Then from the shell enter bash scripttwo.sh. You should see a display similar to the one shown in Figure 20.6. Obviously, your display will depend entirely on what text files are in your directory. If you like, you can save blank documents with various names in this directory, just so you can test the script.

Let's examine this script in some detail to make certain you understand it completely. The first line of the script is the same as in the first script we examined. In fact, all of the scripts we work with in this book will begin in this manner. What we see next are three separate calls to the ls command. The first uses the asterisk wildcard to ask for all files, regardless of their name, that end in .txt. This will display all text files in that directory. The second line says to display all files that begin with some letter from a to m, followed by three more letters and ending in a .txt extension. The third line asks for all text files whose names have only two letters. Finally, we come to the exit 0 line, which instructs the script to exit.

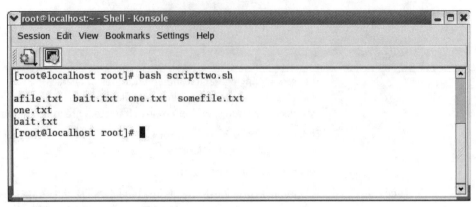

FIGURE 20.6 Running script two.

This second example shows two things. First, it should demonstrate that writing scripts is not particularly hard. Make certain that you always check your spelling and end your script with the exit 0, and everything should be fine. The second thing this script illustrates is the enormous flexibility you have with wildcards.

VARIABLES IN SHELL SCRIPTS

Previously in this chapter, it was stated that Linux shell scripts are very similar to many traditional programming languages, such as C++ and BASIC. In any programming language you will need to store data temporarily. For example, if you want a script to divide two numbers and display the answer, you will need to store those two numbers and the answer. To process information, data must be kept in the computer's RAM memory. RAM memory is divided into small segments, and each segment has a unique number called memory location/address, which is used to hold data. We could designate a specific memory address to store our data, but that would be an absolutely monumental task. You would have to memorize the thousands of possible memory addresses. You also would have to realize that not all the addresses available now will be available the next time you run the script. Fortunately, this problem was solved a long time ago by the creators of the modern programming languages. In your code you declare some name as a representation for a place in memory. The specific address that your name refers to is determined by the system itself; you don't have to do that. This name for a specific location in memory is called a *variable* because its contents can vary. You can change what is stored there. A variable is a name for a location in memory used to store data.

In the Linux shell you have two types of variables: system variables and user-defined variables, also called UDVs. System variables are created and maintained by Linux itself. This type of variable is always written in all capital letters, so they are easy to recognize. The second type of variable, the user-defined variable, is created and maintained by the user. This type of variable is always written in all lowercase letters.

SYSTEM VARIABLES

You can see all the system variables by typing in set at the shell. You will see a rather long list like the one shown in Figure 20.7.

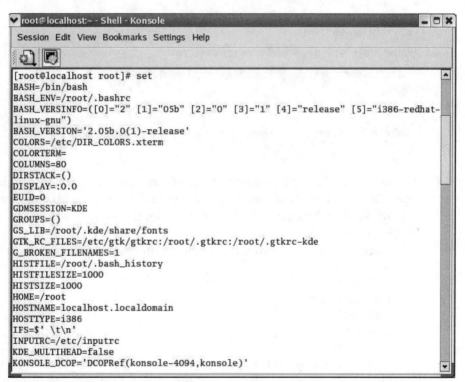

```
[root@localhost root]# set
BASH=/bin/bash
BASH_ENV=/root/.bashrc
BASH_VERSINFO=([0]="2" [1]="05b" [2]="0" [3]="1" [4]="release" [5]="i386-redhat-
linux-gnu")
BASH_VERSION='2.05b.0(1)-release'
COLORS=/etc/DIR_COLORS.xterm
COLORTERM=
COLUMNS=80
DIRSTACK=()
DISPLAY=:0.0
EUID=0
GDMSESSION=KDE
GROUPS=()
GS_LIB=/root/.kde/share/fonts
GTK_RC_FILES=/etc/gtk/gtkrc:/root/.gtkrc:/root/.gtkrc-kde
G_BROKEN_FILENAMES=1
HISTFILE=/root/.bash_history
HISTFILESIZE=1000
HISTSIZE=1000
HOME=/root
HOSTNAME=localhost.localdomain
HOSTTYPE=i386
IFS=$' \t\n'
INPUTRC=/etc/inputrc
KDE_MULTIHEAD=false
KONSOLE_DCOP='DCOPRef(konsole-4094,konsole)'
```

FIGURE 20.7 The system variables.

Table 20.2 lists some of the more commonly used system variables and their functions.

TABLE 20.2 System Variables

System Variable	Meaning
BASH=/bin/bash	The name of the shell
BASH_VERSION=1.1	The shell version name
COLUMNS=80	The number of columns wide the screen should be
HOME=/home/ceasttom	The home directory
LINES=25	The number of vertical rows the screen should be
LOGNAME=ceasttom	The login name
OSTYPE=Linux	The operating system
PATH=/usr/bin:/sbin:/bin:/usr/sbin	The path settings
PS1=[\u@\h \W]\$	The prompt settings
PWD=/home/students/Common	The current working directory
SHELL=/bin/bash	The shell name
USERNAME=jsmith	Username currently logged in to this PC

You can use the echo command to print any of these variables from inside a script. The echo command means to display to the screen. This command also works in Windows batch files. Let's look at a script that displays some of the system variables to the screen.

Type the following into your favorite text editor and save it as scriptthree.sh:

```
#!/bin/bash
echo $USERNAME
echo $HOME
echo $SHELL
```

You should then go to the shell and enter bash scriptthree.sh. You will see something similar to what is shown in Figure 20.8. Of course, your display will be slightly different because your username and home directory are different.

So you can see that writing a script to display the system variables is not particularly difficult. Before we continue too far, we should examine this echo command a bit more closely. In addition to using echo to display system commands to the screen, you also can use it to echo simple text. You can use this text to inform the user of anything you want. Let's look at the previous script, written to use the echo command to clarify the data we are displaying.

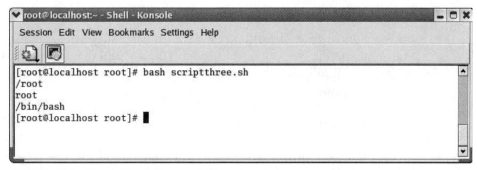

FIGURE 20.8   Displaying system variables.

```
#!/bin/bash
echo Hey this script will display your current
echo home directory, user name, and shell
echo Home directory is $HOME
echo Username is $USERNAME
echo shell is $SHELL
exit 0
```

If you save this as scriptfour.sh and run it from the shell, you should see something like what is shown in Figure 20.9.

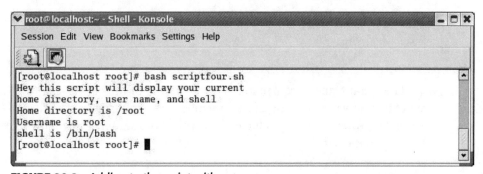

FIGURE 20.9   Adding to the script with echo.

As you can see, this script is more user friendly that the first one. Instead of displaying a list of values, it tells the user what it intends to display, and then it labels each value. You will find your scripts more user friendly if you use the echo command to provide the user with some additional information.

User-Defined Variables

As we mentioned, a user-defined variable is, as its name suggests, a variable you create for some specific purpose in your script. You will find that most scripts of any complexity at all will require variables. The generic syntax for defining a user-defined variable is shown here:

```
variable name=value
```

This means you provide some name for your variable, followed by an initial value to put in that variable. For example, you might have a variable that is designed to hold a person's age. You would declare that in the following manner:

```
age=20
```

Of course, you can store more than numbers in a variable. Perhaps you want a variable to store last names. You would declare that variable in this manner:

```
lastname=Smith
```

You have a great deal of flexibility in naming variables, but there are some rules that must be obeyed. Variable names must begin with an alphanumeric character or underscore character (_), followed by one or more alphanumeric characters. The following are all examples of valid variable names:

```
lastname
_lastname
variable7
```

The second rule to remember regards the use of the equals sign (=) to assign values to your variables. You must remember to not put spaces on either side of the equals sign when assigning value to a variable. For example, the following variable declaration is correct:

```
no=20
```

The following variable declarations are all in error:

```
age =20
age= 20
age = 20
```

The third rule for you to remember is that variable names, like everything in Linux, are case sensitive. The following creates three variables named age, Age, and AGE, each with an initial value of 20.

```
age=20
Age=20
AGE=20
```

This actually creates three variables named age, each with an initial value of 20.

The fourth rule regarding variable declaration regards null variables. A null variable is defined as one without any initial value. You can define a null variable by not assigning it any value after the equals sign, as you see here:

```
age=
lastname=
```

Creating a variable is not particularly difficult. Let's examine a brief script that creates a couple of variables and prints their values to the screen.

```
#!/bin/bash
lastname=Easttom
firstname=Chuck
echo My name is $firstname $lastname
exit 0
```

Save this script as scriptfive.sh and run it from the shell. You should see what is shown in Figure 20.10.

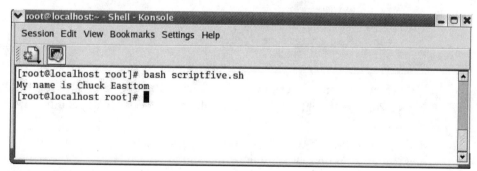

FIGURE 20.10 Using variables.

Now we see how to create variables, but they will not be of much use unless we can do two things. The first is to put data in them. This will often be data from the user, so we need to explore how to get data from the user. We will also need to manipulate data arithmetically. Both topics will be examined in the next two portions of this chapter.

GETTING INPUT FROM THE USER

As was previously mentioned, variables will often get their values from user input. We need some method to take the data that the user types in at the keyboard and put it into the variables in our script. The vehicle for accomplishing this is the read statement. The read statement takes whatever is typed in, up to the point of the user pressing the Enter key, and puts that value into the designated variable. The following is an example of the syntax:

```
somevariable=
read somevariable
```

Let's examine a script that has the user enter data and uses the echo statement to print the data to the screen. Type the following into your favorite text editor and save it as scriptsix.sh:

```
#!/bin/bash
lastname=smith
firstname=john
echo Please type in your first name
read firstname
echo Please type in your last name
read lastname
echo
echo Hello $firstname $lastname it is good to meet you.
exit 0
```

When you run this script you should see something similar to what is shown in Figure 20.11, although your display will vary, of course, depending on the name you enter.

You see this is a rather friendly script! It also demonstrates how to create a variable and how to fill that variable with data the user provides. Notice that when we display the values of the variables to the screen, we get the values the user typed in, not the initial values we put in our script. The contents of the variables were overwritten by the data the user entered. If you will recall, we stated earlier that they are called variables because their content can vary.

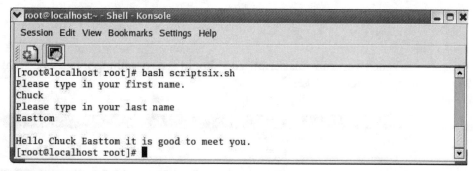

FIGURE 20.11   Getting user input.

MATH IN SCRIPTS

In addition to getting input from the user, you often will want to perform some basic arithmetic operations. This is a place where scripts can be particularly useful. If you have some calculations you need to perform on a regular basis, you can use a script to automate that task. The generic syntax used is this:

```
expr operator1 math-operator op2
```

For example, you can add two numbers by typing in

```
expr 20 +2
```

The math you can do in a Linux shell script is very limited. Essentially you can do very simple arithmetic operations on two operators. One or both of the operators can be a variable, so you could write a script that asks the user for two numbers and adds or subtracts them. For more advanced math you will need a more advanced scripting language, and that is beyond the scope of this book. However, let's take a moment to look at a script that does use the limited math capabilities available. Type the following into the text editor of your choice and save it as script-seven.sh:

```
#!/bin/bash
numone=0
numtwo=0
echo Please enter the first number
read numone
echo Please enter the second number
read numtwo
```

```
echo $numone added to $numtwo is `expr $numone + $numtwo`
exit 0
```

When you run this script, you should see something much like what is displayed in Figure 20.12.

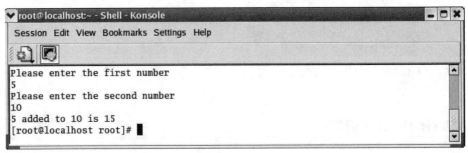

FIGURE 20.12   Basic script math.

Admittedly this is not particularly advanced math or even very interesting! But it does illustrate the very basic arithmetic capabilities of a Linux shell script. You may have noticed what appear to be single quotes on each side of the `expr $numone + $numtwo` statement. These are not actually single quotes, they are backquotes. On most keyboards, to the left of the number one key, you will see a key that has a ~ and a ` mark. The first is called a tilde, and the second is the backquote. It is imperative that you use the backquote rather than the single quote that is to the right of your colon/semicolon key.

IF STATEMENTS IN SCRIPTS

In any programming or scripting language, you need to take alternative actions depending on some input. If some condition is true, then execute one set of code, and if it's not, execute a different set. The following is a generic example of the syntax used:

```
if condition
then
  condition is zero (true - 0)
  execute these commands

else
  if condition is not true then
  execute these commands
fi
```

NOTE

fi *indicates a finished* if *statement.*

Let's look at a script that illustrates this. In your favorite text editor, enter the following lines and save it as `scripteight.sh`:

```
#!/bin/bash
num=0
echo Please enter an integer
read num
if test $num -gt 0
then
  echo $num is positive
else
  echo $num is a negative number
fi
exit 0
```

If you run this script from the shell, you should see something similar to what is displayed in Figure 20.13.

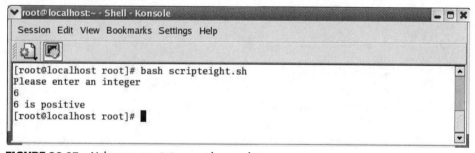

FIGURE 20.13   Using an if statement in a script.

There are several items in this particular script that we need to pay attention to. The first line that is different from what we have previously seen is if test $num -gt 0. This line says to see if the variable num is greater than (gt) zero. If it is, then proceed to the code found under the then statement. If it is not, then proceed to the code found under the else statement. Complete the if with the fi statement.

The if statement is a construct that is common to virtually all scripting and programming languages. Whether you are doing a Linux shell script, a Windows batch file, a JavaScript, or a C++ program, you will have if statements that follow essentially the same structure as you see here. The syntax will be a bit different from one language to the next, but the basic structure is essentially the same.

You also can have an entire `if` statement, including the `fi`, inside of another `if` statement. These are referred to as *nested* `if` statements. If you think about this for a moment, it's not so strange. You use nested `if` statements in your day-to-day thinking. For example, before going to work in the morning, you might say to yourself that if the freeway is busy, take a side route. Then if the freeway is busy, you might say if alternate side route A is busy, take side route B. A nested `if` statement, whether it is in a Linux shell script or in your day-to-day thinking, works like this:

```
if some condition is true
then
 if some other condition is true
then
  do action a
else
  do action b
else
  do action c
```

Using a nested `if` inside of a Linux shell script is not much different. Let's look at an example of a nested `if`. Type the following code into your favorite text editor and save it as `scriptnine.sh`.

```
#!/bin/bash
age=0
echo Please enter your age
read age
if test $age -gt 16
  then
    if test $age -gt 18
      then
      echo You are old enough to vote!
      else
        echo you are old enough to drive, but not to vote.
      fi
  else
    echo You are too young to drive.
  fi
exit 0
```

If you run this script from the shell, you should see what is shown in Figure 20.14.

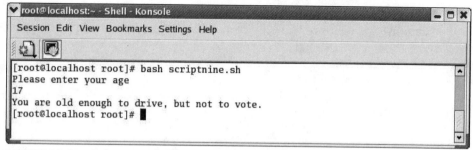

FIGURE 20.14   Using nested `if` statements in a shell script.

You can see that a nested `if` is not really as complicated as it sounded. The important thing to remember is to complete the inner `if` statement with an `fi`. If you do not complete the inner `if` statement, you will get an error, and your script will not function properly.

LOOPS IN SCRIPTS

From time to time anyone who writes scripts will find an occasion to repeat a set of commands for a certain number of times. This is referred to as a *loop*. The type of loop used most often in Linux shell scripts is the `for` loop. The general concept of a `for` loop is *for as long as some condition is true, keep looping*. The general concept of a `while` loop is similar. It is *while some condition is true, keep looping*.

There are a few rules that apply to all loops in shell scripts.

- The variable used in the loop condition must be initialized before execution of the loop begins.
- A test to see if the loop's conditions are met is made at the beginning of each iteration.
- The body of a loop ends with a statement that modifies the value of the test variable.

The basic syntax of a `for` loop is this:

```
for { variable name } in { list }
do
execute one for each item in the list until the list is
not finished (and repeat all statement between do and done)
done
```

Let's take a look at a script that illustrates the for loop. Type the following lines into the text editor of your choice and save it as scriptten.sh:

```
#!/bin/bash
echo Count down
for i in 1 2 3 4 5
do
  echo $i
done
echo blast off!
exit 0
```

If you run this from the shell, you should see something like what is displayed in Figure 20.15.

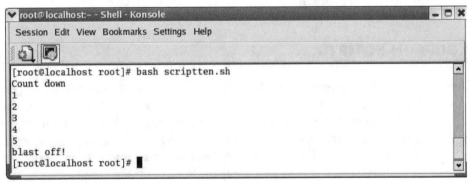

FIGURE 20.15 The for loop.

You can see that a for loop is simple. Take a variable named i and count through the numbers 1 through 5, assigning that variable to i in each loop. Each time, echo that value to the screen. In other words, take the variable i, start it off with a value of 1, and keep incrementing through a value of 5.

SUMMARY

In this chapter, we delved into the world of Linux shell scripts. You saw how to write a basic script, how to echo commands to the screen, how to use variables, how to construct if statements, and how to create loops. At this point you should be, essentially, comfortable with Linux shell scripts. You will find that scripting is a powerful tool, especially for system administrators. You can use shell scripts to automate a variety of tasks.

REVIEW QUESTIONS

1. What does the ? designate?
2. What line must all shell scripts end with?
3. What would you enter to invoke a script named `myscript.sh`?
4. What is a variable?
5. What is a UDV?
6. What does the `echo` command do?
7. What does `fi` do?

21

Advanced Shell Functions

In This Chapter

- Advanced Shell Commands
- Shell Editors
- Advanced Shell Scripting

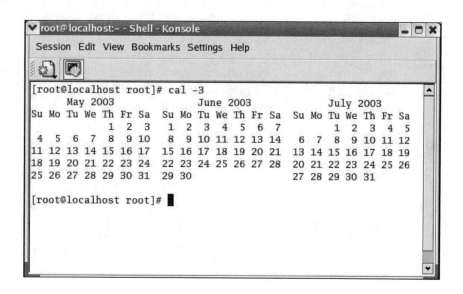

INTRODUCTION

In the preceding chapters we have explored the Linux shell in some depth. You have seen how to use basic Linux shell commands, how to perform administration of a Linux machine from the shell, and even how to write some simple shell scripts. For the casual Linux user, a home user just wanting to get on the Internet and type documents, this is more than enough knowledge. However, some readers will want to delve deeper into these topics. This chapter is provided for the reader who wants to go into more depth with the shell. We will explore more shell commands, how to edit documents from the shell, and some more complex shell scripts. If you are a casual Linux user, feel free to skip this chapter altogether.

Unfortunately, there is no direct Windows corollary for much of what we will examine in this chapter. This means that we will have to forego our usual method of examining how something is done in Linux and comparing it to a similar task in Windows.

ADVANCED SHELL COMMANDS

We have looked at a lot of shell commands in this book. Most were pretty easy to work with. You could devote an entire book just to Linux shell commands, so obviously we will not be examining all of them. However, there are a few more interesting ones that we will take a look at in this section. You may be wondering why these commands were held off until now. Some did not fit neatly into any previous category. Others are a bit more complex and probably are best shown to you after you have had a little experience with shell commands.

cal

This is an interesting command and quite useful. From a purely aesthetic view point, it probably is the most appealing of the shell applications. The cal command displays a calendar in your shell. This can be very useful. If you enter cal at the shell, you should see a calendar much like the one shown in Figure 21.1.

This command is very easy to use. However, like most shell commands, it has several flags you can pass to it if you want. Table 21.1 lists several of the more common flags used with cal.

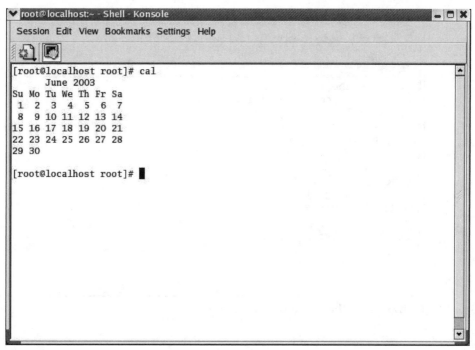

FIGURE 21.1   The cal command.

TABLE 21.1   cal Flags

Flag	Purpose
-3	This causes the calendar to show the previous, current, and next month. The number three causes three months to be displayed.
-s	This causes the calendar to use Sunday as the first day of the week.
-m	This causes the calendar to use Monday as the first day of the week.
-j	This will cause the calendar to display using Julian dates.

There are more flags than this, of course, and you can see them all by entering man cal at the shell. However, these flags are enough to demonstrate how the calendar works differently with different flags. For example, the cal –m command is shown in Figure 21.2.

In Figure 21.3 you can see the past, current, and next month displayed using the cal –3 command.

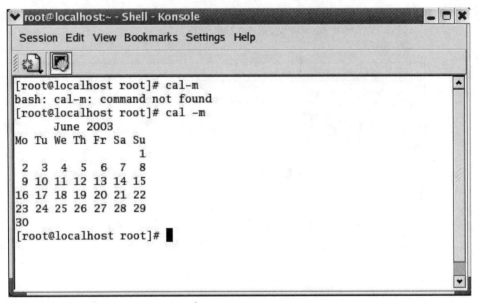

FIGURE 21.2 The cal –m command.

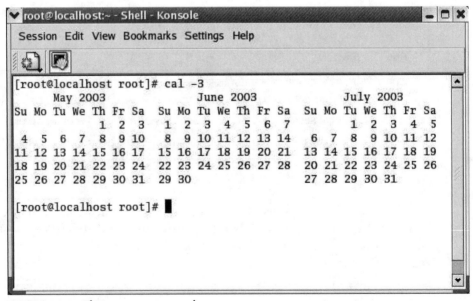

FIGURE 21.3 The cal –3 command.

The cal command may be one of the easiest to use shell commands we have discussed. However, it is quite useful and does not fit into any previous category.

grep

The grep command is one of the most widely used commands in the Unix/Linux world. It is a search command. It is used to search a file for a particular occurrence. You can search for a single character, entire word, sentence, or more. The format is quite simple:

```
grep [item to search for] filename
```

If you want to search one of your previously written script files from the preceding chapter for the occurrence of the word *else*, you could simply type in

```
grep else scripteight.sh
```

You should see something much like what is shown in Figure 21.4.

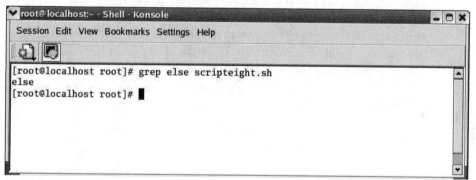

FIGURE 21.4 The grep command.

The grep command is popular with Linux and Unix users because it is so flexible. If you enter man grep at the shell, you will see a rather extensive entry, listing a number of flags you can pass to grep. However, some of the most common flags are listed and described in Table 21.2.

TABLE 21.2 The grep Flags

Flag	Purpose
-i	This instructs grep to ignore case.
-w	This tells grep to look for whole word matches only.
-l	This instructs grep to look for entire line matches only.
-s	This suppresses error messages.

As with all shell commands, you can pass more than one flag to grep. This makes it a very flexible and popular search tool. It is probable that there has never been any book written about Linux that did not give grep at least a passing introduction.

dc

If you will recall, when we explored the KDE interface we discussed the Calculator and compared it to the Calculator found in Windows. You may be pleased to find that the Linux shell also has a calculator, although not nearly so graphically appealing. The dc command puts your shell into Calculator mode. You can then enter the arithmetic operations you want to perform. Much like certain calculators, dc uses a sort of reverse notation. For example, if you enter the following, you should see something much like what is displayed in Figure 21.5.

```
dc
10
5
+
p
15
```

After each character, you will of course press the Enter key. They are not displayed here on separate rows by accident. Each command, number, and arithmetic operator is entered separately, followed by pressing the Enter key.

Notice that the arithmetic operator appears after the second operand, rather than between the two operands. Also notice the letter p. This concludes the arithmetic operations and causes the answer to be printed to the screen.

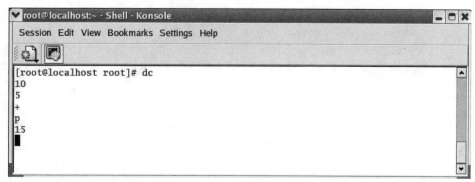

FIGURE 21.5 The dc command.

SHELL EDITORS

When we discussed shells scripts in the preceding chapter, we wrote all the scripts in one of the text editors you had been previously introduced to. However, this is not the only way to write a shell script. Since some machines are running in shell mode only, how would you write a script on those machines? There are text editors that actually work entirely from the shell. The three most common would probably be vi, Pico, and Emacs. Of these, vi is probably the most common, although programmers frequently use Emacs to write program code.

vi

The vi editor works entirely from the shell. To invoke the vi editor and begin an editing session, enter vi, followed by the name of the file you want to edit, and then press Return.

```
% vi filename [Return]
```

For example, if you want to edit the scripttwo.sh file that we created in the previous chapter, you would enter:

```
vi scripttwo.sh
```

You would then see something like what is shown in Figure 21.6.

vi automatically sets aside a temporary buffer as a working space for use during this editing session. If the file you specify when calling vi does not already exist

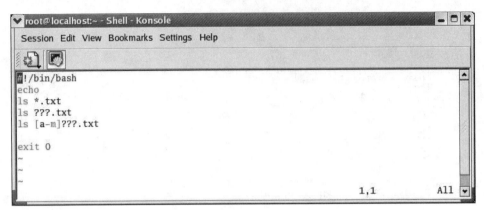

FIGURE 21.6 Opening files with the vi editor.

in your current working directory, a new file will be created with the name you specified. This means that you create a new file with the vi editor the same way you open an existing file; just make certain that the name you use is not already being used by another file in that directory.

There are several points you should note about the vi editor. Perhaps the most important thing is that vi only operates in one of two modes. These are the Insert mode and the Command mode. In Insert mode, whatever you type will be inserted into the file you are editing, up to the point when you exit Insert mode by pressing the Escape key. This is obviously the mode used to actually type in the text of a document. In command mode, you can execute a variety of commands. These commands include cut and paste, move the cursor, search, delete characters, delete entire lines, and so on.

In command mode you need to be very aware that almost every key on the keyboard executes a command, so be careful what keys you press. Since it is possible for you to change your document accidentally, you should be aware of how to undo such changes. Provided your cursor has not left a particular line of text, typing in an uppercase U will undo all the changes that were applied to that line of text, restoring the line to its original state. You also can press a lowercase u to undo the last command, but only the last command.

The vi editor has a long list of commands that can be executed. You should be aware of the more commonly used commands. When the vi editor first starts, it begins in Command mode. You should be aware of this because you cannot begin typing and inserting text. One of your first commands normally will be to move the cursor and start inserting. Table 21.3 summarizes some basic vi editor commands.

TABLE 21.3   Basic vi Commands

Command	Purpose
i	This command inserts text at the current cursor position. All characters typed after i will be inserted. To exit this mode, press the Escape key.
a	This command will append text after the current cursor position. All characters typed after a will be inserted. To exit this mode, press the Escape key.
h, j, k, l	These keys move the cursor in various directions. They move the cursor left, down, up, and right, respectively.
$	This key moves the cursor to the end of the current line.
:1	This key moves the cursor to the first line.
:$	This key moves the cursor to the last line.
dd	Pressing the d key twice deletes the line the cursor is on.
x	Pressing the x key deletes the character the cursor is on.
u	The lowercase u will undo the previous command.
U	This command will undo changes to the current line.
p	This command will paste the last deleted text at the cursor position. This is much like the Ctrl key and the v key being pressed simultaneously in most Windows programs.
q!	This command will discard all of your changes and exit the vi editor.
ZZ	This command will save all of your changes and exit the vi editor.

You will need to keep in mind that while you are inserting text, you will need to type a carriage return at the end of each line. Otherwise, your text will be one very, very, very long line. Unfortunately the vi editor does support automatic word wrapping.

You might think the vi editor seems a bit complex and has a number of archaic commands. You are correct. It might seem curious then that this editor is so popular. However, it is popular among Linux aficionados because it has been around for a long time and has been in widespread use. Of course, proponents of the vi editor would argue that, with its plethora of commands, it is also quite a powerful text editor.

Pico

If you thought the vi editor was a bit too complex, it is quite possible that you will find Pico more to your liking. Pico is a simple text editor. The first thing you will notice when you launch Pico is that the main commands are displayed at the bottom of the screen and that context-sensitive help is provided. This means that you don't have to memorize any commands. This may be the single most important advantage of Pico over vi. The commands you need are shown at the bottom of the screen. When you open a file with Pico, you should see something much like Figure 21.7, where one of the scripts from the preceding chapter is shown open for editing.

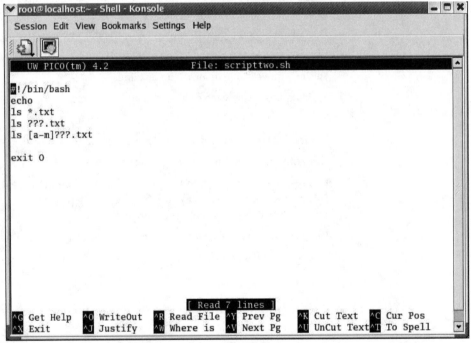

FIGURE 21.7   Opening a file in Pico.

There is no command mode or insert mode in Pico. As you type characters on your keyboard, they are immediately inserted into the text. Any commands you might need are entered using control-key combinations. The Pico editor is an excellent choice for those new to Linux. It is also quite easy for the Windows user to become accustomed to. You launch Pico, and in fact most text editors, the same way you launch vi, by typing in pico, followed by the file you want to open.

```
pico filename
```

If the filename you designate does not already exist, a new file with that name will be created. Changes made to a file do not become permanent until you write them to the system. The command to do this is the Ctrl key followed by lowercase o. You can then exit Pico using the Ctrl key followed by the x key.

Emacs

According to the Emacs manual, Emacs is an extensible, customizable, self-documenting real-time display editor. The name Emacs was originally an abbreviation of Editor MACroS. This is because Emacs was originally used strictly to edit macros. Macros are, in essence, mini programs, not unlike the shell scripts we previously explored. The original Emacs implementation was written for a rather specific system called the Incompatible Timesharing System (ITS). There was a custom of giving such macro packages names ending in the syllable *mac* or *macs*.

Emacs is perhaps the most powerful of the editors, but also the most complex. Entire books have been written on Emacs. This means that we will be touching on only the basics in this chapter. You also will find a lot of documentation on Emacs on the Internet. You can find some help from Web sites listed in Appendix A, "Other Resources," or you can enter "Emacs" into your favorite search engine, and you will get quite a few responses. The Emacs documentation uses some specific terminology. You need to understand some of these terms to be able to use all the free help available on the Internet. Table 21.4 summarizes the more commonly used terms.

TABLE 21.4   Emacs Terminology

Emacs Term	Meaning
buffers	Emacs loads files into internal *buffers*. A buffer is a temporary area in memory often used in many programs and operating systems to hold files that are currently being worked on. In some Emacs documentation, the file you are editing may be referred to as a *buffer*.
frames	One Emacs process can produce a number of separate windows. Emacs calls each of these windows a *frame*.
windows	Each frame can be split into sections that Emacs calls *windows*.
point	This designates the actual *point* where the text cursor currently is.
meta keys	Emacs documentation often refers to the Escape key as a meta key.
Lisp	Emacs is not a self-contained binary. Many of Emacs' commands are written in a language called Lisp. To call one of these functions by name, type M-x function name. The files containing these functions are in the directory /usr/src/editors/Emacs/lisp. You can write your own Lisp functions, but nearly all users will be able to do what they want without having to do this.

The syntax for opening a file with Emacs is much like the syntax for opening a file with Pico or vi:

```
emacs filename
```

When you open a file, such as one of the script files from the previous chapter, you should see something like what is shown in Figure 21.8.

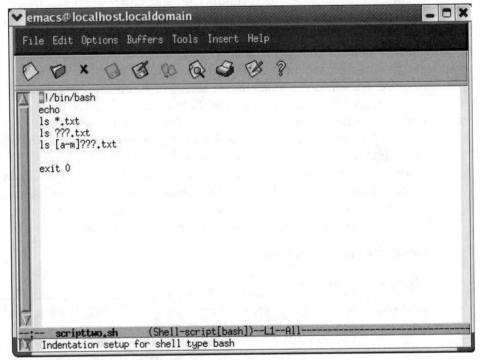

FIGURE 21.8   Opening a file with Emacs.

You should note that when you do this, you launch a new window (if you are using a terminal within some desktop environment such as KDE or GNOME). The Emacs editor is split into two areas. The top area is where you edit your text, and the bottom area is the echo area. The echo area displays the commands you issue and any messages the Emacs editors have for you. You can abort a command by pressing the Ctrl key and the g key in combination.

The text area and the echo area are separated by a line called the mode line. This line shows the current status information of Emacs. Emacs uses a number of symbols to communicate information about the file you are editing. For example, the Emacs editor will place two asterisks (**) in front of the buffer name if changes have been made but not yet saved. Two percent signs (%%) will appear if the file is read-only. Next to the buffer name will be the major mode of the buffer. These modes control the way Emacs behaves with your text and consist of the text, lisp, and c modes. Next to the major mode will be a list of the minor options that can be altered. Next to this will be a display showing the percentage of the file displayed.

Most Emacs commands are based on the use of the Ctrl key or the Escape key (meta key). However, each of these keys works slightly differently. The Ctrl key should be held down while the next key is pressed. The Escape key, however, should be pressed and then released before entering the next key sequence. Also, the Ctrl key should be held only for the next character. For example, the command Ctrl-X U means hold down the Ctrl key and press x and then release the Ctrl key and press the u key. Some commands do not have key sequences assigned to them and must be entered by hand. You can exit the Emacs editor by either using Ctrl-X or Ctrl-C.

ADVANCED SHELL SCRIPTING

In the preceding chapter we looked at shell scripting. If you will recall, we examined the basics of scripting as well as how to write some basic programming techniques in a script. After studying that chapter, you should be basically competent at writing simple shell scripts in Linux. If you will recall, we mentioned that entire books have been written on scripting. That means that a single chapter touched the basics. This chapter certainly won't make you an expert at writing shell scripts. However, we should take a moment to examine a few items that you might find useful in script writing.

case Statements

We looked at `if` statements when we initially examined shell scripts. `if` statements work for many situations where you need to make some sort of decision in the execution of your script. However, what happens when you have a series of decisions to make? Do you simply write a series of five, six, or more `if` statements? Yes that works, but it is certainly not an elegant choice. This is where `case` statements come in. A `case` statement allows you take one of many choices.

The basic format of a `case` statement is that you put the word `case`, followed by the variable, then the word `in`. After that you list the choices. Each choice is followed by a parenthesis and two semicolons. The entire `case` statement ends with the keyword `esac`. Here is a generic example:

```
case somevariable in
  choice one);;
  choice two);;
  choice three);;
esac
```

Let's look at an example script:

```
#!/bin/bash
echo 1. Windows
echo 2. Macintosh
echo 3. Linux
echo 4. OS2
echo Please choose your operating system
read opsys
case $opsys in
  1) echo What? Haven't you been reading this book?;;
  2) echo Good grief...;;;;
  3) echo Alright! Now you got it!;;
  4) echo What planet are you on?;;
esac
exit 0
```

If you type this into your favorite text editor, you can save it as `scriptcase.sh`, then run it from the shell. If you run it from the shell, you should see something like what is shown in Figure 21.9.

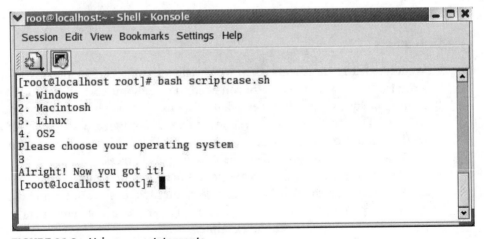

FIGURE 21.9 Using case statements.

This may look a little complicated, and there are several rules to remember. Each choice must end with a double semicolon, the entire case statement must end with esac, and each choice is followed by a parenthesis. This may seem like a lot to remember, but with a little practice it will become very natural. This is also another technique that is common to most programming languages.

Multiple Statements on One Line

Sometimes in your script you might have several related statements to write. You might want to put them all on one line. You could do this either to save space or to group commands that belong together logically. For whatever reason, doing it is simple. You separate each command on the line with a single semicolon, as you see here:

```
statement one; statement two; statement three
```

Open your favorite text editor and enter the following. Then save it as script-multiple.sh and run it.

```
#!/bin/bash
ls; ps;who;logname;
exit 0
```

When you run this, it will work just as if you had placed each command on a separate line. You can see the results in Figure 21.10.

Whether or not to place your commands on a single line or space them out is a matter of preference. Linux scripts allow you to do either. Let's take another look at putting multiple commands on a single line. What we will do is to put echo statements in the previous script to explain to the user what we are doing. Your script should look something like this:

```
#!/bin/bash
echo running ls; ls; echo running ps; ps; echo running who; who;
    echo running logname; logname;
exit 0
```

If you run your script now, you will see something like what is shown in Figure 21.11.

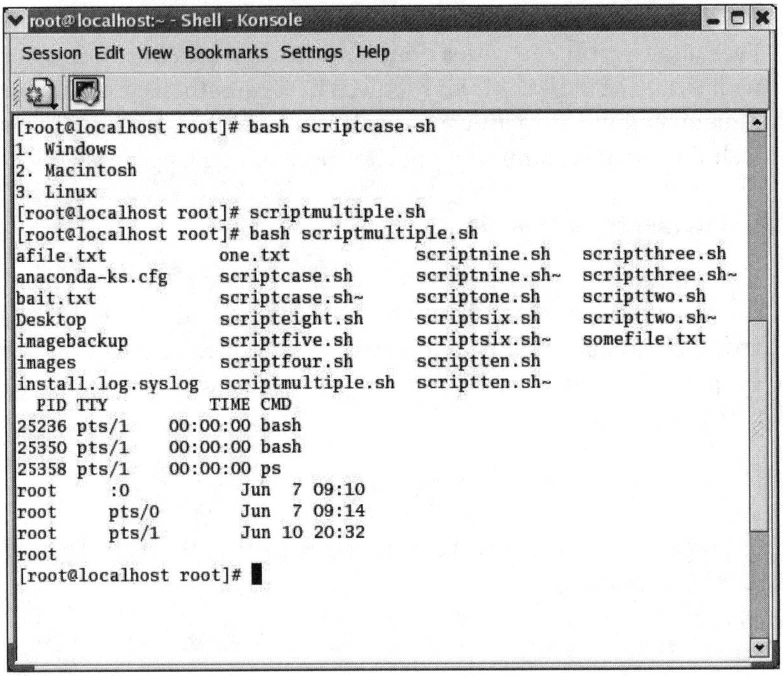

```
root@localhost:~ - Shell - Konsole                              _ □ ✕

Session  Edit  View  Bookmarks  Settings  Help

[root@localhost root]# bash scriptcase.sh
1. Windows
2. Macintosh
3. Linux
[root@localhost root]# scriptmultiple.sh
[root@localhost root]# bash scriptmultiple.sh
afile.txt            one.txt              scriptnine.sh      scriptthree.sh
anaconda-ks.cfg      scriptcase.sh        scriptnine.sh~     scriptthree.sh~
bait.txt             scriptcase.sh~       scriptone.sh       scripttwo.sh
Desktop              scripteight.sh       scriptsix.sh       scripttwo.sh~
imagebackup          scriptfive.sh        scriptsix.sh~      somefile.txt
images               scriptfour.sh        scriptten.sh
install.log.syslog   scriptmultiple.sh    scriptten.sh~
  PID TTY            TIME CMD
25236 pts/1     00:00:00 bash
25350 pts/1     00:00:00 bash
25358 pts/1     00:00:00 ps
root       :0            Jun  7 09:10
root       pts/0         Jun  7 09:14
root       pts/1         Jun 10 20:32
root
[root@localhost root]# █
```

FIGURE 21.10   Multiple commands.

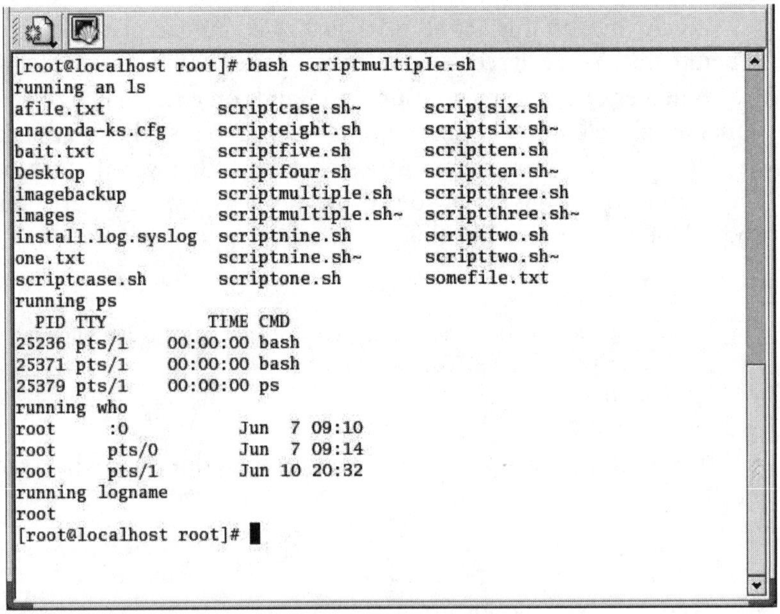

```
[root@localhost root]# bash scriptmultiple.sh
running an ls
afile.txt            scriptcase.sh~       scriptsix.sh
anaconda-ks.cfg      scripteight.sh       scriptsix.sh~
bait.txt             scriptfive.sh        scriptten.sh
Desktop              scriptfour.sh        scriptten.sh~
imagebackup          scriptmultiple.sh    scriptthree.sh
images               scriptmultiple.sh~   scriptthree.sh~
install.log.syslog   scriptnine.sh        scripttwo.sh
one.txt              scriptnine.sh~       scripttwo.sh~
scriptcase.sh        scriptone.sh         somefile.txt
running ps
  PID TTY            TIME CMD
25236 pts/1     00:00:00 bash
25371 pts/1     00:00:00 bash
25379 pts/1     00:00:00 ps
running who
root       :0            Jun  7 09:10
root       pts/0         Jun  7 09:14
root       pts/1         Jun 10 20:32
running logname
root
[root@localhost root]# █
```

FIGURE 21.11   Echoing with multiple commands.

SUMMARY

In this chapter, we have taken your knowledge of the shell to a new level. You saw new shell commands as well as new shell script techniques. However, perhaps the most important thing you saw in this chapter is the use of shell-based editors. You will find that many Linux aficionados prefer the shell-based editors, such as vi, over the graphical editors, such as KWrite. At least a passing familiarity with these shell-based editors is a requirement for working with Linux in a professional setting. With the growing popularity of Linux in the business world, it is entirely possible that some readers may find themselves using Linux in their workplace, either now or in the near future.

REVIEW QUESTIONS

1. What is the most commonly used shell editor in Linux?
2. What does the `grep` command do?
3. What does the `dc` command do?
4. If you enter `cal -3` at the shell, what will be displayed?
5. Unlike the vi editor, what mode is Emacs always in?
6. What advantage does the Pico editor have?

22

Samba, Printing, and More

In This Chapter

- What Is Samba?
- Configuring Samba
- Other Services

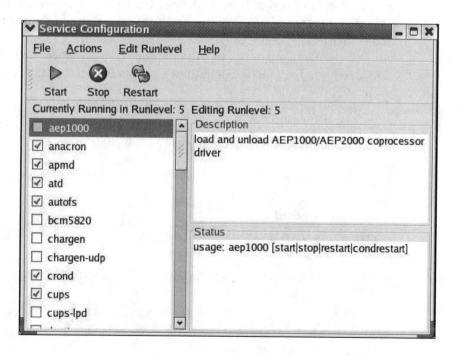

INTRODUCTION

During the time you have been reading this book, you have seen a lot that Linux can do, all at a very low cost and in many cases free. You might feel a rush of excitement and want to completely convert all computers in your home or office over to Linux. Slow down just a moment and let reality tap you gently on the shoulder. It is very unlikely that you will dispense with Windows in one fell swoop. It is not even clear that such a move would be desirable, even if it were possible. The fact is that Linux often is found in a mixed environment, one with both Windows and Linux machines and occasionally Macintosh machines as well. This means that sooner or later you are going to need to share files between a Linux machine and a Windows machine. That is where Samba comes in. Samba is a program that facilitates sharing a Linux drive so that Windows can use it and enabling Linux to access shared drives on Windows machines.

WHAT IS SAMBA?

Samba is a file and print server for Windows-based clients using TCP/IP. TCP/IP is a suite of protocols that is used in most Internet and network communication. This means that Samba is a utility that enables Windows machines to access files and even printers that are connected to a Linux machine. This is an important service because Linux often will be found in mixed environments. Samba was originally developed by Andrew Tridgell but is now being developed by a global team of about 30 active programmers.

You can find a lot of useful details about Samba, if you are interested, at *www.samba.org*. However, the documents you find will use some terminology you should be familiar with. These terms are explained in Table 22.1.

TABLE 22.1   Samba Terminology

Term	Meaning
SMB	This stands for Server Message Block. It is the protocol that Microsoft uses for file and print sharing.
IPC	This means Inter Process Communication. It is a technical way of communicating between different programs.
NetBIOS	This stands for Network Basic Input/Output System. This is a method for communicating on a network that is used by Microsoft.
W2K	Short for Windows 2000.

In much of the Samba documentation you will find, these terms are used but not defined. We define them here so that you can use the online Samba documentation available on the Internet. It is certainly possible to configure and use Samba without going into any extensive research on the topic. In fact, in this chapter you will see how to set up Samba and run it. However, some readers will want to go a little deeper on this topic.

CONFIGURING SAMBA

In the past the only way to configure Samba was via shell commands. Fortunately, that is no longer the case. You can go to the Start menu, find Server Settings, select More Server Settings, and choose Samba Settings. You will then see a screen like the one shown in Figure 22.1.

This screen is simple. Adding a Samba service to your Linux machine with this utility is probably easier than many of the other tasks we have performed. At this point you can either click the Add button on the toolbar or select File and Add Share from the drop-down menu. When you choose that you will see a screen much like the one shown in Figure 22.2.

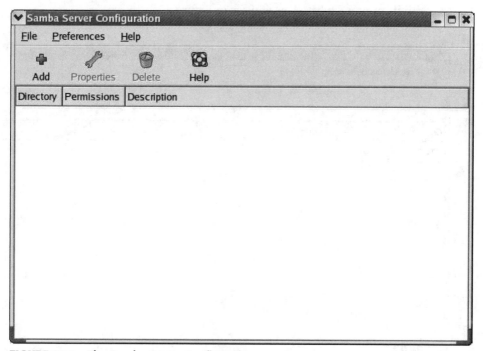

FIGURE 22.1   The Samba Server Configuration screen.

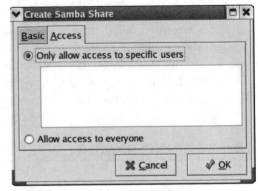

FIGURE 22.2   Adding a new share.   **FIGURE 22.3**   Giving users access.

On this first tab you can use the Browse button to find a directory that you want to share. You also can give this directory a description and set whether or not users who access it can write files to it or only read files from it. The Access tab, shown in Figure 22.3, enables you to decide whether all the users can access this shared drive, or just certain users that you list.

When you are satisfied, click OK, and this share will appear on the main screen with its properties listed, as you see in Figure 22.4.

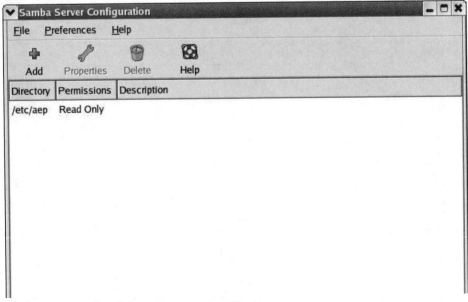

FIGURE 22.4   A list of shares.

If you want to add users to the list of people who can access Samba, go to Preferences and choose Samba Users. You can add any user who exists on your machine. You can see the Add User screen in Figure 22.5. It is important that you realize that you can add only users who have a user account on this machine, so first you will need to add a user account for the person you want to access the Samba shared directory. This makes perfect sense if you think about it. A person cannot access a directory on a machine if he is not first given access to that machine. Remember in earlier chapters we discussed adding users both from KDE and from the shell.

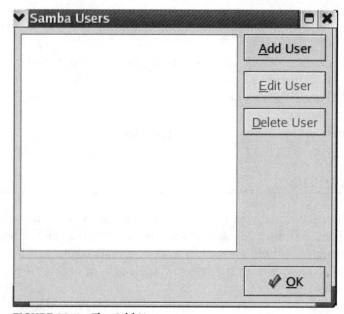

FIGURE 22.5   The Add User screen.

That's all it takes to create a Samba shared directory and give users access to it. Sharing a printer is much simpler than you think. If you will recall, early in this book you were told that Linux views devices as files. Your floppy drive is actually dev/fd0 to Linux. Your printer is a device file as well. When you want to share a printer, go to the /dev folder and pick your printer!

Like most applications, Samba can be configured. If you go to Settings and choose Samba Settings, you will see a screen like the one displayed in Figure 22.6. On the first tab of this screen you can choose the workgroup and username that Samba runs as. Remember when we discussed Apache Web Server? It also runs as a special user account. With user accounts for applications, like the ones for Samba

FIGURE 22.6 Samba settings.   **FIGURE 22.7** Samba Security tab.

and Apache, it is best to leave the default setting unless you have some pressing reason to do otherwise.

There is also a second tab under settings, shown in Figure 22.7. This tab enables you to set the security settings. You can choose how to authenticate login attempts, whether or not to encrypt transmissions, and more.

OTHER SERVICES

Although Samba is an interesting service and very useful, it is not the only one available in Linux. Remember that the words *service* and *daemon* can be used interchangeably. Both words refer to a program that runs in the background and provides some service to the system. In the case of Samba, it is providing access to Windows machines.

Also under Server Settings you will find Service Management. This screen is shown in Figure 22.8. Through this utility you can see every service running on your machine. You also can start or stop any service you want. However, you cannot configure these services from this screen, you can only start or stop them.

One of the most important services for your computer is printing. In our discussion of Samba we mentioned that you can even share your printer with Windows users. It would probably be prudent to make certain that you can add printers to your Linux machine. We discussed this briefly in a previous chapter but not in any depth.

If you go to the Start menu and select System Settings and then Printing, you will see a screen much like the one in Figure 22.9. This screen lists all of the documents waiting in the print queue and the printers. As you can see, we have none connected at this time.

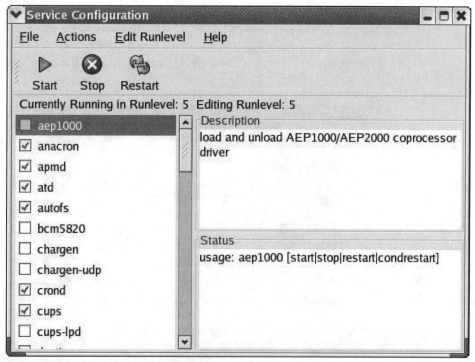

FIGURE 22.8 The Service Configuration screen.

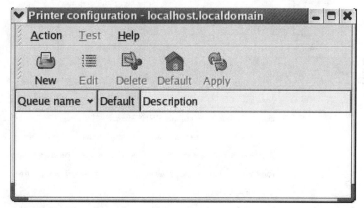

FIGURE 22.9 The print manager.

Let's add a printer. Click on the New button on the toolbar. Your computer will take a few minutes to find out about any printers that are attached and then will start a wizard to set up the print queue. For this exercise we will set up an actual printer. This is not meant as an endorsement of that particular printer model. It is the printer that is connected to the machine the author is using. The first screen of the Print Queue Wizard, shown in Figure 22.10, tells you what is about to happen.

The next screen, seen in Figure 22.11, asks you to give this printer a name and a short description. The name is absolutely required. This is how you will refer to

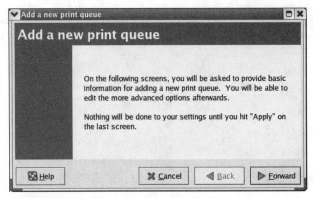

FIGURE 22.10   The Print Queue Wizard screen one.

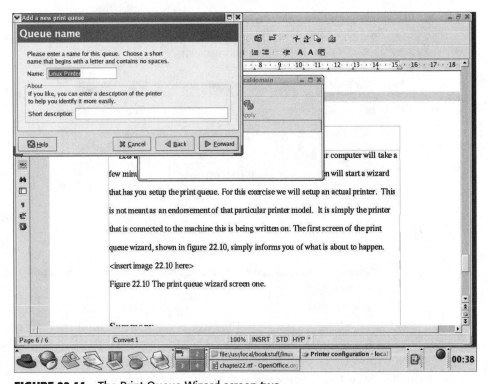

FIGURE 22.11   The Print Queue Wizard screen two.

your printer in various applications you want to print from. The description is optional.

The third screen, shown in Figure 22.12, is the most important. Here you see a list of all locally connected printers that Linux can detect. In this case there is only one. You also can use the drop-down menu at the top to change from looking for locally controlled printers to looking for networked printers. Click once on the printer you want and then click the Forward button.

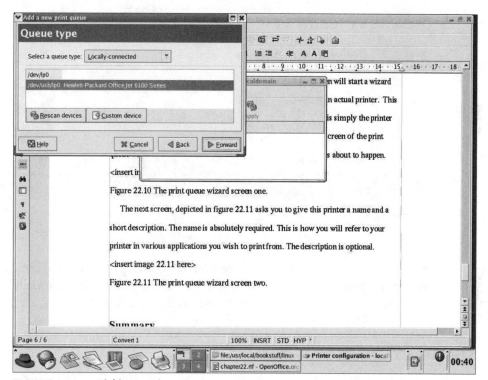

FIGURE 22.12   Picking a printer.

If you know technical details about your printer, you can select the type of printer it is from the list shown in Figure 22.13. However, if you are not sure, or your printer specifics don't appear in the list, choose the Generic printer option.

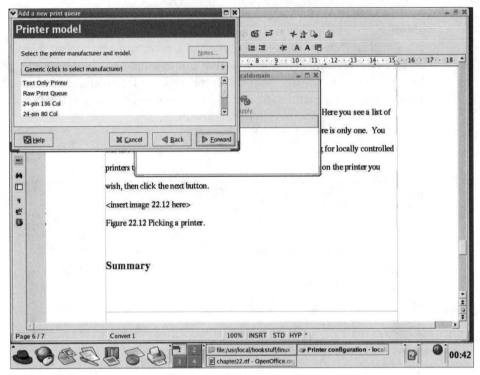

FIGURE 22.13 Printer type.

Once you have selected your specific printer model and type, you can complete the wizard. You will then be asked if you want to print a test page. It usually is a wise idea to do so. As you can see, setting up a printer in Linux is not a difficult task.

SUMMARY

A few very important topics were covered in this chapter. We discussed Samba, a critical utility if you want your Linux machine to be accessible from Windows machines. Samba enables you to run a mixed environment that combines Windows and Linux machines. We also discussed the Service Configuration utility. This is very useful for finding out what services are started, and stopping or starting them as needed.

We completed the chapter with a discussion of adding printers. At some point, most people will want to print from their computers. Using the Print Queue Wizard, you should have no trouble hooking up most printers to your Linux machine.

REVIEW QUESTIONS

1. What is Samba?
2. What is an SMB?
3. What is IPC?
4. How do you configure a service from the Service Configuration screen?

A | Other Resources

This appendix is provided to enable you to further your studies of any of the items presented in this book. Obviously one book cannot cover it all, so these resources are meant to help you. I have picked those resources that I think are your best bet for good solid Linux information.

General Linux Links

Linux Online: *http://www.linux.org/*
Linux.com: *http://www.linux.com/*
The Linux Journal: *http://www.linuxjournal.com*
Linux Today: *http://linuxtoday.com/*
Linux World: *http://www.linuxworld.com/*

Distributions

Red Hat Linux: *http://www.redhat.com/*
Debian Linux: *http://www.debian.org/*
Mandrake Linux: *http://www.mandrakelinux.com/en/*
SuSE Linux: *http://www.suse.com/index_us.html*
Slackware: *http://www.slackware.com/*

Linux Tutorials

Linux Online: *http://www.linux.org/*
Linux Planet: *http://www.linuxplanet.com/linuxplanet/tutorials/*
Linux Guru's: *http://www.linuxguruz.com/z.php?id=2*

Linux Software

Open Office: *http://www.openoffice.org/*
Star Office: *http://wwws.sun.com/software/star/staroffice/6.0/*

Opera Web Browser: *http://www.opera.com/*
Mozilla Web Browser: *http://www.mozilla.org/*
Netscape Web Browser: *http://www.netscape.com/*
VS FTP Server: *http://vsftpd.beasts.org/*
Apache Web Server: *http://www.apache.org*
GIMP: *http://www.gimp.org/*

Linux Games

Linux Games: *http://www.linuxgames.com/*
Loki Games: *http://www.lokigames.com/*
Games for Linux: *http://games.linux.sk/*
Tux Games: *http://www.tuxgames.com/*
Happy Penguin: *http://www.happypenguin.org/*

General PC Tutorials

Introduction to the PC: *http://homepage.cs.uri.edu/tutorials/csc101/pc/intro/*
PC Tutorial: *http://tutorials.beginners.co.uk/read/id/386*
Working inside a PC tutorial: *http://tutorials.freeskills.com/read/id/324*
HTML Tutorial: *http://www.davesite.com/webstation/html/*
Introduction to HTML: *http://www.cwru.edu/help/introHTML/toc.html*
HTML Goodies: *http://www.htmlgoodies.com/*

Samba

Online version of a Samba book: *http://www.oreilly.com/catalog/samba/chapter/book/*
The main Web page for Samba: *http://www.samba.org/*

Apache

Apache main page: *http://www.apache.org*
Apache Week: *http://www.apacheweek.com/*

B Glossary of Linux and Operating System Terms

absolute pathname: A pathname that explicitly identifies all directories from the root directory to an individual file.

account: A combination of a user login and password that is created by the system administrator. The creation of an account also automatically assigns a home directory

admin: Short for administrator, referring to the person responsible for the maintenance of a computer.

alias: An alternate name, or abbreviation, used in place of a command or a sequence of shell commands.

bang: Denoted by the ! character. The shell command !!, which is used to repeat the last command you typed in, for example, is pronounced "Bang! Bang!"

bash: Bourne-again shell, a newer version of the Bourne shell and the most commonly used shell in Linux.

BIOS: Basic Input Output System. This is software embedded in a chip in the PC that tells the PC what to do when it turns on (for example, whether to boot through the CD, floppy drive, or hard drive).

bin: A directory that contains executable programs, the majority of which are stored in binary files (thus the name bin). Most programs/applications are found in the directories /bin and /usr/bin.

bootdisk: A miniature, self-contained Linux system on a floppy diskette. These disks are usually only used to boot the system up either for installing Linux or for repairing some problem.

boot loader: A program that loads an operating system into memory upon bootup.

bootstrap: A ROM (read-only memory) routine that is used to load the operating system is known as the bootstrap. This name is derived from the old expression "pull yourself up by your own bootstraps."

cat: Concatenate files and print on the standard output.

cd: This is the command to change directory. cd .. moves you backwards to the next higher subdirectory level; cd / moves you to the highest directory level.

cron: A Linux daemon that periodically checks the contents of a file called /var/lib/crontab and carries out any tasks due to be performed.

crontab: A short name for file /var/lib/crontab, which contains a list of Linux commands to be performed at specific times. The fact that the commands are timed means that they occur chronologically, thus the name crontab.

daemon: A program that runs in the background, usually performing some essential service. Web servers and FTP servers often run as daemons.

Disk Druid: A disk portioning utility used with Linux.

Evolution: An e-mail client for Linux.

ext2: The native filesystem for Linux that offers long filenames, permissions, error tolerance, and high throughput.

fg: A shell command that will take a process and run it in the foreground.

FTP: File Transfer Protocol, which enables a user to transfer files electronically from remote computers back to the user's computer.

GIMP: Graphics Image Manipulation Program. A graphics program much like Adobe Photoshop.

GNOME: GNU Network Object Model Environment. A GUI for Linux.

GNU: GNU is not Unix.

grub: The most recent boot loader for Linux.

grep: Linux abbreviation for *get regular expression*. A grep tool lets you search through a set of text files for a pattern. The item you are looking for is a *regular expression*.

GUI: Graphical user interface. There are a number of GUIs available for Linux. The most popular are KDE and GNOME.

hard boot: A boot initiated by hardware. An example would be pressing the power switch.

history: A shell command that will list commands the user has previously entered.

init: The first process to run after the system boots and always has a process ID of 1. It is responsible for starting the system in single-user mode or spawning a shell to read the startup files, and for opening ports that are designated as login ports. init also spawns getty processes for each one.

KDE: K Desktop Environment. A commonly used GUI for Linux.

kernel: The core of an operating system.

LAN: Local area network.

Lilo: A commonly used boot loader for Linux.

mbr: Master boot record, which is the first sector of the disk; this is the sector that the BIOS reads in and starts when the machine is first booted.

mkdir: This makes a new directory.

mv: Moves or renames files or directories.

Mozilla: A very commonly used Web browser for Linux.

Open Office: An office suite complete with word processor, presentation tools, and spreadsheet tool. It is available as a free download.

shell: A command-line interface where you type in commands. There are a number of shells available, including the Bourne shell, Bourne-again shell (bash), Korn shell, and C shell.

tar: A file compression and decompression utility.

C Answers to Review Questions

CHAPTER 1

1. What operating system are both Minix and Linux based on?
   Unix
2. What does GNU stand for?
   GNU is not Unix.
3. Who invented Linux?
   Linus Torvalds
4. List two advantages of Linux over Windows.
   Stability and price.
5. List two advantages of Windows over Linux.
   Availability of software and availability of technical support.
6. What filesystem does Linux use by default?
   ext2
7. What filesystem does Windows XP use by default?
   NTFS

CHAPTER 2

1. What are the four options for selecting packages?
   Personal Desktop, Workstation, Server, Custom
2. If your PC has two NICs, what would the second one be named, when you look at firewall or network configuration?
   eth1
3. What is Disk Druid?
   A disk partitioning utility.
4. What is the minimum size for your SWAP partition?
   The same as the size of your memory.

5. What is the maximum size for your SWAP partition?
   Two and one half times the size of your memory.
6. What is GRUB?
   Grand Unified Boot Loader, a boot loader for Linux.
7. What is LILO?
   Linux Load—an older boot later for Linux.
8. What is a NIC?
   A network interface card.
9. What is RAM?
   Random access memory.

CHAPTER 3

1. What does the man command do?
   It brings up a manual page for a specific command.
2. What is the shell command to delete a directory?
   `rmdir`
3. What is the default shell used by Linux?
   bash (Bourne-again shell)
4. What is the Linux command to delete a file?
   `rm`
5. What is found in KDE under Extras?
   Additional items for the other major categories.
6. What is the Linux equivalent of the Windows Recycle Bin?
   Trash Bin
7. The File Manager in Linux operates much like what other type of application?
   Windows Explorer
8. What is the Linux command to view all the files in a directory?
   `ls`

CHAPTER 4

1. What are the three most common means of Internet connection?
   Modem, Ethernet, and cable/DSL
2. How many different desktops does KDE provide, by default?
   Four
3. Under desktop settings, what does the common background setting do?
   It forces all the various desktops to use the same background.

4. What is the rule of thumb for changing hardware settings?
   If you do not know what it is, do not touch it!
5. What is the default browser for KDE?
   Mozilla
6. What drop-down menu do you select in Mozilla to set up your Internet connection settings?
   Edit
7. What is the default e-mail client for KDE?
   Evolution
8. Favorites in Internet Explorer are called what in Mozilla?
   Bookmarks

CHAPTER 5

1. What is the biggest difference between Kate and KWrite?
   KWrite has a spell checker.
2. Kate is most like what Windows application?
   Notepad
3. Which offers more graphics functionality, Windows Paint or Image Magick?
   Image Magick
4. Do you use the Print Screen button to do screen captures in KDE?
   No, you must use the screen capture utility.
5. What are sticky keys?
   Sticky keys cause the machine to remember any key press for a few seconds and to put it with the subsequent key press if the combination creates a command the software recognizes.
6. What are bounce keys?
   With bounce keys turned on, the software will ignore the second press of the same key if it occurs in less than a specified number of seconds.

CHAPTER 6

1. What is a daemon?
   A program that runs in the background. In Windows, this is called a service.
2. What daemon is responsible for scheduling tasks?
   crond
3. Why is your birth date not a good password?
   It would be too easy for someone to guess.

4. What protocol is used for sending e-mail?
   SMTP (Simple Mail Transfer Protocol)
5. What protocol is used for receiving e-mail?
   POP3 (Post Office Protocol)
6. What KDE utility would you use to find out how much memory is being used by your system?
   The System Monitor
7. What is the purpose of the KDE control center?
   To provide a single, convenient location from which to accomplish many common administration tasks.

CHAPTER 7

1. Which Linux word processor has an interface most like Microsoft Word?
   AbiWord
2. What file types can GNumeric Worksheet import?
   Microsoft Excel, Quatro Pro, and Lotus 1-2-3
3. Which graphics program is ideal for cataloging images?
   gThumb
4. What does GNOME stand for?
   GNU Network Object Model Environment
5. When was GNOME 1.0 released?
   March 1999
6. Can GNOME run on non-Linux machines?
   Yes, GNOME can run on any Unix-like system that uses GTK.
7. GNOME's equivalent of Microsoft Paint is called what?
   GPaint

CHAPTER 8

1. What three common text formatting buttons are found in the exact same order in both Microsoft Word and Open Office Writer?
   Bold, italic, and underline.
2. What type of functions are found on the second toolbar in Writer?
   Common or standard word processing functions.
3. Name an advantage that Microsoft Word has over Open Office Writer.
   MS Word has more graphics.

4. What is a common document tool used to organize data in an easily read format?
   A table.
5. Inserting a symbol in Microsoft Word is duplicated in Open Office Writer by inserting a special character.
6. Does Open Office Writer have more field options than Microsoft Word?
   No

CHAPTER 9

1. Name one feature found in Calc, not present in Microsoft Excel.
   The ability to insert Java applets and plug-ins.
2. Why might you want to add some drawing to your spreadsheet?
   To add visual impact to your data.
3. What would you find on the Object toolbar?
   The Object toolbar consists a set of tools that are specific to calculation and cell formatting.
4. What is one thing that Excel and all Microsoft Office products do that Calc does not do?
   Keep a recently opened files list.
5. How would you compute the standard deviation of a column or row?
   By clicking the Autopilot button and selecting the stddev function, after highlighting the cells you want to compute the function for.
6. How do you customize the toolbars in Calc?
   Right-click on the button on the toolbar.
7. What is the difference between using autofill on numbers and dates?
   Dates are incremented to the next month or day, whereas numbers are simply incremented by one.

CHAPTER 10

1. Does Open Office Impress support automatic slide show presentation?
   No
2. What drop-down menu would you use to change the toolbars that are displayed?
   Go to View, then select Toolbars.

3. What drop-down menu would you use to add three-dimensional effects to text?
   Go to Format and then select Text.
4. What is the purpose of the Slides view?
   To arrange your slides in some particular order.
5. What is the difference between rehearse timings in PowerPoint and in Impress?
   In Impress it is simply for your own rehearsal. In PowerPoint the timings are recorded.

CHAPTER 11

1. What is an image map?
   An image map is created when different regions of a single image link to different addresses.
2. How would you make a picture into a link to a Web site?
   Right-click on the picture to change its properties to include a link.
3. Name at least one free Web hosting site.
   www.angelfire.com and *www.geocities.com*
4. List three graphics types that you can insert into your Web page.
   GIF, JPG, BMP
5. What is the purpose of the Open Office Setup utility?
   To alter options normally configured during the initial setup.
6. What is the purpose of Open Office Math?
   To provide a word processor for mathematical formulas.
7. What is the purpose of Open Office Global?
   To set up global parameters that are used throughout Open Office.

CHAPTER 12

1. What does the GIMP acronym stand for?
   Graphics Image Manipulation Program
2. What does the Oilify filter do?
   Change your image so that it appears to be an oil painting.
3. What does the Freehand Selection tool do?
   Allow you to use your mouse to draw an area to select.
4. What does the Eyedropper do?
   Allow you to extract the exact color used in a specific region of an image.

5. How do you change settings for the Airbrush tool?
   You can set it by going to File, selecting Dialogs, and choosing Tool Options, after selecting the airbrush, of course.
6. What tools does the Tool Options dialog work with?
   Any tool
7. What are the two most important properties when airbrushing?
   The pressure and the opacity of your airbrush.
8. What is the purpose of the Clone tool?
   To copy a region of the image.

CHAPTER 13

1. What Microsoft product is Evolution most like?
   Microsoft Outlook
2. What is POP3?
   Post Office Protocol Version 3, used to retrieve e-mail.
3. A bookmark in Mozilla is most like Favorites in Internet Explorer.
4. Mozilla is most like the Netscape Navigator browser.
5. What is the most useful feature of KMail?
   The ability to filter incoming mail.
6. What is the default port for FTP?
   21
7. What is the process to retrieve your e-mail in KMail?
   Go to File, and choose Check Mail.

CHAPTER 14

1. Which Linux application is most like RealPlayer or QuickTime?
   KsCD
2. What is GNOME Pilot for?
   PDAs
3. The sound recorder uses what type of file by default?
   .wav
4. What is GNOME Toastmaster?
   A CD writer
5. What application do you use to send a fax from KDE?
   KDEPrintFax

6. How do you send a document using that application?
Click on the Add File button. You will then be able to browse your machine's hard drive and attach any file you wish. In the field marked Fax Number, simply type in the number you want to fax to. You then simply go to Fax, and select Send Fax.

CHAPTER 15

1. What protocol do Web browsers use?
HTTP (Hypertext Transfer Protocol)
2. What is the default port for Web servers to listen on?
80
3. In simple terms, what is a Web server?
A computer with a program running that can listen to port 80 and respond.
4. What is HTTP return code 301?
The page has been moved and you are being redirected to the new address.
5. How did Apache server get its name?
Because its creators thought it was A Patchy Server.
6. What is the name of the Apache configuration file?
httpd.conf
7. What is the ServerAdmin setting in the configuration file?
The e-mail address for the Web server administrator.
8. What are four basic troubleshooting steps should you first take when having an Apache problem?
   1. Is your Web server running?
   2. Is it connected to the Internet?
   3. Did you type in the address correctly without misspelling it?
   4. Have you checked the error log for error messages?

CHAPTER 16

1. What port do FTP servers work on?
Port 21
2. What does FTP stand for?
File Transfer Protocol
3. What is the main configuration file for VSFTP?
/etc/vsftp/vsftp.conf
4. What is the most commonly used FTP server?
wu-ftp

5. What happens to a user who is added to the vsftpusers file?
   He is blocked from accessing the FTP server.
6. In vsftp, what does the ftpd_banner setting do?
   Shows that message to each user when he logs on to your FTP server.

CHAPTER 17

1. What is the name of the Linux golf game described in this chapter?
   Kolf
2. Which operating system ships with more games, Windows or Linux?
   Red Hat Linux
3. What Web site specializes in Linux versions of popular commercial games?
   www.lokigames.com/
4. KMine is most like what Windows game?
   Minesweeper
5. List four major game hits that are available in Linux.
   Civilization Call to Power, Quake III, Descent—Tycoon II, Heretic II

CHAPTER 18

1. What is the primary difference between `ping` and `traceroute`?
   `ping` tells you if an IP is reachable, `traceroute` tells you how it was reached.
2. What does the `finger` command do?
   Provide information about a user account.
3. What is the Windows equivalent for the `diff` command?
   `comp`
4. What is the difference between the `diff` command and the `cmp` command?
   The `diff` command performs a byte-by-byte comparison, the `cmp` command performs a textual comparison.
5. What is the difference between the `ps` command and the `top` command?
   The `top` command provides a great deal more information.
6. What does the `head` command do?
   It returns the first several lines of a file.
7. What is the loopback address?
   127.0.0.1; it is a dummy address that points to your NIC and is used for testing the NIC.

CHAPTER 19

1. What is found in the /bin directory?
   Binary files or programs.
2. What does the command init 6 do?
   Reboot the system.
3. What is the shell command to activate your network card?
   `ifconfig -up`
4. What is in the /mnt directory?
   Temporary storage devices such as floppy drives and CD-ROMs.
5. What is /dev/fp0/ ?
   The floppy drive.
6. Where would you look to change the message of the day?
   /etc/motd
7. Why should an inexperienced person never alter anything in /etc/inittab?
   It is where you configure the init process. Misconfiguration of this process can cause your system to be completely unbootable.
8. What is the purpose of the `pwd` command?
   To give the complete path to your current directory.
9. What command is used to see how much free memory you have on your system?
   `free`

CHAPTER 20

1. What does the ? designate?
   A single character wildcard.
2. What line must all shell scripts end with?
   exit 0
3. What would you type in to invoke a script named myscript.sh?
   bash myscript.sh
4. What is a variable?
   A name designating an address in memory to hold data.
5. What is a UDV?
   A user-defined variable.
6. What does the `echo` command do?
   Displays to the screen
7. What does `fi` do?
   Finishes an `if` statement

CHAPTER 21

1. What is the most commonly used shell editor in Linux?
   The vi editor.
2. What does the grep command do?
   Search a file for specific characters or words.
3. What does the dc command do?
   Launch a shell-based calculator.
4. If you type in cal –3 at the shell, what will be displayed?
   A calendar for the previous, current, and next month
5. Unlike the vi editor, what mode is Emacs always in?
   Insert
6. What advantage does the Pico editor have?
   It is much easier to use.

CHAPTER 22

1. What is Samba?
   It is a utility for giving Windows users access to Linux directories.
2. What is an SMB?
   Server Message Block, a Microsoft networking protocol.
3. What is IPC?
   Inter Process Communication
4. How do you configure a service from the service configuration screen?
   You don't. You can only start or stop services.

D PC Hardware*

You do not need to be an electrical engineer or even a PC technician in order to use Linux or any other operating system. However, it is important that you have a basic understanding of PC hardware. It's going to be hard for you to configure your operating system if you don't even know what the parts to your PC are. This appendix is designed to help readers who don't have this knowledge. If you already have a basic knowledge of PC hardware and terminology, then you can skip this appendix.

WHAT IS IN A PC?

First of all, in case you were not aware, PC is short for *personal computer*. People sometimes refer to the basic box (the one you plug the keyboard and monitor into) as the CPU. This is really inaccurate. This box *contains* the CPU, but itself is not the CPU. A more appropriate name would be to call it the system. There are lots of parts that you would find if you opened up your PC, and we will discuss each of these parts in this appendix. The primary parts are summarized in Table D.1 and covered in more detail later in this appendix.

It is not recommended that you actually open your PC. If it has a warranty, then opening the box will probably void your warranty.

* Figures D.1, D.4, and D.5 are courtesy of *PC Repair and Maintenance: A Practical Guide*; Figure D.6 is courtesy of *Essential Electronics for PC Technicians.* © 2004 Charles River Media. All rights reserved.

TABLE D.1   PC Parts

PC Part	Purpose
Power supply	A basic power box that takes incoming power from your building's electrical outlets and converts it to DC voltage.
Motherboard	This is the primary circuit board. All other parts are either directly or indirectly connected to the motherboard.
CPU	The central processing unit. This is essentially the brains of the system.
RAM	Random access memory. The memory in your PC.
Hard drive	The storage space on your PC.
Drives drives, etc.	These are for disks. This can be floppy drives, CD drives, DVD.
Cards	There are additional circuit cards for almost anything. Your monitor plugs into a video card. If you have an internal modem, it is a card. Your speakers plug into a sound card.
BIOS	This is the Basic Input Output System. It is usually a chip on your motherboard that has the basic commands on how your system should start up.

Motherboards

The motherboard is the master circuit board for your PC. It is simply a basic circuit board that all other PC boards plug into. Your PC's CPU (central processing unit) is found on the motherboard. If you purchase a sound card or video card, it will plug into the motherboard. Figure D.1 shows a standard motherboard. This is sometimes also called the *main board*. Either term is acceptable, but in recent years, the term *motherboard* has become much more commonplace.

CPU

A CPU, or central processing unit, is a chip that essentially does the thinking for your PC. All the PC's instructions are ultimately carried out by the CPU. The choice of CPU for your computer is very important, as it will affect what software you can run. Figure D.2 shows an Intel Pentium IV CPU. A great deal of research and money has gone into developing newer and more powerful CPU chips. These chips are the heart of your computer. Perhaps the most important consideration when buying a new computer is the CPU type it has.

FIGURE D.1   A motherboard.

FIGURE D.2   Pentium IV CPU.

You measure CPUs based on two factors. The first is the CPU type, and the second is the speed of the processor. Originally, Intel gave numeric designations to each new generation of CPUs. One of their early CPU designs, used in the late 1980s, was the 8088 chip. These were used in IBM XT PCs and IBM XT clones, like the one shown in Figure D.3.

Subsequent CPU models were given numeric designations 80286, 80386, and 80486. These were popular throughout the early and mid-1990s. Often these PCs were simply referred to by the last three digits of the numeric designation of the processor. For example, a salesperson at a commercial electronics store might have asked you if you were looking for a 486 PC. Several other vendors created clones of Intel's 8086 series, and Intel was looking for a way to prevent these companies from using the same name as Intel did. However, you cannot copyright a number, so Intel chose to call its next generation of chips the Pentium, a name that they could and did copyright. As the years passed, the Pentium was superseded by the Pentium II, Pentium III, and currently the Pentium IV.

Each chip generation brought an increase in the speed at which commands could be processed. The fastest 80486 chip could only process at 66 megahertz per second. Often such a PC was referred to as a 486 66 PC. The 80386 chip had never been able to do more than 20 megahertz per second. Today's Pentium IV chips go well beyond 2 gigahertz, or 2000 megahertz, per second. Clearly this is a lot more processing speed and power. The most important things for you to remember are that the CPU is a microchip, it plugs directly into the motherboard, and it is one of the most important considerations when buying a new computer.

FIGURE D.3   IBM XP PC.

FIGURE D.4   A hard drive.

Drives

Your PC needs to store information. Permanent storage of data takes place on some type of drive. Your hard drive is an internal device, plugged into a controller card that is in turn plugged into your motherboard. Hard drives, depicted in Figure D.4, are measured in how many megabytes of data they can store. A megabyte is 1 million bytes, and a byte is generally eight characters. Modern hard drives have so much storage capacity that they are measured in gigabytes, or billion bytes of data. A gigabyte is 1000 megabytes. Modern hard drives range from 20 to 200 gigabytes.

The internal workings of a hard drive are beyond the scope of this book. For our purposes, you should simply realize that, when it comes to hard drives, bigger is better. Oddly enough, the hard drive, while being important, is not as critical a decision in buying a new computer. It is relatively easy and inexpensive to replace a hard drive with a bigger one, or simply to add on an additional one, in conjunction with the existing one. This means that if you err and get too small a hard drive when you buy a computer, it's fairly easy to fix later.

In addition to permanently storing data in an internal hard drive, you may frequently wish to store data on some external media such as a floppy disk or CD-ROM. Both of these require drives. A floppy drive or CD-ROM drive will plug into a controller card that is mounted on the motherboard. Often this is the same controller card that the hard drive plugs into. A floppy drive is shown in Figure D.5, and a CD-ROM drive is shown in Figure D.6.

FIGURE D.5 Floppy drive.

FIGURE D.6 CD-ROM drive.

Floppy disks hold a maximum of 1.44 megabytes of data. There is not really much difference between floppy drives. In fact, floppy drives have not changed much in the past decade, so there is really not much to consider regarding floppy drives when you purchase a new computer. CD-ROM drives, however, come in varying speeds. The higher the speed, the quicker data will be found on a CD-ROM. The speeds are measured against the speed of the original CD-ROM drives. For example, a 4X CD-ROM drive is four times faster than the original CD-ROM drives. Most modern CD-ROM drives are 40X speed and also allow you to write data to a blank CD. Also, many modern computers come with the option of a DVD drive. The DVD looks and works almost exactly like your CD drive, only it uses a more sophisticated technology for reading and writing to disks.

It is also becoming common for people to buy computers with special CD drives that not only read CDs but will create them. These CD writers will take files you designate and write them to a CD. The average CD has a capacity of about 600 megabytes or the equivalent of 389 floppy disks. You can see why this is so useful. CD writers are often referred to as CD *burners*, and the process of creating a CD is often called *burning a CD*.

Video

There are two computer devices that work in conjunction to provide you with video output. The first, and most obvious, is the monitor. Monitors come in a variety of sizes, shapes, and specifications. The higher the resolution the better. For example, a monitor that uses 1024 × 1078 is better than a monitor that uses 600 × 800. These numbers designate how many dots or pixels are used to draw the complete screen.

The numbers represent the number of vertical pixels by the number of horizontal pixels. The more pixels that are used, the finer and more detailed a picture you get.

The second element that your PC uses to create video is the video card. When you plug your monitor cable into the back of your PC, you are plugging it into the end of your video card. Video cards have their own memory, called video RAM. The more video RAM your card has, the better. So, a video card with 64 megabytes of video RAM is much better than one with 16 megabytes of video RAM. The video card, like all cards, is a specialized circuit board that is mounted on the motherboard.

Modems and Network Cards

Most people who use a computer today do so to access the Internet. The Internet is simply a loose connection of independent computers that share information in the form of e-mail, Web pages, or files. You connect to the Internet via some company that is hooked into the Internet. Such a company is usually called an Internet service provider or ISP. You connect to your ISP through some type of connection. The most common types of connections one might use would be the phone line, cable connection, or DSL (digital subscriber line). In order for your PC to communicate with either of these communication mediums, it will require appropriate hardware.

If you connect via a modem, then you probably plug a phone line into a standard phone jack in the back of your computer. The standard phone jack is known in the industry as an RJ-11 connector. The plug that you connect to on the back of your PC is really simply the outer interface of yet another PC circuit board. This one is called a modem. Modem stands for modulator demodulator. The purpose of the modem is to take the analog signal of your phone line and translate it into a digital signal that your computer can understand. It also will translate the digital output of your PC into analog transmission for the Internet.

Modems are ranked by their speed, measured in what is called baud. Baud is sometimes defined as bits per second; although this is not exactly accurate, it is pretty close. Very old modems operated at 1200 baud. The author first used a 1200 baud modem. Later speeds included 2400, 9600, 14,400, 28,800, and 56,600 baud modems. Obviously, the faster the better.

If you use DSL or cable, then there is probably a box near your computer that has an outside line coming in and then a short cable connected to your computer. The cable connected to your computer has connectors on each end that look like rather large phone jacks. These connectors are referred to as RJ-45 connectors.

Where your cable connects to your PC is actually the outer interface of yet another circuit board in your PC, much like the modem. This board is called a network interface card, or NIC. It is used to connect to cable that is used in standard networks. To connect to most cable and DSL boxes, and to connect to almost any local area network, you will need a network interface card. NICs are classed by their speed. Current speeds are either 10 megabits per second or 100 megabits per second.

Conclusion

These are the essential internal parts of your PC. This appendix will not make you a PC hardware expert, but it should give you enough information that you can understand your operating system and how it interacts with the hardware. The goal of this appendix has been to ensure that you are basically familiar with PC hardware.

E | Red Hat Packages

While much of this book is pertinent to any Linux distribution, the primary focus is on Red Hat Linux. Within this book we examine many of the programs/packages that come with Red Hat 9.0. Obviously, we don't cover all of them. Some readers might find it useful to have a complete list of the packages that are on the Red Hat 9.0 CD-ROM for you to install. Frankly, this list is huge. There are large numbers of programs available on the CD for you to install. Some are very important major applications, and some are small utilities. It is likely that at least some of the items in this list will not be applications you need. It is even possible that some will be applications you won't even quite understand. However, if you are curious as to what comes with Red Hat 9.0, this list is complete.

Many items in this list are source code or extensions for various applications. While many readers of this book may not be professional programmers, you should be aware that one of the hallmarks of open source software is the fact that you get the source code as well. You can then, if you so desire, alter and recompile the program to suit your needs. For example, anything with C++ in its name is probably for programmers using the C++ programming language. Also, if you see the words *Python* or *Perl*, these refer to programming languages as well.

Package	Version	Description
4Suite	0.11.1	These are tools and libraries for XML processing and databases with the Python programming language.
Canna	3.6	This gives you Japanese characters.
Canna-devel	3.6	Header file and library for developing programs that use Canna.
Canna-libs	3.6	The runtime library for Canna.
ElectricFence	2.2.2	This is a debugging tool that detects memory allocation violations.
FreeWnn	1.11	This is a Japanese character set conversion system.

Package	Version	Description
FreeWnn-common	1.11	These are files needed for Wnn Kana-to-Kanji conversion.
FreeWnn-devel	1.11	This is a development library and header files for FreeWnn.
FreeWnn-libs	1.11	This is the runtime library for FreeWnn.
GConf	1.0.9	This is the GNOME configuration system.
GConf-devel	1.0.9	This is the GNOME configuration system development package.
GConf2	2.2.0	Another configuration system.
GConf2-devel	2.2.0	Headers and libraries for GConf development. For readers who don't know, headers and libraries are used by programmers in the creation of applications.
Glide3	20010520	This is the Glide, a runtime for the 3Dfx Voodoo family of cards.
Glide3-devel	20010520	Development libraries and headers for Glide.
Gtk-Perl	0.7008	Perl extensions for GTK+.
Guppi	0.40.3	This is a utility for GNOME Data Analysis and Visualization.
Guppi-devel	0.40.3	These are the libraries and include files to develop Guppi-based applications.
ImageMagick	5.4.7	This is a graphics program. This program is discussed in this book.
ImageMagick-c++	5.4.7	ImageMagick Magick++ library.
ImageMagick-c++ -devel	5.4.7	C++ bindings for the ImageMagick library.
ImageMagick-devel	5.4.7	Static libraries and header files for ImageMagick app development.
ImageMagick-perl	5.4.7	ImageMagick Perl bindings.
LPRng	3.8.19	The LPRng print spooler.
MAKEDEV	3.3.2	This is a program used for creating the device files in /dev.
Maelstrom	3.0.5	This is a space combat game.
MagicPoint	1.09a	This package is a presentation program.
MyODBC	2.50.39	ODBC drivers for MySQL.
MySQL-python	0.9.1	An interface to MySQL.
ORBit	0.5.17	A CORBA Object Request Broker.

Package	Version	Description
ORBit-devel	0.5.17	Development libraries, header files, and utilities for ORBit.
ORBit2	2.6.0	A CORBA Object Request Broker.
ORBit2-devel	2.6.0	Development libraries, header files, and utilities for ORBit.
Omni	0.7.2	The Omni Print Driver System.
Omni-foomatic	0.7.2	Foomatic data for the Omni Print Driver System.
PyQt	3.5	Python bindings for Qt.
PyQt-devel	3.5	Files needed to build other bindings based on Qt.
PyQt-examples	3.5	Examples for PyQt.
PyXML	0.7.1	XML libraries for Python.
SDL	1.2.5	A multimedia library.
SDL-devel	1.2.5	Files needed to develop DirectMedia Layer applications.
SDL_image	1.2.2	A sample image loading library for SDL.
SDL_image-devel	1.2.2	Development files for the SDL image loading library.
SDL_mixer	1.2.4	A multichannel audio mixer library for SDL.
SDL_mixer-devel	1.2.4	Development files for the SDL_mixer audio mixer library.
SDL_net	1.2.4	SDL portable network library.
SDL_net-devel	1.2.4	Libraries and includes to develop SDL networked applications.
SysVinit	2.84	Programs for controlling basic system processes.
VFlib2	2.25.6	A vector font library used for Japanese document processing.
VFlib2-VFjfm	2.25.6	Extra files and scripts for use with the VFlib library.
VFlib2-conf-ja	2.25.6	Japanese vfontcap for use with the VFlib library.
VFlib2-devel	2.25.6	The header files and static library for VFlib v2.24.0.
Wnn6-SDK	1.0	A client library for Wnn6.
Wnn6-SDK-devel	1.0	Files needed for development of Wnn6 clients.
XFree86-100dpi-fonts	4.3.0	A set of 100dpi resolution fonts for the X Window System.
XFree86	4.3.0	The basic fonts, programs, and docs for an X workstation.
XFree86-75dpi-fonts	4.3.0	A set of 75dpi resolution fonts for the X Window System.

Package	Version	Description
XFree86-ISO8859-14-100dpi-fonts	4.3.0	ISO8859-14-100dpi-fonts.
XFree86-ISO8859-14-75dpi-fonts	4.3.0	ISO8859-14-75dpi-fonts.
XFree86-ISO8859-15-100dpi-fonts	4.3.0	ISO8859-15-100dpi-fonts.
XFree86-ISO8859-15-75dpi-fonts	4.3.0	ISO8859-15-75dpi-fonts.
XFree86-ISO8859-2-100dpi-fonts	4.3.0	A set of 100dpi Central European language fonts for X.
XFree86-ISO8859-2-75dpi-fonts	4.3.0	A set of 75dpi Central European language fonts for X.
XFree86-ISO8859-9-100dpi-fonts	4.3.0	ISO8859-9-100dpi-fonts.
XFree86-ISO8859-9-75dpi-fonts	4.3.0	ISO8859-9-75dpi-fonts.
XFree86-Mesa-libGL	4.3.0	A 3D graphics library that uses an OpenGL-like API.
XFree86-Mesa-libGLU	4.3.0	Commonly used GL utility library.
XFree86-Xnest	4.3.0	A nested XFree86 server.
XFree86-Xvfb	4.3.0	A virtual framebuffer X Window System server for XFree86.
XFree86-base-fonts	4.3.0	The collection of XFree86 core base fonts.
XFree86-cyrillic-fonts	4.3.0	Cyrillic fonts for X.
XFree86-devel	4.3.0	X11R6 static libraries, headers, and programming man pages.
XFree86-doc	4.3.0	Documentation for various X11 programming interfaces.
XFree86-font-utils	4.3.0	Font utilities required for installing fonts.
XFree86-libs	4.3.0	Shared libraries needed by the X Window System Version 11 Release 6.4.
XFree86-libs-data	4.3.0	Common architecture independent data required by XFree86-libs.
XFree86-syriac-fonts	4.3.0	XFree86 Syriac TrueType fonts by Beth Mardutho.
XFree86-tools	4.3.0	Various tools for XFree86.

Package	Version	Description
XFree86-truetype-fonts	4.3.0	XFree86 Luxi TrueType fonts by Bigelow and Holmes.
XFree86-twm	4.3.0	A simple window manager.
XFree86-xauth	4.3.0	X authority file utility.
XFree86-xdm	4.3.0	X Display Manager.
XFree86-xfs	4.3.0	A font server for the X Window System.
Xaw3d	1.5	A version of the MIT Athena widget set for X.
Xaw3d-devel	1.5	Header files and static libraries for development using Xaw3d.
Xbae	4.50.0	The Motif matrix and caption widgets.
Xbae-devel	4.50.0	Static library and header files for Xbae development.
Xlt	9.2.9	The Xlt Widget Set.
Xlt-devel	9.2.9	Static library and header files for Xlt development.
a2ps	4.13b	Converts text and other types of files to PostScript.
abiword	1.0.4	This is a word processor. This program is discussed in this book.
ac-archive	0.5.39	autoconf extensions archive.
acl	2.2.3	These are access control list utilities.
adjtimex	1.13	A utility for adjusting kernel time variables.
alchemist	1.0.26	A multisourced configuration backend.
alchemist-devel	1.0.26	Files needed for developing programs that use alchemist.
am-utils	6.0.9	Automount utilities, including an updated version of Amd.
amanda	2.4.3	A tape backup program.
amanda-client	2.4.3	The client component for the Amanda tape backup system.
amanda-devel	2.4.3	Libraries needed for development of Amanda applications.
amanda-server	2.4.3	The server side of the Amanda tape backup system.
ami	1.2.2	A Korean Input Method System (IMS).
anaconda	9.0	The Red Hat Linux installation program. You saw this if you were carefully watching the installation process.
anaconda-help	9.0	Help files for use in the Red Hat Linux installer.
anaconda-images	9.0	Images used in the Red Hat Linux installer.

Package	Version	Description
anaconda-runtime	9.0	Red Hat Linux installer portions needed only for fresh installs.
anacron	2.3	A cron-like program that can run jobs lost during downtime.
apel	10.4	A portable Emacs library.
apel-xemacs	10.4	A portable [X]Emacs library.
apmd	3.0.2	Advanced Power Management (APM) BIOS utilities for laptops.
arpwatch	2.1a11	Network monitoring tools for tracking IP addresses on a network.
arts	1.1	A modularized sound system for KDE.
arts-devel	1.1	Development files for the aRts sound server.
ash	0.3.8	A smaller version of the Bourne shell (sh).
asp2php	0.76.2	An ASP-to-PHP converter.
asp2php-gtk	0.76.2	This package contains a GUI GTK+ interface for the asp2php file format converter.
aspell	0.33.7.1	A spelling checker.
aspell-ca	0.1	Catalan files for aspell.
aspell-da	1.4.22	Danish files for aspell.
aspell-de	0.1.1	German files for aspell.
aspell-devel	0.33.7.1	Static libraries and header files for Aspell development.
aspell-en-ca	0.33.7.1	A Canadian English dictionary for aspell.
aspell-en-gb	0.33.7.1	A British English dictionary for aspell.
aspell-es	0.2	Spanish files for aspell.
aspell-fr	0.6	French files for aspell.
aspell-it	0.1	Italian files for aspell.
aspell-nl	0.1	Dutch files for aspell.
aspell-no	0.3	Norwegian files for aspell.
aspell-pt	0.1	Portuguese files for aspell.
aspell-pt_BR	2.4	An aspell dictionary for Brazilian Portuguese.
aspell-sv	1.3.8	Swedish files for aspell.
at	3.1.8	Job spooling tools.
at-spi	1.1.8	Assistive Technology Service Provider Interface.

Package	Version	Description
at-spi-devel	1.1.8	Development libraries and headers for at-spi.
atk	1.2.0	Interfaces for accessibility support.
atk-devel	1.2.0	System for layout and rendering of internationalized text.
attr	2.2.0	Utilities for managing the filesystem extended attributes.
audiofile	0.2.3	A library for accessing various audio file formats.
audiofile-devel	0.2.3	Development files for audio file applications.
aumix	2.7	An ncurses-based audio mixer.
aumix-X11	2.7	A GTK+ GUI interface for the Aumix sound mixer.
authconfig	4.3.4	Text-mode tool for setting up NIS and shadow passwords.
authconfig-gtk	4.3.4	Graphical tool for setting up NIS and shadow passwords.
autoconf	2.57	A GNU tool for automatically configuring source code.
autoconf213	2.13	A GNU tool for automatically configuring source code.
autoconvert	0.3.7	Chinese HZ/GB/BIG5 encodings auto-converter.
autoconvert-xchat	0.3.7	Auto-convert xchat plug-ins.
autofs	3.1.7	A tool for automatically mounting and unmounting filesystems.
automake	1.6.3	A GNU tool for automatically creating Make files.
automake14	1.4p6	A GNU tool for automatically creating Make files.
automake15	1.5	A GNU tool for automatically creating Make files.
autorun	3.10	A CD-ROM mounting utility.
awesfx	0.4.3a	Utility programs for the AWE32 sound driver.
balsa	2.0.6	An e-mail client for GNOME.
basesystem	8.0	The skeleton package that defines a simple Red Hat Linux system.
bash	2.05b	The GNU Bourne-again shell (bash). This program is discussed in this book.
bash-doc	2.05b	Documentation for the GNU Bourne-again shell (bash).
bc	1.06	GNU's bc (a numeric processing language) and dc (a calculator).
beecrypt	2.2.0	An open source cryptography library.
beecrypt-devel	2.2.0	Files needed for developing applications with beecrypt.

Package	Version	Description
bg5ps	1.3.0	Converts Big5 encoded Chinese into printable PostScript.
bind	9.2.1	A domain name system (DNS) server.
bind-devel	9.2.1	Include files and libraries needed for bind DNS development.
bind-utils	9.2.1	Utilities for querying DNS name servers.
binutils	2.13.90.0.18	A GNU collection of binary utilities.
bison	1.35	A GNU general-purpose parser generator.
bitmap-fonts	0.3	Selected set of bitmap fonts.
bitmap-fonts-cjk	0.3	Selected cjk bitmap fonts for Anaconda.
blas	3.0	The BLAS (Basic Linear Algebra Subprograms) library.
blas-man	3.0	Man pages for BLAS (Basic Linear Algebra Subprograms) routines.
bluez-libs	2.3	Bluetooth libraries.
bluez-libs-devel	2.3	Development libraries for Bluetooth applications.
bluez-utils	2.2	Bluetooth utilities.
bogl	0.1.9	A terminal program for displaying Unicode on the console.
bogl-bterm	0.1.9	A Unicode-capable terminal program for the Linux frame buffer.
bogl-devel	0.1.9	Development files required to build BOGL applications.
bonobo	1.0.22	Library for compound documents in GNOME.
bonobo-activation	2.2.0	Activation framework for Bonobo component system.
bonobo-activation-devel	2.2.0	Libraries and headers for Bonobo activation.
bonobo-conf	0.16	Bonobo configuration moniker.
bonobo-conf-devel	0.16	Libraries and include files for the configuration moniker.
bonobo-devel	1.0.22	Libraries and include files for the Bonobo document model.
bootparamd	0.17	A server process that provides boot information to diskless clients.
booty	0.19	A sunoke Python boot loader configuration library.
bridge-utils	0.9.3	Utilities for configuring the Linux Ethernet bridge.
bridge-utils-devel	0.9.3	Utilities for configuring the Linux Ethernet bridge.
bug-buddy	2.2.0	A bug reporting utility for GNOME.

Package	Version	Description
busybox	0.60.5	Statically linked binary providing simplified versions of system commands.
busybox-anaconda	0.60.5	Version of busybox configured for use with Anaconda, the Red Hat install program.
byacc	1.9	A public domain Yacc parser generator.
bzip2	1.0.2	A file compression utility.
bzip2-devel	1.0.2	Files needed to develop applications that will use bzip2.
bzip2-libs	1.0.2	Libraries for applications using bzip2.
caching-nameserver	7.2	The configuration files for setting up a caching name server.
cadaver	0.20.5	A command-line WebDAV client.
cdda2wav	2.0	A utility for sampling/copying .wav files from digital audio CDs.
cdecl	2.5	Encoding/decoding utilities for C/C++ function declarations.
cdicconf	0.2	Canna dictionary maintainance tool.
cdlabelgen	2.3.0	Generates frontcards and traycards for inserting in CD jewelcases.
cdp	0.33	An interactive text-mode program for playing audio CD-ROMs.
cdparanoia	alpha9.8	A Compact Disc Digital Audio (CDDA) extraction tool (or ripper).
cdparanoia-devel	alpha9.8	Development tools for libcdda_paranoia (*Paranoia III*).
cdparanoia-libs	alpha9.8	Libraries for libcdda_paranoia (*Paranoia III*).
cdrdao	1.1.7	Writes audio CD-Rs in disk-at-once (DAO) mode.
cdrecord	2.0	A command-line CD/DVD recording program.
cdrecord-devel	2.0	The libschily SCSI user-level transport library.
chkconfig	1.3.8	A system tool for maintaining the /etc/rc*.d hierarchy.
chkfontpath	1.9.7	Simple utility for editing the font path for the X font server.
chromium	0.9.12	*Chromium* is an arcade-style space shooting game.
cipe	1.4.5	A kernel module and daemon for providing an encrypted IP tunnel.
ckermit	8.0.206	The quintessential all-purpose communications program.
cleanfeed	0.95.7b	A spam filter for Usenet news servers.

Package	Version	Description
compat-db	3.3.11	The Berkeley DB database library for Red Hat Linux 7.x compatibility.
compat-gcc	7.3	The GNU Compiler Collection for Red Hat Linux 7.3 compatibility.
compat-gcc-c++	7.3	C++ support for Red Hat 7.3 backward compatibility compiler.
compat-gcc-g77	7.3	FORTRAN 77 support for Red Hat 7.3 backward compatibility compiler.
compat-gcc-java	7.3	Java support for Red Hat 7.3 backward compatibility compiler.
compat-gcc-objc	7.3	Objective-C support for Red Hat 7.3 backward compatibility compiler.
compat-libgcj	7.3	The Java runtime compatibility library for gcc.
compat-libgcj-devel	7.3	Compatibility libraries for Java development using gcc.
compat-libstdc++	7.3	Standard C++ libraries for Red Hat Linux 7.3 backwards compatibility.
compat-libstdc++-devel	7.3	Header files and libraries for Red Hat Linux 7.3 backward compatibility C++ compiler
compat-pwdb	0.62	The password database library.
compat-slang	1.4.5	The shared library for the S-Lang extension language.
comps-extras	8.0.94	Images for components and tools for working with the comps file.
comsat	0.17	A mail checker client and the comsat mail checking server.
control-center	2.2.0.1	The GNOME Control Center.
coreutils	4.5.3	The GNU core utilities: a set of tools commonly used in shell scripts.
cpio	2.5	A GNU archiving program.
cpp	3.2.2	The C Preprocessor.
cproto	4.6	Generates function prototypes and variable declarations from C code.
cracklib	2.7	A password-checking library.
cracklib-dicts	2.7	The standard CrackLib dictionaries.
crontabs	1.10	Root crontab files used to schedule the execution of programs.

Package	Version	Description
ctags	5.4	A C programming language indexing and/or cross-reference tool.
cups	1.1.17	Common Unix Printing System.
cups-devel	1.1.17	Common Unix Printing System—development environment.
cups-libs	1.1.17	Common Unix Printing System—libraries.
curl	7.9.8	A utility for getting files from remote servers (FTP, HTTP, and others).
curl-devel	7.9.8	Files needed for building applications with libcurl.
cvs	1.11.2	A version control system.
cyrus-sasl	2.1.10	The Cyrus SASL library.
cyrus-sasl-devel	2.1.10	Files needed for developing applications with Cyrus SASL.
cyrus-sasl-gssapi	2.1.10	GSSAPI support for Cyrus SASL.
cyrus-sasl-md5	2.1.10	CRAM-MD5 and DIGEST-MD5 support for Cyrus SASL.
cyrus-sasl-plain	2.1.10	PLAIN and LOGIN support for Cyrus SASL.
db4	4.0.14	The Berkeley DB database library (Version 4) for C.
db4-devel	4.0.14	Development files for the Berkeley DB (Version 4) library.
db4-java	4.0.14	Development files for using the Berkeley DB (Version 4) with Java.
db4-utils	4.0.14	Command-line tools for managing Berkeley DB (Version 4) databases.
dbskkd-cdb	1.01	A dictionary server for the SKK Japanese input method system.
ddd	3.3.1	A GUI for several command-line debuggers.
ddskk	11.6.0	Daredevil SKK—Simple Kana to Kanji conversion program for Emacsen.
ddskk-xemacs	11.6.0	Daredevil SKK—Simple Kana to Kanji conversion program for XEmacs.
dejagnu	1.4.2	A front end for testing other programs.
desktop-backgrounds-basic	2.0	Desktop background base set.
desktop-backgrounds-extra	2.0	Desktop background images.

Package	Version	Description
desktop-file-utils	0.3	Utilities for manipulating .desktop files.
desktop-printing	0.1.10	Nautilus desktop print icon.
dev	3.3.2	The most commonly used entries in the /dev directory.
dev86	0.16.3	A real mode 80x86 assembler and linker.
devlabel	0.26.08	Consistent/persistent storage device access through symlinking.
dhclient	3.0pl1	Development headers and libraries for interfacing to the DHCP server.
dhcp	3.0pl1	A Dynamic Host Configuration Protocol server and relay agent.
dhcp-devel	3.0pl1	Development headers and libraries for interfacing to the DHCP server.
dia	0.90	A diagram drawing program.
dialog	0.9b	A utility for creating TTY dialog boxes.
dictd	1.5.5	DICT protocol (RFC 2229) command-line client.
dietlibc	0.21	A small libc implementation.
diffstat	1.31	A utility that provides statistics based on the output of diff.
diffutils	2.8.1	A GNU collection of diff utilities.
diskcheck	1.4	A hard drive space monitor.
dmalloc	4.8.1	Memory allocation debugging routines.
docbook-dtds	1.0	XML document type definition for DocBook 4.1.2.
docbook-style-dsssl	1.76	Norman Walsh's modular stylesheets for DocBook.
docbook-style-xsl	1.58.1	Norman Walsh's XSL stylesheets for DocBook XML.
docbook-utils	0.6.12	Shell scripts for managing DocBook documents.
docbook-utils-pdf	0.6.12	A script for converting DocBook documents to PDF format.
dos2unix	3.1	A text file format converter.
dosfstools	2.8	Utilities for making and checking MS-DOS FAT filesystems on Linux.
doxygen	1.2.18	A documentation system for C/C++.
doxygen-doxywizard	1.2.18	A GUI for creating and editing configuration files.
dtach	0.5	A simple program that emulates the detach feature of screen.

Package	Version	Description
dump	0.4b28	Programs for backing up and restoring filesystems.
dvdrecord	0.1.2	A command-line CD/DVD recording program.
dvgrab	1.01	Utility to capture video from a DV camera.
e2fsprogs	1.32	Utilities for managing the second extended (ext2) filesystem.
e2fsprogs-devel	1.32	ext2 filesystem-specific static libraries and headers.
ed	0.2	The GNU line editor.
eel2	2.2.1	Eazel Extensions Library.
eel2-devel	2.2.1	Libraries and include files for developing with EEL.
efax	0.9	A program for faxing using a Class 1, 2, or 2.0 fax modem.
eject	2.0.13	A program that ejects removable media using software control.
elfutils	0.76	A collection of utilities and DSOs to handle compiled objects.
elfutils-devel	0.76	Development libraries to handle compiled objects.
elfutils-libelf	0.76	Library to read and write ELF files.
elinks	0.4.2	A text-mode Web browser.
emacs	21.2	The GNU Emacs text editor.
emacs-el	21.2	The sources for elisp programs included with Emacs.
emacs-leim	21.2	Emacs Lisp code for input methods for international characters.
emacspeak	17.0	A speech interface for Emacs.
enscript	1.6.1	A plain ASCII to PostScript converter.
eog	2.2.0	Eye of GNOME image viewer. This program is discussed in this book.
epic	1.0.1	An ircII chat client.
eruby	1.0.1	An interpreter of embedded Ruby language.
eruby-devel	1.0.1	Development files for eRuby.
eruby-libs	1.0.1	Library for eRuby.
esound	0.2.28	Allows several audio streams to play on a single audio device.
esound-devel	0.2.28	Development files for EsounD applications.
ethereal	0.9.8	Network traffic analyzer.

Package	Version	Description
ethereal-GNOME	0.9.8	Red Hat GNOME integration for ethereal and ethereal-usermode.
ethtool	1.6	Ethernet settings tool for PCI ethernet cards.
evolution	1.2.2	GNOME's next-generation groupware suite.
exmh	2.5	The exmh mail handling system.
expat	1.95.5	A library for parsing XML.
expat-devel	1.95.5	Libraries and include files to develop XML applications with expat.
expect	5.38.0	A tcl extension for simplifying program-script interaction.
expect-devel	5.38.0	A program-script interaction and testing utility.
expectk	5.38.0	A program-script interaction and testing utility.
fam	2.6.8	FAM, the File Alteration Monitor.
fam-devel	2.6.8	FAM, the File Alteration Monitor development files.
fbset	2.1	Tools for managing a frame buffer's video mode properties.
festival	1.4.2	A free speech synthesizer.
festival-devel	1.4.2	Development files for the festival speech synthesizer.
fetchmail	6.2.0	A remote mail retrieval and forwarding utility.
file	3.39	A utility for determining file types.
file-roller	2.2.1	File Roller is a tool for viewing and creating archives.
filesystem	2.2.1	The basic directory layout for a Linux system.
findutils	4.1.7	The GNU versions of find utilities.
finger	0.17	The finger client.
finger-server	0.17	The finger daemon.
firstboot	1.0.5	Initial system configuration utility.
flex	2.5.4a	A tool for creating scanners (text pattern recognizers).
flim	1.14.4	Library to provide basic features about message for Emacs.
flim-xemacs	1.14.4	Library to provide basic features about message for XEmacs.
fontconfig	2.1	Font configuration and customization library.
fontconfig-devel	2.1	Font configuration and customization library.
fontilus	0.3	Font extensions for Nautilus.
fonts-ISO8859-2	1.0	Central European language fonts for the X Window System.

Package	Version	Description
fonts-ISO8859-2-100dpi	1.0	ISO 8859-2 fonts in 100dpi resolution for the X Window System.
fonts-ISO8859-2-75dpi	1.0	A set of 75dpi Central European language fonts for X.
fonts-KOI8-R	1.0	Russian and Ukrainian language fonts for the X Window System.
fonts-KOI8-R-100dpi	1.0	KOI8-R fonts in 100dpi resolution for the X Window System.
fonts-KOI8-R-75dpi	1.0	A set of 75dpi Russian and Ukrainian language fonts for X.
fonts-hebrew	0.71	Fonts for Hebrew.
fonts-ja	8.0	Japanese fixed fonts for X11.
foomatic	2.0.2	Foomatic printer database.
freeciv	1.13.0	The *Freeciv* multiplayer strategy game.
freetype	2.1.3	A free and portable TrueType font rendering engine.
freetype-demos	2.1.3	A collection of FreeType demos.
freetype-devel	2.1.3	Header files and static library for development with FreeType.
freetype-utils	2.1.3	Utilities for manipulating and examining TrueType fonts.
ftp	0.17	The standard Unix FTP (File Transfer Protocol) client.
ftpcopy	0.5.2	An FTP site mirroring tool.
g-wrap	1.3.4	A tool for creating Scheme interfaces to C libraries.
g-wrap-devel	1.3.4	Include files and libraries needed for g-wrap development.
gail	1.2.0	Accessibility implementation for GTK+ and GNOME libraries.
gail-devel	1.2.0	Files to compile applications that use GAIL.
gaim	0.59.8	A GTK+ clone of the AOL Instant Messenger client.
gal	0.23	GNOME widgets and utility functions.
gal-devel	0.23	Files for GNOME Application Library development.
galeon	1.2.7	GNOME browser based on Gecko.
gawk	3.1.1	The GNU version of the awk text processing utility.
gcc	3.2.2	The GNU cc and gcc C compilers.
gcc-c++	3.2.2	C++ support for the GNU gcc compiler.

Package	Version	Description
gcc-g77	3.2.2	Fortran 77 support for gcc.
gcc-gnat	3.2.2	Ada 95 support for GCC.
gcc-java	3.2.2	Java support for gcc.
gcc-objc	3.2.2	Objective C support for gcc.
gconf-editor	0.4.0	Editor/admin tool for GConf.
gd	1.8.4	A graphics library for quick creation of PNG or JPEG images.
gd-devel	1.8.4	The development libraries and header files for gd.
gd-progs	1.8.4	Utility programs that use libgd.
gdb	5.3post	A GNU source-level debugger for C, C++ and other languages.
gdbm	1.8.0	A GNU set of database routines that use extensible hashing.
gdbm-devel	1.8.0	Development libraries and header files for the gdbm library.
gdk-pixbuf	0.18.0	An image loading library used with GNOME.
gdk-pixbuf-devel	0.18.0	Files needed for developing apps to work with the GdkPixBuf library.
gdk-pixbuf-GNOME	0.18.0	GNOMECanvas support for displaying images.
gdm	2.4.1.3	The GNOME Display Manager.
gedit	2.2.0	A text editor for GNOME.
genromfs	0.3	Utility for creating romfs filesystems.
gettext	0.11.4	GNU libraries and utilities for producing multilingual messages.
gftp	2.0.14	A multithreaded FTP client for the X Window System.
ggv	1.99.97	GNOME Ghostview (ggv) is a frontend for Ghostscript.
ghostscript	7.05	A PostScript interpreter and renderer.
ghostscript-devel	7.05	Files for developing applications that use Ghostscript.
ghostscript-fonts	5.50	Fonts for the Ghostscript PostScript™ interpreter.
giftrans	1.12.2	A program for making transparent GIFs from non-transparent GIFs.
gimp	1.2.3	The GNU Image Manipulation Program. This program is discussed in this book.
gimp-data-extras	1.2.0	Extra files for the GIMP.

Package	Version	Description
gimp-devel	1.2.3	The GIMP plug-in and extension development kit.
gimp-perl	1.2.3	Perl extensions and plug-ins for GIMP.
gimp-print	4.2.4	A collection of high-quality printer drivers.
gimp-print-cups	4.2.4	CUPS drivers for Canon, Epson, HP, and compatible printers.
gimp-print-devel	4.2.4	Files for developing applications that use gimp-print.
gimp-print-plugin	4.2.4	GIMP plug-in for gimp-print.
gimp-print-utils	4.2.4	Utility programs from gimp-print.
gkrellm	2.1.5	Multiple stacked system monitors: 1 process.
glade	0.6.4	A GTK+ GUI builder.
glade2	1.1.3	A GTK+ GUI builder.
glib	1.2.10	A library of functions used by GDK, GTK+, and many applications.
glib-devel	1.2.10	GIMP ToolKit (GTK+) and GIMP Drawing Kit (GDK) support library.
glib2	2.2.1	A library of handy utility functions.
glib2-devel	2.2.1	The GIMP ToolKit (GTK+) and GIMP Drawing Kit (GDK) support library.
glibc	2.3.2	The GNU libc libraries.
glibc	2.3.2	The GNU libc libraries.
glibc-common	2.3.2	Common binaries and locale data for glibc.
glibc-debug	2.3.2	Shared standard C libraries with debugging information.
glibc-devel	2.3.2	Header and object files for development using standard C libraries.
glibc-kernheaders	2.4	glibc header files from the Linux kernel.
glibc-profile	2.3.2	The GNU libc libraries, including support for gprof profiling.
glibc-utils	2.3.2	Development utilities from GNU C library.
glut	3.7	GL Utility Toolkit (GLUT).
glut-devel	3.7	GLUT Development environment.
gmp	4.1.2	A GNU arbitrary precision library.
gmp-devel	4.1.2	Development tools for the GNU MP arbitrary precision library.
GNOME-applets	2.2.0	Small applications for the GNOME panel.

Package	Version	Description
GNOME-audio	1.4.0	Sounds for GNOME events.
GNOME-audio-extra	1.4.0	Files needed for customizing GNOME event sounds.
GNOME-desktop	2.2.0.1	Package containing code shared among GNOME-panel, GNOME-session, nautilus, etc.
GNOME-desktop-devel	2.2.0.1	Libraries and headers for GNOME-desktop.
GNOME-games	2.2.0	GNOME games.
GNOME-icon-theme	1.0.0	Base GNOME icons.
GNOME-kerberos	0.3.1	Kerberos 5 tools for GNOME.
GNOME-libs	1.4.1.2.90	The main GNOME libraries.
GNOME-libs-devel	1.4.1.2.90	Libraries and headers for GNOME application development.
GNOME-lokkit	0.50	A firewall configuration application for an average end user.
GNOME-media	2.2.1.1	GNOME media programs.
GNOME-mime-data	2.2.0	MIME type data files for GNOME desktop.
GNOME-panel	2.2.0.1	GNOME panel.
GNOME-pilot	0.1.71	GNOME pilot programs.
GNOME-pilot-devel	0.1.71	GNOME pilot libraries, includes, etc.
GNOME-print	0.37	Printing libraries for GNOME.
GNOME-print-devel	0.37	Libraries and include files for developing GNOME applications.
GNOME-python2	1.99.14	The sources for the GNOME Python extension module.
GNOME-python2-applet	1.99.14	Python bindings for GNOME Panel applets.
GNOME-python2-bonobo	1.99.14	Python bindings for interacting with Bonobo.
GNOME-python2-canvas	1.99.14	Python bindings for the GNOMECanvas.
GNOME-python2-gconf	1.99.14	Python bindings for interacting with GConf.
GNOME-python2-GNOMEvfs	1.99.14	Python bindings for interacting with GNOME-vfs.
GNOME-python2-gtkhtml2	1.99.14	Python bindings for interacting with gtkhtml2.
GNOME-python2-nautilus	1.99.14	Python bindings for interacting with Nautilus.

Package	Version	Description
GNOME-session	2.2.0.2	GNOME session manager.
GNOME-spell	0.5	Bonobo component for spell checking.
GNOME-system-monitor	2.0.4	Simple process monitor.
GNOME-terminal	2.2.1	GNOME Terminal.
GNOME-themes	2.2	Themes collection for GNOME.
GNOME-user-docs	2.0.1	GNOME User Documentation.
GNOME-utils	2.2.0.3	GNOME utility programs.
GNOME-vfs	1.0.5	The GNOME virtual filesystem libraries.
GNOME-vfs-devel	1.0.5	Libraries and include files for developing GNOME VFS applications.
GNOME-vfs-extras	0.2.0	The GNOME virtual filesystem extra modules.
GNOME-vfs2	2.2.2	The GNOME virtual filesystem libraries.
GNOME-vfs2-devel	2.2.2	Libraries and include files for developing GNOME VFS applications.
GNOME-vfs2-extras	0.99.10	Extra modules for Version 2 of the GNOME virtual filesystem.
GNOMEmeeting	0.96.0	A GNOME-based H323 teleconferencing application.
gnucash	1.8.1	GnuCash is an application to keep track of your finances. This program is discussed in this book.
gnucash-backend-postgres	1.8.1	Backend for storing GnuCash data in a PostgreSQL database.
gnuchess	5.02	The GNU chess program.
gnumeric	1.0.12	A spreadsheet program for GNOME.
gnumeric-devel	1.0.12	Files necessary to develop gnumeric-based applications.
gnupg	1.2.1	A GNU utility for secure communication and data storage.
gnuplot	3.7.3	A program for plotting mathematical expressions and data.
gperf	2.7.2	A perfect hash function generator.
gphoto2	2.1.0	Software for accessing digital cameras.
gphoto2-devel	2.1.0	Headers and links to compile against the libgphoto2 library.
gpm	1.19.3	A mouse server for the Linux console.
gpm-devel	1.19.3	Libraries and header files for developing mouse driven programs.

Package	Version	Description
gqview	1.2.1	An image viewer.
grep	2.5.1	The GNU versions of grep pattern matching utilities.
grip	3.0.4	A GTK+ based frontend for CD rippers and MP3 encoders.
groff	1.18.1	A document formatting system.
groff-gxditview	1.18.1	An X previewer for groff text processor output.
groff-perl	1.18.1	Parts of the groff formatting system that require Perl.
grub	0.93	GRUB—the Grand Unified Boot Loader.
gsl	1.1.1	The GNU Scientific Library for numerical analysis.
gsl-devel	1.1.1	Static libraries and header files for GSL development.
gstreamer	0.6.0	GStreamer streaming media framework runtime.
gstreamer-devel	0.6.0	Libraries/include files for GStreamer streaming media framework.
gstreamer-plugins	0.6.0	GStreamer Streaming-media framework plug-ins.
gstreamer-plugins-devel	0.6.0	Libraries/include files for GStreamer plug-ins.
gstreamer-tools	0.6.0	tools for GStreamer streaming media framework.
gthumb	2.0.1	Image viewer, editor, organizer.
gtk+	1.2.10	A library for creating GUIs for X.
gtk+-devel	1.2.10	Development tools for GTK+ (GIMP ToolKit) applications.
gtk-doc	0.10	An API documentation generation tool for GTK+ and GNOME.
gtk-engines	0.11	Theme engines for GTK+.
gtk2	2.2.1	The GIMP ToolKit (GTK+), a library for creating GUIs for X.
gtk2-devel	2.2.1	Development tools for GTK+ applications.
gtk2-engines	2.2.0	Theme engines for GTK+ 2.0.
gtkam	0.1.7	A GTK frontend for gPhoto2.
gtkam-gimp	0.1.7	GIMP plug-in for digital camera access through gPhoto2.
gtkglarea	1.2.2	An OpenGL widget for the GTK+ GUI library.
gtkhtml	1.1.8	gtkhtml library.
gtkhtml-devel	1.1.8	Libraries, includes, etc. to develop gtkhtml applications.
gtkhtml2	2.2.0	An HTML widget for GTK+ 2.0.

Package	Version	Description
gtkhtml2-devel	2.2.0	Libraries, includes, etc. to develop Gtkhtml2 applications.
gtoaster	1.0beta6	A versatile CD recording package for both sound and data.
guile	1.6.0	A GNU implementation of Scheme for application extensibility.
guile-devel	1.6.0	Libraries and header files for the GUILE extensibility library.
gv	3.5.8	An X frontend for the Ghostscript PostScript interpreter.
gzip	1.3.3	The GNU data compression program.
h2ps	2.06	Korean Hangul converter from text file to PostScript.
hanterm-xf	2.0.5	Hangul Terminal for X Window System.
hdparm	5.2	A utility for displaying and/or setting hard disk parameters.
hesiod	3.0.2	Hesiod libraries and sample programs.
hesiod-devel	3.0.2	Development libraries and headers for Hesiod.
hexedit	1.2.2	A hexadecimal file viewer and editor.
hotplug	2002_04_01	A helper application that loads modules for USB devices.
hotplug-gtk	2002_04_01	GTK control interface for Hotplug PCI.
hpijs	1.3	HP Printer Drivers.
hpoj	0.90	HP OfficeJet low level driver infrastructure.
hpoj-devel	0.90	Headers required to compile against the hpoj library.
htdig	3.2.0	A Web indexing system.
htdig-Web	3.2.0	Scripts and HTML code needed for using ht://Dig as a Web search engine.
htmlview	2.0.0	A script that calls an installed HTML viewer.
httpd	2.0.40	Apache HTTP server.
httpd-devel	2.0.40	Development tools for the Apache HTTP server.
httpd-manual	2.0.40	Documentation for the Apache HTTP server.
hwbrowser	0.8	A hardware browser.
hwcrypto	1.0	Hardware cryptographic accelerator support.
hwdata	0.75	Hardware identification data.
im-sdk	20030118	IIIMF.
imap	2001a	Server daemons for IMAP and POP network mail protocols.

Package	Version	Description
imap-devel	2001a	Development tools for programs that will use the IMAP library.
imlib	1.9.13	An image loading and rendering library for X11R6.
imlib-cfgeditor	1.9.13	A configuration editor for the Imlib library.
imlib-devel	1.9.13	Development tools for Imlib applications.
indent	2.2.9	A GNU program for formatting C code.
indexhtml	9	The Webpage you see after installing Red Hat Linux.
inews	2.3.4	Sends Usenet articles to a local news server for distribution.
info	4.3	A stand-alone TTY-based reader for GNU texinfo documentation.
initscripts	7.14	The inittab file and the /etc/init.d scripts.
inn	2.3.4	The InterNetNews (INN) system, a Usenet news server.
inn-devel	2.3.4	The INN (InterNetNews) library.
intltool	0.25	Utility for internationalizing various kinds of data files.
ipchains	1.3.10	Tools for managing Linux kernel packet-filtering capabilities.
iproute	2.4.7	Advanced IP routing and network device configuration tools.
iptables	1.2.7a	Tools for managing Linux kernel packet filtering capabilities.
iptables-ipv6	1.2.7a	IPv6 support for iptables.
iptraf	2.7.0	A console-based network monitoring utility.
iputils	20020927	Network monitoring tools including ping.
ipxutils	2.2.1	Tools for configuring and debugging IPX interfaces and networks.
irb	1.6.8	The Interactive Ruby.
irda-utils	0.9.14	Utilities for infrared communication between devices.
iscsi	3.1.0.3	iSCSI daemon and utility programs.
isdn4k-utils	3.1	Utilities for configuring an ISDN subsystem.
isdn4k-utils-devel	3.1	Static library and header files for capi development.
isdn4k-utils-vboxgetty	3.1	ISDN voice box (getty).
isicom	3.05	Multitech Intelligent Serial Internal (ISI) support tools.
itcl	3.2	Object-oriented mega-widgets for Tcl.

Package	Version	Description
jadetex	3.12	TeX macros used by Jade TeX output.
jcode.pl	2.13	A Perl library for Japanese character code conversion.
jdkgcj	0.2.3	A free Java software development kit (SDK).
jed	0.99.15	A fast, compact editor based on the S-Lang screen library.
jfsutils	1.0.17	Utilities for managing the JFS filesystem.
jisksp14	0.1	A set of Japanese fonts.
jisksp16-1990	0.1	16 dot JIS auxiliary Kanji fonts.
joe	2.9.7	An easy to use, modeless text editor.
joystick	1.2.15	Utilities for configuring most popular joysticks.
jpilot	0.99.2	Jpilot pilot desktop software.
jwhois	3.2.1	Internet whois/nicname client.
kakasi	2.3.4	A Japanese character set conversion filter.
kakasi-devel	2.3.4	Files for development of applications that will use KAKASI.
kakasi-dict	2.3.4	The base dictionary for KAKASI.
kappa20	0.3	20 dot Japanese fonts.
kbd	1.08	Tools for configuring the console (keyboard, virtual terminals, etc.).
kcc	2.3	A Kanji code converter.
kdbg	1.2.6	A GUI for gdb, the GNU debugger, and KDE.
kde-i18n-Afrikaans	3.1	Afrikaans language support for KDE.
kde-i18n-Brazil	3.1	Brazil Portuguese language support for KDE.
kde-i18n-British	3.1	British English support for KDE.
kde-i18n-Catalan	3.1	Catalan language support for KDE.
kde-i18n-Chinese	3.1	Chinese (simplified Chinese) language support for KDE.
kde-i18n-Chinese-Big5	3.1	Chinese (Big5) language support for KDE.
kde-i18n-Czech	3.1	Czech language support for KDE.
kde-i18n-Danish	3.1	Danish language support for KDE.
kde-i18n-Dutch	3.1	Dutch language support for KDE.
kde-i18n-Estonian	3.1	Estonian language support for KDE.
kde-i18n-Finnish	3.1	Finnish language support for KDE.

Package	Version	Description
kde-i18n-French	3.1	French language support for KDE.
kde-i18n-German	3.1	German language support for KDE.
kde-i18n-Greek	3.1	Greek language support for KDE.
kde-i18n-Hebrew	3.1	Hebrew language support for KDE.
kde-i18n-Hungarian	3.1	Hungarian language support for KDE.
kde-i18n-Icelandic	3.1	Icelandic language support for KDE.
kde-i18n-Italian	3.1	Italian language support for KDE.
kde-i18n-Japanese	3.1	Japanese language support for KDE.
kde-i18n-Korean	3.1	Korean language support for KDE.
kde-i18n-Norwegian	3.1	Norwegian (Bokmaal) language support for KDE.
kde-i18n-Norwegian-Nynorsk	3.1	Norwegian (Nynorsk) language support for KDE.
kde-i18n-Polish	3.1	Polish language support for KDE.
kde-i18n-Portuguese	3.1	Portuguese language support for KDE.
kde-i18n-Romanian	3.1	Romanian language support for KDE.
kde-i18n-Russian	3.1	Russian language support for KDE.
kde-i18n-Serbian	3.1	Serbian language support for KDE.
kde-i18n-Slovak	3.1	Slovak language support for KDE.
kde-i18n-Slovenian	3.1	Slovenian language support for KDE.
kde-i18n-Spanish	3.1	Spanish language support for KDE.
kde-i18n-Swedish	3.1	Swedish language support for KDE.
kde-i18n-Turkish	3.1	Turkish language support for KDE.
kde-i18n-Ukrainian	3.1	Ukrainian language support for KDE.
kde2-compat	2.2.2	Compatibility libraries for KDE 2.2.x.
kdeaddons	3.1	KDE plug-ins.
kdeadmin	3.1	Administrative tools for KDE. These programs are discussed in this book.
kdeartwork	3.1	Additional artwork for KDE.
kdebase	3.1	K Desktop Environment—core files.
kdebase-devel	3.1	Development files for kdebase.
kdebindings	3.1	KDE bindings to non-C++ languages.

Package	Version	Description
kdebindings-devel	3.1	Development files for kdebindings.
kdeedu	3.1	Educational applications for KDE.
kdeedu-devel	3.1	Header files for kdeedu.
kdegames	3.1	KDE—games.
kdegames-devel	3.1	Development files for kdegames.
kdegraphics	3.1	KDE—graphics applications.
kdegraphics-devel	3.1	Development files for kdegraphics.
kdelibs	3.1	KDE—libraries.
kdelibs-devel	3.1	Header files and documentation for compiling KDE applications.
kdemultimedia	3.1	Multimedia applications for KDE.
kdemultimedia-devel	3.1	Development files for aRts plug-ins.
kdenetwork	3.1	KDE—network applications.
kdenetwork-devel	3.1	Development files for kdenetwork.
kdepim	3.1	PIM (Personal Information Manager) for KDE.
kdepim-devel	3.1	Development files for kdepim.
kdesdk	3.1	The KDE Software Development Kit (SDK).
kdesdk-devel	3.1	Development files for kdesdk.
kdetoys	3.1	KDE—toys and amusements.
kdeutils	3.1	KDE—utilities.
kdeutils-devel	3.1	Development files for kdeutils.
kdevelop	2.1.5	Integrated Development Environment for C++/C.
kdoc	3.0.0	Documentation for KDE.
kernel	2.4.20	The Linux kernel (the core of the Linux operating system).
kernel-BOOT	2.4.20	The version of the Linux kernel used on installation boot disks.
kernel-bigmem	2.4.20	The Linux Kernel compiled with options for machines with more than 4 gigabytes of memory.
kernel-doc	2.4.20	Various pieces of documentation found in the kernel source.
kernel-pcmcia-cs	3.1.31	The daemon and device drivers for using PCMCIA adapters.

Package	Version	Description
kernel-smp	2.4.20	The Linux kernel compiled for SMP machines.
kernel-smp	2.4.20	The Linux kernel compiled for SMP machines.
kernel-source	2.4.20	The source code for the Linux kernel.
kernel-utils	2.4	Kernel and Hardware related utilities.
kinput2-canna-wnn6	v3.1	The kinput2 input system for both Canna and Wnn6.
knm_new	1.1	The revised version of the Kaname-cho font.
koffice	1.2.1	A set of office applications for KDE.
koffice-devel	1.2.1	Development files for KOffice.
kon2	0.3.9b	A Kanji emulator for the console.
kon2-fonts	0.3.9b	Fonts for the KON Kanji emulator for the console.
kpppload	1.04	A PPP connection load monitor for KDE.
krb5-devel	1.2.7	Development files needed to compile Kerberos 5 programs.
krb5-libs	1.2.7	The shared libraries used by Kerberos 5.
krb5-server	1.2.7	The server programs for Kerberos 5.
krb5-workstation	1.2.7	Kerberos 5 programs for use on workstations.
krbafs	1.1.1	A Kerberos to AFS bridging library, built against Kerberos 5.
krbafs-devel	1.1.1	Development files for use with the krbafs package.
krbafs-utils	1.1.1	Kerberos/AFS utilities.
kterm	6.2.0	A Kanji (Japanese character set) terminal emulator for X.
kudzu	0.99.99	The Red Hat Linux hardware probing tool.
kudzu-devel	0.99.99	Development files needed for hardware probing using kudzu.
lam	6.5.8	The LAM (Local Area Multi-computer) programming environment.
lapack	3.0	The LAPACK libraries for numerical linear algebra.
lapack-man	3.0	Documentation for the LAPACK numerical linear algebra libraries.
less	378	A text file browser similar to more, but with additional functionality
lesstif	0.93.36	An OSF/Motif clone.
lesstif-devel	0.93.36	Static library and header files for LessTif/Motif development.
lftp	2.6.3	A file transfer program.

Package	Version	Description
lha	1.14i	An archiving and compression utility for LHarc format archives.
libIDL	0.8.0	Library for parsing IDL (Interface Definition Language).
libIDL-devel	0.8.0	Development libraries and header files for libIDL.
libacl	2.2.3	Dynamic library for access control list support.
libacl-devel	2.2.3	Access control list static libraries and headers.
libaio	0.3.93	Linux-native asynchronous I/O access library.
libaio-devel	0.3.93	Development files for Linux-native asynchronous I/O access.
libao	0.8.3	Cross Platform Audio Output Library.
libao-devel	0.8.3	Cross Platform Audio Output Library Development.
libart_lgpl	2.3.11	Library of graphics routines used by libGNOMECanvas.
libart_lgpl-devel	2.3.11	Libraries and headers for libart_lgpl.
libattr	2.2.0	Dynamic library for extended attribute support.
libattr-devel	2.2.0	Extended attribute static libraries and headers.
libavc1394	0.3.1	AV control lib for 1394.
libavc1394-devel	0.3.1	Development libs for libavc1394.
libbonobo	2.2.0	Bonobo component system.
libbonobo-devel	2.2.0	Libraries and headers for libbonobo.
libbonoboui	2.2.0	Bonobo user interface components.
libbonoboui-devel	2.2.0	Libraries and headers for libbonoboui.
libcap	1.10	Library for getting and setting POSIX.1e capabilities.
libcap-devel	1.10	Development files for libcap.
libcapplet0	1.4.0.1	GNOME 1 control center library compatibility package.
libcapplet0-devel	1.4.0.1	Header files for GNOME 1 control center library compatibility package.
libdbi	0.6.5	Database Independent Abstraction Layer for C.
libdbi-dbd-mysql	0.6.5	MySQL plug-in for libdbi.
libdbi-dbd-pgsql	0.6.5	PostgreSQL plug-in for libdbi.
libdbi-devel	0.6.5	Development files for libdbi.
libesmtp	0.8.12	SMTP client library.
libesmtp-devel	0.8.12	Headers and development libraries for libESMTP.

Package	Version	Description
libf2c	3.2.2	FORTRAN 77 runtime for GCC 3.1.
libgail-gnome	1.0.0	Accessibility implementation for GTK+ and GNOME libraries.
libgal21	0.23	The GNOME application library.
libgcc	3.2.2	GCC Version 3.0 shared support library.
libgcj	3.2.2	The Java runtime library for gcc.
libgcj-devel	3.2.2	Libraries for Java development using gcc.
libghttp	1.0.9	GNOME HTTP client library.
libghttp-devel	1.0.9	Files for development using libghttp.
libglade	0.17	The libglade library for loading user interfaces.
libglade-devel	0.17	The files needed for libglade application development.
libglade2	2.0.1	The libglade library for loading user interfaces.
libglade2-devel	2.0.1	The files needed for libglade application development.
libgnat	3.2.2	GNU Ada 95 runtime shared libraries.
libgnome	2.2.0.1	GNOME base library.
libgnome-devel	2.2.0.1	Libraries and headers for libGNOME.
libgnomecanvas	2.2.0.1	GNOMECanvas widget.
libgnomecanvas-devel	2.2.0.1	Libraries and headers for libGNOMECanvas.
libgnomeprint	1.116.0	Printing library for GNOME.
libgnomeprint-devel	1.116.0	Libraries and include files for developing GNOME applications.
libgnomeprint15	0.37	Printing libraries for GNOME.
libgnomeprint22	2.2.1.1	Printing library for GNOME.
libgnomeprint22-devel	2.2.1.1	Libraries and include files for developing GNOME applications.
libgnomeprintui	1.116.0	GUI support for libGNOMEprint.
libgnomeprintui-devel	1.116.0	Libraries and headers for libGNOMEprintui.
libgnomeprintui22	2.2.1.1	GUI support for libGNOMEprint.
libgnomeprintui22-devel	2.2.1.1	Libraries and headers for libGNOMEprintui.
libgnomeui	2.2.0.1	GNOME base GUI library.
libgnomeui-devel	2.2.0.1	Libraries and headers for libGNOME.

Package	Version	Description
libgsf	1.6.0	GNOME Structured File library.
libgsf-devel	1.6.0	Support files necessary to compile applications with libgsf.
libgtop	1.0.12	A library that retrieves system information.
libgtop-devel	1.0.12	Files needed to develop LibGTop applications.
libgtop2	2.0.0	libgtop library (Version 2).
libgtop2-devel	2.0.0	Libraries and include files for developing with libgtop.
libjpeg	6b	A library for manipulating JPEG image format files.
libjpeg-devel	6b	Development tools for programs that will use the libjpeg library.
libmng	1.0.4	A library that supports MNG graphics.
libmng-devel	1.0.4	Development files for the LibMNG library.
libmng-static	1.0.4	A statically linked version of the LibMNG library.
libmrproject	0.9	Support libraries for Mr. Project.
libmrproject-devel	0.9	The files needed for libmrproject application development.
libobjc	3.2.2	Objective-C runtime.
libogg	1.0	The Ogg bitstream file format library.
libogg-devel	1.0	Files needed for development using libogg.
libole2	0.2.4	The Structured Storage OLE2 library.
libole2-devel	0.2.4	Files needed for development of libole2 applications.
libpcap	0.7.2	A system-independent interface for user-level packet capture.
libpng	1.2.2	A library of functions for manipulating PNG image format files.
libpng-devel	1.2.2	Development tools for manipulating PNG image format files.
libpng10	1.0.13	Old version of libpng, needed to run old binaries.
libpng10-devel	1.0.13	Development tools for version 1.0 of libpng.
libraw1394	0.9.0	Library providing low-level IEEE-1394 access.
libraw1394-devel	0.9.0	Development libs for libraw1394.
librep	0.16.1	A shared library that implements a Lisp dialect.
librep-devel	0.16.1	Include files and link libraries for librep development.
librsvg	1.0.2	An SVG library based on libart.
librsvg-devel	1.0.2	Libraries and include files for developing with librsvg.
librsvg2	2.2.3	An SVG library based on libart.

Package	Version	Description
librsvg2-devel	2.2.3	Libraries and include files for developing with librsvg.
libsane-hpoj	0.90	SANE driver for scanners in HP's multifunction devices (from HPOJ).
libstdc++	3.2.2	The GNU Standard C++ Library v3.
libstdc++-devel	3.2.2	The header files and libraries needed for C++ development.
libtabe	0.2.6	Chinese lexicons library for xcin-2.5.2.
libtabe-devel	0.2.6	Header files and libraries for developing apps that will use libtabe.
libtermcap	2.0.8	A basic system library for accessing the termcap database.
libtermcap-devel	2.0.8	Development tools for accessing the termcap database.
libtiff	3.5.7	A library of functions for manipulating TIFF format image files.
libtiff-devel	3.5.7	Development tools for programs that will use the libtiff library.
libtool	1.4.3	The GNU libtool that simplifies the use of shared libraries.
libtool-libs	1.4.3	Runtime libraries for GNU libtool.
libtool-libs13	1.3.5	The GNU libtool, that simplifies the use of shared libraries.
libungif	4.1.0	A library for manipulating GIF format image files.
libungif-devel	4.1.0	Development tools for using the libungif library.
libungif-progs	4.1.0	Programs for manipulating GIF format image files.
libunicode	0.4	A Unicode manipulation library.
libunicode-devel	0.4	Files for development of programs that will use libunicode.
libusb	0.1.6	A library that allows userspace access to USB devices.
libusb-devel	0.1.6	Development files for libusb.
libuser	0.51.7	A user and group account administration library.
libuser-devel	0.51.7	Files needed for developing applications that use libuser.
libvorbis	1.0	The Vorbis General Audio Compression Codec.
libvorbis-devel	1.0	Development tools for Vorbis applications.
libwnck	2.2.1	Window Navigator Construction Kit.
libwnck-devel	2.2.1	Libraries and headers for libwnck.
libwvstreams	3.70	WvStreams is a network programming library written in C++.

Package	Version	Description
libwvstreams-devel	3.70	Development files for WvStreams.
libxml	1.8.17	An XML library.
libxml-devel	1.8.17	Files for developing libxml applications.
libxml2	2.5.4	Library providing XML and HTML support.
libxml2-devel	2.5.4	Libraries, includes, etc. to develop XML and HTML applications.
libxml2-python	2.5.4	Python bindings for the libxml2 library.
libxslt	1.0.27	Library providing XSLT support.
libxslt-devel	1.0.27	Libraries, includes, etc. to develop XML and HTML applications.
libxslt-python	1.0.27	Python bindings for the libxslt library.
licq	1.2.3	An ICQ clone for online messaging.
licq-GNOME	1.2.3	GNOME frontend for licq.
licq-kde	1.2.3	KDE frontend for licq.
licq-qt	1.2.3	Qt frontend for licq.
licq-text	1.2.3	This is a text based front-end for licq.
lilo	21.4.4	The boot loader for Linux and other operating systems.
linc	1.0.1	This is a utility for writing network programs.
linc-devel	1.0.1	Development libraries and header files for linc.
linuxdoc-tools	0.9.20	A text formatting package based on SGML.
lm_sensors	2.6.5	Hardware monitoring tools.
lm_sensors-devel	2.6.5	Development files for programs that will use lm_sensors.
lockdev	1.0.0	A library for locking devices.
lockdev-devel	1.0.0	The header files and a static library for the lockdev library.
logrotate	3.6.8	Rotates, compresses, removes and mails system log files.
logwatch	4.3.1	A log file analysis program.
lokkit	0.50	Firewall configuration application for an average end user.
losetup	2.11y	Programs for setting up and configuring loop back devices.
lrzsz	0.12.20	The lrz and lsz modem communications programs.
lslk	1.29	A lock file lister.
lsof	4.63	A utility that lists open files on a Linux system.

Package	Version	Description
ltrace	0.3.29	Tracks runtime library calls from dynamically linked executables.
lv	4.49.4	A multilingual file viewer.
lvm	1.0.3	Linux Logical Volume Manager utilities.
lynx	2.8.5	A text-based Web browser.
m2crypto	0.09	Support for using OpenSSL in python scripts.
m4	1.4.1	The GNU macro processor.
macutils	2.0b3	Utilities for manipulating Macintosh file formats.
magicdev	1.1.4	A GNOME daemon for automatically mounting/playing CDs.
mailcap	2.1.13	Associates helper applications with particular file types.
mailman	2.1	Mailing list manager with built-in Web access.
mailx	8.1.1	The /bin/mail program for sending quick e-mail messages.
make	3.79.1	A GNU tool that simplifies the build process for users.
man	1.5k	A set of documentation tools: man, apropos, and whatis.
man-pages	1.53	Manual pages from the Linux Documentation Project.
man-pages-cs	0.16	Czech man pages from the Linux Documentation Project.
man-pages-da	0.1.1	Danish man pages from the Linux Documentation Project.
man-pages-de	0.4	German man pages from the Linux Documentation Project.
man-pages-es	1.28	Spanish man pages from the Linux Documentation Project.
man-pages-fr	0.9.7	French man pages from the Linux Documentation Project.
man-pages-it	0.3.0	Italian man pages from the Linux Documentation Project.
man-pages-ja	0.6	Japanese man pages from the Linux Documentation Project.
man-pages-ko	1.48	Korean man pages from the Linux Documentation Project.
man-pages-pl	0.22	Polish man pages from the Linux Documentation Project.
man-pages-ru	0.7	Russian man pages from the Linux Documentation Project.
mars-nwe	0.99pl20	NetWare file and print servers that run on Linux systems.
mc	4.6.0	A user-friendly file manager and visual shell.
mdadm	1.0.1	mdadm controls Linux md devices (software RAID arrays).
memprof	0.5.1	A tool for memory profiling and leak detection.
metacity	2.4.34	Metacity window manager.

Package	Version	Description
mew	3.1	Mew—Messaging in the Emacs World.
mew-common	3.1	Mew—Common files of Messaging in the Emacs World.
mew-xemacs	3.1	Mew—Messaging in the Emacs World for XEmacs.
mgetty	1.1.30	A getty replacement for use with data and fax modems.
mgetty-sendfax	1.1.30	Provides support for sending faxes over a modem.
mgetty-viewfax	1.1.30	An X Window System fax viewer.
mgetty-voice	1.1.30	A program for using your modem and mgetty as an answering machine.
mikmod	3.1.6	A MOD music file player.
mingetty	1.01	A compact getty program for virtual consoles only.
miniChinput	0.0.3	A Chinese XIM server.
minicom	2.00.0	A text-based modem control and terminal emulation program.
mkbootdisk	1.5.1	Creates a boot floppy disk for booting a system.
mkinitrd	3.4.42	Creates an initial ramdisk image for preloading modules.
mkisofs	2.0	Creates an image of an ISO9660 filesystem.
mktemp	1.5	A small utility for safely making /tmp files.
mod_auth_mysql	1.11	Basic authentication for the Apache Web server using a MySQL.
mod_auth_pgsql	0.9.12	Basic authentication for the Apache Web server using a PostgreSQL.
mod_perl	1.99_07	An embedded Perl interpreter for the Apache Web server.
mod_python	3.0.1	An embedded Python interpreter for the Apache Web server.
mod_ssl	2.0.40	Cryptography support for the Apache Web server.
modutils	2.4.22	Kernel module management utilities.
modutils-devel	2.4.22	Kernel module management utilities development libraries.
mount	2.11y	Programs for mounting and unmounting filesystems.
mozilla	1.2.1	A Web browser.
mozilla-chat	1.2.1	IRC client integrated with Mozilla.
mozilla-devel	1.2.1	Files needed for development of Mozilla.

Package	Version	Description
mozilla-dom-inspector	1.2.1	A tool for inspecting the DOM of pages in Mozilla.
mozilla-js-debugger	1.2.1	JavaScript debugger for use with Mozilla.
mozilla-mail	1.2.1	A Mozilla-based mail client.
mozilla-nspr	1.2.1	Netscape Portable Runtime.
mozilla-nspr-devel	1.2.1	Development Libraries for the Netscape Portable Runtime.
mozilla-nss	1.2.1	Network Security Services.
mozilla-nss-devel	1.2.1	Development Libraries for Network Security Services.
mozilla-psm	1.2.1	SSL support for Mozilla.
mpage	2.5.3	A tool for printing multiple pages of text on each printed page.
mrproject	0.9	MrProject.
mrtg	2.9.17	Multi Router Traffic Grapher.
mt-st	0.7	A tool for controlling tape drives.
mtools	3.9.8	Programs for accessing MS-DOS disks without mounting the disks.
mtr	0.52	A network diagnostic tool.
mtr-gtk	0.52	The GTK+ interface for mtr.
mtx	1.2.16	A SCSI media changer control program.
mutt	1.4	A text mode mail user agent.
mx	2.0.3	A collection of Python software tools.
mysql	3.23.54a	MySQL client programs and shared library.
mysql-devel	3.23.54a	Files for development of MySQL applications.
mysql-server	3.23.54a	The MySQL server and related files.
namazu	2.0.12	Namazu is a full-text search engine.
namazu-cgi	2.0.12	A CGI interface for Namazu.
namazu-devel	2.0.12	Libraries and include files of Namazu.
nasm	0.98.35	A portable x86 assembler that uses Intel-like syntax.
nasm-doc	0.98.35	Documentation for NASM.
nasm-rdoff	0.98.35	Tools for the RDOFF binary format, sometimes used with NASM.

Package	Version	Description
nautilus	2.2.1	Nautilus is a network user environment.
nautilus-cd-burner	0.3.2	Easy to use CD burning for GNOME.
nautilus-media	0.2.1	A Nautilus media package with views and thumbnailers.
nc	1.10	Reads and writes data across network connections using TCP or UDP.
ncftp	3.1.5	Another FTP client.
ncompress	4.2.4	Fast compression and decompression utilities.
ncpfs	2.2.1	Utilities for the ncpfs filesystem, a NetWare client for Linux.
ncurses	5.3	A CRT screen handling and optimization package.
ncurses-c++-devel	5.3	C++ bindings to ncurses.
ncurses-devel	5.3	The development files for applications that use ncurses.
ncurses4	5.0	A backwards compatible version of ncurses.
nedit	5.3	A GUI text editor for systems with X and Motif.
net-snmp	5.0.6	A collection of Simple Network Management Protocol (SNMP) tools and libraries.
net-snmp-devel	5.0.6	The development environment for the NET-SNMP project.
net-snmp-utils	5.0.6	Network management utilities using SNMP, from the NET-SNMP project.
net-tools	1.60	Basic networking tools.
netatalk	1.5.5	AppleTalk networking programs.
netatalk-devel	1.5.5	Headers and static libraries for Appletalk development.
netconfig	0.8.14	A text-based tool for simple configuration of Ethernet devices.
netdump	0.6.8	Client setup for network kernel message logging and crash dumps.
netdump-server	0.6.8	Server for network kernel crash dumps.
netpbm	9.24	A library for handling different graphics file formats.
netpbm-devel	9.24	Development tools for programs that will use the netpbm libraries.
netpbm-progs	9.24	Tools for manipulating graphics files in netpbm supported formats.
newt	0.51.4	A development library for text mode user interfaces.

Package	Version	Description
newt-devel	0.51.4	Newt windowing toolkit development files.
nfs-utils	1.0.1	NFS utilities and supporting daemons for the kernel NFS server.
nhpf	1.42	Hangul Printing Filter for a Netscape (2.0 or later) PS-saved file.
njamd	0.9.2	A debugger that detects memory allocation violations.
nkf	2.01	A Kanji code conversion filter.
nmap	3.00	Network exploration tool and security scanner.
nmap-frontend	3.00	Gtk+ frontend for nmap.
nmh	1.0.4	A mail handling system with a command line interface.
nptl-devel	2.3.2	Header files and static libraries for development using NPTL library.
nscd	2.3.2	A Name Service Caching Daemon (nscd).
nss_db	2.2	An NSS library for the Berkeley DB.
nss_db-compat	2.2	An NSS compatibility library for Berkeley Databases and glibc 2.0.x.
nss_ldap	202	NSS library and PAM module for LDAP.
ntp	4.1.2	Synchronizes system time using the Network Time Protocol (NTP).
ntsysv	1.3.8	A tool to set the stop/start of system services in a run level.
nut	1.2.0	Tools for monitoring UPS equipment.
nut-cgi	1.2.0	CGI utilities for use with NUT.
nut-client	1.2.0	Client monitoring utilities for NUT.
nvi-m17n	1.79	Common files for the nvi text editor.
nvi-m17n-canna	1.79	The nvi text editor with support for Canna.
nvi-m17n-nocanna	1.79	The nvi text editor without support for Canna.
oaf	0.6.10	Object activation framework for GNOME.
oaf-devel	0.6.10	Libraries and include files for OAF.
octave	2.1.40	A high-level language for numerical computations.
open	1.4	A tool that will start a program on a virtual console.
openh323	1.11.2	Library for H323 spec.

Package	Version	Description
openh323-devel	1.11.2	Development package for openh323.
openjade	1.3.1	A DSSSL implementation.
openldap	2.0.27	The configuration files, libraries, and documentation for OpenLDAP.
openldap-clients	2.0.27	Client programs for OpenLDAP.
openldap-devel	2.0.27	OpenLDAP development libraries and header files.
openldap-servers	2.0.27	OpenLDAP servers and related files.
openmotif	2.2.2	Open Motif runtime libraries and executables.
openmotif-devel	2.2.2	Open Motif development libraries and header files.
openmotif21	2.1.30	Compatibility libraries for Open Motif 2.1.
openoffice	1.0.2	OpenOffice.org comprehensive office suite.
openoffice-i18n	1.0.2	OpenOffice.org internationalization.
openoffice-libs	1.0.2	OpenOffice.org shared libraries.
openssh	3.5p1	The OpenSSH implementation of SSH protocol Versions 1 and 2.
openssh-askpass	3.5p1	A passphrase dialog for OpenSSH and X.
openssh-askpass-GNOME	3.5p1	A passphrase dialog for OpenSSH, X, and GNOME.
openssh-clients	3.5p1	OpenSSH clients.
openssh-server	3.5p1	The OpenSSH server daemon.
openssl	0.9.7a	The OpenSSL toolkit.
openssl	0.9.7a	The OpenSSL toolkit.
openssl-devel	0.9.7a	Files for development of applications that will use OpenSSL.
openssl-perl	0.9.7a	Perl scripts provided with OpenSSL.
openssl096	0.9.6	Secure Sockets Layer Toolkit.
openssl096b	0.9.6b	The OpenSSL toolkit.
oprofile	0.4	System wide profiler for ix86 processors.
pam	0.75	A security tool that provides authentication for applications.
pam-devel	0.75	Files needed for developing PAM-aware applications and modules for PAM.
pam_krb5	1.60	A Pluggable Authentication Module (PAM) for Kerberos 5.

Package	*Version*	*Description*
pam_smb	1.1.6	A Pluggable Authentication Module (PAM) for use with SMB servers.
pan	0.13.3	A GNOME/GTK+ news reader for X.
pango	1.2.1	System for layout and rendering of internationalized text.
pango-devel	1.2.1	System for layout and rendering of internationalized text.
parted	1.6.3	The GNU disk partition manipulation program.
parted-devel	1.6.3	Files for developing apps that will manipulate disk partitions.
passivetex	1.21	Macros to process XSL formatting objects.
passwd	0.68	The passwd utility for setting/changing passwords using PAM.
patch	2.5.4	The GNU patch command, for modifying/upgrading files.
patchutils	0.2.19	A collection of programs for manipulating patch files
pax	3.0	A file archiving tool.
pccts	1.33mr33	The Purdue Compiler-Compiler Tool Set.
pciutils	2.1.10	PCI bus-related utilities.
pciutils-devel	2.1.10	Linux PCI development library.
pcre	3.9	Perl-compatible regular expression library.
pcre-devel	3.9	Development files for pcre.
pdksh	5.2.14	A public domain clone of the Korn shell (ksh).
perl	5.8.0	The Perl programming language.
perl-Archive-Tar	0.22	Archive-Tar Perl module.
perl-BSD-Resource	1.20	BSD-Resource Perl module.
perl-Bit-Vector	6.1	Bit-Vector Perl module.
perl-CGI	2.81	CGI modules for Perl.
perl-CPAN	1.61	CPAN module for Perl.
perl-Compress-Zlib	1.16	A module providing Perl interfaces to the zlib compression library.
perl-Crypt-SSLeay	0.45	Crypt-SSLeay module for Perl (/disk1/nfs/CPAN/modules/by-category/14_Security_and_Encryption/Crypt).
perl-DBD-MySQL	2.1021	An implementation of DBI for MySQL.

Package	Version	Description
perl-DBD-Pg	1.21	A PostgresSQL interface for Perl.
perl-DBI	1.32	A database access API for Perl.
perl-DB_File	1.804	DB_File module for Perl.
perl-Date-Calc	5.3	Date-Calc Perl module.
perl-DateManip	5.40	DateManip module for Perl (/disk1/nfs/CPAN/authors/id/S/SB/SBECK).
perl-Devel-Symdump	2.03	Devel-Symdump module for Perl (Development_Support/Devel).
perl-Digest-HMAC	1.01	Digest-HMAC Perl module.
perl-Digest-SHA1	2.01	Digest-SHA1 Perl module.
perl-File-MMagic	1.16	A Perl5 module that guesses file types based on their contents.
perl-Filter	1.29	Filter Perl module.
perl-Filter-Simple	0.78	Filter-Simple Perl module.
perl-Frontier-RPC	0.06	Frontier-RPC module for Perl (String_Lang_Text_Proc/Frontier).
perl-HTML-Parser	3.26	HTML-Parser module for Perl.
perl-HTML-Tagset	3.03	This module contains data tables useful in dealing with HTML.
perl-Inline	0.44	Inline Perl module.
perl-NKF	1.71	A Perl extension for nkf, the Network Kanji Filter.
perl-Net-DNS	0.31	Net-DNS Perl module.
perl-PDL	2.3.4	PDL Perl module.
perl-Parse-RecDescent	1.80	Parse-RecDescent Perl module.
perl-Parse-Yapp	1.05	Parse-Yapp module for Perl.
perl-RPM2	0.48	RPM2 Perl module.
perl-SGMLSpm	1.03ii	A Perl library for parsing the output of nsgmls.
perl-TermReadKey	2.20	TermReadKey Perl module.
perl-Text-Kakasi	1.05	A KAKASI library module for Perl.
perl-Time-HiRes	1.38	Time-HiRes module for Perl (Data_Type_Utilities/Time).
perl-TimeDate	1.1301	TimeDate module for Perl (/disk1/nfs/CPAN/modules/by-module/Time).

Package	Version	Description
perl-URI	1.21	URI module for Perl (World_Wide_Web_HTML_HTTP_CGI/URI).
perl-XML-Dumper	0.4	Perl module for dumping Perl objects from/to XML.
perl-XML-Encoding	1.01	XML-Encoding module for Perl.
perl-XML-Grove	0.46alpha	XML-Grove module for Perl.
perl-XML-Parser	2.31	A Perl module for parsing XML documents.
perl-XML-Twig	3.09	XML-Twig module for Perl.
perl-libwww-perl	5.65	Libwww-perl module for Perl.
perl-libxml-enno	1.02	The libxml-enno module for Perl.
perl-libxml-perl	0.07	The libxml-perl module for Perl.
perl-suidperl	5.8.0	suidperl, for use with setuid Perl scripts.
php	4.2.2	The PHP HTML-embedded scripting language.
php-devel	4.2.2	Files needed for building PHP extensions.
php-imap	4.2.2	An Apache module for PHP applications that use IMAP.
php-ldap	4.2.2	A module for PHP applications that use LDAP.
php-manual	4.2.2	The PHP manual, in HTML format.
php-mysql	4.2.2	A module for PHP applications that use MySQL databases.
php-odbc	4.2.2	A module for PHP applications that use ODBC databases.
php-pgsql	4.2.2	A PostgreSQL database module for PHP.
php-snmp	4.2.2	A module for PHP applications that query SNMP-managed devices.
pidentd	3.0.14	An implementation of the RFC1413 identification server.
pilot-link	0.11.5	File transfer utilities between Linux and Palm Pilots.
pilot-link-devel	0.11.5	Palm Pilot development header files.
pilot-link095-compat	0.9.5	Compatibility libraries for File transfer utilities between Linux and Palm Pilots.
pine	4.44	A commonly used, MIME-compliant mail and news reader.
pinfo	0.6.6	An info file viewer.
pkgconfig	0.14.0	A tool for determining compilation options.
plugger	4.0	A utility that calls helper applications for Navigator.
pmake	1.45	The BSD 4.4 version of make.

Package	Version	Description
pnm2ppa	1.04	Drivers for printing to HP PPA printers.
popt	1.8	A C library for parsing command line parameters.
portmap	4.0	A program that manages RPC connections.
postfix	1.1.11	Postfix Mail Transport Agent.
postgresql	7.3.2	PostgreSQL client programs and libraries.
postgresql-contrib	7.3.2	Contributed source and binaries distributed with PostgreSQL.
postgresql-devel	7.3.2	PostgreSQL development header files and libraries.
postgresql-docs	7.3.2	Extra documentation for PostgreSQL.
postgresql-jdbc	7.3.2	Files needed for Java programs to access a PostgreSQL database.
postgresql-libs	7.3.2	The shared libraries required for any PostgreSQL clients.
postgresql-odbc	7.2.5	The ODBC driver needed for accessing a PostgreSQL DB using ODBC.
postgresql-pl	7.3.2	The PL procedural languages for PostgreSQL.
postgresql-python	7.3.2	Development module for Python code to access a PostgreSQL DB.
postgresql-server	7.3.2	The programs needed to create and run a PostgreSQL server.
postgresql-tcl	7.3.2	A Tcl client library and the PL/Tcl procedural language for postgres.
postgresql-test	7.3.2	The test suite distributed with PostgreSQL.
postgresql72-libs	1	The shared libraries required for any PostgreSQL clients.
PPP	2.4.1	The PPP (Point-to-Point Protocol) daemon.
prelink	0.2.0	An ELF prelinking utility.
printman	0.0.1	A tool for monitoring print queues from GNOME.
privoxy	3.0.0	Privoxy—privacy enhancing proxy.
procinfo	18	A tool for gathering and displaying system information.
procmail	3.22	The procmail mail processing program.
procps	2.0.11	System and process monitoring utilities.
psacct	6.3.2	Utilities for monitoring process activities.
psgml	1.2.3	A GNU Emacs major mode for editing SGML documents.
psmisc	21.2	Utilities for managing processes on your system.

Package	Version	Description
pspell	0.12.2	Portable Spell Checker Interface Library.
pspell-devel	0.12.2	Static libraries and header files for pspell.
pstack	1.1	Display stack trace of a running process.
psutils	1.17	Utilities for use with PostScript documents.
pump-devel	0.8.14	Development tools for sending DHCP and BOOTP requests.
pvm	3.4.4	Libraries for distributed computing.
pvm-gui	3.4.4	A Tcl/Tk GUI frontend for monitoring and managing a PVM cluster.
pwlib	1.4.7	Portable Windows Library.
pwlib-devel	1.4.7	Development package for pwlib.
pxe	0.1	A Linux PXE (Preboot eXecution Environment) server.
pyOpenSSL	0.5.1	Python wrapper module around the OpenSSL library.
pychecker	0.8.11	A Python source code checking tool.
pydict	0.3.0	English/Chinese Dictionary written with python/gtk.
pygtk2	1.99.14	Python bindings for the GTK+ widget set.
pygtk2-devel	1.99.14	Files needed to build wrappers for GTK+ addon libraries.
pygtk2-libglade	1.99.14	A wrapper for the libglade library for use with PyGTK.
pyorbit	1.99.3	Python bindings for ORBit2.
pyorbit-devel	1.99.3	Files needed to build wrappers for ORBit2 add-on libraries.
python	2.2.2	An interpreted, interactive, object-oriented programming language.
python-devel	2.2.2	The libraries and header files needed for Python development.
python-docs	2.2.2	Documentation for the Python programming language.
python-optik	1.4	Powerful, flexible, easy-to-use, command-line parsing library
python-tools	2.2.2	A collection of development tools included with Python.
pyxf86config	0.3.5	Python wrappers for libxf86config.
qmkbootdisk	1.0.1	Graphical frontend to generating boot disks.
qt	3.1.1	The shared library for the Qt GUI toolkit.
qt-MySQL	3.1.1	MySQL drivers for Qt's SQL classes.
qt-ODBC	3.1.1	ODBC drivers for Qt's SQL classes.

Package	Version	Description
qt-PostgreSQL	3.1.1	PostgreSQL drivers for Qt's SQL classes.
qt-Xt	3.1.1	An Xt (X Toolkit) compatibility add-on for the Qt GUI toolkit.
qt-designer	3.1.1	Interface designer (IDE) for the Qt toolkit.
qt-devel	3.1.1	Development files and documentation for the Qt GUI toolkit.
qt2	2.3.1	The shared library for the Qt 2.x GUI toolkit.
qt2-Xt	2.3.1	An Xt (X Toolkit) compatibility add-on for the Qt GUI toolkit.
qt2-designer	2.3.1	An interface designer for the Qt toolkit.
qt2-devel	2.3.1	Development files and documentation for the Qt GUI toolkit.
qt2-static	2.3.1	A version of the Qt GUI toolkit for static linking.
qtcups	2.0	CUPS front-end and library for Qt.
qtcups-devel	2.0	CUPS front-end and library for Qt.
quanta	3.1	An HTML editor for KDE.
quota	3.06	System administration tools for monitoring users' disk usage.
radvd	0.7.2	A Router Advertisement daemon.
raidtools	1.00.3	Tools for creating and maintaining software RAID devices.
rarpd	ss981107	The RARP daemon.
rcs	5.7	Revision Control System (RCS) file version management tools.
rdate	1.3	Tool for getting the date/time from a remote machine.
rdesktop	1.2.0	A Windows Terminal Server desktop in X.
rdist	6.1.5	Maintains identical copies of files on multiple machines.
readline	4.3	A library for editing typed command lines.
readline-devel	4.3	Files needed to develop programs that use the readline library.
readline41	4.1	A library for editing command lines.
recode	3.6	Conversion between character sets and surfaces.
recode-devel	3.6	Header files and static libraries for development using recode.
redhat-artwork	0.73	Artwork for Red Hat default look-and-feel.
redhat-config-bind	1.9.0	A Red Hat DNS configuration tool.
redhat-config-date	1.5.9	A graphical interface for modifying system date and time.

Package	Version	Description
redhat-config-httpd	1.0.1	Apache configuration tool.
redhat-config-keyboard	1.0.3	A graphical interface for modifying the keyboard.
redhat-config-kickstart	2.3.6	A graphical interface for making kickstart files.
redhat-config-language	1.0.4	A graphical interface for modifying the system language.
redhat-config-mouse	1.0.5	A graphical interface for configuring mice.
redhat-config-network	1.2.0	The Network Administration Tool for Red Hat Linux.
redhat-config-network-tui	1.2.0	The NEtwork Administration Tool for Red Hat Linux.
redhat-config-nfs	1.0.4	NFS server configuration tool.
redhat-config-packages	1.1.8	Package manager for Red Hat Linux. It supports installation of interesting packages from CD.
redhat-config-printer	0.6.47	A printer configuration backend/frontend combination.
redhat-config-printer-gui	0.6.47	A GUI frontend for printconf.
redhat-config-proc	0.21	A configuration tool for operating system tunable parameters.
redhat-config-rootpassword	1.0.2	A graphical interface for modifying the root password.
redhat-config-samba	1.0.4	Samba server configuration tool.
redhat-config-securitylevel	1.1.1	A graphical interface for modifying the system security level.
redhat-config-services	0.8.4	redhat-config-services is an initscript and xinetd configuration utility.
redhat-config-soundcard	1.0.4	A graphical interface for detecting and configuring sound cards.
redhat-config-users	1.1.5	A graphical interface for administering users and groups.
redhat-config-xfree86	0.7.3	A graphical interface for configuring XFree86.
redhat-logos	1.1.12	Red Hat-related icons and pictures.
redhat-logviewer	0.8.5	A graphical interface for viewing log files.
redhat-lsb	1.3	LSB support for Red Hat Linux.
redhat-menus	0.38	Configuration and data files for the desktop menus.
redhat-release	9	The Red Hat Linux release file.
redhat-rpm-config	8.0.21	Red Hat specific RPM configuration files.

Package	Version	Description
redhat-switch-mail	0.5.17	The Mail Transport Agent Switcher for Red Hat Linux.
redhat-switch-mail-GNOME	0.5.17	A GUI interface for Mail Transport Agent Switcher.
redhat-switch-printer	0.5.16	The Printing System Switcher for Red Hat Linux.
redhat-switch-printer-GNOME	0.5.16	A GUI interface for Printing System Switcher.
reiserfs-utils	3.6.4	Tools for creating, repairing, and debugging ReiserFS filesystems.
rep-gtk	0.17	GTK+ bindings for librep Lisp environment.
rhn-applet	2.0.9	Panel applet for indication that newer Red Hat packages are available.
rhnlib	1.0	Python libraries for the RHN project.
rhpl	0.93	Library of Python code used by programs in Red Hat Linux.
rmt	0.4b28	Provides certain programs with access to remote tape devices.
rootfiles	7.2	The basic required files for the root user's directory.
routed	0.17	The routing daemon that maintains routing tables.
rp-pppoe	3.5	A PPP over Ethernet client (for xDSL support).
rpm	4.2	The RPM package management system.
rpm-build	4.2	Scripts and executable programs used to build packages.
rpm-devel	4.2	Development files for manipulating RPM packages.
rpm-python	4.2	Python bindings for apps that will manipulate RPM packages.
rpmdb-redhat	9	The entire RPM database for the Red Hat Linux distribution.
rsh	0.17	Clients for remote access (rsh, rlogin, rcp).
rsh-server	0.17	Servers for remote access (rsh, rlogin, rcp).
rsync	2.5.5	A program for synchronizing files over a network.
ruby	1.6.8	An interpreter of object-oriented scripting language.
ruby-devel	1.6.8	A Ruby development environment.
ruby-docs	1.6.8	Manuals and FAQs for scripting language Ruby.
ruby-libs	1.6.8	Libraries necessary to run Ruby.

Package	Version	Description
ruby-mode	1.6.8	Emacs Lisp ruby-mode for the scripting language Ruby.
ruby-tcltk	1.6.8	Tcl/Tk interface for scripting language Ruby.
rusers	0.17	Displays the names of users logged into machines on the local network.
rusers-server	0.17	Server for the rusers protocol.
rwall	0.17	Client for sending messages to a host's logged in users.
rwall-server	0.17	Server for sending messages to a host's logged in users.
rwho	0.17	Displays who is logged in to local network machines.
samba	2.2.7a	The Samba SMB server.
samba-client	2.2.7a	Samba (SMB) client programs.
samba-common	2.2.7a	Files used by both Samba servers and clients.
samba-swat	2.2.7a	The Samba SMB server configuration program.
sane-backends	1.0.9	Scanner access software.
sane-backends-devel	1.0.9	The SANE (a universal scanner interface) development toolkit.
sane-frontends	1.0.9	Graphical frontend to SANE.
sash	3.4	A statically-linked shell, including some built-in basic commands.
sawfish	1.2	An extensible window manager for the X Window System.
screen	3.9.13	A screen manager that supports multiple logins on one terminal.
scrollkeeper	0.3.11	ScrollKeeper is a cataloging system for documentation on open systems.
sed	4.0.5	A GNU stream text editor.
sendmail	8.12.8	A widely used Mail Transport Agent (MTA).
sendmail-cf	8.12.8	The files needed to reconfigure Sendmail.
sendmail-devel	8.12.8	Extra development include files and development files.
sendmail-doc	8.12.8	Documentation about the Sendmail Mail Transport Agent program.
setserial	2.17	A utility for configuring serial ports.
setup	2.5.25	A set of system configuration and setup files.
setuptool	1.12	A text mode system configuration tool.

Package	Version	Description
sgml-common	0.6.3	Common SGML catalog and DTD files.
shadow-utils	4.0.3	Utilities for managing accounts and shadow password files.
shapecfg	2.2.12	A configuration tool for setting traffic bandwidth parameters.
sharutils	4.2.1	The GNU shar utilities for managing shell archives.
sip	3.5	SIP—Python/C++ Bindings Generator.
sip-devel	3.5	Files needed to generate Python bindings for any C++ class library.
skkdic	20030211	The SKK dictionary.
skkinput	2.06.3	A Japanese language input application for X.
slang	1.4.5	The shared library for the S-Lang extension language.
slang-devel	1.4.5	The static library and header files for development using S-Lang.
slocate	2.6	Finds files on a system via a central database.
slrn	0.9.7.4	A threaded Internet news reader.
slrn-pull	0.9.7.4	Offline news reading support for the SLRN news reader.
sndconfig	0.70	The Red Hat Linux sound configuration tool.
soup	0.7.10	Soup, a SOAP implementation.
soup-devel	0.7.10	Header files for the Soup library.
sox	12.17.3	A general purpose sound file conversion tool.
sox-devel	12.17.3	The SoX sound file format converter libraries.
spamassassin	2.44	Spam filter for e-mail that can be invoked from mail delivery agents.
specspo	9.0	Red Hat package descriptions, summaries, and groups.
splint	3.0.1.7	A C code checker.
squid	2.5.STABLE1	The Squid proxy caching server.
squirrelmail	1.2.10	SquirrelMail Webmail client.
star	1.5a08	An archiving tool with ACL support.
stardict	1.31	An English to Chinese online dictionary.
startup-notification	0.5	Library for tracking application startup.
startup-notification-devel	0.5	Development portions of startup-notification.
statserial	1.1	A tool that displays the status of serial port modem lines.

Package	Version	Description
strace	4.4.95	Tracks and displays system calls associated with a running process.
stunnel	4.04	An SSL-encrypting socket wrapper.
subversion	0.17.1	A Concurrent Versioning system similar to, but better than, CVS.
subversion-devel	0.17.1	Development package for Subversion developers.
sudo	1.6.6	Allows restricted root access for specified users.
swig	1.1p5	Connects C/C++/Objective C to some high-level programming languages.
switchdesk	3.9.8	A desktop environment switcher.
switchdesk-GNOME	3.9.8	A GNOME interface for the Desktop Switcher.
switchdesk-kde	3.9.8	A KDE interface for the Desktop Switcher.
sylpheed	0.8.9	A GTK+ based, lightweight, and fast e-mail client.
symlinks	1.2	A utility that maintains a system's symbolic links.
sysklogd	1.4.1	System logging and kernel message trapping daemons.
syslinux	2.00	A simple kernel loader that boots from a FAT filesystem.
sysreport	1.3.1	Gathers system hardware and configuration information.
sysstat	4.0.7	The sar and iostat system monitoring commands.
taipeifonts	1.2	Taipei Chinese Big 5 fonts.
talk	0.17	Talk client for one-on-one Internet chatting.
talk-server	0.17	The talk server for one-on-one Internet chatting.
tar	1.13.25	A GNU file archiving program.
tcl	8.3.5	An embeddable scripting language.
tcl-html	8.3.5	Tcl/Tk manual in HTML format.
tcllib	1.3	A library of utility modules for Tcl.
tclx	8.3	Extensions for Tcl.
tcp_wrappers	7.6	A security tool that acts as a wrapper for TCP daemons.
tcpdump	3.7.2	A network traffic monitoring tool.
tcsh	6.12	An enhanced version of csh, the C shell.
telnet	0.17	The client program for the Telnet remote login protocol.
telnet-server	0.17	The server program for the Telnet remote login protocol.

Package	Version	Description
termcap	11.0.1	The terminal feature database used by certain applications.
tetex	1.0.7	The TeX text formatting system.
tetex-afm	1.0.7	A converter for PostScript font metric files, for use with TeX.
tetex-doc	1.0.7	The documentation files for the TeX text formatting system.
tetex-dvips	1.0.7	A DVI to PostScript converter for the TeX text formatting system.
tetex-fonts	1.0.7	The font files for the TeX text formatting system.
tetex-latex	1.0.7	The LaTeX frontend for the TeX text formatting system.
tetex-xdvi	1.0.7	An X viewer for DVI files.
texinfo	4.3	Tools needed to create Texinfo format documentation files.
tftp	0.32	The client for the Trivial File Transfer Protocol (TFTP).
tftp-server	0.32	The server for the Trivial File Transfer Protocol (TFTP).
time	1.7	A GNU utility for monitoring a program's use of system resources.
timidity++	2.11.3	A software wave table MIDI synthesizer.
tix	8.1.4	A set of capable widgets for Tk.
tk	8.3.5	The Tk GUI toolkit for Tcl, with shared libraries.
tkinter	2.2.2	A graphical user interface for the Python scripting language.
tmake	1.7	Makefile generator.
tmpwatch	2.8.4	A utility for removing files based on when they were last accessed.
tora	1.3.9.2	A GUI-based database development program.
traceroute	1.4a12	Traces the route taken by packets over a TCP/IP network.
transfig	3.2.3d	Utilities for creating TeX documents with portable graphics.
tree	1.2	A utility that displays a tree view of the contents of directories.
tripwire	2.3.1	A system integrity assessment tool.
tsclient	0.104	Client for VNC and Windows Terminal Server.
ttcp	1.12	A tool for testing TCP connections.
ttfonts-ja	1.2	Free Japanese TrueType fonts.
ttfonts-ko	1.0.11	Baekmuk Korean TrueType fonts.

Package	Version	Description
ttfonts-zh_CN	2.12	Arphic TrueType Font[md]GB ming and kai face.
ttfonts-zh_TW	2.11	Arphic TrueType Font[md]Big5 ming and kai face.
ttfprint	0.9	PostScript filter for Chinese.
ttmkfdir	3.0.9	Utility used to create fonts.scale files for truetype fonts.
tux	2.2.9	User-space component of TUX kernel-based threaded HTTP server.
tuxracer	0.61	Tux Racer.
umb-scheme	3.2	An implementation of the Scheme programming language.
unarj	2.63a	An uncompressor for .arj format archive files.
units	1.80	A utility for converting amounts from one unit to another.
unix2dos	2.2	A Unix to DOS text file format converter.
unixODBC	2.2.3	A complete ODBC driver manager for Linux.
unixODBC-devel	2.2.3	Development files for programs that will use the unixODBC library.
unixODBC-kde	2.2.3	KDE driver manager components for ODBC.
unzip	5.50	A utility for unpacking zip files.
up2date	3.1.23	Determines that system packages need to be updated via RHN.
up2date-GNOME	3.1.23	A GUI interface for Update Agent.
urw-fonts	2.0	Free versions of the 35 standard PostScript fonts.
usbutils	0.9	Linux USB utilities.
usbview	1.0	A USB topology and device viewer.
usermode	1.67	Tools for certain user account management tasks.
usermode-gtk	1.67	Graphical tools for certain user account management tasks.
utempter	0.5.2	A privileged helper for utmp/wtmp updates.
util-linux	2.11y	A collection of basic system utilities.
uucp	1.06.1	The uucp utility for copying files between systems.
vconfig	1.6	Linux 802.1q VLAN configuration utility.
vim-X11	6.1	The VIM version of the vi editor for the X Window System.
vim-common	6.1	The common files needed by any version of the vim editor.

Package	Version	Description
vim-enhanced	6.1	A version of the vim editor that includes recent enhancements.
vim-minimal	6.1	A minimal version of the vim editor.
vixie-cron	3.0.1	The Vixie cron daemon for executing specified programs at set times.
vlock	1.3	A program that locks one or more virtual consoles.
vnc	3.3.3r2	A remote display system.
vnc-doc	3.3.3r2	Complete documentation for VNC.
vnc-server	3.3.3r2	A VNC server.
vorbis-tools	1.0	The Vorbis General Audio Compression Codec tools.
vsftpd	1.1.3	vsftpd—Very Secure Ftp Daemon.
vte	0.10.25	An experimental terminal emulator.
vte-devel	0.10.25	Files needed for developing applications that use vte.
w3c-libwww	5.4.0	An HTTP library of common code.
w3c-libwww-apps	5.4.0	Applications built using Libwww Web library.
w3c-libwww-devel	5.4.0	Libraries and header files for programs that use libwww.
w3m	0.3.2.2	A pager with Web browsing abilities.
w3m-el	1.3.3	W3m interface for emacsen.
w3m-el-common	1.3.3	Common files for W3m interface of emacsen.
w3m-el-xemacs	1.3.3	W3m interface for XEmacs.
watanabe-vf	1.0	The Watanabe font in SYOTAI CLUB format.
Webalizer	2.01_10	A flexible Web server log file analysis program.
wget	1.8.2	A utility for retrieving files using the HTTP or FTP protocol.
which	2.14	Displays where a particular program in your path is located.
wireless-tools	25	Wireless Ethernet configuration tools.
wl	2.10.0	An IMAP4, POP, and NNTP client for GNU Emacs.
wl-common	2.10.0	An IMAP4, POP, and NNTP client for XEmacs.
wl-xemacs	2.10.0	An IMAP4, POP, and NNTP client for XEmacs.
words	2	A dictionary of English words for the /usr/share/dict directory.
wordtrans	1.1pre12	Multi Language Word Translator for Linux.

Package	Version	Description
wordtrans-kde	1.1pre12	KDE frontend for wordtrans.
wordtrans-Web	1.1pre12	Web frontend for wordtrans.
wvdial	1.53	A heuristic autodialer for PPP connections.
x3270	3.2.19	An X Window System–based IBM 3278/3279 terminal emulator.
x3270-text	3.2.19	An IBM 3278/3279 terminal emulator for text mode.
x3270-x11	3.2.19	IBM 3278/3279 terminal emulator for the X Window System.
xawtv	3.81	A TV application for video4linux-compliant devices.
xawtv-tv-fonts	3.81	Bitmap fonts for xawtv.
xboard	4.2.6	An X Window System graphical chessboard.
xcdroast	0.98a13	An X Window System–based tool for creating CDs.
xchat	1.8.11	A GTK+ IRC (chat) client.
xcin	2.5.3.pre3	An X input method server for Chinese.
xcpustate	2.5	An X Window System–based CPU state monitor.
xdelta	1.1.3	A binary file delta generator and an RCS replacement library.
xdelta-devel	1.1.3	Static library and header files for Xdelta development.
xemacs	21.4.12	An X Window System–based version of GNU Emacs.
xemacs-el	21.4.12	The .el source files for XEmacs.
xemacs-info	21.4.12	Information files for XEmacs.
xferstats	2.16	Compiles information about file transfers from logfiles.
xfig	3.2.3d	An X Window System tool for drawing basic vector graphics.
xhtml1-dtds	1.0	XML document type definition for XHTML 1.0.
xinetd	2.3.10	A secure replacement for inetd.
xinitrc	3.32	The default startup script for the X Window System.
xisdnload	1.38	An ISDN connection load average display for the X Window System.
xloadimage	4.1	An X Window System–based image viewer.
xml-common	0.6.3	Common XML catalog and DTD files.
xmltex	20000118	Namespace-aware XML parser written in TeX.
xmlto	0.0.12	A tool for converting XML files to various formats.
xmms	1.2.7	An MP3 player for X that resembles Winamp.

Package	Version	Description
xmms-devel	1.2.7	Static libraries and header files for Xmms plug-in development.
xmms-skins	1.2.7	Skins for the xmms multimedia player.
xojpanel	0.90	Graphical tool displaying the contents of the LCD of HP printers.
xosview	1.8.0	An X Window System utility for monitoring system resources.
xpdf	2.01	A PDF file viewer for the X Window System.
xpdf-chinese-simplified	2.01	Chinese simplified support.
xpdf-chinese-traditional	2.01	Chinese traditional support.
xpdf-japanese	2.01	Japanese support.
xpdf-korean	2.01	Korean support.
xsane	0.89	An X Window System frontend for the SANE scanner interface.
xsane-gimp	0.89	A GIMP plug-in that provides the SANE scanner interface.
xscreensaver	4.07	A set of X Window System screensavers.
xsnow	1.42	An X Window System–based dose of Christmas cheer.
xsri	2.1.0	A program for displaying images on the background for X.
xtraceroute	0.9.0	An X and GTK+–based graphical display of traceroute's output.
yelp	2.2.0	A system documentation reader from the GNOME Project.
yp-tools	2.7	NIS client programs.
ypbind	1.11	The NIS daemon that binds NIS clients to an NIS domain.
ypserv	2.6	The NIS (Network Information Service) server.
ytalk	3.1.1	This is a chat program for multiple users.
zebra	0.93b	This is a routing daemon.
zip	2.3	This is a file compression utility compatible with PKZIP.
zisofs-tools	1.0.4	Utilities that are used to compress CD-ROM filesystems.
zlib	1.1.4	The zlib compression and decompression library.
zlib-devel	1.1.4	Header files and libraries for Zlib development.
zsh	4.0.6	This is a a shell similar to ksh, but with improvements.

Index

A